Causation in International Relations

World political processes, such as wars and globalisation, are engendered by complex sets of causes and conditions. Although the idea of causation is fundamental to the field of International Relations, what the concept of cause means or entails has remained an unresolved and contested matter. In recent decades ferocious debates have surrounded the idea of causal analysis, some scholars even questioning the legitimacy of applying the notion of cause in the study of International Relations. This book suggests that underlying the debates on causation in the field of International Relations is a set of problematic assumptions (deterministic, mechanistic and empiricist) and that we should reclaim causal analysis from the dominant discourse of causation. Milja Kurki argues that reinterpreting the meaning, aims and methods of social scientific causal analysis opens up multi-causal and methodologically pluralist avenues for future International Relations scholarship.

MILJA KURKI is a lecturer in the Department of International Politics at Aberystwyth University. Her research on the concept of cause in International Relations theory has been awarded prizes by the British International Studies Association and the Political Studies Association.

CAMBRIDGE STUDIES IN INTERNATIONAL RELATIONS: 108

Causation in International Relations

Cambridge Studies in International Relations is a joint initiative of Cambridge University Press and the British International Studies Association (BISA). The series will include a wide range of material, from undergraduate textbooks and surveys to research-based monographs and collaborative volumes. The aim of the series is to publish the best new scholarship in International Studies from Europe, North America and the rest of the world.

CAMBRIDGE STUDIES IN INTERNATIONAL RELATIONS

107 *Richard M. Price*
Moral Limit and Possibility in World Politics

106 *Emma Haddad*
The Refugee in International Society
Between sovereigns

105 *Ken Booth*
Theory of world security

104 *Benjamin Miller*
States, nations and the great powers
The sources of regional war and peace

103 *Beate Jahn (ed.)*
Classical theory in international relations

102 *Andrew Linklater and Hidemi Suganami*
The English School of international relations
A contemporary reassessment

101 *Colin Wight*
Agents, structures and international relations
Politics as ontology

100 *Michael C. Williams*
The realist tradition and the limits of international relations

99 *Ivan Arreguín-Toft*
How the weak win wars
A theory of asymmetric conflict

98 *Michael Barnett and Raymond Duvall*
Power in global governance

97 *Yale H. Ferguson and Richard W. Mansbach*
Remapping global politics
History's revenge and future shock

96 *Christian Reus-Smit*
The politics of international law

Series list continues after index

Causation in International Relations

Reclaiming Causal Analysis

MILJA KURKI

CAMBRIDGE UNIVERSITY PRESS
Cambridge, New York, Melbourne, Madrid, Cape Town, Singapore, São Paulo, Delhi

Cambridge University Press
The Edinburgh Building, Cambridge CB2 2RU, UK

Published in the United States of America by Cambridge University Press, New York

www.cambridge.org
Information on this title: www.cambridge.org/9780521709507

First published 2008

Printed in the United Kingdom at the University Press, Cambridge

A catalogue record for this publication is available from the British Library

Library of Congress Cataloging-in-Publication Data
Kurki, Milja.
Causation in international relations: reclaiming causal analysis / Milja Kurki.
p. cm. – (Cambridge studies in international relations; 108)
Includes bibliographical references and index.
ISBN 978-0-521-88297-2 (hardback) – ISBN 978-0-521-70950-7 (pbk.)
1. International relations–Study and teaching. 2. International relations–Research.
3. International relations–Philosophy. I. Title. II. Series.

JZ1237.K87 2008
327.101 – dc22

2007050507

ISBN 978-0-521-88297-2 hardback
ISBN 978-0-521-70950-7 paperback

For Raimo, Pirjo and Catherine

Contents

Figures

Acknowledgements

This book argues that the concept of cause should be liberated from the deterministic and mechanistic connotations that it has in much of modern philosophy, social theory and International Relations scholarship. It is argued that we should look towards alternative philosophies of science in order to grasp the multiplicity of meanings that the notion of cause can have and for the many non-deterministic senses in which causes work to be appreciated. If the argument here is accepted and causes are seen to refer to all those things that we talk of, not only as 'pushing and pulling' causes, but also as 'becauses', as 'influences', or as 'constraining and enabling' conditions, then there are many causes to this work itself. It has by no means been predetermined in its outcome or process, but nevertheless has been shaped by many 'enabling' causal conditions. Since causal accounts, it seems, should entail recognition of manifold causal forces, I must begin by expressing my personal gratitude to the many people and institutions that have facilitated, encouraged and influenced this work.

First, since many of the arguments developed in this book were formulated during my doctoral research at the University of Wales, Aberystwyth, I want to thank the Economic and Social Research Council and the University of Wales, Aberystwyth (now Aberystwyth University) for the financial support that their research studentships provided between 2001 and 2004. Furthermore, I want to extend warm thanks to the Centre of Excellence in Global Governance Research at the University of Helsinki for providing me with the time and resources to finish this project in 2007.

I also want to thank the eclectic collection of supervisors and colleagues who have had a hand in shaping the arguments expressed in this book. First, I owe an immense debt to Colin Wight for his support, supervision and friendship over the past six years. Colin's interest and insight in conceptual matters has been an invaluable help and inspiration to me: quite simply I would have been lost without his guidance. In addition I want to thank Steve Smith: for the inspiration that his work has provided me ever since I first picked up Hollis and Smith's *Explaining and Understanding International Relations* as an undergraduate, as well as for Steve's enthusiasm and belief in the somewhat unorthodox doctoral project that provided the groundwork for this book. Heartfelt thanks are also due to Jonathan Joseph for all his guidance in philosophy of science and to William Bain for pushing me to think 'outside the box' about causation and especially about the structure of this work. I also want to acknowledge the detailed and extremely useful comments provided by Colin Hay, Hidemi Suganami and anonymous referees on earlier drafts of the manuscript. I also wish to thank Alex Wendt and Heikki Patomäki for sharing their insights on causation, and Adriana Sinclair, Alex Pritchard and Susanne Kempe for their (unimaginable) willingness to debate issues of causation and philosophy during our shared years at Aberystwyth. Many thanks also to Heidi Kivekäs for help with compilation of the bibliography, and to James O'Connor for help with final read-throughs.

I should also mention that the vibrant research culture of the Department of International Politics at Aberystwyth has played a very important part in the preparation of the arguments expressed here, as have discussions with and the support of colleagues, notably of Tim Dunne, at the Department of Politics at Exeter between 2004 and 2006. No doubt thanks are due also to those teachers, colleagues and students that I have failed to mention here but who have shared their perspectives on the ongoing controversy over causation in international relations and social sciences more widely.

Certain sections of the argument expressed within this book, most notably in chapter 6, reproduce in an adapted form material previously published in 'Causes of a Divided Discipline: Rethinking the Concept of Cause in International Relations Theory', *Review of International Studies* 32(2) (2006): 189–216 (copyright British International Studies Association, reproduced with permission).

I wish to dedicate this book to my parents, Raimo and Pirjo, and to Catherine. Their support has been invaluable, not least in enabling me to keep my wits about me through the past few years of entanglement with the complexities of philosophy of causation.

Milja Kurki
Helsinki

Introduction: the problem of causation and the divided discipline of International Relations

The guiding aim of the discipline of International Relations (IR) at its inception in the aftermath of the First World War was the study of the causes of war. Scholars engaged in the new field of International Relations sought to uncover the causes of the Great War, and of wars in general, in the hope of thereby being able to avoid disastrous conflicts in the years to come.[1] In the course of the twentieth century the causal questions that have been of interest to IR scholars have proliferated widely beyond those pertaining to the causes of interstate war: scholars in the discipline of IR have studied subjects ranging from the causes of democratic peace and the causes of globalisation, to the causes of global terrorism and the causes of global inequalities. Although studying causal relations has been fundamental to IR research from the start and continues to occupy scholars in the discipline, debates over causation have also been highly controversial.

During the past century it has become clear that theorists from different schools of thought have tended to disagree sharply over their substantive causal accounts of international politics. For example, the causes of war are still as contested as ever: just compare the variety of accounts given for the war in Iraq. While some believe that the war was initiated because the USA, and the coalition states, had a national interest in securing themselves against a threat posed by weapons of mass destruction and 'rogue states', others insist that it had more to do with long-standing economic interests in the oil in the region, or a wish to ensure access to markets in the area. Others yet emphasise the relative importance of more idealistic reasons for engagement in the region, such as the wish to promote human rights and democratic norms. Heated disagreements also characterise debates over other key world political trends: causes of global poverty, for example, are deeply contested between different actors and theoretical positions, as are

[1] Dickinson (1917: v).

the causes of global terrorism. Contestation between different causal interpretations has been not only theoretically important in gaining an understanding of the key forces that shape international politics, but in many cases also consequential for how political actors or actions have been morally and politically judged.

As if these debates over the causes of global political trends were not enough, the contestation surrounding the concept of cause has increased significantly in the discipline of IR during the past two decades. This is because many IR theorists have come to question, not just the scope and the plausibility of each other's causal accounts of world politics, but also the very legitimacy of the notion of cause in analysing world politics. Deep philosophical rifts have come to divide the discipline of IR between *causal* and *non-causal* forms of theorising.

The advocates of a scientific study of international relations, often termed 'positivist' or 'rationalist'[2] scholars in the discipline, have called for the study of international politics through systematic methods of causal analysis. These scholars have argued that the standards of a 'scientific' model of causal analysis should be upheld throughout IR scholarship in order for the discipline to generate useful and reliable empirical knowledge about causes and consequences in international politics.[3] The scientific approach to causal analysis has entailed that we study general patterns in international relations: for example, regular patterns of state behaviour. One example of a general pattern that has been identified in international relations is that democracies do not tend to fight other democracies. In trying to decipher whether democracy can really be said to 'cause' peace, rationalist causal analysts in IR have formulated many specific hypotheses regarding the relationship between democracy and peace, which they have then tested against

[2] Rationalism is a term famously used by Robert Keohane to describe approaches that believe in the validity of the 'scientific' approach to international relations inquiry as well as in the utility of rational choice models. Keohane (1988). Positivism can be seen as a term that is in many ways interchangeable with the term rationalism, although the former suffers from many prejudicial historical connotations, from which most theorists like to distance themselves. Thus, most scientifically inclined theorists in contemporary IR prefer to refer to their work as rationalist rather than as positivist. Because of its less prejudicial and more precise connotations the term 'rationalism' will be preferred here, although it is seen as interchangeable with what some theorists would classify as positivism. Positivism will be discussed in more detail in following chapters.

[3] Exemplified especially by King, Keohane and Verba (1994). See also Nicholson (1996a).

patterns in large-scale data gathered about state behaviour. Some scholars have concluded that certain causal hypotheses, for example one suggesting a link between democratic norms within a state and peaceful state behaviour, can be considered 'robust' in reference to the data, hence providing an indication of the causal significance of democracy for peace.[4] Differing interpretations have also been advanced: some scholars have rejected the significance of the link between democracy and war in the data, and other causal factors, such as the level of wealth, or alliance structures, have been measured and tested as possible causal variables that explain peace between Western democratic states.[5] Regardless of their differing conclusions, many rationalist social scientists have accepted that the study of causal connections between observable variables in such a manner constitutes the key task of IR scholarship. These kinds of causal studies can provide grounds for progressive accumulation of knowledge in the study of international relations.[6]

However, since the 1980s, a variety of 'critical approaches' – critical theory, poststructuralism, feminism, and constructivism – have challenged the mainstream approaches to the study of world politics.[7] Importantly, many of the so-called 'reflectivist' approaches[8] have rejected the mainstream 'positivist' methods and many of them also the idea of causal analysis: they have sought to carve out room for a 'postpositivist' form of inquiry centred on examining how world politics is socially, normatively or discursively 'constituted'. This idea of constitutive analysis has been applied in analysis of 'traditional' IR matters, such as interstate war and democratic peace, but also in new subject areas, such as the study of global gender relations.[9]

[4] See Maoz and Russett (1993).

[5] See, for example, Layne (1994) and Spiro (1994). For a more detailed discussion see chapters 3 and 7.

[6] See, for example, Chernoff (2004).

[7] See, for example, Cox (1981); Ashley (1989); Walker (1993); Onuf (1989); Enloe (1990).

[8] Reflectivism is also a term coined by Keohane to refer to those IR scholars who reject the scientific approach to social science of the mainstream rationalists and the utility of rational choice methods, preferring instead historical and sociological study of world politics. Keohane (1988: 384). For a more detailed discussion of the term see chapter 4.

[9] More traditional territory has been intervened in, for example, by Campbell (1998a, 1998b); Fierke (2005); Zehfuss (2002); Barkawi and Laffey (2001b); Cox (1987). New aspects, such as gender relations, have been explored, for example, by Sylvester (1994); Weber (1999); Zalewski and Parpart (1998).

David Campbell's insightful analysis of US foreign policy provides one example of a 'reflectivist' analysis that rejects the classical methods and terminology of IR scholarship. Campbell studies not general observational patterns that characterise US foreign policy behaviour, but rather how US foreign policy has been discursively constituted by the so-called 'discourse of danger'. He traces how the discursive constitution of enemies has been entangled with the discursive construction of the United States itself.[10] This kind of analysis has gone against the grain of traditional social scientific IR scholarship in explicitly refusing to analyse the 'underlying causes' of US foreign policy in accordance with traditional theoretical frameworks, such as realism and liberalism, and in rejecting the methods of social scientific causal analysis. In fact, Campbell has fiercely attacked the idea that a social scientific causal model should be enforced in analysis of the ways in which global political dynamics are constituted.[11]

A significant divide has appeared in the discipline between those interested in scientific analysis of causes in world politics, and those vehemently opposed to the very idea of causal analysis. What has given rise to this dichotomy? In their influential book *Explaining and Understanding International Relations* Martin Hollis and Steve Smith sought to give a philosophical grounding for the emerging divisions between the rationalist 'causal' and reflectivist 'non-causal' forms of theorising in IR.[12] Hollis and Smith aimed to explain the theoretical divisions in IR by drawing on the terms of debate between the 'positivist' and the 'hermeneutic' theorists in the philosophy of social science. They argued that there are always 'two stories to tell' in IR, as there are in other social sciences: one can attempt either to 'explain' international politics through causal analysis that seeks general patterns in world political processes, or to 'understand' world politics through inquiring into the constitution of meaning and the 'reasons for' particular actions. They also contended that, while 'explanation' was about finding causes, 'understanding', or the inquiry into the meaningful context of action, was essentially a non-causal form of inquiry.[13] These two approaches to the social world, they claimed, have different aims but

[10] For reflectivist interventions in more classical IR territory see, for example, Campbell (1998a, 1998b).

[11] Campbell (1998b: 207–27).

[12] Hollis and Smith (1990).

[13] Hollis and Smith (1990: 3).

are both legitimate in their own ways. Crucially, it was argued that the two forms of theorising cannot be combined: they refer to fundamentally different forms of inquiry embedded in fundamentally different views on the nature of the social world.[14]

Hollis and Smith's philosophical justification for the separation of the two forms of social inquiry seems to have made sense to many IR theorists – across the theoretical divides. During the past decade, the postpositivist approaches, although widely divergent in their specific theoretical claims, have largely accepted the common assumption that it is possible and legitimate to study world politics without conducting causal analysis or using causal terminology. Many of them reject the possibility of 'cataloging, calculating and specifying the "real causes"', as David Campbell puts it.[15] On the other hand, while the rationalists have seen their own scientific approach as the most reliable and systematic form of research in IR, they have also come to accept the existence of 'reflectivist' non-causal theorising and the division of IR into two distinct theoretical camps.[16] Both the rationalist and the reflectivist theoretical 'camps' see themselves as engaging in different, largely incommensurable, forms of inquiry, utilising different methods, epistemological criteria and theoretical assumptions in dealing with world politics. Some constructivist theorists have tried to mitigate the implications of this division, but even their 'synthesising' efforts have tended to accept the underlying separation of the two forms of inquiry.[17] The division between causal and constitutive theorising has, then, come to shape the contemporary disciplinary 'self-image' in IR in important ways: it has become embedded within the discursive frameworks through which theorists position themselves in relation to others and justify their own theoretical stances.[18]

What is interesting about the contemporary rationalist–reflectivist, or positivist–postpositivist, divide in IR is that it has not entailed a detailed analysis of the concept that plays a central role in legitimating the division of the forms of social inquiry: *the concept of cause*. Despite

[14] Hollis and Smith (1990: 1). [15] Campbell (1998b: 4).

[16] Keohane (1988); Nicholson (1996a: 2–3). See also Katzenstein, Keohane and Krasner (1999b).

[17] Ruggie (1999: 215–24); Onuf (1998b); Wendt (1999b). See also chapter 4.

[18] See, for example, Steve Smith (1995). See also Wæver (1996). The acceptance of this division is also evident in recent IR textbooks. See, for example, Burchill (2001a).

the increasing controversy over causation in IR, what is meant by the concept of cause has not been explored in any detail – not by the self-proclaimed causal theorists, or by those who reject the legitimacy of the notion of cause.

This book seeks to remedy this important omission in contemporary IR theorising by subjecting the concept of cause to detailed scrutiny and by re-examining the theoretical divisions in IR in the light of such analysis. When the debates on causation in IR are analysed in detail, and positioned within wider discussions in the philosophy of science and social science, it emerges that these debates have been hindered by the fact that they have been deeply informed by the guiding assumptions of a dominant, yet by no means self-evident or unproblematic, discourse on causation, the key principles of which can be traced to the philosophical works of David Hume. The so-called Humean conception of causation, which has been deeply entwined with the empiricist tradition in modern philosophy, has entailed that

1 causal relations are tied to regular patterns of occurrences and causal analysis to the study of patterns of *regularities* in the world around us;
2 causal relations are regularity relations of patterns of *observables*;
3 causal relations are *regularity-deterministic*; it has been assumed that, given certain observed regularities, when A type of events take place, B type of events can be assumed to follow (at least probabilistically); and
4 beyond these strictly empiricist assumptions, it has also been assumed that causes refer to 'moving' causes, that is, that they are *efficient causes* that 'push and pull'.

These assumptions about the concept of cause are deeply embedded in modern philosophy of science and social science and, owing to the lack of detailed attention that causation has received in IR, they have also come to inform IR theorists' views on causation, even if often implicitly or inadvertently. The dominance of a Humean discourse of causation[19] has given rise to various meta-theoretical and theoretical problems in IR, problems often not adequately understood in the

[19] The term 'Humean' is used here because the assumptions identified in the current discourse can be seen to be in line with the key principles often attributed to Hume's philosophy of causation. However, as is discussed in

discipline owing to scholars' poor appreciation of the nature and role of the particular causal discourse at the centre of the disciplinary debates. For example, it is the dominance of the Humean discourse of causation that justifies the division of IR into two distinct camps – causal and non-causal. Also, as will be seen, this discourse has led IR approaches – on both sides of the division – to adopt certain (regularity-)deterministic and mechanistic assumptions about causation, to associate the idea of causal analysis solely with the 'empiricist-positivist' idea of science, and to accept certain reductionist tendencies in analysis of causal forces in the study of world politics.

While it is not a negative development that many rationalist social scientists have sought to develop increasingly sophisticated methods of causal analysis for the purposes of IR research, it is somewhat unfortunate that the self-avowed causal theorists in IR, and their critics, have failed to recognise the role that a Humean background discourse of causation has had in shaping and delimiting the very starting points for the development of models and methods of causal analysis in the discipline. I argue that the mainstream positivist or 'rationalist' IR theorising, as a result of the acceptance of Humean assumptions with regard to causation, is characterised by certain systematic limitations associated with the underlying philosophical approach to causal analysis. While the Humean model of causal analysis has its strengths in systematising empirical analysis of general patterns, it is methodologically, epistemologically and ontologically constrained in important ways: methodologically it does not give an adequate role to historical, qualitative, discursive and interpretive methods and approaches; epistemologically it provokes theorists to set overly objectivist aims for social knowledge; and ontologically it has a difficult time in dealing with unobservable causes, such as ideas and reasons, and the social construction of social life. Such weaknesses are *not* characteristic of causal approaches more widely conceived, but are typical of those approaches that accept a Humean background discourse on causation.

The reflectivist or postpositivist camp has noted that the rationalist Humean causal analyses of world political processes are problematic

chapter 1, it is not at all self-evident that Hume's philosophy is as straightforwardly empiricist, and indeed 'Humean', as is often assumed. Hence the term should be taken not as a direct reference to Hume but as a description of a set of assumptions associated with his philosophy.

in their explanatory range and nuance.[20] However, through a closer analysis of the reflectivist literature we can see that the reflectivists have also bought into the Humean assumptions concerning causation, and that this has given rise to various inconsistencies and confusions in their theorising. The reflectivists reject causation on the basis of accepting Humean causal analysis as their reference point. The reflectivist rejection of causal descriptions on these bases is problematic, not only because it has entailed inadequate engagement with non-Humean philosophies of causation and, therefore, reinforces Humeanism as the 'only game in town' with regard to causal analysis, but also because the rejection of Humeanism prevents the reflectivists from seeing that their own work advances certain causal (although non-Humean) claims, even if only, rather narrowly, concerning the role of ideas, norms, rules and discourses in social life.

This book attempts to liberate IR theorising from the grip of the dominant Humean discourse of causation and to reclaim an alternative conception of causal analysis for the purposes of world political research. It is argued here that the Humean philosophy of causation represents only one of the potential 'solutions' to the problem of causation and a 'solution' that has certain important weaknesses despite its taken-for-granted status in the twentieth-century philosophy of science, social science and, indeed, in the discipline of IR. Through a philosophical and theoretical critique of the influence of Humeanism in IR, it seeks to open up avenues towards post-Humean thinking on causation in the discipline.

It should be noted that the approach adopted here is unashamedly theoretical and philosophical in nature. While philosophical, or metatheoretical, discussions have often been subjected to criticism from the more empirically minded IR scholars, in my view philosophical reflection on the key concepts we use frequently, such as causation, is fundamental in the social sciences, IR among them. This is because, as Colin Wight puts it, 'conceptual inquiry is a necessary prerequisite to empirical research'.[21] Without an adequate understanding of the ways in which we apply concepts, appreciation of the reasons for our conceptual choices, and recognition of the strengths and the weaknesses

[20] See, for example, Cox (1981); Campbell (1998a, 1998b); Edkins (1999). See chapter 4 for a more specific discussion.
[21] Wight (2006: 290).

that our use of key concepts entail, we run the risk of conducting empirical studies that we cannot justify or that amount to nothing more than aimless fact-finding. Also, we risk not being able to understand how and why our accounts might differ from those of others and, hence, are not able to engage in constructive debate with other perspectives. This book is motivated by the belief that IR has *not* become too theoretical or philosophical at the expense of empirical inquiry:[22] rather it still remains inadequately reflective towards many fundamental concepts used in empirical analyses. While meta-theoretical, or philosophical, debate is clearly in and of itself not the sole or the central aim of International Relations scholarship, it should not be forgotten that the ways in which we 'see' and analyse the 'facts' of the world political environment around us are closely linked to the kinds of underlying assumptions we make about meta-theoretical issues, such as the nature of science and causation. Indeed, the analysis here is motivated by the belief that whenever we make factual, explanatory or normative judgements about world political environments, important meta-theoretical filters are at work in directing the ways in which we talk about the world around us, and these filters are theoretically, linguistically, methodologically, and also potentially politically consequential.[23] It follows that philosophical investigation of key concepts such as causation should not be sidelined as 'hair-splitting' or 'meta-babble',[24] but embraced – or at least engaged with – as one important aspect of the study of international relations.

Challenging Humeanism: a deeper and broader notion of cause

Reclaiming causal analysis from the Humean assumptions dominant among rationalist causal researchers and reflectivist constitutive theorists in IR, involves the development of a coherent and comprehensive alternative to the Humean conception of causation. This in turn necessitates in-depth engagement with philosophies of causation outside of the dominant Humean tradition. We will discover that there are some important philosophical alternatives to Humeanism in the fields of philosophy of science and philosophy of social science that

[22] An accusation made for example by William Wallace (1996).
[23] See Kurki and Wight (2007).
[24] See also Hidemi Suganami's reflections on this issue (1996: 2–3).

we can draw on. It is seen that the pragmatist and the philosophically realist approaches specifically provide important philosophical insights that allow us to challenge the Humean assumptions concerning causation. It is seen that by drawing on these alternative philosophies of causation, a few IR theorists – Hidemi Suganami, Alexander Wendt, David Dessler, Colin Wight and Heikki Patomäki[25] – have already taken important steps to avoid the Humean framing of causation, and the consequent theoretical dichotomisations in IR. The philosophical alternatives to Humeanism, and their IR applications, have opened important new avenues in framing issues of causation and causal analysis. However, some problems and gaps still characterise the existing attempts to overcome Humeanism – philosophically and in IR context – and hence a re-theorisation of the issue of causation is necessary in order for a consistent alternative to the Humean discourse of causation to be developed in IR. The argument advanced here aims to go beyond the previous attempts to confront Humeanism: it is proposed that we challenge Humeanism in two respects. First, we should *deepen* the meaning of the notion of cause by providing it with a 'deep ontological' grounding, something that the Humeans have avoided doing. Second, we should *broaden* the assumptions associated with the notion of cause by disentangling it from the notion of 'efficient cause'.

In seeking to avoid 'metaphysical questions', modern philosophy has predominantly reduced the problem of causation to an *epistemological* problem (Can we know causes? How do we come to make knowledge claims about causes?) or a *methodological* one (What methods should we use for causal analysis? How do we justify a causal link and how do we test causal theories/hypotheses?). Here, the meaning of the concept of cause is 'deepened' by opening up the *ontological* aspect of the problem of causation. Drawing on philosophical realism, a school of philosophy that maintains that we must accept that the world exists independently of our efforts to understand it,[26] I argue that ontological questions (What constitutes a cause and causation? Are causes ontologically real, and how? Are there different types of causes and what

[25] Suganami (1996); Wendt (1999b); Dessler (1991); Wight (2006: 21–2, 29–32, 272–9); Patomäki (1996). See also Kurki (2006, 2007).

[26] Philosophical realism as it is utilised in this book draws on Roy Bhaskar's work (1978, 1979, 1989, 1991). For philosophical realism in general see also, for example, Ellis (2001) and Psillos (1999).

are their causal powers?) are, in fact, fundamental to understanding causation and its role in science, natural as well as social. The account here follows the philosophical realists in rejecting the Humean 'regularity criteria' for causal analysis. Causes are seen to consist in the real causal powers of ontological entities, not in regularity relations of patterns of events. It follows that causal analysis is understood as consisting not of analysis of regularities or laws, but of developing understandings of the nature and the causal powers of 'ontologically deep' objects with the aim of thereby rendering intelligible the concrete events and processes that we can observe. 'Deep ontology' is necessary in conducting causal analysis because 'what is' (ontology) is not reducible to 'what is perceived', as empiricist Humeanism has entailed.[27]

The acceptance of such an ontologically grounded conception of cause has important implications for causal analysis in the social sciences. It allows us to recognise the reality and causal nature of such aspects of social life as rules, norms, ideas, reasons, discourses, as well as, importantly, of 'structures of social relations'. Also, giving deeper ontological grounding to causes allows us to recognise that there is no singular strictly defined scientific method by which social scientific inquiry should abide, as the empiricists argue. Instead, epistemological relativity and methodological pluralism can be accepted: it can be recognised that there are many ways to understand and to approach the world and its complex causal powers and processes, as indeed the practice of social science, outside the rigorous empiricist prescriptions, seems to indicate. Because reasons, ideas and discourses play crucial roles in the social world, interpretive and discursive approaches should be recognised as playing an important role in world political causal explanation.

Besides deepening the meaning of the notion of cause by giving it ontological grounding, I argue that broadening the meaning of the notion of cause is equally important. Modern philosophy has unhelpfully narrowed down the meaning of the term cause: causes have been seen as 'pushing and pulling' forces or, as Aristotle put it, as 'efficient' or 'moving causes'.[28] This assumption has been deeply embedded in the Humean understanding of causation but also, interestingly,

[27] The argument here follows Roy Bhaskar's account. Bhaskar (1975: 21–62).
[28] Aristotle (1998: 115).

has been accepted by many of the philosophically realist approaches. Re-examination of the Aristotelian 'four causes account' helps us to move away from the mechanistic pushing and pulling connotations often attached to the notion of cause in modern philosophy, especially in modern philosophy of social science. Aristotle recognised that 'since many different things can be called causes', we should understand that 'many different things can all be causes . . . not, however, causes in the same way'.[29] He conceptualised four types of causes: material, formal, efficient and final. Understanding change, for Aristotle, involved understanding the role, not just of efficient causes ('movers'), but also of material causes (the passive potentiality of matter), formal causes (defining shapes or relations) and final causes (purposes that guide change). Any account of things or changes in the world would, for Aristotle, have to refer to all these four different types of causes and their complex interaction.

The rich and flexible Aristotelian understanding of causation is helpful in 'broadening' the meaning of the notion of cause in IR. On the basis of the Aristotelian system, we can still hold on to the notion of 'active' causes (efficient causes) while conceptualising these causes in relation to final causes and, crucially, within a 'constitutive', or causally conditioning, environment understood through material and formal causes. The notion of formal cause allows us to understand the causal role of ideas, rules, norms and discourses. Instead of treating ideas, rules, norms and discourses as non-causal, as has been the tendency in much of interpretive social theory, these factors can be seen as 'constraining and enabling' conditioning causes of social action. The Aristotelian conceptualisation also allows us to understand the causal role of material resources and properties: instead of treating them as 'pushing and pulling' forces, or ignoring them, they are conceptualised as ubiquitous but 'passive' conditioning causes. Crucially, the Aristotelian philosophy requires us always to embed different types of causes in relation to each other and thereby to concentrate causal analysis on the complex interaction of different types of causes. This allows us to steer clear of theoretically reductionist accounts, whether materialist, idealist, agential or structural.

Mention of Aristotelian philosophy may startle some readers: this philosophy after all has been out of favour among commentators and

[29] Aristotle (1970a: 28–30: lines 194b–195a32).

practitioners of modern science, who consider this framework to have been decisively proved wrong with the rise of empirical science during the Renaissance. Modern sciences have been hugely successful in explaining physical and biological realities and building new means of production and destruction alike. It should be noted then that it is *not* the aim of this book to argue for a return to Aristotelian metaphysics. It is the aim here to argue not that Aristotelianism is the only or the most productive basis for philosophy of science, or even for philosophy of social science, but simply, more narrowly, that certain aspects of the Aristotelian account of causation can be useful in elucidating the nature of different senses in which we might apply the concept of cause in the social sciences, and specifically in IR. On a related point, it should also be noted that the relationship between philosophies, or discourses, of science and the practice of science is a complex and complicated one. The presuppositions that underlie scientific practices and theoretical self-understandings of scientists may be quite different.[30] Discourses of philosophy of science, and of causation, are seen here as 'conditioning causes' that constrain and enable knowledge claims, not as 'when A, then B' type causes of specific scientific theories. This is important to recognise, both because it goes some way to explain why an Aristotelian conceptual framework might be useful in clarifying the nature of causal analysis in International Relations and also because it allows us to understand why Humean theories in science, social science or IR should not simply be rejected as uninsightful, even if the discourse of causation that informs them can be considered problematic in certain respects. Tracing the complex interactions between philosophies of science, and between the practice of science and theories of science, is a complicated task, and holistic analysis of such links is beyond the scope of the present book. However, some idea of the complex interaction between discourses of science and causation, and their links to the practice of scientific inquiry, will be provided within the detailed discussions of key trends in philosophy of science, philosophy of social science and International Relations discourses discussed in chapters 1, 2, 3 and 4.

[30] As many philosophical realists such as Bhaskar (1978) and Psillos (1999), for example, argue, the practice of science is better understood through philosophical realist assumptions rather than through empiricist assumptions, despite the dominance of an empiricist-positivist discourse in philosophy of science.

Implications of rethinking the concept of cause in the divided discipline

The deeper and broader conception of cause advanced here seeks to provide an alternative framework for conducting causal analysis in IR research: an alternative that claims to overcome some of the problematic aspects of existing approaches to causal analysis in the discipline. The deeper and broader account of cause presented here, first, addresses some of the central theoretical problems characteristic of the rationalist and the reflectivist approaches to causal analysis and, importantly, provides IR theorists and researchers with more holistic and pluralistic conceptual and methodological tools in analysis of world political causes. Second, the conception of cause advanced here also entails an objection to the self-images that characterise positions in the discipline: it allows us to challenge the divisive causal vs. non-causal theory self-image in IR scholarship. Third, the reconceptualisation of causation has certain implications for concrete research in the discipline – the kinds of causal questions we ask and the way in which we frame our causal analyses – as well as for our understandings of the nature and the scope of IR as a discipline. Let's examine these contributions in a little more detail.

First, by questioning the received wisdom on causal analysis in the discipline, the approach advanced here poses some challenging questions to the dominant form of causal theorising in the contemporary IR, that is, rationalist Humean causal theorising. The Humean approach to causation can be seen to have its uses in that it is recognised that analysis of general patterns and associational connections between variables can be of use in describing certain general aspects of global realities. However, in terms of *causal explanation*, the framing of causation advanced here poses a deep challenge to rationalist causal theorising. It does so methodologically, epistemologically and ontologically.

Methodologically, causal analysis is not seen to be dependent on quantitative 'regularity analysis'. Instead, causal analysis is seen to consist of forming conceptual systems that allow us to grasp the underlying causal structures and relations that are involved in bringing about concrete processes or patterns of events. The conception of causal analysis advocated here accepts the social scientific legitimacy of various kinds of methods and data – quantitative, historical and qualitative as well as discursive. It also emphasises the role, not just of observational measurement of variables, but also of interpretation of social meanings, contexts and reasons. On the basis of this methodological pluralism the scientific legitimacy of many marginalised IR theories, including post-structuralism, can be maintained.

Also, the rationalist *epistemological* reliance on observational knowledge is challenged. There are many avenues through which to grasp social life; I argue that observational knowledge is only one of them. Further, it is argued that we must accept that social inquiries are not neutral or objective, as the rationalists often assume. In fact, all social inquiries are seen as socially and politically embedded and fallible. Science, by its nature, is a social activity and its descriptions and analysis socially engendered and embedded. Crucially, while rejecting objectivism of the rationalist kind, the account here is not relativist: it is argued that we can still accept that, in principle, some causal analyses grasp the world better than others. It is accepted here that we can, and do, judge between accounts of the world. While our judgements are made in social and political contexts, and have social and political impacts, all accounts are not 'equally valid'.

Rationalist, or positivist, approaches to causal analysis can also be challenged on the *ontological* level. I argue that ontologically these accounts are often 'flat' in that they are not conceptually equipped to theorise 'deep causes'. Owing to their concentration on observable-based variables and their relations across time, rationalists have not been able adequately to theorise the complex 'underlying' structures, relations and processes of world politics. I aim to demonstrate that the 'atomistic' ontological assumptions of mainstream IR research should be replaced by a deeper and more complexity-sensitive social ontology involving the causal powers of complex 'conditioning' social forces (including rules, norms, discourses, material resources as well as social structures).

While the approach here supports many postpositivist insights – indeed, causal analysis as advocated here is closely linked to the interpretive tradition in the social sciences – it also challenges the 'reflectivist' theorists' rejection of causation. The reflectivists accept the Humean view of causation as characteristic of causal approaches: this is unnecessary and misleading. I want to suggest that if the post-positivist theorists in IR engaged with non-Humean philosophies of causation with more depth, they might realise that their accounts are not as 'non-causal' as they think: their analyses, in fact, contain not just assumptions concerning the causal nature of ontological objects in the social world (the 'constitutive' nature of social constructions), but also straightforward causal claims ('constitution' matters because it has consequences for social action). The constitutive theorists have not understood the causal nature of their inquiries because they have accepted the regularity-deterministic assumptions of Humeanism as characteristic of causation. Ignoring the possibility that causal analysis can be non-Humean, and that causes can be 'conditioning', rather than 'pushing and pulling', has been responsible for much of their confusion about causation.

Cause, as it is understood here, is a pragmatic human concept but, crucially, a concept that reflects the fact that we live in a world where 'nothing comes from nothing'. As quantum physicist David Bohm has powerfully stated, there is no account, scientific or otherwise, that has challenged the basic principle that 'everything comes from other things and gives rise to other things'.[31] Cause here is seen as a broad concept referring to a variety of things, actions, processes, structures or conditions that we can talk of as being responsible for directing outcomes, actions, states of affairs, events or changes. When the self-evidence of the surprisingly restrictive assumptions of the Humean approach are criticised we can recognise that causal analysis is much more widespread, and common-sensical, than the Humean discourse has led us to believe: causal analysis is something that we all, including the reflectivist theorists, engage with continuously. When our conception of causes is 'deepened' and 'broadened', causal analysis can be seen to reach far beyond what is normally perceived as 'causal' in IR.

It follows that the self-image of IR premised on the dichotomisation of causal and constitutive approaches is misleading. In the light of the reconceived notion of cause advanced here, the rigid dichotomy between causal and constitutive forms of inquiry has to be rejected, or at least radically reformulated. The causal–constitutive divide becomes redundant in that constitutive theorising can be seen as a form of theorising that is intimately bound up with causal theorising and causal claims. This means that we can see the causal–constitutive divide that the disciplinary 'camps' have reproduced for more than a decade, not as a fundamental incommensurable philosophical dichotomy, but as a

[31] Bohm (1984: 1).

discursively produced and in many respects unhelpful 'detour' in IR theoretical debates.

The divisive logic of the discipline is also challenged by the Aristotelian categories that allow us to reject the theoretically reductionist tendencies of both the rationalists and the reflectivists in IR. The reflectivists have often concentrated on the study of the 'ideational', normative or discursive aspects of world politics, without asking holistic questions about the material constraints and conditioning of rules, norms and discourses.[32] Structural realists in IR, on the other hand, have attached 'pushing and pulling' connotations to material factors in world politics and, thus, have avoided accounting for 'how' material conditions determine outcomes.[33] The Aristotelian categories allow us to avoid these tendencies to explain things through one or another 'isolated' 'independent' 'determining' factor. While it does not solve specific empirical questions over the role of different causes in world politics – these are for empirical specialists in the areas to study – the Aristotelian framing directs IR researchers to steer clear of reductionist frameworks and to ask questions about many types of causes and their complex interactions. The opening up of the ontological bases of IR suggested here entails not only the re-theorisation of the role of the 'ideational' and the 'material' in IR but, moreover, the introduction of complexity-sensitive structural analysis of 'social relations' that goes beyond the conceptual premises of both rationalist and reflectivist approaches.

It is also demonstrated that developing the conceptual apparatuses of IR in such a manner is not just an abstract philosophical or theoretical exercise, but has implications for how IR theorists conceptualise, research and debate world political causal questions. The framework advanced opens up a number of analytical questions and avenues in concrete world political causal research that the Humean approach has sidelined. In the light of the revised notion of cause that I present here, the study of world politics is opened up towards the possibility of conducting ontologically and conceptually more nuanced, epistemologically and methodologically pluralist research. Reframing causation allows IR theorists not only to ask deeper and broader causal questions disallowed by Humeanism, but also, in doing away with divisive

[32] Koslowski and Kratochwil (1995).
[33] Waltz (1979); Mearsheimer (1995); Grieco (1988).

theoretical terminology, to conduct more constructive disciplinary debates over complex causal puzzles such as democratic peace and the end of the Cold War. The reconceptualised approach to causal analysis also allows us to reassess the relationship of IR and other social science disciplines. On the basis of the broad causal ontology accepted here, the 'taken-for-granted' nature of IR as a separate discipline must be questioned. Indeed, in order for IR to come up with explanatorily adequate causal accounts of complex global realities, it should open up to analysis of social relations beyond the traditional scope of 'Inter*national* Relations'.

A note on structure, methodology and style

The argument advanced here proceeds in three parts. Part I seeks to understand the nature of the Humean philosophy of causation in contemporary philosophy of science, social science and IR, and to examine its consequences for the forms of analysis that have characterised these fields. Chapter 1 introduces the philosophical problem of causation, the Humean solution to it and the nature of causal theorising in twentieth-century philosophy of science. In chapter 2 philosophy of social science debates over causation are examined: it is seen that the controversy over causes in the social sciences has been informed by a distinctly Humean understanding of causation. Chapters 3 and 4 examine how the Humean framing of the concept of cause has penetrated IR theorisations and what consequences this has. The structure of the discussion follows the traditional faultlines of the contemporary 'divided discipline': chapter 3 analyses the positivist or 'rationalist' theorists and their assumptions about causal analysis, while chapter 4 examines the 'reflectivist' critiques of positivist causal approaches, alongside discussion of constructivist theorisations. It is argued that each theoretical camp has been deeply informed by Humean assumptions about causation and that this has entailed certain problematic effects on rationalist, reflectivist and constructivist theorising.

Part II seeks to move beyond Humeanism in IR by exploring possibilities for reconceptualising the notion of cause. Chapter 5 examines two philosophies of causation that have sought to challenge Humeanism – pragmatism and philosophical realism – and points to IR theorists who have sought to draw on these approaches. Chapter 6, then, aims to build an alternative to Humeanism, a deeper and broader reconceptualisation of the notion of cause. Subsequently Part III examines the consequences of rethinking causation in IR. Chapter 7 seeks to illustrate how the reconceptualisation of causation influences IR scholars' engagement with causal puzzles in world politics, such as democratic peace and the end of the Cold War. Chapter 8, on the other hand, reflects on the implications that rethinking causation has for the 'self-image' of IR as a discipline.

Given the nature of the object of study, much of the analysis here is premised on critical literature and critical discursive analysis. The aim is to draw out the main assumptions and claims of different philosophical and theoretical approaches through a close reading of the key texts in philosophy of science, social science and IR. The approach taken here is not 'literalist': indeed, as will be seen, often assumptions about causation are not explicitly apparent and have to be extrapolated from the wider discursive framework. The alternative to Humeanism advanced in Part II is developed out of literature-based engagement with alternative philosophies of causation. However, it is not reducible to these previous engagements but instead seeks to provide a new, more comprehensive way of integrating philosophical discourses and conceptual systems.

A few terminological and stylistic clarifications also need to be made. According to the usual convention, the academic discipline of International Relations is referred to in capitals while the object of study of this discipline, the international and world political processes, actions and trends, is referred to in lower case. As will be clarified in chapter 7, because of the holistic ontological framework advocated here, 'world politics' is a term considered more apt in describing the object of study of the discipline, than the ontologically narrower terms inter*national* politics or inter*national* relations.

It should be noted that lower case will also be used here for individual IR theoretical schools of thought. Since this book analyses a variety of philosophical, social theoretical, as well as IR theoretical frameworks, this might leave some room for confusion over whether notions such as 'realism', which are part of the lexicon in both philosophy of science and IR (and have entirely different meanings in these fields), are used in a philosophical sense or in an IR theory sense. To avoid any confusion in this regard, I have sought to define which type of realism is referred to: that is, I have used the terms philosophical realism and critical realism to refer to specific philosophical theories, and the term political or structural realism to refer to IR theory realisms. As for causal terminology, the notion 'causality' is typically used when referring to the (often Humean) philosophers and theorists who use it themselves. My own preference is to use the notions 'cause' and 'causation', notions which have stronger ontological connotations.

PART I

The Humean philosophy of causation and its legacies

1 The Humean philosophy of causation and its legacies in philosophy of science

David Hume famously stated that 'there is no question, which on account of its importance, as well as difficulty, has caus'd more disputes both among antient and modern philosophers, than this concerning the efficacy of causes, or that quality which makes them follow'd by their effects'.[1] The contestation over the meaning of the idea of cause that Hume refers to, however, has escaped many IR theorists, who have unwittingly worked within the confines of an influential but also a rather narrow discourse of causation initiated by Hume's philosophy of causation. This book seeks to reclaim contestation over the concept of cause and also advances an approach to causation that goes beyond the Humean approach. Development of an alternative post-Humean discourse of causation in IR, however, necessitates that we first deal with some important preliminary questions such as 'what is Humeanism?', 'what exactly is its role in philosophy of science and in IR?' and 'what are the consequences of adherence to Humeanism?' The first part of the book seeks to address such questions.

The first task we are presented with is that we must understand what the Humean approach to causation consists of, and how it fits within wider philosophical disputes over the meaning of causation. To this end, chapter 1 aims to examine the context, the core assumptions and the influence of the Humean perspective on causation in philosophy of science. The chapter first traces the 'decline' of the concept of cause: that is, the gradual rejection of 'metaphysical' ancient Greek notions of cause in favour of a much 'narrowed down' and 'emptied out' meaning of the concept. I will then examine Hume's conception of cause and point to the key assumptions that a Humean framing of causation entails: the acceptance of regularity analysis of causal relations; the equation of causal relations with regularity relations of observables; the treatment of causal necessity as 'regularity-deterministic' (given

[1] Hume (1978: 156).

regularities, 'when A, then B'); and the acceptance of the image of causes as 'efficient causes'. The latter part of the chapter analyses how these assumptions have become deeply embedded within twentieth-century philosophy of science, albeit in a variety of forms.

Two things need to be noted at the outset. First, the discussion here focuses on the Humean philosophy of causation, not because Humeanism is the only possible philosophy, or discourse, on causation, but rather because it is believed that its central assumptions have played a highly influential role in how the concept of cause has been treated in philosophical and theoretical discussions during the modern era, especially during the twentieth century. As will be seen, the Humean philosophy of causation has become deeply embedded in twentieth-century philosophy of science, and also philosophy of social science (the subject of chapter 2), and has become deeply entwined with the dominant empiricist, or positivist, conceptions of what science consists in.[2] Second, it should be noted that it is impossible to provide here a full account of the reasons for the dominance of Humeanism, and the wider discourse of empiricism, during the past few hundred years. This would entail an inquiry into the sociology of knowledge of those centuries. Although an exploration of the complex history of empiricism and positivism would be an interesting task and would involve interesting questions about the interconnections between these traditions of thought and the rise of currents of thought such as liberalism, it is too much to take on here. Hence, here the rise of Humeanism is but documented in key philosophical writings. This kind of literary examination suffices to give us an indication of the way in which the Humean solution to the problem of causation has become the 'benchmark' that all causal accounts, including the non-Humean accounts that the second part of the book examines and draws on, have had to grapple with.

[2] Empiricism refers to a particular epistemological conception of the nature of knowledge, while positivism refers to philosophies of science that have drawn on certain empiricist premises in defining the scientific method. The interactions between Humeanism, empiricism and positivism are complex. As will be seen the Humean philosophy of causation is a theory of causation that has become widely accepted by many empiricist philosophers and positivist philosophers of science. Yet, it should be noted that Humeanism as a philosophy of science does not exhaust empiricism or positivism, nor is empiricism or positivism defined exclusively by Humeanism.

The history of philosophy of causation: from Aristotle to Hume

The origins of the concept of cause

The origins of the notion of cause lie in the Greek philosophies of nature. The pre-Socratic philosophical schools started to develop the notion of cause from superstitious, or semi-religious, ideas concerning the 'powers' of nature. The early ancient philosophers began to inquire into 'powers' that make and enable things to be what they are and for changes in them and between them to take place. The aim was to dispose of the mythical qualities of nature through finding nature's guiding 'first principles'. In referring to powers of nature the common term used in pre-Socratic philosophy was *arche* (fundamental principle). *Arche* referred to those principles that pre-existed concrete entities (yet in some way co-existed with them) and provided a reason for their existence. The pre-Socratic philosophers, especially in the Ionian and Eleatic schools, located the 'first principles' of nature and change in the constitution of matter.[3]

This was something that Plato came to reject. Plato critiqued the materialist philosophies of nature through developing the so-called theory of forms,[4] which divided the world into distinct spheres: the ideational reality – the world of forms – and the sense-world, which was seen as the imitation of the 'real' unobservable world of forms. Interestingly, the 'idea-ist' philosophy of Plato made a crucial contribution to defining the notion of cause. Plato specified the pre-Socratic *arche* to the notion of *aition* (plural *aitia*) ('cause', also previously denoting guilt and responsibility). Plato's particular concern was with ideas (or forms) as *aitia*. Forms, Plato argued, 'participate in' or are presupposed in the phenomenal objects: it was forms that 'were behind' and 'explained' things that we observe (sense-objects). Instead of reducing explanations of the state of the world to material principles, Plato argued that 'formal' 'aetiological' explanations should be used to make sense of the world.[5] Causal, or aetiological, intelligibility of the world in this sense was a fundamental commitment for Plato.

[3] For more detailed accounts of cause in the different pre-Socratic schools see Hankinson (1998). See also Aveling (2001).

[4] See Wallace (1972a: 18). [5] Plato (1993: 51–5).

It was Aristotle, however, who truly developed the notion of cause and gave it a central place in Western philosophy. Aristotle aimed to synthesise and systemise the diverse ideas that had revolved around the notions of *arche* and *aition*. Accounting for *aitia* had a fundamentally important role for Aristotle's conception of science and knowledge: knowledge for him consisted of efforts to understand why things happen. Crucially, it was *aitia* that were seen to give answers to these why-questions.[6] Causal, or aetiological, explanation was, for Aristotle, a central epistemological tool of science: it was through asking why-questions and answering them through accounting for *aitia* that science could provide knowledge of nature. It is because of this emphasis on explanation through *aitia* that Aristotle made an important distinction between a mere 'fact' and a 'reasoned fact'; the former denoted merely an observation, the latter a fact that had been explained through its *aitia*.[7]

Crucially, for Aristotle, the concept of cause did not refer simply to an epistemological category of thought through which to understand the world: Aristotle's account of causes was *ontologically grounded*. While the concept of cause was recognised to be a 'human concept', it referred to something 'out there': indeed, causes, for Aristotle, referred to really existing (ontological) things or powers in the world. Aristotle's account started from a philosophically realist metaphysical premise, that is, the assumption that people live in the world that is real and that pre-exists them, and a world in which things give rise to other things, where 'nothing comes from nothing'. The causal why-questions, and thus *aitia,* refer to independently existing ontological entities in the world: '"the why" is an objective feature of the world'.[8]

Aristotle's term for cause, *aition*, also had a rather broad meaning. In Aristotle's framework the meaning of *aition* was something close to the modern English meaning of 'causal condition' or 'causal antecedent', which included within it many kinds of possible causes.[9] Indeed, the notion of cause could refer to many different kinds of things. In *Physics* and *Metaphysics* Aristotle charts the contributions and faults of each of the many pre-existing 'aetiological' accounts and, in the end, opts for a synthetic account, the so-called 'four causes' account of causation. From the Ionians Aristotle picked up the idea of material explanation,

[6] Lear (1988: 6). [7] Wallace (1972a: 12).
[8] Lear (1988: 26). [9] Matthen (1987: 5–7).

from Empedocles and Anaxagoras vague ideas concerning agential causation, from Plato the notion of formal causes, and from his own system the notion of final cause.[10] Aristotle argued that there are many types of *aitia*: 'since many different things can be called causes, it follows that many different things can all be causes . . . not, however, causes in the same way'.[11]

Aristotle proceeds to discuss four different types of causes. First, he conceptualises 'material causes'; an *aition* is defined as 'that from which . . . a thing comes into being'.[12] Matter to Aristotle was fundamentally important in any explanation. However, matter was conceived as 'indeterminate potentiality'. Matter was a cause through providing the material from which a thing comes to be, such as marble as the cause of a statue. The substance of marble is a cause in that without it the statue could not exist, but also in the sense that the properties of the substance 'constrain and enable' how matter can be shaped.[13] Crucially, matter, for Aristotle, is of little significance in and of itself, and it is ultimately unintelligible: we cannot make sense of marble as the cause of the statue without considering what it is being moulded into.

To define or specify material causes, Aristotle thinks we require understanding of the second type of cause, formal cause. Formal causes refer to the forms, ideas or essences of things. The formal cause, as the cause of a statue, would be the idea, image or shape that the sculptor moulds the marble into. Formal cause, then, denotes the 'form or pattern of a thing';[14] formal causes define and 'actualise' material potentiality into things or substances.

Third, Aristotle conceptualises agential, or what he calls efficient causes, which he sees as 'the primary sources of change'.[15] These sources of change could, for Aristotle, entail any agential mover or more broadly an act of doing something. The efficient cause of the bronze statue, then, would be the sculptor or the act of sculpting.

The fourth category of Aristotle's four-fold categorisation of causes is the notion of final cause – 'that for the sake of which' something comes to be. To utilise the sculptor analogy again: the final cause is the purpose for which the sculpture is being moulded. Aristotle saw

[10] Edel (1982: 412).
[11] Aristotle (1970a: 28–30: lines 194b–195a32). [12] Aristotle (1970b: 4).
[13] For a discussion of compound of form and matter see Aristotle (1970b: 184–6).
[14] Aristotle (1970b: 4). [15] Aristotle (1970a: 28–9: line 194b30).

'striving' for something as a different way of talking about causes. 'In answer to the question, Why does one walk? we reply "In order to be healthy"; and in saying so we believe we have assigned the cause.'[16] Aristotle did not argue that there is a conscious nature that determines things, merely that nature, and human acts, can often be understood better in relation to their purposefulness or intentionality.

It should be noted that Aristotle's four causes account was flexible and sensitive to pragmatic concerns of explanation. Aristotle recognised that causal explanation always takes place in pragmatic explanatory settings. It follows that although causal explanations get at 'real causes' in the world, for practical purposes we might not need to cite them all, just the crucial ones from the point of view of our inquiry. Also, Aristotle recognised that the categories can be used in different ways in different contexts. He accepted that while the four causes can be conceptualised as different categories, in practice different causes often 'mesh together' or 'coincide'. This was the case especially with formal, efficient and final causes.[17] Aristotle's account of causes was, though all-encompassing and ontologically grounded, also a very flexible and, indeed, for want of a better word, a 'common-sensical'[18] account. The Aristotelian account of cause is dealt with in more detail in chapter 6 as the insights of this account of cause are transposed to the debates in the social sciences. However, there are some questions of interpretation that are worth discussing in more detail at this juncture.

First, we must clarify the meanings of 'causal necessity' and 'determinism' in the Aristotelian framework.[19] The idea of causal necessity plays an important role for Aristotle. However, crucially Aristotle recognises many kinds of 'aetiological' necessity.[20] He recognises that

[16] Aristotle (1970b: 4).

[17] In substantial explanations the lines between the different types of causes could blur. For example, in the statue example, the formal cause (image of object) can be seen as closely intertwined with the agent, the 'image' of the object in his head and the purpose of sculpting (to make marble into this image). Aristotle (1970a: 38: line 198a25).

[18] The notion 'common-sensical' is potentially a very loaded term. In the context of this book it is taken to mean that which seems to make 'practical sense' to a number of people, that which seems intuitively satisfactory.

[19] For a discussion of necessity and determinism in Aristotle see Edel (1982: 390–5).

[20] For Aristotle's discussion of various forms of necessity see, for example, Aristotle (1970b: 10–11).

there are statements which necessitate each other logically: 'because demonstration cannot go otherwise than it does'.[21] This logical necessity, however, is distinguished from natural necessity. Natural necessity refers to the ontological causal relation that arises from within the constitution of a substance and/or from the interaction of different ontological substances, or *aitia*. Crucially, natural necessity is not 'deterministic' in the sense that a cause strictly necessitates an effect (when A, then B): this is because natural necessity is always contextual. Although things or changes are 'determined' (caused), they are always 'co-determined' by many naturally necessitating *aitia*. For example, Aristotle argues that potentiality of matter is a 'necessary' cause, but this refers to a naturally (ontologically) necessitating relation that implies a 'non-deterministic' kind of necessity in the sense that, though matter is a necessary (ontological) cause of a thing/change, it is determining in a 'constraining and enabling' sense and is never the only 'determining' cause.

Also, Aristotle's conception of 'voluntary action' demonstrates that he is not a determinist in the sense often implied. If Aristotle had been a determinist in the sense pejoratively implied by this notion (owing to a 'regularity-deterministic' understanding of the term discussed later), there would have been no room in his account for voluntary actions of people, or moral responsibility; this, however, is not the case. On the contrary, Aristotle is very interested in the 'voluntary actions' and the ethical considerations that arise from such actions. Aristotle believes that there are no 'fresh starts' (uncaused bases) for human action, yet for him this does not entail negation of voluntary action.[22] Although he admits that character is caused both internally and externally, it is still the locus of voluntary actions: we have many feelings/beliefs/desires that, although they are caused, we can choose from, which in turn builds our character.[23] The Aristotelian conceptions of causal necessity and determinism differ greatly from the more modern conceptions of these notions, as will be seen.

21 For example, $2 + 2 = 4$. Aristotle (1998: 121).

22 Sorabji (1980: 227–42). For a fascinating discussion of Aristotle's idea of voluntary action and responsibility see also Meyer (1993).

23 Moreover, it should be noted that Aristotle discusses extensively the notion of chance. Chance and accidents, for Aristotle, are not uncaused events but rather events with 'indefinite causes' from the point of view of the person who considers something as 'chance' or 'accidental'. See Aristotle (1998: 150).

It should also be noted that attempts to associate Aristotle's notion of causal explanation with the search for universal regularities and laws are misplaced. Although Aristotle put great emphasis on empirical data as means to understand the world, this did not mean that he espoused the regularity accounts of cause that have come to dominate in modern philosophy.[24] For Aristotle, even though a pattern or a generalisation is one way to gain knowledge of the world, it is not principally required, or necessarily interesting, in answering our why-questions.[25] Causal explanations, for him, consist of accounting for the coming together of (ontological) causal factors, not from observation of regular patterns of events or laws.

The Aristotelian account of causation remained the norm in philosophical debates up until the seventeenth century. It was especially powerful during medieval times in the frameworks of the Scholastic philosophers.[26] Throughout the medieval period the universe and its substances were understood through material and formal causes (hylomorphism). Also, efficient causes played a role during this period and, in fact, gained some precision through the development of the theories of local motion.[27] However, the most crucial category in the Scholastic philosophy was the notion of final cause, which became linked to the idea of God: God came to be seen as the ultimate final cause.[28] However, seventeenth-century Renaissance scientists started to challenge, and slowly dispose of, the 'broad' Aristotelian categorisation of causes in favour of a much more 'specific' concept of cause.

The anti-Aristotelian turn and the 'narrowing down' of the concept of cause

The early modern scientists were sceptical of achieving knowledge of the 'ultimate causes' in the world on Aristotelian lines. Against the Aristotelian 'speculations' concerning the constitution of the world, there was a shift towards a systematic observation-led view of science. This

[24] The origins of the regularity account can, in fact, be traced to the Stoics who saw causation not only as a universal principle in the world but also as a determinist principle. They introduced to philosophy the notion of 'exceptionless cause' and linked this with the notion of regularity. See, for example, Sorabji (1980: 64–8).

[25] Sorabji (1980: 65). [26] See White (2005). [27] Suarez (1994).

[28] See, for example, Aquinas (2006: 24–7; 1905: 2.15).

entailed prioritising 'observed facts' over the Aristotelian 'reasoned facts'. This shift can be seen in the works of the leading figures of the emerging experimental science: Galileo, Gilbert, Kepler and Newton.[29] Despite the increasing hostility towards the Aristotelian framework, which was associated with the 'static' Scholastic philosophy and science, it should be noted that the emergent 'empiricist' thinking was still balanced by the continuing belief in the notion of *verae causae*, that is, the assumption that there are real unobservable ontological causes behind observational knowledge of patterns of facts.[30] Also, the Aristotelian categories of cause were still used, although scientists started emphasising certain categories over others.[31]

Crucial shifts in the concept of cause started taking place, however, during the hundred years or so after the publication of René Descartes' *Meditations* in 1637: this is when the concept of cause was first 'narrowed down' to efficient causes by Descartes and then 'emptied out' of ontological meaning by the empiricist sceptics, notably by David Hume.

Descartes' thinking had its background in Scholastic philosophy. However, the purpose of his philosophy was to escape the Scholastic doctrine and to provide a new way of thinking about the world and the emerging experimental science. Central to Descartes' philosophy, which aimed to provide a rational basis for certain knowledge, was the rejection of the Aristotelian schema of causes. First and foremost, Descartes rejected the Scholastic doctrine that had emphasised the notion of final cause as the most important causal category: 'we must not inquire into the final, but only the efficient causes', Descartes states.[32] According to him, final causes cannot be known since only God knows the purposes of things. Also, Descartes wanted to avoid accepting the Aristotelian metaphysics of 'substances'. He argued that forms are an unnecessary part of scientific explanation: he was adamant that things cannot be assumed to have 'little souls' (that shape their existence). Descartes also remained largely indifferent to

[29] Wallace (1972a: 191–5).

[30] Thus, philosophically realist assumptions still held sway in early modern science. Clatterbaugh (1999: 181–2); Wallace (1972a: 159–210).

[31] Thus, Kepler focused on mathematical 'formal' explanations, while Galileo was interested in understanding the world through efficient causes. See Wallace (1972a: 191–5).

[32] Descartes (1997: 287).

material causes, especially the Aristotelian notion of material potentiality. Instead, he argued that the material world (body) can only be explained through 'pushing and pulling' or 'moving' forces. Efficient causes, then, became the central category of cause for Descartes.[33]

Since Descartes argued that we must avoid assigning 'occult qualities'[34] to objects of science, not only did efficient causes become the sole philosophically valid category of cause but they also became narrowed down in their content. Since Descartes ruled out 'forms' pre-existing within the efficient causes, efficient causes were no longer conceived of as 'self-moving' (that is, in the sense that powers for moving would be conceived to arise from internal structure or substance).[35] The conception of efficient cause used became 'mechanical': efficient causes referred, quite simply, to 'pushing and pulling' forces in the universe. The universe, and change in it, was understood mechanically: causes were seen as analogous to cogwheels in clocks where the various parts push each other along. To use the Aristotelian sculptor example, the sculptor is now conceived as a mechanical cause (that which chips marble) rather than as a substance with a particular form (and hence possessing causal powers of sculpting) with a goal (final cause) and an image of object (form) in mind. The deeper, embedded meaning of efficient cause advanced by Aristotle was abandoned in favour of this more precise, and singular, concept of cause.

Arguably, Descartes' denial of the wider causal categories created a trend towards mechanistic interpretations of causation, exemplified by the philosophy of Thomas Hobbes.[36] The idea of cause, however, was still fundamentally important for Descartes and the rationalist philosophers: Descartes may have initiated the disintegration of the Aristotelian categories of thinking about causation, but he was not a sceptic on causation.[37]

[33] Descartes stretched the meaning of efficient cause to two senses. First, since God is omnipotent, God is the first (and only) efficient cause in the universe. Descartes is often seen to be on the borderlines of a rather curious causal theory called 'occasionalism'. According to this view – which was later developed in Malebranche's and Berkeley's philosophies – God is the only 'efficient and total cause' in the universe. Yet, Descartes also does give a place to 'created things' as causes. He is interested in the emerging empirical science and volunteers many explanations for worldly phenomena, thus charting worldly, or secondary, efficient causes in 'created things'. Wallace (1972b); Nadler (1993).

[34] Chávez-Arvizo (1997: ix). [35] Descartes (1997: 3–15).

[36] Hobbes (1905). See also Clatterbaugh (1999: 9–10).

[37] Clatterbaugh (1999: 5). See also Wallace (1972b: 5–16).

John Locke's philosophy was one of the first to contain scepticism of the idea of 'necessary connection' between causes and effects, and specifically, scepticism about the ontological grounding of causes. Locke feared that the lack of human capacity to understand natural things beyond their empirical facets forced some limitations upon the search for causes as a way to certain knowledge. He argued that instead of talking about unobservable causes, and assuming the 'real existence' of these unobservable ontological causes, science would be better justified if it relied on 'sense-experience'.[38] Locke, then, laid down the first empiricist critique of classical metaphysical and Renaissance rationalist understandings of causation, although he did not develop this empiricism to a systematic rejection of these positions.[39]

George Berkeley took up Locke's incipient scepticism on causation. Berkeley also drew on the tradition of occasionalism, that is, the theory of causation that asserted that there are no causes in the world besides God as the efficient and total cause.[40] The outcome of this combination of intellectual backgrounds was the development of the scepticist ontologically 'empty' notion of cause. Berkeley argued that 'natural causes' have no real ontological status – nor do they have 'active power' in them. All causal power ultimately relates back to God. Because of his sceptical stance on worldly natural causes Berkeley came to argue that all earthly science does is observe the law-like occurrences in the world – without speculating on their metaphysical status ('reality').[41] This step is crucial in leading up to the sceptical empiricist philosophy of causation of David Hume.

David Hume and empiricist scepticism on causation

David Hume's solution to the problem of causation, or as he rephrases it, the problem of causal relation, is not only one of the most oft-quoted in modern philosophy; it is also, for our purposes, the most crucial one to understand, for it is this conception of causation that can be seen

[38] Wallace (1972b: 29).

[39] However, despite advancing empiricist ideas Locke did not dispense fully with the idea of causation or the notion of 'causal powers'. Behind his pessimism about humans finding out necessary causal connections, he seems to acknowledge that this does not mean that there are no real causes in the world (even if they are often beyond our understanding). Locke (1970: 335).

[40] Loeb (1981: 229–68). [41] Wallace (1972b: 36–7).

to have fundamentally influenced philosophy of science since. Hume advanced the first radically sceptic empiricist philosophy of causation, directly challenging both metaphysically realist and philosophically rationalist stances on causation.[42] The main contribution of Hume's philosophy, it is commonly agreed, is that it aimed to extend to its logical conclusions the sceptical critique of knowledge that emerged in modern philosophy with Locke and Berkeley. The question that Hume was grappling with was 'how can we really say we know anything for certain?', or perhaps more precisely, 'given we cannot know anything for certain, how can we justify science and knowledge?'[43] For Hume the 'solution' to the problem of knowledge lay in recognising that all knowledge arises purely from experience. The bases of knowledge – and the limits of our knowledge – are defined by what our perceptions transmit to us.

Hume promised to draw 'no conclusions but where he is authorised by experience'.[44] Against the rationalist philosophers such as Descartes, Hume argued that our ideas are not innate within us but arise from experience. Experiential impressions precede our ideas, our ideas are causally dependent on our impressions.[45] Instead of inquiring into ideas, we should, he argued, inquire into what is 'behind' the ideas that we hold, that is, the impressions that precipitate these particular ideas. In his *Inquiry Concerning Human Understanding* Hume states: 'By bringing ideas in so clear a light we may reasonably hope to remove all dispute which may arise concerning their nature and reality.'[46] Against the philosophical realist premises of the 'antient' philosophers and many Renaissance scientists, Hume famously argued that it is impossible to conceptualise the nature of reality beyond our impressions: because we have no way of justifying knowledge beyond our impressions and (impression-derived) ideas. Any claim to knowledge beyond experience is simply meaningless, he argued. Hume, thus, initiated the radical empiricist critique of metaphysics according to

[42] The critiques of modern Sceptics are in many ways developed on the same lines as the ancient Greek scepticism of Pyrrhos and Aenesidemus. See Hankinson (1998: 269).

[43] There was then a positive not just a sceptical element to his thought too. See Norton (1993a: 1).

[44] Hume (1978: 646).

[45] In that they are regularly conjoined with ideas and precede them. Norton (1993a: 6).

[46] Hume (1955: 29).

which the human mind and perceptions take precedence over 'reality'. As a result, any claims concerning external objects outside perceptions were to be 'committed to the flames' as metaphysical.[47]

The human mind, for Hume, is 'nothing more than a faculty of compounding, transposing, augmenting or diminishing the materials afforded to us by senses and experience'.[48] Our 'associations between ideas', he argues, arise from three things: '*resemblance, contiguity* in time and place and *cause* and *effect*'.[49] Importantly, Hume is careful in defining the most important form of the 'associations between ideas', that is, the relation between cause and effect. Hume did not think it was possible to define causes on the basis of 'efficacy, agency, power, force, energy, necessity, connexion or productive quality' as many previous philosophers had assumed.[50] These definitions, Hume points out, are all 'metaphysical' (refer to what cannot be experienced) and, thus, cannot be used to define causation.[51]

Hume argues that 'instead of searching for the idea [of cause and effect] in these definitions' we must 'look for it in impressions, from which it originally derived'.[52] He argues that there is nothing that can be perceived about causal relation *per se* in terms of 'powers', 'energy' or 'necessity' between cause and effect.[53] What the idea of causal relation, and the belief in the 'necessary connection' between cause and effect, come down to is the experience of 'constant conjunctions' of observable impressions, which our mind through 'custom' comes to 'link' together. We talk of 'causes and effects', he argues, when we have perceived certain observables or events regularly following each other: when we observe billiard balls colliding in regular successions we come to assume that the movement of one ball is the cause of the movement of the other.

Hume argues that a cause should be defined as 'an object precedent and contiguous to another, and where all the objects resembling the former are plac'd in like relations of precedency and contiguity to those objects which resemble the latter'.[54] Causation, or causal relation between a cause and an effect, is but an 'illusion' created in our minds through habit and imagination when we have observed certain constant conjunctions of observables or events in regular succession.

[47] See, for example, Rosenberg (1993: 67–70). [48] Hume (1955: 27).
[49] Hume (1978: 11). [50] Hume (1978: 157). [51] Hume (1978: 77).
[52] Hume (1978: 157). [53] Hume (1978: 161–3). [54] Hume (1978: 170).

> Upon the whole, *necessity is something that exists in the mind, not in objects*: nor is it possible for us ever to form the most distant idea of it considered as a quality of bodies. Either we have no idea of necessity, or *necessity is nothing but that determination of the thought to pass from causes to effects and from effects to causes, according to their experienced union.*[55]

Being simply an 'imagined' relation between successively observed events there are no metaphysical constraints on Humean causes: as long as regularities are present 'any thing may produce any thing'.[56] The one important qualification Hume insists on is that causes must be prior to their effects: indeed, in order to identify what is 'cause' and what an 'effect' Hume needs to define cause as the 'precedent event', that is, the type of event that is observed temporally prior to the effect.

This definition of cause is characterised by certain key assumptions – assumptions that will here be termed Humean assumptions. The guiding light of all these assumptions is the empiricist principle that all knowledge is derived from empirical experience.

First, Hume's definition of cause entails that all that can be said about causes must be derived from analysis of regular successions of perceptions: the idea of cause emerges in our heads only when we have observed certain types of events or occurrences in 'constant conjunctions'. Beyond regular successions of perceived events or occurrences there is no meaning to the notion of cause, and no basis for making claims about causal relations between causes and effects. Thus, the only way to find out what caused a billiard ball to move is to examine regular instances in which the billiard ball moved, for example, particular kinds of collisions between billiard balls.[57] These regular experiences provide us with the only valid grounds to make a 'causal statement' about the relations of the objects.

Second, Hume reduces causal relation to a relation between 'observables': since all we can know is what we observe, causal relations cannot but be regularity relations between observables, that is, relations of observable objects (billiard balls), or perhaps rather more specifically, relations of statements pertaining to observable 'events' (billiard balls colliding). It should be noted that this assumption of observability

[55] Hume (1978: 165–6). Italics added.
[56] Hume (1978: 173). [57] Hume (1978: 652).

entails that the objects Humean approaches talk about are 'ontologically flat', or 'atomistic', that is, they do not interest us beyond their observable facets. Since all we can know is what we observe, questions about the nature or constitution of objects beyond observability cannot be talked about meaningfully. For example, questions concerning the 'nature' and 'properties' of the billiard balls, let alone the 'powers' and 'capabilities' of the players, the table, or gravity, fall outside the limits of justifiable empiricist knowledge.

Third, the Humean definition denies the notion of 'natural necessity', that is, the idea that causes and effects are linked ontologically. Instead causal relations are characterised by another form of necessity: what is perhaps most accurately characterised as a psychological form of necesity, but has also been interpreted as close to a form of logical necessity. Hume tried to reduce the problem of causation to an epistemological issue, thus avoiding all ontological aspects of the problem of causation. He also avoided describing causal relations as in any way 'necessary'. However, it is difficult for him to avoid presuming some sort of necessary relation between causes and effects. For example, if we have observed billiard ball A hitting ball B for N amount of times, we have, on Humean grounds, a basis for saying A is the cause of B's movement. But what is the nature of this connection between A and B for Hume? It is, he argues, a connection derived from the psychological workings of the mind. However, interestingly, the form of psychological connection Hume describes is close to a form of logic, which is arguably why many followers of Hume have come to talk about the causal relations between regularly conjoined types of events as 'logically necessary'. There seems to be confusion between logical and psychological forms of necessitation in the Humean account, although it is not clear whether this is Hume's confusion or his followers'.[58] It certainly seems that for Hume's followers causal inference can be described as follows: 'given past regularities involving A and B, our minds seem to logically assume when A, then B': A and B, or statements pertaining to them, it seems, are related as a result of a logical deduction (based on past observations).[59] The assumption of something close to a logical necessitation

[58] See, for example, Mackie (1974: 27).

[59] As Hume puts it: 'when by any clear experiment we have discover'd the causes or effects of any phenomenon, we immediately extend our observation to every phenomenon of the same kind'. Hume (1978: 173–4).

seems to be embedded in the Humean, and in most empiricist accounts of causal relation that follow the general Humean assumptions.[60]

This (psycho)'logical' conception of causal connection is important to note because it carries within it a particular form of determinism, so-called regularity-determinism. Basing analysis of causal relations on relations of regularities entails the implicit assumption that, when we account for regularities, we can make causal claims of the form 'given that regularities connect type A and type B events, we have the basis for assuming when A, then B'. Despite Hume's scepticism of relying on inductive inference, his account seems to assume that when regularities are present we come to deduce 'logically' what will happen in a given instance. This assumption has subsequently come to play an important role in Hume's followers' accounts and gives rise to the particular 'closed system', and predictive, view of causation characteristic of twentieth-century approaches to science: given regularities we can logically deduce, or predict, a given event, even if only probabilistically.

Finally, it has to be noted that the Humean discussion of causation takes place strictly within the 'efficient cause' definition of cause marked out by Descartes: 'There is no foundation for [the] distinction... betwixt efficient causes, and formal, and material... and final causes. For as our idea of efficiency is deriv'd from the constant conjunction of two objects, wherever this is observ'd, the cause is efficient; and where there is not, there can never be a cause of any kind.'[61] Even though Hume rejects any ontological definition of cause (efficient or otherwise), the efficient cause metaphor plays a crucial role in the Humean accounts. The 'imagined' relation between causes and effects on the basis of regularities is imagined as an efficient one. Indeed, the regularity-deterministic 'given regularities, when A, then B' assumption evidences this well.

These assumptions of Humean philosophy have been widely influential in the philosophy of science in the late nineteenth century and in the twentieth century, as will be seen. However, before moving on to examine Hume's legacy in philosophy of science, it is vital to point to an often-ignored inconsistency in Hume's thought.

[60] Popper, for example, accepts that this is the fundamental contradiction within all empiricist thought (deriving all truths and knowledge from experience but being sceptical of experience as the way to certain knowledge). Popper (1959: 42).

[61] Hume (1978: 171).

Through his scepticist empiricism, Hume is considered to have destroyed any traditional philosophical justification for the concept of cause and for the old metaphysical maxim 'everything must have a cause' – in the ontological 'naturally necessitating' sense.[62] However, the philosophically realist strand of interpretation maintains that Hume does, in contradiction to his empiricist principles, accept the reality of non-observational objects and their causal powers.[63] Some interpreters point to the fact that, although his empiricist philosophical bases dictate that Hume should not talk of 'distinctions between objects and perception', Hume still regularly talks 'of things whereof he should be silent'.[64] In many passages Hume accepts that external (non-perceptual) objects are (ontologically) real and have real unobservable properties, even though we cannot necessarily know them through our ideas or impressions – hence, his frequent references to them as 'the unknown powers'.[65] Hume argues that 'These ultimate springs and principles are totally shut off from human curiosity and enquiry. Elasticity, gravity, cohesion of parts, communication of motion by impulse; these are probably the *ultimate causes and principles* which we shall never discover.'[66]

If metaphysical realism is defined as the belief in a mind-independent ontological reality of the world and its objects,[67] it seems that Hume, in contradiction with his empiricist scepticism, in fact, accepts the ontological nature of reality beyond our knowledge about it.[68] Despite

62 Wallace (1972b: 40).

63 The realist interpretation of Hume has a long history. Already some of Hume's contemporaries noticed his realism intertwining with empiricism. More recently, especially John P. Wright has been associated with this strand of interpretation (1983). See also Strawson (1989). An alternative 'projectivist' interpretation is developed in Helen Beebee (2006).

64 Wallace (1972b: 41).

65 There are numerous passages that imply this. See, for example, Hume (1978: 159, 267) and (1955: 75, 96).

66 Hume (1955: 45).

67 For a more detailed discussion of philosophical realism see chapters 5 and 6.

68 This implicit metaphysical realism, the philosophically realist interpreters argue, is also evident in Hume's second, often ignored, definition of cause as 'an object precedent and contiguous to another, and so united with it, that the idea of the one determines the mind to form the idea of the other and the impression of the one to form a more lively idea of the other'. Hume (1978: 170). This statement implies that Hume accepts that our minds are 'determined' to pass from one idea or impression to another and that, hence,

arguing that our knowledge is limited to 'constant conjunctions', Hume accepts that causal powers, in a 'metaphysical' sense, still exist beyond our empirical knowledge.[69]

This is a crucial thing to note, not just because it exposes an often-ignored incoherence in the thinking of this supposed 'arch-empiricist', but also because it allows us to realise that perhaps 'heroic Humeanism', with the deficiencies associated with it, is not Hume's position.[70] It follows that we must be cautious in defining Humeanism and in analysing Humean approaches. Humeanism is defined here through the three empiricist assumptions drawn out in this section (regularity, observability and regularity-determinism) and is also seen to be associated with efficient causality (although this does not characterise only Humean approaches). It is argued here that an approach is seen as Humean if it accepts, explicitly or implicitly, these assumptions. However, it is crucial to note that neither Hume himself, nor other scholars, as will be seen, are necessarily 'simply Humean'. This book focuses on drawing out the Humean assumptions in philosophers' and theorists' thinking, but this does not entail that people's views on causation are informed exclusively or coherently by such assumptions. The Humean discourse of causation has, as we shall see, been dominant in modern engagements with causation but its assumptions have played themselves out in various forms – hard and moderate, explicit and implicit – and they have often been accompanied – even if incoherently – with non-Humean assumptions.

The legacy of Humeanism in twentieth-century philosophy of science

The aim of the latter part of this chapter is to inquire into the ways in which Humean assumptions informed the twentieth-century philosophy of science. It is argued that the Humean assumptions have become dominant in how scientific causal explanation is framed. This is because these assumptions – albeit in a variety of forms – have become an essential ingredient of the philosophies of science that dominated twentieth-century philosophy. However, before discussing the legacy

Hume sees imagination and custom (the fundamental basis of his philosophy of causal relation) as real neurological, 'mechanical power' of the human mind. See also Hume (1978: 55, 84–6, 94–5, 104–5, 108).

[69] Hume (1978: 60). [70] Beauchamp and Rosenberg (1981: 32).

of Hume in the twentieth-century philosophy of science, I will first make a brief comment on the first influential philosophical systems to be deeply informed by Hume: Immanual Kant's and John Stuart Mill's.

Kant and Mill

Hume's discussion of causality famously awoke Kant from his 'dogmatic slumber'[71] and precipitated the ambitious Kantian system of philosophy that aimed to synthesise empiricism and rationalism. Hume had argued that causal necessity was but an illusion to which regular experiences gave rise. Kant was disturbed by Hume's sceptical conclusions and sought to give new philosophical grounds for causality. Kant wanted to justify the notion of causal necessity by rooting it in the *a priori* categories of the mind.

For Kant, there are two aspects to knowledge: sensation (passive observation) and thought (spontaneous act of mind). These 'ways of knowing' take place in space and time, intuitions that Kant deduces to be *a priori* categories of the mind.[72] Causality, for Kant, is an important example of an *a priori synthetic* relation that combines both ways of knowing and provides an important justification of human cognition.[73] Kant roots causality in the *a priori* categories of the mind: causal relation is necessary in thought, although not necessary in the world. He justifies causal necessity by arguing that causality is based on the 'necessary intuitions' of space and time that impose necessity on perceptions and thought. He argues that causal relations are 'necessary' because without necessary relation between causes and effects (in thought) experience becomes impossible: causality connects *a priori* categories with experience, thus justifying the role of human cognition.

However, it should be noted that this justification for causation is still squarely within the Humean fold. Although the relation between cause and effect is seen as a 'necessary relation' it is a relation not in the world but in thought. Also, crucially, Kant still sees causality as based on experience, and specifically, on 'the succession of the manifold'.[74] Like Hume's, Kant's conception of causation works on the basis of experienced regular successions: it is still a relation known through

[71] Kant quoted in Ewing (1924: 1). [72] Kant (1993: 48–75).
[73] Kant (1993: 177–80). [74] Kant (1993: 146).

experience and a relation that has no real value beyond experience of regular instances.[75]

Kant's treatment of causality should be noted for another reason besides its embeddedness in the core Humean assumptions as defined here. It is important to note that Kant initiated an important division in modern thought by divorcing causality in the phenomenal world from the sphere of ideas. The 'noumenal' sphere of moral and rational reasoning is, for Kant, divorced from deterministic causal laws of the phenomenal world; in the noumenal sphere free will can be seen to have autonomy from the exercise of causal laws.[76] Recognising this division is important as it has given rise to a dualistic logic in modern philosophy: causality has become associated with deterministic laws of nature and the noumenal has been seen as a separate 'ideational' non-causal/non-caused field entirely divorced from these 'deterministic' laws of the phenomenal world.[77]

In contrast to Kant's attempts to give a role to *a priori* faculties of the mind in justifying the category of causality, J. S. Mill continued the bold English tradition of empiricism. For Mill, all human reasoning was based on experience. It followed that the principle of causality was also derived from empirical experience: Mill argues that we can establish the 'universal law of causality' through the method of induction.[78] Mill's account of cause is fundamentally Humean in that the inductive logic takes causal knowledge to be co-extensive with regularities of observables.

However, Mill also extended Humean arguments in a new direction. He defines causes not just in terms of the classic Humean logic, but also in terms of 'consequents' and 'antecedents': 'every consequent is connected ... with some particular antecedent or set of antecedents; for every event there exists some combination of objects or events ... the

[75] For discussion of Hume and Kant and their similarities see Beauchamp (1974c: 1–35).

[76] Ewing (1924: 196–235).

[77] For a good account of the impact of this dualistic logic see Patomäki (2002: 89).

[78] Mill (1970: 203). Unlike Hume, Mill is not critical of the principle of induction but asserts that inductive method if properly developed can provide basis for all knowledge. Hume saw no self-evident certainty in induction. See, for example, Hume (1955: 40–54). For a discussion as to the extent of his scepticism of induction see Beauchamp and Rosenberg (1981: 33–79).

occurrence of which is always followed by that phenomenon'.[79] Crucially, Mill emphasises that causal analysis tries to determine those antecedents that can be shown to be crucial for an effect. He puts forward the so-called Method of Agreement as a way of explicating these singular causes. He argues that a cause can be called a cause if it can be shown that when effect E is present, cause C is also present. Crucially, he also introduces the so-called Method of Difference which aims to demonstrate, through a counterfactual argument, that effect E would not have taken place were it not for cause C (that is, E is absent when C is absent).

Although Mill makes room for talking about what seem to be 'singular' causal antecedents (causal statements that do not explicitly invoke regularities), it should be noted that causal antecedents are seen to be underlined by regularities in nature. To say 'if C, then E' or 'if no C, no E' entails, for Mill, the acceptance of a regularity connection that links 'C to E'. The logic of the argument is also tied to the regularity-deterministic assumption that characterises the Humean account of cause: we have grounds for making 'if C, then E' and 'if no C, then no E' statements precisely because causal relations are seen as characterised by 'closed system' relations; when regularities are observed we have a basis for making regularity-deterministic statements of the 'when A, then B' or 'if no A, then no B' kind.

Despite Kant's and Mill's acceptance of basic Humean premises, Humeanism did not flourish fully until the twentieth century. During the twentieth century the Humean assumptions became deeply embedded within the dominant currents in the philosophy of science. I will now turn to discuss the most influential twentieth-century philosophies of science and examine how they have been informed by the Humean assumptions. I will first discuss the anti-causal Humeanism that characterised phenomenalism, conventionalism and logical positivism, and, then, the more moderate form of Humeanism that informed the most widely accepted form of twentieth-century Humeanism, DN-model positivism. Finally, I will also examine certain theories of causation that have not generally been noted as being influenced by Humeanism but nevertheless implicitly buy into its core assumptions, notably the counterfactual theories of causation.

[79] Mill (1970: 213–14).

Radical empiricism and the anti-causal turn

For Hume, Kant and Mill, despite the acceptance of some key empiricist assumptions, the notion of cause still played a fundamental role in scientific terminology and knowledge claims. However, at the beginning of the twentieth century there was a distinct turn against the very notion of cause in scientific and philosophical circles, a turn premised on following the Humean assumptions to 'radically empiricist' conclusions.

Ernst Mach was one of the first radical empiricists. Mach based his phenomenalist philosophy on the basic empiricist assumption: 'what is knowable must be perceivable'.[80] However, he took this principle to its extreme logical conclusions: he denied outright the existence of 'things' (external objects) in nature. For Mach, all we can know *and* all that exists are sense-impressions. The job of science is to catalogue these sense-impressions for practical purposes and, hence, all references to 'real objects' and 'external reality' must be abandoned since:

> The world consists only of sensations and the assumption of the nuclei referred to, or of a reciprocal action between them from which sensations proceed, turns out to be quite idle and superfluous. Such a view can only suit a half-hearted realism or a half-hearted philosophical criticism... What I aimed at was merely to obtain a safe and clear philosophical standpoint... shrouded in no metaphysical clouds.[81]

The 'conventionalists' concurred with this anti-realist conclusion. Henri Poincaré and Pierre Dühem proposed that what we think are scientific facts are only what we think are convenient ways of thinking about the world. This entailed a whole-scale rejection of independent reality beyond the human mind, an assumption that had been fundamental for Aristotle and was also implicitly accepted by Hume.[82]

Crucially, the logical positivist philosophers of science who became influential in the early part of the twentieth century followed these empiricist lines of thought: they aimed to give the new radical empiricist premises solid grounding through 'logical analysis of language'. The principle at the heart of logical positivism was Ludwig Wittgenstein's 'verification principle', which maintained that all propositions of

[80] Mach (1959: 46). [81] Mach (1959: 12, 47).
[82] Dantzig (1954: 12). See also Jaki (1984).

science should be analysable by deducing them down to more elementary statements that can be verified through observation.[83] Instead of resorting to tautological analytic statements, such as 'a sleep-inducing powder has dormitive power', or speculative synthetic statements, such as 'all bachelors are drunkards', which are not clearly verifiable, science must base itself on clearly verifiable statements such as 'all observable bodies of the type A, with the observable qualities x, y, z . . . , tend to, in given circumstances a, b, c . . . , be observed to behave in C ways', the truth of which can then be clearly established through observation.[84] The logical positivist account of science aims to provide the ultimate bulwark against 'ontological', or 'metaphysical', approaches to science. Indeed, the import of the verification principle was that any non-observation-based statements could be rejected as 'meaningless', since 'we have no idea of what [they are] supposed to signify'.[85]

How did these radical empiricists conceptualise causation? Most radical empiricists interestingly came to abandon all references to causes. Mach and the conventionalists, for example, rejected the notion of cause as an unreliable, rudimentary and 'conventional' notion with no real practical purpose in the new twentieth-century science.[86] The countless controversies in metaphysics seemed to prove that there has never been, nor can there ever be, agreement on the metaphysical question of causation: as a result, it was argued that science had better accept that there is no 'essential' causation.[87] Others, such as Bertrand Russell, similarly concluded that 'the law of causality . . . like much that passes among philosophers is a relic of a by-gone age'.[88]

On the whole, the issue of causation came to be replaced by a new focus, the analysis of laws, since:

> It is more fruitful to replace the entire discussion of the meaning of causality by an investigation of the various kinds of laws that occur in science. When these laws are studied it is a study of the kinds of causal connections that have been observed. The logical analysis of laws is certainly a clearer, more precise problem than the problem of what causality means.[89]

[83] Wittgenstein (1961). See also Hanfling (1981: 7).
[84] M. Smith (1998: 98–9). See also Ayer (1974: 7).
[85] Schlick quoted in Hanfling (1981: 8).
[86] Poincaré quoted in Dantzig (1954: 93). [87] Wallace (1972b: 168–80).
[88] Bertrand Russell quoted in Wallace (1972b: 181).
[89] Carnap (1966: 204).

The phenomenalist, conventionalist and logical positivist view of science came to be based upon looking for empirical regularities of 'facts', which could (with enough verification, that is, repetition) be inferred into 'general laws'.

Crucially, laws were conceived of in line with Humean assumptions. They were seen as 'factual generalisations', that is, generalisations consisting of observed 'factual' regularities. Since laws were conceived of simply as describing regular patterns of observation, following Hume, causal relations in any deeper 'ontologically necessary' sense were not deemed to concern science. Indeed, the radical empiricists saw references to 'real' causal relations or 'powers' as meaningless. Thus, to say, for example, that 'gravity has causal power' is meaningless because this statement cannot be verified through experience. To talk of such things as gravity meaningfully, we have to construct empirically verifiable statements, such as 'all material bodies with weight X fall to earth', which, when empirically verified (through regular observations), can be inferred to refer to the empirical 'law of gravity'.

This conception of science based on the analysis of laws was, crucially, firmly rooted in the acceptance of the Humean assumptions. Indeed, the radical empiricists acknowledge their roots in Hume and Mill and the tradition of 'English empiricism'.[90] However, they also make clear that what they want to pick up from this tradition is the strictly empiricist premises. They argue that Humean assumptions, when developed coherently, can be used to do away with all the 'vague' discussions of external reality but also, paradoxically, to dispose of the very notion of cause (which Hume, Kant and Mill accepted). The acceptance of Humean assumptions in their pure form, it is pointed out, leads to the obsolescence of the very concept of cause: it is, in fact, a vague notion that must be abandoned in favour of the more precise notion of laws.

It is important to emphasise that although these approaches were largely anti-causal in terminology, they entailed the acceptance of the Humean assumption of regularity-determinism, logical necessity and 'closed systems'. This can clearly be detected in the radical empiricist penchant for talking about 'functional necessitation', 'mathematical functions' and 'prediction', in the place of causation:

[90] Ayer (1974: 73–4).

> The notion of cause possesses significance only as a means of provisional knowledge or orientation. In any exact or profound investigation of an event, the inquirer must regard the phenomena as dependent on one another in the same way that the geometer regards the sides and angles of a triangle as dependent on one another . . . The concept of cause is replaced . . . by the concept of function; the determining of the dependence of phenomena on one another, the economic exposition of actual facts, is proclaimed as the object, and physical concepts as a means to an end solely.[91]

While 'functional' and 'mathematical' necessity was not termed 'causal' in the work of these theorists, the emphasis on 'functional determination' and 'mathematical necessity' exemplified the regularity-determinist way of framing relationships of explanatory regularities or laws. When observational regularities have been observed (that is, laws, such as heavy objects fall to the ground), we can deduce predictions from them (that is, when a pen is dropped it will fall). Laws and their relations make up 'closed systems' within which 'when A, then B' type statements can be formulated. The radical empiricists saw the world, and science, as characterised by 'closed systems' where regularities (laws), or statements pertaining to them, were seen as logically related.[92] Within this system causal laws (for example, the causal law of gravity) are conceived as functionally or logically necessitating of outcomes, but they are not conceived as 'naturally' necessitating forces in the world.

It is on the basis of this closed system view of causation that these approaches also emphasised the role of prediction: regularity assumption allows these theorists to talk about not just 'laws' but also predictability.[93] Given that certain regularities, or laws, have been observationally verified, scientists can predict (logically deduce) expected events. Furthermore, the notion of probability is greatly developed as a way of introducing openness to the otherwise regularity-deterministic closed system view of causation. Indeed, the problem of induction (cannot always obtain observationally perfect laws) is solved by resorting to 'probability inferences', that is, probability measurements of the degrees of certainty that an empirical law has (probabilistic theories will be discussed in more detail shortly).[94]

[91] Ernst Mach quoted in Wallace (1972b: 171). See also Mach (1959: 89–92).
[92] See Schlick (1959: 85–7). [93] Carnap (1966: 192).
[94] See, for example, Carnap (1950).

Deductive-nomological causal explanation

From the 1930s onwards the influential logical positivist account of science was challenged 'from within'. What came to replace the dominance of logical positivism in philosophy of science was the 'standard positivism' of Carl Gustav Hempel and Karl Popper. These philosophers of science were ingrained within logical positivism but attacked its excessive reliance on inductive inference. Popper argued that scientific knowledge does not arise simply from inductive observation but, rather, from deductive testing of hypotheses. Popper accepted that scientists hold many theoretical and conceptual (or 'metaphysical') preconceptions before engaging in empirical testing.[95] He also accepted that verification by empirical testing *never* proves conclusively a scientific truth, as the logical positivist view of science had assumed. He maintained that by rejecting the logical positivist inductive view of science in favour of a 'deductive' and 'falsifiability-based' model of science we can justify the practice, rationality and progress of science far more adequately.

Popper argued that the key to a scientific (as opposed to non-scientific) theorising is that it is falsifiable, that any other person can empirically test the theory, and, thereby, either corroborate or falsify it. Science does not need to, nor should it, advance absolute truths: science is about being critical of knowledge claims by subjecting all claims to the possibility of falsification. Popper stipulates that a scientific explanation has to follow a particular method of inference to avoid 'unscientific' and 'unfalsifiable' conclusions. This method of scientific inference is well summarised by Hempel as the so-called 'deductive-nomological' (DN-) model of explanation. The DN- or covering law model claims that the explanatory and predictive logic of science requires that we analyse events (explanandums) through a logically deductive analysis of two kinds of empirical statements, general laws and initial conditions (explanans).[96] Popper argues that 'to give a causal explanation of an event means to deduce a statement which describes it, using as premises of the deduction one or more universal laws, together with certain singular statements, the initial conditions'.[97] This means that to explain something causally we have to describe (a) the universal laws that have been observed (e.g. whenever a weight put on a thread

[95] Popper (1959: 38). [96] Hempel (1966: 50–4). [97] Popper (1959: 59).

exceeds the tensile strength of the thread, it will break), and (b) the initial conditions referring to a particular time and place (e.g. tensile strength of thread X is 1 pound and a weight of 2 pounds is put on the thread); we can then (c) deduce the 'event' to be explained (e.g. the thread breaks).[98]

Contra radical empiricists, Hempel and Popper do not reject the concept of cause. However, it must be noted that the DN-model understanding of science and causality is deeply empiricist and, indeed, Humean. Popper makes it clear that he rejects the metaphysical principle of causation (assumption that everything has an ontological cause), settling, instead, on seeing causal explanations (in the deductive mode prescribed) as a 'guiding methodological rule' of empirical science.[99] Crucially, causal analysis, as a methodological rule, is firmly tied to observation of regular patterns of events. Popper admits that the initial conditions of the deduced event are often referred to as the 'cause' of the event.[100] However, he points out that mere initial conditions *do not* explain: statements of universal causal laws are necessary for any causal explanation. Causal explanation, then, is based squarely on the analysis of regularities. Scientific causal statements require, or more weakly, presuppose, the notion of causal laws (conceived as regularities). Any account that makes a singular causal statement without advancing the laws on which it is presupposed is, as Hempel puts it, only an 'explanatory sketch' that needs to be validated by search for the relevant regularities.[101] To say that placing a weight on a thread was the cause of the thread breaking is only an explanatory sketch that needs validation by laws (observation-based regularities) to qualify as a 'causal explanation'. The general laws are still arrived at through observing regularities of events and the 'general laws' are still the crux of the scientific 'causal' explanation.

Also, the causal statements are still based on regularities of observed events. Science is concerned with generalisations about observations. Hence, 'deep ontological' assumptions about the nature of observables are not necessary for scientific knowledge. For knowledge to be reliable, scientific inquiry must not veer into making unjustifiable speculative claims about unobservables. Popper admits that scientific theories make many theoretical assumptions about unobservables but,

[98] Popper (1959: 60). [99] Popper (1959: 61).
[100] Popper (1959: 60). [101] Hempel (1965: 423).

crucially, emphasises that the confirmation of the plausibility of a scientific account must conform to the logic of the empirical observation specified.[102]

Importantly, it must also be noted that the regularity theory in the DN-model form also entails the assumption of logical necessity and regularity-determinism, that is, if 'laws' have been detected and initial conditions are outlined certain events can be 'logically' deduced. Causal relations refer to logically necessitating relations between statements rather than naturally necessitating causal relationships. The regularity-deterministic assumption is also accepted: it is assumed that 'for every event Y there is an event X, or set of events X1 ... Xn, such that X, or X1 ... Xn, and Y are regularly conjoined under some set of descriptions; thus *whenever X (or X1 ... Xn), then Y*'.[103] Causal explanation and prediction, then, are justified on the basis of a 'closed system' model of causation. Owing to this Humean regularity-deterministic framing of the issue of causation, explanation, prediction and causality come to be seen as mutually dependent, symmetrical processes in the DN-model: causality (understood in terms of regularities) equals explanation equals predictive capability. If prediction is not possible, neither is a scientifically valid causal account nor an explanation of a set of observations.

Probability theories of causation

Popper and Hempel recognised the problem that the strict tying together of 'causality' (conceived of as regularities), prediction and explanation entailed, given how difficult prediction in many sciences is. To deal with this problem of prediction, standard positivism developed the opening for the 'probabilistic' mode of explanation. This mode of explanation works in the same format as the DN-model but

[102] Even though, arguably, the treatment of the notion of cause with Popper acquires some deeply problematic overtones owing to his inability to distinguish between logical and natural necessity and his occasional references to causal laws as 'ontologically' or 'metaphysically' necessary. Indeed, there seems to be an amount of 'slippage' into philosophically realist assumptions in Popper's work, although these sharply contradict his empiricist Humean premises. See Popper (1959: 438). See also essays by Kneale and Popper in Beauchamp (1974c: 36–63).

[103] Bhaskar (1978: 69).

with the requirement of showing probability rather than deductive certainty.[104] Probabilistic explanations are, as Hempel puts it, 'assertions to the effect that if certain specified conditions are realised, then an occurrence of such and such kind will come about with such and such statistical probability'.[105] Here the logic of inference is perhaps best described as 'inductive-probabilistic' in that, rather than being based on 'necessary' deduction from universal laws, it is based on probabilistic hypothesis based on inductively observed frequencies of certain events happening.[106] This model of explanation is still very closely linked to the DN-model, however. As von Wright has summarised, in the probability inferences 'the covering law, the "bridge" or "tie" connecting the basis with the object of explanation, is a probability-hypothesis to the effect that on an occasion when E1 ... En [initial conditions] are instantiated it is highly probable that E will occur'.[107]

Importantly, a variety of probabilistic theories of causation have prospered in the wake of the DN-model explanation.[108] This is because through the probabilistic mode of inference the empiricist positivist model of science was provided with a useful way of accepting and dealing with uncertainty of knowledge claims: through the probabilistic model we need not make absolutely regularity-deterministic statements necessitated by the ideal of closed system causality. Probability analysis is useful when 'complete causal analysis is not feasible' because of causal complexity or incompleteness of our data or theories.[109]

It is important to remember that the probability models, in the past and in the present debates, are fundamentally tied to the empiricist Humean assumptions of regularity, observability and, indeed, logical regularity-determinism (although in probabilistic form). The resort to probability explanations provides a way for empiricist Humean accounts to recognise – while being premised on a 'closed' model of causality – that perfect prediction and deterministic 'when X, then Y' statements are not always possible.

In many ways the discussions in the burgeoning area of probabilistic causal theorising still focus on the old paradox of empiricist theories of causation: on what grounds may we talk of causal relations when

[104] Hempel (1966: 58–69). [105] Hempel (2001: 279).
[106] Von Wright (1971: 13–15). [107] Von Wright (1971: 13).
[108] See, for example, Eells (1991); Suppes (1970); Spirtes, Glymour and Schienes (1999); Hitchcock (1993).
[109] Suppes (1970: 8).

all we can really have knowledge about are observable statistical regularities? How can we derive causal interpretations from statistical data and mathematical forms of knowledge? Contemporary causality and probability modellers recognise that causation does not equal correlation. Nevertheless, it is assumed that statistical methods that measure correlations are what fundamentally give us access to 'causal relations'. What much of the discussion in probabilistic theories of causation is now focused on is discussions of what counts as 'causality' among statistical and mathematical relations and around provision of methods or equations that provide us with what can be described as causal, rather than non-causal, inferences and conclusions.[110]

Implicit legacies of Humeanism

The logical positivist account of science dominated philosophy of science for the first part of the twentieth century. Since the 1950s the Popperian (post)positivist[111] view of science has been dominant, even if criticised with regard to its account of the 'growth of knowledge'. Both versions of the positivist philosophy of science are seen to have been supported by scientific developments in quantum physics and chaos theory. These new areas of science are seen to have demonstrated the uselessness of talking of 'reality' or 'ontological causal powers' and, hence, to have validated the empiricist 'ontologically flat' form of scientific inquiry focused on analysing logical relations of statements and statistical relations of quantifiable variables.[112] It should be noted, however, that the self-evidence of these interpretations is now vehemently contested: it is not clear whether empiricist frameworks have

[110] See especially the discussions surrounding Spirtes, Glymour and Schienes' book *Causation, Prediction and Search* (1999). Interesting discussions can be found in Vaughn R. McKim and Stephen P. Turner's *Causality in Crisis? Statistical Methods and Search for Causal Knowledge* (1997). See also Hausman (1999).

[111] Popper conceived of his own conception of science as postpositivist in relation to logical positivism. However, it is nowadays widely discussed as a variant of a general positivist philosophy of science. See chapter 2 for the definition of positivism applied here.

[112] This assumption has certainly guided the so-called orthodox quantum physics of Heisenberg (1930). See also Born (1949) and Gribbin (1991: 162). Anti-realist interpretations have also been advanced by Quine (1960, 1969).

reflected or contributed to the anti-realist trends in early quantum and chaos theory.[113]

Because of the dominance of empiricist positivist views of science, most philosophy of science debates have, in the past four decades, been debated within the confines of the Humean analysis of causation they have entailed. Humean assumptions have been so dominant that they have, by and large, been accepted as a given in twentieth-century philosophy of science. The debate on the 'growth of knowledge', for example, has been conducted largely within the confines of the Humean assumptions. Although the logical positivist and Popperian models of scientific progress have come under criticism from philosophers such as Thomas Kuhn, Imre Lakatos and Paul Feyerabend,[114] these attacks have not challenged the Humean notion of cause embedded in the positivist accounts of scientific progress.[115]

Because of the largely unproblematised nature of the empiricist positivist views of science, the Humean assumptions, it must be noted, are accepted not just explicitly and knowingly, but increasingly also inadvertently. It is important to point to some of these implicitly Humean legacies in philosophical approaches.

One of the influential theories of causation that has increasingly been adopted by many philosophers of science has been the counterfactual theory of causation. Mill was the first to advance a counterfactual definition of causation but it did not gain wide acceptance until the 1970s when David Lewis developed his counterfactual theory of causation.[116] The counterfactual theory of causation has complicated philosophical justifications involving the 'similarity relations' between possible worlds. The basic idea, however, is simple: E (effect) causally depends on C (cause) if and only if E would not have happened had it not been for C's occurrence. To give a concrete example often utilised by

[113] Recent developments suggest that relativity theory, quantum theory and chaos theory are all commensurable with an ontologically realist and causal approach. See, for example, Fine (1986); Christopher Norris (2000); Bohm and Hiley (1993); Cushing, Fine and Goldstein (1996), Cushing and McMullin (1989); Williams (1997); Bell (1987). See also Bunge (1959, 1979) and Krips (1987).

[114] Lakatos and Musgrave (1970); Kuhn (1962); Feyerabend (1993); Laudan (1978). See also discussion in Chalmers (1996).

[115] Although the empiricist positivist idea of science was questioned by Feyerabend, the empiricist notion of cause, and the attendant form of scientific causal theorising, was never fully attacked. See Feyerabend (1981, 1989).

[116] D. K. Lewis (1973). For revised ideas see D. K. Lewis (1999).

counterfactual accounts: Suzy's throw was a cause of a bottle breaking because, had she not thrown the stone at the bottle, it would not have broken. Essentially this means that causation is defined as a dependency relation between observed events. This assumes an asymmetry between causes and effects, that is, an effect is seen as counterfactually dependent on the cause in a way that the cause is not dependent on the effect.[117] The counterfactual theorists have come up with a variety of 'causal puzzles' to extend and clarify the logic of counterfactual definition of causation.[118] However, for our purposes, it is not necessary to go into these puzzles in great detail; instead what needs to be ascertained is that the counterfactual accounts of causation are often premised on Humean assumptions.

How can Humeanism be seen to play a role in these accounts? First, counterfactual causation of the kind advocated by most philosophers of causation is based squarely on observables: the counterfactual theories analyse the relationships of observed events such as Suzy's throwing of a stone and a bottle breaking. In this sense, these theories conform to the Humean focus on observable events as the focus of causal analysis: they do not touch upon or even claim to investigate the nature of underlying causal powers or mechanisms in science.

Second, their analysis often proceeds on the basis of examining the logical relation between these observed events: the focus is on finding logical patterns in the way in which we assign something as a cause.[119] Counterfactual theory, then, is often conceived of as an epistemological theory: its aim is not to make 'deep ontological' causal claims concerning powers or structures underlying observable instances or events, but to find logical relations between events. This is also seen in the refusal to acknowledge the reality of the theoretical terms used in the discussion. While David Lewis himself was a modal realist with regard to the possible worlds logic that underpins his counterfactual theory of causation,[120] 'most contemporary philosophers . . . would distanc[e] themselves from full-blown realism about possible worlds' and would

[117] For an account of causal asymmetries see Hausman (1998).

[118] See, for example, debates between Lewis and his critics. Collins (2000); D. K. Lewis (2002). See also Collins and Paul (2002).

[119] Hitchcock (2002).

[120] Other theorists such as Peter Menzies (1999) also developed more realist accounts.

'even treat them instrumentally as useful theoretical entities having no independent reality'.[121]

Furthermore, and most interestingly, although counterfactual theories put the focus on singular cases of causal relation, these singular cases often assume a Humean account of laws. Singular claims, as in Mill's account of cause, for example, are based on generalised observational patterns – the breaking of the bottle was counterfactually dependent on Suzy's throw because it is assumed that in the past we have learned through successive observations that when hard objects encounter glass bottles at sufficient speed they tend to break them. As Daniel Hausman's discussion of counterfactuality, for example, evidences, counterfactual theories are discussed in conjunction with a view of causation as 'lawful co-variation', a 'relation fallibly but reliably indicated by correlations and probabilistic dependencies'.[122]

Humeanism of counterfactuality is evidenced also in the fact that counterfactual theories accept a form of regularity-deterministic logic: it is important to note that the 'when no A, no B' logic is but a reversal of the regularity-deterministic deduction 'if A, then B'. Indeed, some philosophers such as Hausman have come to demand that counterfactuality is tied to prediction: 'suppose one accepts a counterfactual of the form, if I were to push the button, the alarm would go off. Such a counterfactual ought to license one to predict that the alarm will go off if one in fact pushes the button.'[123] Much like causality for the DN-model, counterfactual logic for many theorists becomes tied to logical deduction of predictive inferences from known causal regularities.

Another influential account in recent years has been the so-called INUS-condition account developed by J. L. Mackie. A cause for Mackie can usefully be defined as 'an *insufficient* but *non-redundant* [necessary] part of an *unnecessary* but *sufficient* condition'.[124] To give a simple example, what this means is that through the INUS-condition framing we can consider the lighting of a match as a necessary but insufficient element of the background conditions that were unnecessary but together sufficient to produce a result, that is, fire. The INUS-condition account has seemed very appealing to many theorists as it can claim to account for various complexes of causes in a logically coherent manner.

[121] Menzies (2001). [122] Hausman (1996: 62).
[123] Hausman (1996: 64). [124] Mackie (1974: 62).

Interestingly, it has been of particular interest to empiricist and positivist scholars who wish to retain an essentially Humean conception of causation, despite the fact that Mackie himself was not an obvious advocate of empiricist Humeanism, but interested in accounting for causation 'in the world': indeed, he clearly states that causation 'is not merely, as Hume says, *to us*, also *in fact*, the cement of the universe'.[125] What might be interpreted to be Humean about his account?

While Mackie's account suggests that regularities do not exhaust causation in the world, and seems to introduce certain philosophically realist premises (philosophical realism is discussed in more detail in chapter 5) into his overall account, his INUS-condition theory can be interpreted as a descendant of the Humean regularity theory of causation, as a variant of 'modern regularity theory'.[126] First, Mackie's INUS-condition account is both sympathetic to Hume's formulation of causation and compatible with a regularity theory of causation. In many ways it is designed to provide the context for analysis of complex regularities, which is why many empiricists have come to read Mackie's INUS-condition account as an empiricist one: as a 'refinement of the theories of D. Hume and of J. S. Mill'.[127] For a Humean, what is interesting about Mackie's theory is that it can account for more complex conditions of causal regularities, while still allowing us to derive causal statements from regularities of events previously observed. The INUS-condition account has been, for example, used to justify a Humean interpretation of the relationship between cancer and smoking: the theory allows a Humean to call on a regularity relation of smoking and cancer, while still allowing him or her to argue that many other causes (regularity-based intervening variables) have, also, to be accounted for in order to give a 'full account' of INUS-conditions.

Also, it is notable that Mackie's INUS-condition account still eschews accounting for causes in terms of 'deep ontological' causal necessity.[128] In many ways, it could be said that the INUS-condition account, like counterfactual theories of causation, provides a logical structure for how we might characterise causation, rather than an ontological account of causes as producers of outcomes. As will be seen in

[125] Mackie (1974: 2). He accepts realist premises and also a role of natural necessity. Mackie (1974: 215, 228–30).

[126] Beauchamp (1974b: 75). [127] Horsten and Weber (2005: 955).

[128] A criticism Bhaskar (1979: 207, fn 23) and Patomäki (2002: 76) advance.

chapter 5, however, the application of the INUS-condition idea of cause need not be Humean: it can, when reformulated away from the regularity premise, also be linked to a non-empiricist non-positivist 'deep ontological' conception of causality.

Another aspect of counterfactual and INUS-condition theories of causation is also worth a mention at this point. What is striking about these theories of causation is that they tend to search for a unified language of causality: what they are seeking to do is define a coherent logic for causal statements, such that will apply in all kinds of cases. While specifying the logic of how we should apply the concept of cause in science is of course important, this search for the perfectly formulated singular logic of causation can be seen as problematic in that it presumes that there is a singular logic of causation to be found. Instead of looking for a generally applicable theory of counterfactual causation, perhaps accepting that there might be different kinds of causes and causal conditions, which entail very different kinds of causal intuitions in us, should be recognised more readily in these discussions.[129] This is an issue that will be picked up in chapter 6 as the broadening out of the conceptualisation of the concept of cause is advanced.

Conclusion

The notion of cause has developed significantly over the years. From the broad and ontologically grounded conception of cause, the meaning of the term has been systematically 'narrowed down' in scope to efficient causes, and then 'emptied out' of 'deep ontological' meaning. Hume's empiricist philosophy, in which these two trends culminated, sought to solve the problem of causation by solving the epistemological problem of causation: how do we come to know causes? By arguing that all we have to base causal claims on is observational empirical regularities, Hume assumed that he had provided solid foundations for thinking about causation. The key assumptions that characterise the Humean approach to causal analysis have been identified here as follows.

[129] An example of a positive step in current theories of causation is Cartwright's recent work (2004, 2007) which holds open the possibility of pluralistic theories of causation.

1 Causal relations are tied to *regularities*, and causal analysis to observation of regular patterns.
2 Causal relations are seen as regularity-relations of patterns of *observables*. Statements concerning 'causal ontology' or 'causal powers' are, as unobservable, taken to be meaningless.
3 Causal relations are characterised by *regularity-determinism*: it is assumed that, given certain observed regularities, when A type of events take place, B type of events can be assumed logically to follow. Humeanism, especially in the twentieth century, is based on the assumption of logical necessitation, that is, a 'closed system' view of causation that gives grounds also for prediction.
4 Beyond these strictly Humean assumptions, causes have been understood through the notion of *efficient cause*. Causes are 'moving' causes that 'push and pull'.

These assumptions have become widely accepted in twentieth-century philosophy of science. They were first appealed to by the radical empiricists who turned the discussion of causality into the analysis of the logical relations between observation-based laws. The Popper–Hempel DN-model moderated the excesses of the logical positivist view of science. However, the Humean assumptions have informed the DN-model of scientific explanation, too. Causal explanation has been tied to regularity analysis of observables and is seen to be characterised by regularity-deterministic rather than ontological 'natural' causal necessity.

Crucially, the Humean assumptions have coincided with, and reinforced, a particular conception of science, that is, the empiricist positivist conceptions of science that sees science as defined by 'a scientific method' based on 'systematic' empirical observation. Positivist philosophies of science, informed strongly by empiricist epistemology, consider science as a provider of knowledge that, based as it is on empirical observation of general patterns, provides 'truth-approximating', predictive knowledge of the empirical world around us. The Humean conception of causation, and of science, has become widely accepted as 'self-evident' in much of the philosophy of science and has formed the implicit and unquestioned backdrop for most debates in the philosophy of science in past decades. Indeed, even when it is stated that 'moisture is the cause of the rusting of the knife' or that 'had Suzy not thrown the rock the glass would not have broken', it is accepted that this 'loose' causal talk is always premised, even if implicitly, on the Humean assumptions (past experiences prove that exposing metal to moisture is followed by appearance of rust; Suzy's throw takes place in the context of regular patterns that make up natural laws). This is because it is accepted that, outside the Humean criteria, there is no meaning to the concept of cause.[130] So internalised has the Humean idea of cause become that the idea of causal analysis has quite simply become equated with adherence to Humean assumptions in one form or another.

This philosophy of cause, however, presents but one philosophical approach to causal analysis among many. The goal of this book is to argue that the Humean solution to the problem of causation is not self-evident in framing causation and causal explanation. This book will seek to draw on theories of causation that, as a consequence of the dominance of Humeanism, have been largely marginalised in the philosophy of science but that, nevertheless, provide consistent and fruitful views on causation and causal analysis. However, before moving on to discuss the philosophical alternatives to Humeanism, the following chapters will concentrate on examining the consequences of the dominance of the Humean framing of causation in the philosophy of social science and in the discipline of International Relations.

[130] Bas Van Fraassen (1980: 113–15) has, in fact, pointed out that empiricists must be careful in using 'loose' causal language because it opens up their accounts to critiques from the scientific realists.

2 Controversy over causes in the social sciences

The Humean discourse on causation has played a crucial role in the history of philosophy of science as chapter 1 demonstrated: it has provided the dominant account of what the concept of cause means and what causal analysis entails, especially during the twentieth century. This chapter will examine the assumptions concerning causation that underlie the philosophy of social science debates. It is seen that the Humean assumptions have played a foundational role in informing these debates, too. Having drawn on the accounts of cause that have been dominant in philosophy of science more widely, the main traditions in the philosophy of social science have also primarily turned to the Humean philosophy of causation in grappling with the concept of cause. Crucially, the acceptance of the Humean assumptions has given rise to some foundational controversies in social theorising over the legitimacy of 'social scientific causal analysis' and has gone towards bringing about a highly dichotomistic view of forms of social inquiry.

The classic debate in the philosophy of social science has been over the question of 'naturalism'. Philosophers of social science have disagreed sharply over whether there are crucial differences between 'natural' and 'social' facts and, consequently, over whether social phenomena can be studied through the same 'scientific' methodology as the natural sciences.[1] Crucially, the Humean notion of cause has played an important role in this foundational debate between the 'positivist' and the 'hermeneutic' traditions. The positivist 'naturalists' have argued, not just for naturalism but, crucially, for a Humean understanding of causal analysis as the basis for this naturalism. The advocates of the hermeneutic tradition, on the other hand, have contended that 'social kinds' are distinctly different from natural kinds since they are meaning/concept/rule-dependent and that, hence, social inquiry must

[1] For a comprehensive account of these debates see, for example, Collin (1997).

involve 'empathic understanding' and 'interpretive methods', rather than simply generalisation about patterns of behaviour. The hermeneutic tradition, it has followed, has denied the legitimacy of 'causal analyses' of the social world. However, it will be argued here that the hermeneutic theorists have also been embedded within the Humean discourse: although they have rejected causes and causal analysis, this rejection has been based on the prior acceptance of the Humean conception of causal analysis as unproblematically characteristic of a causal approach to social inquiry.

Understanding the role of causation in the debates between the positivist and hermeneutic strands of social theorising is crucial because the discipline of International Relations, as will be seen in the following chapters, has drawn on these debates, thus carrying the Humean assumptions, and the divisive logic they have given rise to with regard to forms of social inquiry, into the disciplinary debates.

Positivist Humean social science

As was seen in the previous chapter, the concept of cause has undergone some important transformations in the course of the past several centuries. Crucially, it was argued in chapter 1 that the so-called Humean assumptions have gained prominence in informing engagements with causation and causal analysis. Following Hume's scepticist philosophy of causation, (1) causes have been associated with, and analysed through, regularities; (2) causal relations have been understood as regularity relations of observables; and (3) causal relations have entailed logical necessity and the assumption of regularity-determinism (when given regularities have been observed we have the basis for making 'when A, then B' statements about causal relations). Moreover, (4) these Humean empiricist assumptions have worked within the confines of an 'efficient cause' understanding of causation: since Descartes cause and effect relations have been seen to refer to 'pushing and pulling' relations.

In the social sciences the Humean assumptions have most clearly and explicitly been associated with the so-called 'positivist' tradition. Positivism is a term that is infamously difficult to define and includes within it many different variants. I shall here use the notion of 'positivism' to refer to those approaches that (1) believe in 'a scientific method' that is applicable across sciences, (2) assume naturalism, (3) assume empiricism, (4) believe in value-neutrality of scientific method and (5) emphasise the importance of instrumental (predictive) knowledge.[2] Humeanism is the dominant discourse of causation within the positivist tradition. This is because it provides an especially good fit with the key assumptions of empiricism, an epistemological cornerstone of positivism. This section will discuss different forms of positivism in the social sciences: the early positivism of Comte and Durkheim, the radical empiricism of the logical positivists and the behaviourists, as well as the social science versions of DN-model positivism. Although these approaches differ in some crucial respects, they can all be seen to share a commitment to the key Humean assumptions.

Early positivists

The origins of positivism and the application of the regularity theory of causation in the social sciences can be traced to Auguste Comte, the nineteenth-century 'founding father' of modern sociology. Comte maintained that, in order to steer social inquiry clear of speculative, theological and superstitious claims, the study of social phenomena was best pursued through following the precepts of 'positive philosophy'. Comte's conception of 'positive philosophy' was in line with the Humean assumptions. He accepted the empiricist assumption that reliable knowledge should be based on the perceivable and, hence, that social inquiry should proceed through the analysis of regularities of observable human behaviour. Consequently, he argued, social inquiry should search for patterns of 'succession and resemblance' in social life, thereby uncovering laws of society.[3] On these bases, Comte also advocated 'naturalism': he equated the study of patterns in society to the study of patterns in the natural sciences.[4] He believed that the laws

[2] Delanty (1997: 12–13). For discussions of positivism in social sciences see, for example, Achinstein and Barker (1969); Giddens (1974).

[3] Comte also turned the Humean assumptions into an anti-causal argument: he relegated causes to the 'metaphysical' stage in the progression of knowledge and replaced the search for causes with the search for laws. Gordon (1991: 290). However, he did not subscribe to the radical empiricist assumptions that the later logical positivists became fixated on, that is, crude objectivism, the reliance on logical analysis of scientific statements and the use of mathematical logic. Crotty (1998: 22).

[4] Comte quoted in Thompson (1976: 44–5). See also M. J. Smith (1998: 79).

of social behaviour were analogous to natural scientific laws and, also, that through uncovering the laws of social life, 'social engineering' to cure the ills of society would be possible.

Another early positivist social scientist who drew on the Humean assumptions was Emile Durkheim. In order to gain insight into 'social currents', Durkheim argued, we should analyse social facts through a quantitative empirical approach. Durkheim has been considered a positivist *par excellence* because his studies, most famously his study of suicide, attempted to establish general statistical relations between empirical variables. Indeed, Durkheim's method for making 'causal' claims about social facts was based on a method he called concomitant variation: an analysis of 'nomological macro-laws' that could be used to link particular causes to particular effects.[5] Thus, for example, quantitative study of the empirical regularities in suicide rates would yield the most important 'causal variables' in explaining suicide (or rather suicide rates). Although on many occasions Durkheim wanted to insist that social causes exist outside human minds in 'collective' ideas and sentiments as real (ontological) causal forces,[6] he did accept the empiricist assumption that only observation of patterns of events gives us reliable knowledge of such forces.[7]

The positivist study of social behaviour became popular in the social sciences owing to the influence of early 'foundational' figures like Comte and Durkheim, although early positivism was taken more as a practical guide to knowledge construction than as a clearly defined philosophical school. However, positivism as a school of thought gained coherence and precision with the rise of the logical positivist and behaviourist approaches in the social sciences.

[5] Lukes (1982: 7).

[6] See Lukes (1982: 3–8). It must also be noted that Durkheim's assumptions were not all in line with empiricist assumptions. It could be argued that despite accepting a Humean methodology, deeper ontological assumptions underlie his theorising. First, being an adamant advocate of holism, the study of empirical generalisations, for Durkheim, took place on the level of the social, not of the individual, as many Humeans before him had argued (e.g. Mill). Significantly, Humean approaches have often worked on the basis of individualistic ontological assumptions because this ontology is more easily 'observable', but Durkheim did not consider this an impediment to his studies. Indeed, it seems that Durkheim was something of a philosophical realist about social objects.

[7] Delanty (1997: 27).

Logical positivism and behaviourism

In the 1920s and 1930s Otto Neurath, drawing on the logical positivist movement in the philosophy of natural science, aimed to give a new radically empiricist basis for knowledge in the social sciences. Neurath saw social science as part of the wider 'Unified Sciences'. This meant that he rejected the 'uniqueness' of social science and its methods: he conceived of the social sciences as part of the general sciences and argued that the social world could be studied through the same empirical scientific methods as the natural sciences. Neurath despised the use of 'emotional' and 'magical' (non-verifiable) terminology in the social sciences. The *Verstehen* approach was his most specific target: 'empathy, understanding (*Verstehen*) and the like may help the research worker, but they enter the totality of scientific statements as little as does a good cup of coffee, which also furthers a scholar's work'.[8]

Neurath took it upon himself to outline a more logically rigorous basis for the social sciences. To steer clear of 'metaphysical speculations', he avoided according objects of science any 'essences' or 'depths'. Neurath argued that the social sciences involved quite simply the empirical study of the patterns of behaviour of 'physical systems' called humans. Logical positivist 'physicalism' entailed the belief that everything in science had to be 'expressible in solely spatio-temporal' terms 'or else vanish from science'.[9] As a consequence, Neurath argued against the use of 'mentalistic' words, such as 'mind' and 'motive', and against the use of 'metaphysical speculations', such as 'nation', 'ethical forces' and 'religious ethos'.[10]

Neurath also rejected the notion of cause: indeed, the notions of 'cause' and 'effect' were relegated to his list of forbidden 'metaphysical' words. Instead of talking about causation, he argued that the analysis of general laws, derived from rigorous observation of human behavioural patterns, gives us the only legitimate scientific insights into the social world.

Neurath's attempt to unify social sciences with the other Unified Sciences never succeeded. However, a number of his arguments gained currency in the social sciences in the 1950s and 1960s through the 'behaviourist revolution'. Drawing on logical positivism, an approach

[8] Otto Neurath quoted in Neurath and Cohen (1973: 357).
[9] Neurath and Cohen (1973: 325). [10] Hempel (1969: 168).

called behaviourism (or logical behaviourism) continued the search for a 'truly scientific' knowledge of the social world. To provide social sciences with objective knowledge the behaviourists argued that we must abandon belief in 'human consciousness'.[11] They maintained that, although terminology about 'mental states' of various kinds is ripe in our everyday language, in social scientific investigations these concepts have no meaning. Social science should concentrate firmly and strictly on studying patterns of observable behaviour.

Behaviourism was deeply informed by the Humean assumptions. First, the behaviourist school, following Neurath, argued that the only 'safe' method of study in the social sciences was the subsumption of types of behaviour under established general laws.[12] The main motivation was to make social sciences 'scientific' by imposing regularity-criteria on social scientific analyses. This, it was hoped, would enable them to come through with their 'great promise', which had so far eluded them because of the proliferation of 'non-scientific' methods.[13]

Second, observability was prioritised and, since the focus was on the observable, human actors were seen as atomistic ontologically 'flat' entities, whose internal constitution, feelings or motivations do not matter: what mattered is that they 'behave' in certain measurable and generalisable ways. Society, on the other hand, was seen as a conglomeration, or a sum, of the measurable behaviour of individual human actors.

Third, the behaviourist conception of social analysis also entailed the acceptance of the assumption of regularity-determinism and, hence, a 'closed system' view of the social world. It was assumed that when laws of behaviour have been observed, on the basis of these regularities we can predict human behaviour.[14]

Despite its supposedly clear-cut answers to many philosophical problems, behaviourism in its full form has decreased in credibility, although its legacies have continued to influence the social sciences. The more influential and lasting positivist approach to social science has proved to be the Popperian 'standard positivist' model of explanation.

[11] See, for example, MacKenzie (1977). [12] Scriven (1969: 201).

[13] Behaviourists and logical positivists always had 'great hope' in the 'rise' of the social sciences once they sorted out their philosophical and methodological basis. See von Mises (1956); Festinger and Katz (1965).

[14] Hempel (1969: 173–4). See also Festinger and Katz (1965).

Standard positivism

Popper's and Hempel's 'standard positivism' became influential in the post-war social sciences, as it did in the natural sciences. The central tenet of this form of positivism was the belief in a systematic scientific analysis on the lines of the deductive-nomological (DN-) model of explanation, which emphasised that all scientific explanation must be tied to the discovery of general laws from which specific effects, in specified initial conditions, can be deduced. Standard positivism avoided the extremes of logical positivism in avoiding reliance on induction but, nevertheless, followed the core empiricist assumptions derivative to Hume.

DN-model positivism, just as logical positivism, was based on a unified conception of the nature of explanation in the different sciences. The only difference between the natural and the social sciences, Hempel argued, was that in the natural sciences 'generalisations' were explicit, whereas in the social sciences, history for example, theorists often failed to make explicit the general regularities that underpinned their accounts.[15] Even in the social sciences, he argued, all 'causal' statements are derived from empirical regularities. Sometimes the prediction-explanations, he argued, can be based on more 'deterministic' laws (universal regularities), more often on mere 'probabilistic regularities'; nevertheless, laws based on observational regularities form the essence of historical explanation. Crucially, 'empathic understanding' of the meanings and reasons underlying patterns of behaviour, Hempel argues, is only a 'heuristic device' and one that 'does not constitute an explanation'.[16]

However, it should be noted that Hempel and Popper did not defend their DN-model causal explanation as strongly in the social sciences as they did in the natural sciences; on the contrary, they often downplayed their claims about causal laws in the social sciences. Popper was, in fact, wary of applying the covering law model to social inquiry. This was largely triggered by his aversion to forms of Marxism and 'historicism'. In *The Open Society and its Enemies* Popper argued against social scientists who wanted to explain the social world and history in terms

[15] Hempel (1965: 236).

[16] Hempel (1965: 239). It should be noted, however, that laws for Hempel could quantify many things: not just patterns of events but also 'reasons' and 'motives' for action.

of universal laws.[17] In a paradoxical way, Popper stood for unity of method between the sciences but took the nature of causality in the social world to be contingent and not comparable to causality in the natural sciences, where it was, in his view, characterised by invariable regularities. Also, Popper was averse to efforts to predict social affairs; one must, he argues, make a clear distinction between prediction in the natural sciences and prediction in the social sciences where it is nothing but self-fulfilling historical prophecy.[18] This meant that the DN-model based squarely on the prediction–explanation nexus seemed to falter in the social sciences.

However, it was not clear what this meant for the social sciences: that they were characterised by less certain 'probability-explanations' or that they were not properly 'scientific' at all? The nature of causation, as it was so closely tied to empirical regularities and prediction in the DN-model, became rather vague with Popper's qualifications about the nature of social generalisations.

Many practising social scientists, however, have ignored Popper's uncertainty about finding causal laws in the social world and have proceeded to use the DN-model explanation extensively in social explanation, even if often in a weaker probabilistic form. Indeed, despite the fall of behaviourism, and Popper's own scepticism about the applicability of the DN-model to the social world, positivist assumptions are still very much around in the philosophy and practice of social science. The DN-model still forms the basis of most textbook accounts of research methods, and, indeed, the core of research training programmes for many social sciences. As a result, many social researchers follow the Popperian assumptions in conducting and justifying their empirical work. Even when social theorists/researchers do not explicitly identify themselves as empiricists or positivists, they mostly conduct their studies through identifying and indexing variables and seeking to explain the relationships of these variables.[19] Indeed, the form of causal explanation that is seen as 'scientific' has by and large been understood through the Humean assumptions.

The appeal of positivism has been improved by the fact that contemporary empiricist approaches have devised a number of answers to

[17] Popper (1974b: 81–8). See also Popper (1974a: 2–3; 1957).

[18] Popper (1974a: 3). See also Delanty (1997: 32–3).

[19] See Ekström (1992). See also, for example, Frankfurt-Nachmias and Nachmias (1994).

many of the well-rehearsed objections from the interpretivist corner.[20] Also, many positivist approaches now accept the validity of historical and qualitative data, even though they argue that these data should be subjected to rigorous scientific examination. This 'rigorous scientific examination' has entailed that historical and qualitative data should be moulded into clear testable hypotheses, which can be measured in reference to clearly identifiable observational data. Not only should our methods be explicit and public – because the content of science is its method[21] – but also our observational data should aim to incorporate 'as many observable implications of our theory as possible'.[22]

Humean assumptions embedded into the positivist approaches, then, still play an important part in structuring many social scientists' views concerning 'causal explanation'. Causes are often associated with regularities, observational methods are prioritised in causal analysis and ontology is often geared around individualistic assumptions (required by demand for observability). Also, prediction, which presumes the acceptance of regularity-deterministic assumptions, is widely accepted as a legitimate goal of social scientific inquiry. In addition, interpretive social science approaches and methods are still often marginalised as 'unscientific', certainly if they do not appear 'systematic' in accordance with empiricist criteria.

The positivist study of the social world aims to be systematic and rigorous. Yet, its systematic and rigorous approach to empirical observation and generalisation has failed to convince some social theorists who point out that the positivist approach seems to miss out the complexity and 'meaningful' nature of the social world. The hermeneutic and interpretive theorists have argued that the social world cannot be adequately understood through the methods of empiricist science and its Humean conception of causal analysis.

Hermeneutic and interpretive approaches

In opposition to the positivist approaches to the study of social affairs, an alternative tradition of philosophy of social science has

[20] For example, positivists now refute 'reasons accounts' through arguing that reasons are causes. However, the bases of this argument are very different from the critical realist ones, advocated in later chapters of this book. See Papineu (1978: 78–81).

[21] King, Keohane and Verba (1994: 9).

[22] King, Keohane and Verba (1994: 12).

developed from the mid-nineteenth century onwards. Against the positivist emphasis on 'science' of human behaviour, the hermeneutic philosophies put emphasis on analysing the role of consciousness and intentionality in human action and on understanding the meaning-defining rule context in which social action takes place. The hermeneutic and interpretive theorists have argued that the meaning- and concept-dependent nature, and the complexity, of social life make the positivist efforts to generalise about human behaviour inadequate in providing us with knowledge of the social world. The hermeneutic theorists have rejected the empiricist positivist scientific approach to studying social life, and crucially, the Humean conception of causal analysis it has entailed. However, it will be seen that despite its rejection of positivist precepts, the hermeneutic tradition is itself, paradoxically, tied to the Humean conception of causation.

Traditional hermeneutics

The hermeneutic approach has its origins in the medieval methods of translating religious texts but gained currency in social inquiry in the mid-nineteenth century. Wilhelm Dilthey, one of the first hermeneutic philosophers, outlined the basic assumptions of hermeneutic interpretation by arguing that the social world differs in crucial ways from the natural world and that this should be taken into account in the methodology of social studies. Historical and social analysis, he argued, should involve the researcher joining in a 'hermeneutic circle' with the author, the texts and the contexts to be analysed. Hence, the goal of historical and social studies, for Dilthey, was not locating scientific laws or general facts, but 'the retrieval of the purpose, intention, unique configuration of thoughts and feelings which precede social phenomena'.[23] In opposition to the so-called nomothetic (lawful) natural sciences, which dealt with general relations of cause and effect, the historical and social studies came to be seen as idiographic, that is, concentrated on the particular.[24] Edmund Husserl developed these hermeneutic insights in his phenomenological approach. Husserl's phenomenology focused on the questions of intentionality and representation and involved the study of different forms of conscious human experience. The goal, contra

[23] Baumann (1978: 12).

[24] However, from the analysis of the 'particular' in its historical and subjective context one could also draw wider conclusions. May (1996: 35).

nomothetic explanation, was to 'understand' social life through a detailed description of experiences.[25]

Dilthey and Husserl, arguably, saw hermeneutics as an important methodological tool in understanding human beings and society, objects of study that, unlike natural objects, were seen as fundamentally tied to 'conscious experience' and 'intentionality', this giving them a unique nature. Husserl's student Martin Heidegger, on the other hand, began to develop hermeneutics from a methodological approach to social explanation towards a deeper 'ontological' understanding of interpretive relations. Heidegger rejected the methodological approach to interpretation of the early hermeneuticians and, specifically, Husserl's 'bracketing' of the interpreter's subjectivity in the process of interpretation. For Heidegger, in the process of interpretation, the interpreter's foreknowledge becomes fundamentally entwined within his or her 'existential understandings' of the world.[26] Heidegger also emphasised the deep role that language had in interpretations of the world: it did not simply express experience but defined experience. Moreover, Heidegger became interested in studying the wealth of (hidden) meanings that could be 'excavated' from language, its syllables, words and phrases,[27] and came to subvert many of the traditional categories of meaning in modern philosophy: he emphasised significance over fact, relation over substance, understanding over knowledge.[28] The impact of Heidegger's thought on social theory has been significant: it provided the basis for questioning traditional ways of knowing and helped put renewed emphasis on the understanding of 'life-worlds' through interpretation of meanings.

Hans-Georg Gadamer, too, developed the hermeneutic tradition in a new direction by arguing that hermeneutic understanding is not just a method: the world itself is characterised by a continually expanding 'spiral' of hermeneutic relations.[29] The goal of interpreters of the world is to gain an understanding of the objects of study through the so-called 'fusion of horizons'. This notion emphasised the fact that we cannot

[25] Interestingly, despite being associated with the hermeneutic tradition, Husserl's goal was paradoxically reminiscent of the logical positivist purposes in that empirical description was for Husserl seen as prior to any metaphysical 'depths', and Husserl's method of 'bracketing' meant that we should abstain from positing the existence of a natural world around us when it came to analysing human consciousness.

[26] Heidegger (1967). [27] Steiner (1982: 15).

[28] Weinsheimer (1985: 5). [29] Weinsheimer (1985: 40).

simply 'come to know' a tradition of thought, for example, 'objectively' from the outside but must 'fuse' our own interpretive self with the meaning contexts of the object. The process of understanding, then, is never a simple 'one-way' process through which we can fix the meaning and nature of the object of understanding, but a complex meeting of interpretive horizons.[30]

The significant unifying element of the hermeneutic approaches has been the rejection of the positivist 'lawful' approaches to the social world. Hermeneutic theorists reject the positivist assumptions that 'social facts' and 'laws' of human behaviour can be derived simply from observation and through the use of natural science methods. Rather, the interpretive approaches argue that social kinds differ from 'natural facts' in that they are not mind-independent but involve intentionality, human cognition and representation through language and symbols, the meaning of which must be 'understood from within'. Hermeneutic theorists, then, reject the positivist approach to the so-called human sciences: social inquiry does not, in their view, derive its value from their degree of conformity to the positivist 'scientific' methodology.[31]

This anti-positivism has led to an aversion to the notion of 'science', but also to the notion of cause. Crucially, the interpretive approaches reject causation as a concept applicable to the social world. For Husserl, for example, the notion of cause was a notion applicable only to the natural world and, hence, in no way to the 'spiritual' sphere.[32] For Husserl the equivalent of causation in the sphere of the Mind was the notion of motivation: causes connect events in the material nature, motivation in the human 'conscious' domain.[33] Husserl implied that the 'motivational impetus' could perhaps be seen as a type of cause,[34] but to prevent dragging metaphysical baggage into the phenomenological science, he did not want to talk of this 'motivational causation' in explicitly causal terms. Gadamer, on the other hand, was opposed to the use of the language of laws, which was associated with causal language, since it implied determinism and fixity of social life that was not in conformity with the fluidity and deep interpretive nature of social life that the hermeneutic circle implied.[35]

The interpretivists' treatment of causation needs to be unpacked. It could be argued that the rejection of causation by the hermeneutic

[30] Gadamer (1975: 273). [31] Outhwaite (1987: 62); Weinsheimer (1985: 4).
[32] D. W. Smith (1995: 366). [33] D. W. Smith (1995: 354).
[34] Mohanty (1995: 66). [35] Weinsheimer (1985: 33).

theorists is based squarely on the rejection of positivism. Positivism is the target that the hermeneutic approaches attack: whether its nomothetical methods (Dilthey) or its simple-minded 'objectivism' about social affairs (Heidegger, Gadamer). However, because causes are associated with science and science with 'objectivist' positivism,[36] causes too have to be rejected. On a closer analysis, it becomes clear that the hermeneutic theorists are wedded to the positivist understanding of science and causal explanation: they do not inquire into the nature of science or causation outside of the positivist and Humean criteria.

Thus, when we observe hermeneutic theorists arguing against causes, we must keep in mind that the object of attack is the 'lawful' positivist form of causal explanation (regularity analysis) and the assumption of regularity-determinism (given regularities we can make 'when A, then B' statements and predict) assumed within it.[37] Also, under attack are the notions of observability – that the objects of social inquiry should be observable behaviour – and of value-neutrality – the assumption that causal analysis pertains to factual explanations only, not to normative or political questions. Outside the regularity-based, regularity-deterministic, observation-based and objectivist conception of causality, the concept of cause is pondered on very little. This implicit and inadvertent acceptance of the Humean premises concerning causation is also evident in the most influential 'strand' of hermeneutic thought, the Wittgensteinian linguistic hermeneutics.

Linguistic hermeneutics: reasons vs. causes, constitutive vs. causal approaches

Ludwig Wittgenstein, in his later philosophy, came to reject the correspondence theory of truth and language and, instead, outlined the so-called philosophy of language games.[38] Language, for Wittgenstein, was the most important carrier of meaning in social life: all meaning arises from language. Wittgenstein's key insight was that the world can be seen to consist of 'life-worlds' made up of different language games, which do not, in any straightforward sense, refer to anything outside the language games themselves. 'Reality', instead of being external and independent of humans, is actually made or carried within our language

[36] Outhwaite (1987: 66).
[37] Weinsheimer (1985: 33).
[38] Wittgenstein (1966; 1967).

and concepts. Wittgenstein argued that in understanding life-worlds one should, instead of studying the world as an 'external' reality, concentrate on the interpretation of meanings and rules that define our understandings, including our 'causal understandings', of the world.[39]

This insight was picked up by Peter Winch, who developed Wittgenstein's linguistic interpretation of social life in analysis of the nature of social sciences. Winch followed the Wittgensteinian notion of concept-dependence, arguing that 'our idea of what belongs to the realm of reality is given for us in the concepts we use'.[40] Social analysis, he argued, is fundamentally complicated by the fact that the researcher is entwined in the very conceptual frameworks that (s)he wants to study and by the fact that there is no other way to describe social events/processes except through the already socially produced concepts.

More importantly, however, Winch also argued that the social world should be understood to consist of, and analysed through the notion of, rule-following: 'all behaviour which is meaningful (therefore all specifically human behaviour) is *ipso facto* rule-governed'.[41] Winch argued that there is no escaping rule-following in social life, in the same sense that we cannot escape language games more widely. Without understanding the constitutive rules of social life 'from within', Winch argued, one could make no sense of social activity. As Hollis explains:

> A visiting Martian, seeing a human being shift a small piece of wood a small distance on a squared surface, would not know that a pawn had been moved. To recognise a pawn as a pawn the visitor needs to grasp the rules and the point of the activity. Without its rules, indeed, there would be no such activity as chess and no pawns to move ... Rules of language define a 'game' which would not exist without them.[42]

Examining the social world through understanding internal rules and meanings in such a manner, the linguistic hermeneutic philosophers came to the conclusion that, *contra* empiricists and positivists, causal explanations of behaviour are not sufficient or even legitimate in accounting for human action. Wittgenstein argued that interpreting 'how to go on' in the social world involves interpreting a rule, and this interpretation process is not causal.[43] Anscombe and Winch,

[39] See, for example, Wittgenstein (1967: 170, 198).
[40] Winch (1990: 15).
[41] Winch (1990: 52).
[42] Hollis (1994: 152).
[43] Wittgenstein (1967: 59–60, 72–3; 1966: 15).

following Wittgenstein, proceeded to question whether human 'motives' could be treated as a species of causal explanation, and were sceptical of treating 'reasons' as something generalisable.[44] Instead, what became central for them was treatment of the 'self' as an intentional object whose 'reasons' and motives for action are distinct from 'causes' of an external kind.[45] This rejection of causation – in favour of a 'reasons account' of social action – has given rise to some powerful dichotomies in the twentieth-century philosophy of social science, most specifically between non-causal and causal approaches to social theory, and between theories of intentional, or 'reasoned', action and those of 'caused' behaviour.[46]

It is important, however, to examine closely the premise on which causality is rejected in the Wittgensteinian tradition. Wittgensteinians argue that our 'reasons' for action are not causal or, in any straightforward sense, caused because relations between events, rules and human reasons for action in the social world are seen as 'internal' and not necessitated by 'causes', which are considered 'independent' and 'external' to meanings and understanding. 'Causal explanation' is deemed impossible because the causal approach cannot get at the internal relationship between rules, reasons and actions: this can only be achieved through 'understanding' the meanings of rules, reasons and actions. Since human life is seen as an intricate web of meanings and rules, seeking prediction and determinate explanations, associated with causal explanation, is seen as a wasted effort.[47] However, as with the rest of the hermeneutic tradition, causation in this line of argument is, in fact, conceived of in accordance with the Humean assumptions. Causal explanation is equated with the positivist model of explanation. For example, Winch clearly sees causal analysis as a question of 'generalisation'. However, the expectation that causes have to involve regularities (lawfulness) and prediction is a typically Humean one. Moreover, besides generalisation, it is assumed that causal analysis entails that cause and effect are 'external' and 'independently existing' (as independently observable events/objects). A classically Humean notion of

[44] Winch (1990: 75, 86–8).

[45] For development of Wittgenstein's thought see Anscombe (1957); Anscombe and Teichmann (2000); Winch (1990).

[46] See, for example, Armstrong and Malcolm (1984); Davidson (1980); Papineau (1978).

[47] Winch (1990: 92).

observability and resulting criteria of 'independence' is being applied here. Also, Winch's arguments are based on a Humean regularity-deterministic understanding of the relationship of causes and effects: indeed, reasons are seen to apply in the social world because causation conceived in the Humean mode – given regularities, we can make legitimate 'when A, then B' statements – does not seem to work.

Interestingly, in the second edition of *Idea of Social Science*, Winch states:

> I found myself at times denying that human behaviour can be understood in causal terms, when I should have been saying that our understanding of human behaviour is not elucidated by anything like the account given of cause by Hume . . . The important point to remember is that the word 'cause' (and related words) are used in a very wide variety of contexts. Hume's account applies perhaps pretty well to some of these uses, to others hardly at all. We *do* use causal language when we are exploring people's motives. 'What made him do that?' 'What was the cause of him doing that?' 'It was a combination of ambition, greed and jealousy.' And there is of course nothing wrong with this way of talking.[48]

Thus, he admits that his conception of causation is in line with the Humean regularity theory and that this created an unjustified anti-causal prejudice in his work. Yet, despite Winch's telling admission, the Wittgensteinian approaches have arguably not sought to get away from the largely Humean conception of causation that they are premised upon, nor the dichotomisation of causal and non-causal (reasons) approaches they have given rise to. Although Winch recognised the crucial role Humeanism played in his rejection of causal descriptions, many of his followers have not.

The reasons and causes dichotomisation has given rise to another misleading conceptual dichotomisation in social sciences: dichotomisation of constitutive and causal approaches. An important contemporary figure arguing for the separation of causal and constitutive theorising is Charles Taylor. He has been one of the most explicit recent defenders of the hermeneutic approach to the study of the social world. He contends that the naturalistic tradition in the social sciences by its very nature excludes from social science that which actually truly

[48] Winch (1990: xii).

accounts for social events. He argues that modern social science – conceived in positivist terms – works on the basis of a notion of agency, of freedom and of understanding that gets in the way of making sense of the social world around us.

He asserts that in order to account for the social world properly, we must study the 'constitutive rules' of social life. Language and intersubjective meanings, he powerfully argues, have a role not just in depicting and making intelligible things 'outside', but also in 'constituting' ourselves. This means that in trying to understand anything in the social world we must interpret language and its meanings and, hence, in doing social science, there is no getting away from the hermeneutic circle.[49] Contra the positivists, Taylor contends, there is no such thing as certainty in social science. Predictions in social science are laughable: 'human science is largely *ex post* understanding'.[50] There are no closed systems; all social systems are open systems. There is no brute data; everything has to be interpreted. Crucially, interpretation means that knowledge is never objective and 'value-neutral' as it always arises from the context of the more or less 'subjective' points of view of the inquirer.

What is the relationship of 'constitutive' accounts to causal accounts? Disappointingly, Taylor does not address the issue directly. However, he assures readers that causal relationships are not the focus of social inquiry. He argues that the focus of social inquiry should be on the 'constitutive' meanings and these do not refer to 'causal' relationships.[51] What he takes causation to be remains something of a mystery; presumably it involves 'closed systems' and exists outside the realm of language (and hence outside social relations too) – and, thus, is by definition something that social studies should not talk about. The notion of 'constitutive rules', just as the notion of 'reasons', is built up as the 'opposition' to scientific causal explanations. However, this dichotomisation is founded on a Humean understanding of causal explanation and, hence, the hermeneutic theorists arguably attack a straw-man of causal explanation. As will be seen in later chapters, if causation is conceptualised in a non-Humean manner, the hermeneutic approaches' aversion to causal terminology can be seen as unjustified: it will be seen that reasons as well as 'constitutive rules' can, in fact, be considered to be causes.

[49] Taylor (1985: 24). [50] Taylor (1985: 56). [51] Taylor (1985: 8).

Caught in the middle: Weber, Habermas, Foucault and Derrida

The dichotomisation of the social sciences between the positivist and the anti-positivist hermeneutic approaches, reasons and causes accounts and constitutive and causal theories has played a fundamental role in the twentieth-century philosophy of social science. However, it must be noted that not all social theorists have followed the divisionary logic religiously. This section will examine Max Weber, Jürgen Habermas, Michel Foucault and Jacques Derrida: theorists who are not easily accommodated within the divisionary logic of twentieth-century philosophy of social science and theorists who seek to avoid reducing causation to Humean assumptions – while, however, failing to advance clearly thought-out or philosophically coherent non-Humean alternatives. A note will also be made on the Marxist framework of thought.

Max Weber, arguably, attempted to transcend the traditional positivist–hermeneutic dichotomies in social science theorising. Like an 'interpretivist', Weber emphasised the importance of interpretive understanding in social research. He considered it important that social researchers understand, not just the physical behaviour of people, but the meanings behind behaviour, what makes behaviour an action. Explanations for him needed to be 'adequate on the level of meaning' (which for him was satisfied when motivations could be understood as rational).[52] Weber's acceptance of the *Verstehen* methods has been interpreted, by many hermeneutic theorists, as a sign that he was an advocate of a non-causal hermeneutic understanding of the social world. However, in Weber's thought, hermeneutic *Verstehen* methodology was coupled with concern about causes. For him, sociology is 'a science which attempts the interpretative understanding of social action in order, thereby, to arrive at causal explanation of its course and effects'.[53] Adequacy 'on the level of meaning' needed to be augmented by 'causal adequacy'.[54] Where did 'causal adequacy' arise from for Weber?

The positivists point out that the causal significance of factors arose, for Weber, from the verified reliability (degree of invariance) of empirical regularities. It is true that Weber's understanding of causes can on some level be compared to Hempel's DN-model causal explanation.[55]

[52] Weber (1970: 98).
[53] Weber quoted in Keat and Urry (1975: 145).
[54] Weber (1970: 22).
[55] Gordon (1991: 465–8).

Weber did argue that 'historical judgement ... does not acquire a valid content until we bring to the "given" reality the whole body of our "nomological" empirical knowledge',[56] a clear statement in favour of a Humean interpretation. Thus, although understanding human actions and motives through engaging with the individual subjective notions was crucial for Weber's sociology, he was, it seems, also equally attached to the positivist tradition in the social sciences and their Humean assumptions about causation.

What are we to make of this two-pronged approach to social explanation: was Weber an interpretivist or a Humean positivist? The hermeneutic theorists have appropriated Weber to the *Verstehen* camp, while the positivists have interpreted him as a 'soft' positivist. Most theorists have argued that there is a tension in his thought as a result of his acceptance of the key principles of both approaches.

In many ways it seems appropriate to conclude that Weber was somewhat confused over what to think about causation: on the one hand, he found it attractive to see causes through the Humean approach in line with many other social scientists of the time, while also refusing to acknowledge that social science objects were captured fully by nomological knowledge.[57] However, it could also be argued that Weber's thought regarding causation has not been fully understood – and not just because he himself was unclear about what exactly causation meant or causal analysis involved, but rather because of the inadequate conceptual capacity of his interpreters to appreciate that he might have been developing a distinct non-Humean approach to causation. Importantly, while many social theorists have asked whether Weber was an empiricist Humean or a *Verstehen* scholar, they have failed to question the suitability of the categories applied to Weber. As the later chapters will attest, if we rethink the notion of cause, we

[56] Weber (1970: 21).

[57] Ekström has emphasised that Weber used the regularity approach merely as a methodology to identify causal puzzles and that he sought to understand these causal puzzles in a 'deeper' sense through the interpretive approach. Ekström argues that causal explanation of social action, for Weber, arises from analysis of the social properties and meanings operating within different contexts, not from analysis of constant conjunctions. It follows that the problem of whether causal accounts could account for motives and reasons ('externality of causes') did not concern Weber as it has concerned the rest of the hermeneutic theorists. This is because he did not conceive causes as Humean 'external' independent forces but conceived of causal explanation as a matter of understanding concrete human actions and motives. See Ekström (1992: 107–22).

can develop a more holistic way of treating causal analysis: one that encompasses both 'positivist' and 'interpretivist' stances, thus doing away with the dichotomistic logic in thinking about forms of doing social science. This allows us to see Weber's theorising, too, in a different light. He could be seen, not as a theorist 'torn' between two mutually opposed approaches, but as a theorist who transcended traditional division through developing, if only in a rudimentary way, a non-Humean 'generative account of cause', which saw reasons as part of causal explanation and, hence, interpretive understanding as part and parcel of causal explanation.[58] This possibility has been missed entirely by many of his interpreters because of the dominance of the Humean discourse of causation, and the dichotomous logic that it has given rise to in the social sciences.

In discussing approaches that have sought to transcend the divisionary logic in the social sciences, we must also consider Jürgen Habermas. Habermas can, on the whole, be associated with the hermeneutic end of social theorising: he has argued that the social sciences must be distinctly separated from the natural sciences on the basis of both subject matter and methodology. Habermas contended that the social sciences could not be exhausted by the positivist methods but should embrace the hermeneutic methods, including not only the traditional hermeneutic but also the 'deeper' insights of linguistic hermeneutics.[59] However, his work on the 'cognitive interests' seeks to moderate the dichotomisation of approaches in the social sciences. Habermas argues that the sciences are directed by their different cognitive interests. He argues that the empirical sciences seek instrumental-technical control and prediction; the historical-hermeneutic sciences aim to gain practical interpretive understanding; and the critical social sciences work on the basis of emancipatory interests and, thereby, combine the two methods above in investigating the obstacles to understanding.[60] Habermas's goal was to expose the 'conditions' of knowledge but also, crucially, to bring explanatory and interpretive approaches 'under one roof' in the conception of critical social sciences.

However, this methodological 'unification' suffers from the fact that it is a unification underlined, in the end, by a Humean account of causation. Although Habermas tried to establish both causal and interpretive methods as the basis for the critical social sciences, he was not

[58] Ekström (1992: 107). [59] Habermas (1988). [60] Habermas (1972: 309).

specifically critical of the positivist Humean account of causation that underlies positivism. Indeed, Habermas still accepted positivism as a legitimate, essentially unproblematic method in the natural sciences – he was only concerned to limit its influence in social theory.[61] As a consequence, Habermas not only understood causes and causal analysis in the Humean sense, but also, in failing to challenge this approach to causation, ended up legitimising the Humean understanding of causation as a valid account of what causation and causal analysis entail.

Foucault and Derrida on causation

As part of our discussion of approaches that do not easily fit the dichotomous logic that has divided the social sciences, we should also comment on Foucault and Derrida. It is often assumed that Foucault's and Derrida's theories are fundamentally anti-causal and fit in with the radically interpretive side of the debate in the social sciences. However, it can be argued that the assumption that these theorists ignore causal analysis owes 'more to hearsay than to first-hand acquaintance with [their] texts'.[62]

Many theorists of the 'postmodernist' inclination do vehemently reject the notion of cause. Lyotard, for example, sees the notion of cause as a form of a modernist 'meta-narrative' of laws, imposed on the world by modern science and philosophy fixated on looking for stability and control.[63] He sees laws and causes as 'associated with the notion that the evolution of system performance can be predicted if all of the variables are known'.[64] He argued that in the emerging post-modern era, evinced by the rise of chaos theories, such deterministic meta-narratives are dying away. Hence, 'postmodern science' concerns itself less with modernist grand narratives (like laws and causes) and more with undecidables, discontinuities, catastrophes, paradoxes and limits of control.[65] This rejection of the concept of cause is in line with the general hermeneutic approaches: causes are understood in

61 Outhwaite (1987: 14).
62 Norris (1997: 79). Norris refers specifically to Derrida's texts.
63 Implied in the discussion of modern and postmodern science. Lyotard (1984: 53–62).
64 Lyotard (1984: 55).
65 Lyotard (1984: 60). The assumption that new forms of science, such as chaos theory, are 'anti-causal' is simplistic. Chaos theory can be seen to challenge the empiricist predictability-based accounts of cause but not all accounts of cause:

a Humean manner (laws, regularities, determinism) and rejected on such a basis. Interestingly, Foucault and Derrida demonstrate a much deeper engagement with causation. They recognise, as Nietzsche did too,[66] that even though you can challenge and deconstruct the notion of cause, this does not mean that you can necessarily do away with all causal concerns.

Foucault aimed to challenge traditional accounts of the development of modern society. Instead of emphasising historical continuities he pointed to the contingencies and discourse-dependencies of modern social institutions, practices and knowledge.[67] His goal was to challenge the traditional structuralist, agency-centric and 'linear' progressive readings of the birth of modern social institutions and to enable thereby a critique of present practices. Foucault is often taken to emphasise the radical indeterminacies in the social world, and this has been taken to mean that he rejects the notion of cause. However, this conclusion is not a straightforward one.

Foucault finds the traditional causal explanations of the birth of modern society inadequate.[68] Social life, for him, consists of the complex interplay of relations of discourses, practices and institutions that do not have clear-cut unidirectional causal relations. Foucault, then, was sceptical of the uses of the notion of cause *as it stands* in modern philosophical and historical discourse. Yet, it is important to note that in many of his works one can discern implicit, and sometimes even more explicit, causal terminology and lines of argumentation.[69] Foucault repeatedly refers to 'forces of production', 'discursive formations' as 'fields of complex social forces', 'affective mechanisms' and 'unobservable social rules and mechanisms'.[70] These, he seems to accept, have some sort of causal 'influence' (even if not a direct and unidirectional one) on people's practices and on the formation of discourses and power-knowledge hierarchies. Foucault's historical accounts suggest that he does work with an implicit notion of cause, even though he

indeed causal descriptions continue to play an important role in chaos theory. See, for example, Williams (1997).

66 Nietzsche's deconstruction pointed out that the effect, in fact, has logical primacy over the cause because identification of cause depends on identification of the effect. Paradoxically, the effect then causes the cause itself. See Culler (1982: 87 fn).

67 Lemert and Gillan (1982: 10). See for example Foucault (1970, 1972, 1991).

68 Foucault (1970: xii–xiii).

69 See, for example, Foucault (1970, 1972, 1991).

70 See Lemert and Gillan (1982: 130–5).

does not posit clear-cut causal relationships.[71] As will be seen in future chapters, not conforming to the Humean conception of causation does not disqualify one from engaging in causal analysis: causal analysis can take place outside of the Humean methods and terminology.

Derrida's deconstruction has also been commonly taken as the archetypal anti-causal approach to the social world owing to its emphasis on radical indeterminacies of textual relations. His deconstruction does, indeed, pose deep challenges to Western 'logo-centric' philosophy and theorising. Derrida placed 'under erasure', as necessary yet unstable concepts, many of the classic concepts of modern philosophy starting with the notion of subject, followed by the notions of object, truth and logic. The purpose of such deconstructions was to show that all key concepts in Western philosophy and science can be destabilised. Instead of searching for stable essences, the key to understanding is the search for a plurality of unstable metaphorical relations.[72] The notion of *différance* is central in Derrida's work: he argues that signs constitute their meaning in difference to and in deferring their meaning in relation to other signs. Hence, there is no stability within signs because a surplus meaning (supplement) will always leave a sign in contestation within itself and in relation to other signs. This means that meanings always change and the meaning the author might want to convey cannot be fixed but remains fundamentally undecidable. No text can escape the inherent instability and undecidability of textual relations.[73]

The notions of intertextuality, undecidability and indeterminacy of meaning have been used widely in the social sciences from the late 1960s onwards. The central claim of 'poststructuralists' who have drawn on Derrida has been that their research is different from other 'standard' social research in that they challenge the 'modern' norms of research premised on fixed or stable concepts that fail to capture the

[71] This is emphasised by the fact that his account is not an 'idealist' account: he does not argue that discourses are just 'ideational' and '(inter-)subjective'. On the contrary, 'discourse is seen as a material relation that interacts with non-discursive practices'. Joseph (2003: 190). Discourses do not work on some 'ideational' noumenal level; they emerge from, and have important – arguably in some sense causal – consequences for, material social relations. It is important to note that it is followers such as Rorty, Laclau and Mouffe that have been responsible for the creation of the 'idealist', 'non-causal' Foucault, not necessarily Foucault himself. Joseph (2003: 190–1); Norris (1997: 79).

[72] M. J. Smith (1998: 256).

[73] Derrida (1978).

contingency and indeterminacy of social (textual) relations. Further, they reject the notion that social research is getting at an 'independent reality': reality is seen to arise from within language. Since there is no fixed arbitrating reality to which we can compare our accounts, it is not viable to assume that our accounts of the world are more 'true' or valid than other perspectives.[74]

However, the non-causal, anti-deterministic and anti-realist reading of poststructuralism cannot be read back to Derrida. In reading his work, one cannot but be struck by how often he refers to 'determinacies' and 'necessities'. Indeed, in *Limited Inc.*, for example, Derrida especially emphasises the fact that undecidability does not mean indeterminacy:

> [U]ndecidability is always a *determinate* oscillation between possibilities (for example, of meaning but also of acts)...The analyses that I have devoted to undecidability concern just these determinations...not at all some vague 'indeterminacy'... I am interested more in relations of force, in differences of force, in everything that allows, precisely, determinations in given situations to be stabilized through a decision of writing...There would be no indecision or *double bind* were it not between *determined* (semantic, ethical, political) poles, which are upon occasion terribly necessary.[75]

Derrida's determinacies do not seem to be anything 'ontologically necessitating'; they refer to relations of logical necessitation within language. Yet, Derrida does not consider conceptual determinations outside of non-conceptual order: he is interested not just in overturning conceptual orders, but also in thereby critiquing the social contexts within which these conceptual orders have been established: conceptual orders are always articulated within non-conceptual ones.[76]

It follows that it is by no means obvious that Derrida is an idealist, or an anti-causal theorist.[77] His concern with causes is aptly revealed in his comments on Foucault. Derrida criticises Foucault for his vagueness on the question of causation in his empirical studies of the history of madness. This history, he argues, is problematic because of Foucault's attempts to account for discourses and relations of social forces

[74] Rorty (1989). [75] Italics in the original. Derrida (1988: 148–9).
[76] Patomäki (2002: 41). [77] Norris (1997: 78–155).

without establishing . . . whether an event such as the creation of a house of internment is a sign among others, whether it is a fundamental symptom or a cause. This kind of question could appear exterior to a method that presents itself precisely as structuralist, that is, a method for which everything within the structural totality is interdependent and circular in such a way that the classical problems of causality themselves would appear to stem from a misunderstanding. Perhaps. But I wonder whether, when one is concerned with history (and Foucault wants to write a history), a strict structuralism is possible, and, especially, whether . . . such a study can avoid all etiological [causal] questions, all questions bearing, shall we say, on the center of gravity of the structure. The legitimate renunciation of a certain style of causality perhaps does not give one right to renounce all etiological demands.[78]

This statement is far from a-causal: it evidences sophisticated reflection on causal argumentation. Indeed, neither Foucault nor Derrida rejects the concept of cause as easily as many hermeneutic theorists or the 'postmodernists', such as Lyotard. They challenge linear accounts of history and lawful mono-causal accounts of the social world. However, they do not reject all meanings of the notion of cause. While showing wariness of a particular kind of causal theorising, they admit that the concept has some relevance to accounts of the social world, including their own. Thus, even though these theorists have not theorised causation systematically, they can be seen to challenge the Humean notion of cause and, indeed, the discursive oppositions constructed in twentieth-century philosophy of social science between causal and non-causal accounts.

A note on Marxism

It should be noted that besides these theorists another current of theorising that has on the whole attempted to avoid Humeanism and the traditional dichotomisations in social science has been the Marxist current of thought. Marx, and the Marxist tradition, are sometimes seen as 'positivist' because of the repeated references to 'laws' of social life in Marx's work.[79] Certainly some Marxists have been advocates of a

[78] Derrida (1978: 43–4).

[79] Arguably, the positivist slant in Marx is a result of Engels's interpetation of Marx. See Thomas (1991: 41).

positivist language of laws and some have adopted sophisticated positivist philosophical premises, such as logical positivist Otto Neurath for example.[80]

However, as von Wright, for example, has noted, Hegel's and Marx's original conceptions of laws are very different from those of positivists and are in many ways closer to the intentionalist logic of explanation of the anti-positivist philosophers.[81] For them, as von Wright puts it, 'the idea of law is primarily that of an intrinsic connection to be grasped through reflective understanding, not that of an inductive generalisation established by observation'.[82] Perhaps then Marx especially is better understood as an advocate of a more interpretive logic over the mechanistic empiricist logic of causal explanation.

Yet another interpretation of Marx has emerged in recent years: some have come to analyse him, not as a positivist or an interpretivist, but as an advocate of a radically different philosophy of science: philosophical realism (a school of thought that will be discussed in more detail in chapters 5 and 6). With Marx's focus on analysis of 'independent reality', 'ontological causes and mechanisms' and 'social relations', philosophical realist rather than empiricist bases could be seen to underlie this current of social theory,[83] although some philosophical realists have rejected this rereading of Marx.[84] It seems plausible, as some interpreters argue, that the dominant interpretation of Marx and Marxists through the lenses of empiricist positivism has resulted in significant misunderstandings of Marx's philosophy. Hence, the Marxist strand of thought is here associated with the philosophical realist framework, albeit tentatively.[85] This school of thought, as will be seen, entails a very different non-Humean account of cause – one that emphasises study of causal powers in objects over study of observable regularities, and hence goes some way to rework the Humean background discourse that has dominated the social sciences.

[80] See discussion in Hempel (2001: 254).

[81] Von Wright (1971: 7). [82] Von Wright (1971: 8).

[83] Farr (1991). See also Sayer (1979); Keat and Urry (1975); Meikle (1985).

[84] See, for example, Patomäki (2002: 6).

[85] Following Meikle (1991). Of course it should be noted that even though Marx may be interpreted better as a philosophical realist, this does not entail the reverse, that philosophical realism entails Marxism.

Conclusion

The issue of causation has been very controversial in the social sciences. The powerful positivist corner has argued that the best way to do causal analysis in the social world is to analyse regularities of observable behaviour. Social reality, then, has been reduced to regularity analysis. This has brought with it the assumption of regularity-determinism, that is, the assumption that given regularities we can make (at least probabilistic) claims of the form 'when A, then B' and predict social affairs. Also, because of the assumption of observability emphasis has been on analysis of individuals and their behaviour, which in turn reproduces a 'flat' and 'atomistic' social ontology.

The hermeneutic theorists, on the other hand, have argued that the social world cannot be explained through regularities of behaviour but should be conceived to consist of webs of meanings and of intersubjective understandings. They point to the concept-dependent and non-observable meaning-defined nature of social reality and draw out the problems that this raises with regard to law-based causal analysis. Causal descriptions of the social world have been rejected in favour of interpretive understanding of subjects.

However, both positions, it seems fair to argue, have been underpinned by a Humean understanding of the notion of cause: Humeanism has dominated the way in which causation has been discussed in the philosophy of social science. There has been very little discussion of what it means to say that social action is caused beyond the Humean assumptions. This inability to think about causes beyond Humeanism has been the key reason for the proliferation of dichotomies between causal and non-causal, explanatory and interpretive, approaches in the philosophy and practice of social sciences.

Developing avenues that explore alternative conceptualisations of causation holds open the possibility of challenging the traditional lines of debate on causation in social science philosophy and social theory. Weber may have developed, at least in a rudimentary fashion, an account that transcends these divisions. However, his insights have been lost as a result of the efforts of both hermeneutic and positivist theorists to read him in their own ways. Habermas has also tried to avoid the dichotomisation, but has still fallen back on the dominant Humean account of cause. Foucault and Derrida have rejected the traditional accounts of cause. They have, however, also refused to do away with the notion of cause or to endorse the dichotomous causal/non-causal framing of social inquiry. Yet, they have not developed a consistent and systematic alternative to the Humean treatment of causation. This is what Part II of this work will aim to achieve. However, before we move to rethink causation we must understand the influence of the Humean framing of causation in the discipline of International Relations.

3 *Humeanism and rationalist causal analysis in International Relations*

Chapters 1 and 2 have sought to demonstrate that Humean assumptions have played a central role in the twentieth-century philosophy of science and philosophy of social science. The focus now turns to the analysis of a specific social science discipline, International Relations (IR). The discipline of IR developed in response to the First World War: its guiding task was to analyse the nature of international politics and the causes of wars between states, with the aim of devising solutions to the problems of international interaction. For much of the twentieth century IR theorising has been dominated by two main schools of thought: the political realists, who argue that war between states is an ever-present condition of international politics – owing either to the self-interested nature of human actors or states, or to the 'anarchic' nature of the international system – and the liberals, who argue that war between states can be moderated, regulated or even overcome through various means such as institutionalisation or economic interaction. While the so-called first debate and the 1970s inter-paradigm debate in IR[1] revolved around these positions and their various permutations, another divide has also characterised IR theorising: there have been deep disagreements between those who see the discipline of IR as one involving a historical or interpretive analysis of world political processes and those who have sought to make the discipline 'scientific' by enforcing systematic methods of empiricist or positivist science on IR research. These disagreements underlay the

[1] It has been common to characterise IR through the notion of 'Great Debates'. See, for example, Hollis and Smith's account (1990: 16–44) or Steve Smith's 'genealogy' of the discipline (1995). The first debate refers to the 'debates' between the idealists and realists during the interwar years, while the third debate refers to the 'inter-paradigm debate' between the 'globalists', the 'realists' and the 'pluralists' recorded well by Viotti and Kauppi (1993). It should be noted that this 'Great Debates' framing of IR is considered dubious by some IR historiographers. Osiander (1988: 409–32); Wilson (1999: 1–17); Schmidt (1998).

so-called 'second debate' between the traditionalists and the behaviouralists in the 1960s, but have developed a new guise in recent years through the rise of the so-called 'fourth debate', which has involved the controversy between the so-called 'rationalist' and 'reflectivist' IR theorists.[2]

It is the goal of this book to examine and to reframe the latest 'discipline-dividing' debate through analysing and critiquing the dominant conception of cause that has informed it. To this end, this and the following chapter aim to examine in detail the treatment of the concept of cause in the contemporary IR discipline. This analysis is necessary because, despite the central role that the concept of cause has played in theoretical debates in IR, an in-depth analysis of the ways in which the meaning of the concept of cause has been understood among IR theorists has been lacking (although Hidemi Suganami's account of analyses of causes of war, discussed in the following chapter, has taken important steps in that direction).[3] This chapter focuses on analysing the concept of cause in the rationalist/positivist mainstream of IR where 'causal analysis' is explicitly advocated, while chapter 4 examines the so-called postpositivist, or reflectivist, 'constitutive' approaches, which are sceptical of the aims and methods of causal analysis.

This chapter argues that the Humean assumptions outlined in chapter 1 characterise most contemporary causal approaches in IR, although it is recognised that scholars can also simultaneously adhere to certain non-Humean assumptions. As we will see, assumptions about causation are not always coherently held or theorised, but Humeanism nevertheless plays a prominent role in directing 'causal approaches' in contemporary IR. The assumptions of regularity, observability, regularity-determinism and efficient causality play important roles in mainstream causal analysis in IR, although the forms that these assumptions take vary. It is pointed out that whether Humean assumptions are accepted in explicit or implicit form, the acceptance of them has some crucial consequences for the kind of theorising and research that the rationalist mainstream conducts. Notably, it directs rationalists towards 'isolating' causal variables and 'additive' theorising. Humeanism also seems to push them to justify causal statements through regularities and to attach regularity-deterministic assumptions

[2] Wæver (1996). [3] Suganami (1996).

to them, even if this might go against the theorists' more 'common-sensical'[4] assumptions and statements about causal forces. Humeanism also directs theorists away from engagement with processes of social construction and towards atomistic observable social ontologies. It should be noted that this chapter does not aim to advance a full-blown critique of Humeanism, although some of the implications of accepting Humeanism can be characterised as problematic. A full critique of Humeanism in rationalist IR will be left for Part II, where an alternative philosophical approach is advanced to address the Humean 'problem-field' in IR research.

The analysis will proceed as follows. First, in order to contextualise the discussion of contemporary approaches, brief comment will be made on the early theoretical approaches in IR as well as on behaviouralist theorising of the 1960s. The central focus, however, will be on examining the contemporary 'rationalist' approaches. I will review and analyse some key sets of 'guidelines' presented in the discipline for the purposes of causal theorising: those advanced by Michael Nicholson and King, Keohane and Verba. Then the chapter will examine how these guidelines are followed in substantive theorising and will seek to draw out some of the consequences that the acceptance of Humean assumptions has for the kind of theorising and research conducted by the rationalist mainstream.

Causal analysis in early IR theorising

The notion of cause has been central in International Relations from the inception of the discipline, owing to the fact that IR arose as a discipline to tackle the causes of war in the aftermath of the First World War. However, the way in which causes have been thought about has not been uniform but has shifted through the years. In order to contextualise the treatment of causation in contemporary IR approaches, it is useful to examine briefly the assumptions that characterised the early 'idealist' and 'realist' IR theorising. It can be seen that the early theorists in IR were not deeply informed by the positivist views on science (which have gained prominence in later IR debates), nor did their assumptions about causation follow the Humean framing. Instead, their approach

[4] Common-sensical is taken here to mean that which seems to make practical sense to a number of people, that which seems intuitively satisfactory.

to causation was more open and 'common-sensical'. Yet, most of these theorists did not explicitly or coherently conceptualise the concept of cause and, as a result, much of their thought on causation was somewhat unsystematic.

The earliest IR theorists in the discipline have often been termed 'idealists' as they have been seen as advocates of a certain type of liberal order that did not manage to prevent war in the international system. Although the goals of the early theorists in IR were 'progressivist', in the sense that IR scholars hoped that the international system would avoid another disastrous war,[5] it should be noted that the early theorists were not seeking easy panaceas, but recognised the complexity of international affairs and of political problems.[6] This could be seen in their analysis of the causes of war.

It is often argued that the early 'idealists' located the causes of the First World War simply in the undemocratic nature of some states or in the misperceptions and misunderstandings that had existed between states and their leaders in the run-up to the war.[7] On a closer analysis it can be seen that the early analyses of the causes of war were not this simplistic. Leonard Woolf, for example, distinguished four dominant (though not exhaustive) types of causes of war – legal, economic, administrative or political and social. These factors, he argued, interacted in various ways in specific historical contexts, and each type would have to be countered in different ways in different contexts.[8] The early inquiries into causes of war were much more multifaceted than is often recognised. The supposed 'idealists' did not envisage simple solutions to problems of world politics because they were very aware of the fact that 'large historical events and movements are moulded by all kinds of different causes'.[9]

What were their assumptions about causation? The liberal internationalist rhetoric espoused a 'scientific' approach to curing the problem of war. However, the early theorists were not advocates of science in the vein of the logical positivists of the time, nor was their conception of causation a Humean one. The 'idealists' did not like to generalise

[5] For classic 'idealist' works see, for example, Woolf (1916, 1917, 1920, 1939); Zimmern (1931, 1936); Dickinson (1917).

[6] Rereadings of the early scholars include, for example, Schmidt (1998) and Osiander (1988).

[7] Hollis and Smith (1990: 18–19).

[8] Woolf (1916: 11).

[9] Woolf (1920: 14–15).

beyond the historical contexts that they were studying, nor did they seek, or isolate, distinct 'causal variables' in world politics. The early theorists, drawing on the traditions of international law and diplomatic history, came to their conclusions through conceptual and historical analyses. They were not interested in finding universal laws of war and peace; rather they saw themselves as historians and pragmatic intellectuals aiming to understand, and advance knowledgeable judgements on, the complex, multiple and changing forces in world politics.

With the coming of the Second World War, and the rise of the self-proclaimed political realist school of international politics, 'idealist' international relations scholarship was attacked ferociously. Political realists argued that the idealists had been clouded by their ideological political views, and had allowed the 'purpose' of their studies (the wish to eradicate war) to drive their analysis.[10] As far as the political realists were concerned, the 'idealists' had not inquired deeply enough into the causes of wars and disorder in the international system. In fact, E. H. Carr argued that the 'utopian' idealists had completely ignored causal analysis – a tendency considered widespread in all 'infant sciences'.[11] To remedy this, Carr emphasised the persistent asymmetry between the 'haves' and 'have-nots' in the international system as an underlying cause of the recurrence of war, while Hans Morgenthau espoused the idea that the instinct for survival at the core of human nature was a persistent incurable ultimate cause for the recurrence of wars.[12] However, despite their critiques of the substantive analyses of world politics advanced by the 'idealists' the conception of causation that informed these early political realists was very much in line with that of the 'idealists'. Crucially, they were not Humeans.

Jim George has argued that because Morgenthau spoke of 'objective laws' of politics he can be seen as a scientific 'positivist' in the sense that has come to dominate the later discipline.[13] It is true that on occasion Morgenthau refers to the objective laws of political life and also uses language that portrays rather Humean sentiments about causation in the natural sciences.[14] However, equating Morgenthau's approach with positivism or Humeanism in analysis of international relations is misleading. On closer analysis, we can see that Morgenthau was, in fact, opposed to efforts to generalise about social life. More important

[10] Carr (2001 [1939]: 8). [11] Carr (2001: 12). [12] Morgenthau (1948).
[13] George (1994: 94). [14] Morgenthau (1947: 114, 130).

than generalising about patterns was to have a deep understanding of historical contexts and the political complexities of world political situations. Indeed, Morgenthau was fiercely opposed to any efforts to pursue predictive social science and, instead, emphasised the complexity and flux of social life and the need for historical and contextual judgements in dealing with world politics.[15] He vehemently resisted any tendencies to talk about causes in the (regularity-deterministic) 'when A, then B' form[16] as he did not see causal relations in the social world as simple or 'stable', but rather as complex and interactive.[17]

E. H. Carr also resisted any attempts to see the relations of causes and effects as generalisable and 'isolatable'; rather he saw the world consisting of 'reciprocal causalities': various structures, agents, events as well as processes exerting influence on each other.[18] Causal forces were seen as complex, multilayered, interactive and did not entail determinism (in the 'when A, then B' form). The role of the theorist or historian was to give their interpretation of the linkages between causal factors and their causal weighting.[19]

Despite the rhetorical strategies that appealed to 'science' and 'laws', neither the idealists nor the political realists in early and mid-twentieth-century IR bought into the Humean discourse on causation in a systematic way. They saw some patterns of behaviour in world politics but explained them through resort to conceptual analysis of complex contextual and historical forces. Why did these theorists not accept Humeanism? Arguably, one of the reasons for this was the fact that these theorists had their background in disciplines such as international law and international history, rather than disciplines such as sociology or economics, where the empiricist-positivist view of science initially had more influence. Since Humeanism played the most central role in those approaches that had been most influenced by the empiricist and positivist approaches to philosophy of science, those scholars who were less dogmatically committed to empiricism and positivism did not feel equally tied to the Humean conception of causal analysis.

However, it should also be noted that these theorists often lacked a clear and explicit approach to the conceptualisation and investigation

15 Morgenthau (1947: 119–20). See also Bain (2000: 449–59).

16 Frei (2001: 191).

17 Morgenthau (1947: 115).

18 See Kubalkova (1998: 30).

19 See Carr (1986: 90).

of causes. Indeed, causation was not conceptualised in a coherent manner by the early theorists, perhaps with the exception of E. H. Carr.[20] Instead, it worked as a common-sensical background assumption in their work: causes referred to various forces and conditions that shaped why and how certain events, changes or processes came about. Because of their lack of a clear conceptualisation of causation, the early theorists did not conceptualise causation as much as they simply 'assumed' the pragmatic utility of talking about causes in referring to world politics. The open but weakly conceptualised framing of causation came under attack by those who, by the 1960s, sought to 'systematise' the study of world politics.

Rise of Humeanism in IR: behaviouralism and causal analysis

The way in which causes and methods of causal analysis were thought about in IR changed drastically with the emergence of behaviouralist approaches in the 1960s. With the rising influence of the empiricist-positivist view of science in the social sciences, the discipline of IR, too, eventually became shaped by the 'scientific' conception of social inquiry, which in turn entailed the systematisation of the concept of cause and of causal analysis: crucially, on Humean lines.

Quincy Wright and Lewis Richardson had already utilised statistical ways of studying the problem of war in the 1940s and 1950s. However, it was not until the 1960s that theorists such as David Singer, Morton Kaplan and Bruce Bueno de Mesquita proceeded to provide a 'scientific' approach with a solid footing in IR. The goal of the new 'scientific' approaches was to apply the empiricist-positivist criteria of science to the explanation of international affairs. The targets of attack were the studies reliant on mere 'intuitive' historical judgements, such as Morgenthau's and Carr's. Their 'conceptual' analyses of world politics were seen as inadequately 'scientific' and, hence, were considered to be in need of rigorous systematisation and empirical testing.

For the new scientific researchers in IR, the 'scientific approach' had as its aim, following Hume, the study of the 'general patterns, not the unique'; the aim was 'not . . . to delineate the particular causes of

[20] Carr's discussion of causation in *What is History?* (1986: 87–105) evidences a sophisticated understanding of philosophical debates on causation. In the light of this work his account of cause can be seen as a mix of pragmatist and philosophically realist assumptions.

a specific war, but to examine a large number of wars to identify the conditions associated with war'.[21] The focus of causal analysis was no more the search for essences or forces in international politics and their out-folding in specific contexts, but rather generalisation about observable patterns of events, notably about the general circumstances in which wars frequently occur.[22] Most behaviouralists in IR still used the word 'cause', unlike some of the more radical empiricists in philosophy of science (see chapters 1 and 2), but they avoided giving it any deeper meaning outside the description of regular patterns and their correlative associations: the question of causes became subsumed under the analysis of 'general laws'.[23] The IR behaviouralists focused the study of IR on the analysis of patterns of behaviour and correlates found within observational data. This entailed, crucially, compilation of extensive ('large-N') statistical data. Various data-gathering projects emerged, for example, the Correlates of War project, Richardson's 'Statistics of Deadly Quarrels' and Bueno de Mesquita's alliance data.

The assumption was that, on the basis of analysing the associations between observable or behavioural patterns, hypotheses about the linkages between some of the key variables in 'war causation' could be either confirmed or rejected. Although the hypotheses could be 'intuitively' derived, their testing and confirmation had to take place according to scientific procedures – conceived of in accordance with the decrees of the empiricist or positivist conception of science. In analysing data and testing hypotheses mathematical methods were the name of the game. To test their 'causal' hypotheses the scientists correlated the patterns they were interested in explaining with other patterns and through bivariate, multivariate, contiguity and regression methods they drew conclusions as to the 'strength of association' between variables. These mathematical methods were viewed as superior to all other methods of data handling because they were seen to allow for methodological manipulation and control of data and made tests replicable.[24]

Singer's account of the behaviouralist research exercise demonstrates the influence of the empiricist Humean characteristics:

[21] Vasquez and Henehan (1992: xx).

[22] A distinct kind of 'causal question' about causes of war, as pointed out by Suganami (1996).

[23] Vasquez and Henehan (1992: xx–xxii). See also Rosenau (1980).

[24] See, for example, Mueller (1969).

Suppose one wanted to test the following hypothesis, not always made explicit, but central to what we call the balance-of-power theory: The *closer* the international system is to bipolarity, the greater the frequency and magnitude of war, and the *further* it is from bipolarity, the less the frequency and magnitude. First the investigator selects that historical period, which holds most theoretical interest for him... His generalisation... normally holds only for that period. Next, he develops quantitative measures of his *independent* variable (polarity of the system) and his *dependent* variables (magnitude of war, frequency of war), and then he goes on to code and score the independent variable and the two dependent variables for each year. Finally, he runs simple statistical correlations between the two sets of variables, and concludes that, for the period under study, the hypothesis is (or is not) strongly (or weakly) disconfirmed... As to the complaint that many factors in the international system *other than* polarity may have accounted for the results, all the investigator can do is go on to study, in a similar fashion, the correlation between *those* factors and his outcome.[25]

Many, mainly political realist hypotheses concerning the associative relations of balance of power, arms races, alliances and capabilities were formulated and tested through these methods.[26] Theorists concentrated on studying observable 'variables' such as military capabilities (amount of military hardware) and incidence of war (defined through quantifiable battle deaths) as these were most readily subjected to the 'scientific' analysis that the positivist criteria of science required. Issues of perception and belief were largely ignored in favour of studying patterns of observable events, observable behaviour or observable 'resources'. Thus, even when the approach taken was not politically realist (for example, 'peace research'), the focus was still largely on quantifying material capabilities or behavioural regularities.[27]

The empirical studies conducted on the basis of these scientific methods stacked up. However, the theoretical contribution of these studies remained rather limited in that the behaviouralists only really advanced correlational evidence of the associations between specific 'independent variables', rather than theoretically insightful explanatory accounts of why and how aspects of the world described by the variables were thus associated. It followed that Humeanism in the form of behaviouralist approaches was not accepted without resistance.

[25] Italics in the original. Singer (1965: 9–10).

[26] Although as Vasquez has shown many of them were falsified. Vasquez (1998: 137–8).

[27] See, for example, Russett (1972: 14).

Hedley Bull, for example, argued vehemently against the rising tide of behaviouralism.[28]

Bull remained extremely sceptical of the behaviouralist attempts to quantify IR. He did not believe in the possibility of the completely value-free, 'objective' and 'scientific' study of politics that the behaviouralists argued for. For Bull, IR was a discipline that should utilise the 'approach to theorising that derives from philosophy, history and law, and that is characterised above all by explicit reliance upon the exercise of judgement'.[29] He argued that the contribution of the behaviouralist methodology to IR was slight since it could not account for history, for sensitive political judgements, or for any normative concerns. The scientific approach according to Bull distorted the nature of politics and impoverished the study of IR by reducing world politics to variables and quantifiables, hence, cutting IR off from historical and philosophical inquiry.[30] Bull did not think that the causes of international society, or of war, can be 'objectively' identified in mere 'correlates of war' or through functional analysis. Rather, he argued, causal analysis in IR should follow the (non-Humean) assumptions of the early theorists.[31] Although Bull recognised that statistical data and methods can have some uses, he contended that, at the end of the day, the contributions of theoretical claims about causality arose from the conceptual and historical judgements made, not from the quantitative data.[32]

Despite Bull's resistance the Humean assumptions that made their way into IR through behaviouralism have persisted as shapers of IR research. Although Humeanism has acquired more moderate and implicit guises in IR research, it is still dominant in the so-called 'rationalist' form of theorising.

Contemporary 'rationalist' causal analysis in IR: the core precepts

Rationalism is a term that has come to be used widely in IR in the past decade or so. Its use has risen with the simultaneous decline of

[28] Bull (1969). [29] Bull (1969: 20). [30] Bull (1969: 28).

[31] It is important to note that Bull's objection to behaviouralism did not arise from an anti-causal 'hermeneutic' premise: causes were still fundamentally important in understanding the world of international politics. Bull (1977: xiv).

[32] Crucially, however, Bull was not a relativist on causes: he accepted that some causal accounts are better than others. Bull (1977: xv).

the use of the term 'positivism', which has increasingly been seen as rather 'vague' and open to contestation. Robert Keohane first used the term rationalism in the Presidential Address to the International Studies Association in 1988 and it has made its way into the IR theory lexicon since then. However, it too is a rather confusing descriptive term in IR, for it is widely used to refer to rational choice approaches that could be described as epistemologically rationalist as well as to scientific approaches that draw on an empiricist epistemology. While there is some incoherence in the use of the term rationalism in IR, this book will conform to the disciplinary usage of the term and conceive 'rationalism' to encompass both empiricist modes of thought and contemporary forms of rationalism, notably rational choice theory.[33] Interestingly, it will be seen that both traditions of thought do, in fact, share important lines of thought, including reproduction of Humean assumptions concerning causation.

In the discipline of IR, rationalists are themselves often identified in comparison with the 'reflectivists': the rationalists, as Keohane argued, can be distinguished from the reflectivists in that they formulate clear research programmes, the assumptions and theoretical propositions of which can be clearly tested by scholars and students of international politics.[34] The key to seeing a theoretical approach as 'rationalist' has been, not the content of the theory, but the way in which the theory has been formulated, justified and tested. Interestingly, one of the criteria for rationalist approaches, it seems, has been whether the approach accepts certain Humean assumptions concerning causal analysis.

It will be seen that Humean assumptions in contemporary 'rationalist' approaches need not take a radical empiricist (or behaviouralist) form. Indeed, even the scientifically inclined theorists in IR have argued that many of the behaviouralist inquiries were characterised by insignificant findings and often nonsensical questions.[35] Humeanism, it should be noted, has acquired new forms in the contemporary discipline. To gain a clearer understanding of this post-behaviouralist Humeanism in IR, I shall first review some of the rationalist methodological guidelines, notably Nicholson's and King, Keohane and Verba's. These guides aptly

[33] For a more detailed discussion of rationalism/reflectivism, and positivist/postpositivism, see Kurki and Wight (2007).
[34] Keohane (1988). [35] Vasquez (1998: 146).

summarise the rationalist post-behaviouralist assumptions about social scientific causal analysis.

Michael Nicholson: Causes and Consequences

The goal of Michael Nicholson's works has been to give a consistent philosophically and methodologically grounded basis for systematic and scientifically rigorous causal analysis in IR. Nicholson has been keen to avoid the excesses of behaviouralism, and has an aversion to the term 'positivism' because of the logical positivist connotations attached to it.[36] However, he openly admits that he follows the empiricist lines of thought. He argues that central in social science research is the analysis of the relations of empirical propositions grounded on observational evidence. He further argues that there is an important level of 'stability' (regular patterns) in social life and that generalising and predictive empirical analysis is what is needed to ground intelligent policy in world politics.[37] These empiricist assumptions inform also his model of causal analysis.

Interestingly, Nicholson never really defines causation. For example, in *Causes and Consequences in International Relations: a Conceptual Study* he curiously never addresses the issue of causation: in fact, he tries his best to avoid discussing the 'philosophically treacherous problem of causation'.[38] Instead of discussing the problem of causation, Nicholson prefers to take the Humean approach to causation as a given and concentrates on examining the Humean question: how are generalisations possible?[39]

Drawing on the Popperian form of Humeanism, Nicholson thinks it is fair that we talk of 'causes' as descriptions of the logical relations between patterns of observables. Causal relations are seen as logical relations that hold between variables, or rather statements pertaining to those variables. Following the empiricist view the key question is

[36] He prefers the term empiricism. Nicholson (1996b: 129).

[37] This stability justifies acceptance of social 'things'. Nicholson (1996b: 131).

[38] Nicholson (1996a: 146). See also his earlier work, *Scientific Analysis of Social Behaviour*, where Nicholson argues that the concept of cause is a useful one in scientific inquiry even though there are 'philosophical doubts' about the nature of particular relationships. His reflections on causation here are explicitly set in the context of seeking to preserve the Humean account of causation (1983: 26–7).

[39] Nicholson (1996a: 145, 155, 31).

epistemological, that is, how do we gain reliable knowledge of the empirical world? The answer to this question is: through systematic unbiased experience. Systematic unbiased experience, for Nicholson, arises from 'regular' experience: the world consists of patterns and these patterns can be discerned through careful observation.[40] Quantification and systematic empirical testing of propositions is central in causal analysis because it ensures that vague and unsystematic accounts of world politics can be avoided.[41]

Nicholson makes some qualifications that allow him to dissociate himself from the behaviouralists. First, although regularities are defined in terms of observables, Nicholson accepts that some 'unobservables' have a valid place in science: references to 'goals', mental states and beliefs are justifiable. However, following Humean scepticism, unobservables can only be 'assumed' to exist. While Nicholson says that we can 'assume' the existence of 'unobservables' ('as if' they existed), crucially, they only count in science in so far as they have regular observable facets or implications.[42]

Second, to avoid Popper's scepticism concerning the nature of causal laws in social science, Nicholson adopts the 'softer' form of Popperian regularity theory: a weaker 'how-possibly' understanding of the DN-model, entailing probabilistic causal analysis.[43] Probabilistic causal explanation, as was seen in chapter 1, avoids the absolutism of the deductive logic of the DN-model, instead settling for probabilistic calculations as the basis for causal deductions. It follows that generalisation, for Nicholson, is about explaining how certain events (such as the Iraq–Iran war) were 'possible' (in light of quantifiable variables and their associations), not why they were 'necessary'.[44] While still squarely relying on the deductive logic of the DN-model and the Humean assumptions of generalisability, observability and (qualified) regularity-determinism, Nicholson can claim to be able to explain events in world politics in a way that is not deterministic in a strict 'when A, then B' manner.

Nicholson's account is widely read as an epistemological and methodological guide to causal analysis in IR. However, an even more influential model of causal analysis is that of King, Keohane and Verba.

[40] Nicholson (1996b: 142).
[41] Nicholson (1996b: 137).
[42] Nicholson (1996b: 139).
[43] Nicholson (1996a: 48–51).
[44] Nicholson (1996a: 49–50).

King, Keohane and Verba: systematising causal inference in political science

During the past decade or so, Gary King, Robert O. Keohane and Sidney Verba have assumed the mantle of methodological role models of 'rationalist' explanation right across the different sub-disciplines of political science. King, Keohane and Verba wanted to advance a 'unified logic of inference' for social scientific disciplines. The goal was to rescue social science from 'vague' and 'unsystematic' social inquiry by showing that the 'scientific logic of inference' can be applied to qualitative as well as the quantitative approaches. By demonstrating that qualitative analysis can become 'scientific', King, Keohane and Verba hoped to force qualitative approaches to 'take scientific inference seriously', hence allowing these approaches to start making 'valid inferences about social and political life'.[45]

King, Keohane and Verba emphasise that causal inference is fundamentally important for science, and indeed, that most approaches do use causal claims, even if implicitly. They argue against those who are against causal analysis owing to the problem of complexity of social life and who choose merely to 'describe' events (interpretivists). Equally, they are opposed to those empiricists who are wary of using causal claims because of the 'correlation does not equal causation'-mantra (logical positivists/behaviourists).[46]

But what is causal inference for King, Keohane and Verba? They start by accepting what they come to call the Fundamental Problem of Causal Inference, that is, the assumption that '[o]ur uncertainty about causal inference will never be eliminated'.[47] They do not claim to have a definitive solution to the problem of causality. However, they do argue that if certain methods are followed we can mitigate the Fundamental Problem of Causal Inference and, hence, have the basis for reasonably trustworthy causal inferences.

Causality, for King, Keohane and Verba, is measured in terms of the 'causal effect' exerted by an 'explanatory' variable on the 'dependent variable'. They propose that we measure 'causal effect' as 'the difference between the systematic component of observations made when the explanatory variable takes one value and the systematic component

[45] King, Keohane and Verba (1994: ix, 3).
[46] King, Keohane and Verba (1994: 75–6).
[47] King, Keohane and Verba (1994: 76).

of comparable observations when the explanatory variable takes on another value'.[48] In other words, when we assess causal relations we try to see what effect changing the value of the explanatory variable has for the 'dependent variable'. Their account of causation is based on virtually 'replaying' an event, or rather pattern of events, with all other elements held constant except for the explanatory variable. Important for this definition of causality is the notion of counterfactual conditionality: the causal effect is the difference between the 're-run' variable and the state of affairs had that variable not been there.[49] They acknowledge that owing to the Fundamental Problem of Causal Inference we can never completely securely 're-run' explanatory variables (as perfectly controlled experiments), but argue that, through careful observation of some central rules of causal inference – falsifiability, consistency, careful selection of dependent variables, maximisation of 'concreteness' and of 'encompassing qualities'[50] – we can minimise this 'disturbance' in causal explanations of the social world.

Importantly, King, Keohane and Verba argue that this logic of causal inference applies equally to the quantitative and the qualitative inferences. They maintain that even in qualitative inference, scientific credibility lies in the careful definition of the 'causal effect'. For example, to find out whether presidential or parliamentary systems are more politically stable we should run hypothesised experiments with both systems and see what the respective causal effects have been. Then, 'we define the *mean causal effect* to be the average of the realized causal effects across replications of experiments'.[51]

Not only is this definition of cause applicable across methodological approaches, it is also considered logically prior to other definitions of causality, for example the 'causal mechanism' and the 'multiple cause' accounts. They argue that the causal mechanism and multiple cause approaches themselves rely upon an understanding of causal effects as they define it.[52]

[48] King, Keohane and Verba (1994: 81–2).
[49] King, Keohane and Verba (1994: 77).
[50] King, Keohane and Verba (1994: 99–114).
[51] King, Keohane and Verba (1994: 84).
[52] King, Keohane and Verba (1994: 85–9). They regard the 'mechanism' approach as vague in that it quickly leads to 'infinite regress' as it cannot give a precise definition or measurement of any one causal effect at any time. King, Keohane and Verba (1994: 86). Their account of mechanisms is, however, problematic in that it misunderstands the way in which philosophical realists treat mechanisms. See Wight (2006: 31).

On a closer analysis we can see that this approach is steeped in Humeanism, though it might not be immediately obvious. The regularity theory of causation is not insisted on as strongly or explicitly as by the behaviourists: King, Keohane and Verba do not take mere correlation to be causation, nor do they see large-N studies as the only way to gain causal knowledge. However, underneath the 'relaxed' rhetoric, the Humean regularity assumption still plays a fundamentally important role. First, there is an expectation that the qualitative variables will be expressed in quantified terms and also that the larger the samples or numbers the better the validity of the inquiry (numbers add 'efficiency').[53] Moreover, the idea of causal effect itself is dependent on quantification, for how do we study, say, the 'stability' of a political system if it is not through operationalisation of some indicators of stability (quantifiable) that we can then compare with the (indexed) stability in the other cases?

Second, *Designing Social Inquiry* is characterised by deep empiricism with regard to observability: causal effects are relations between patterns of observables, not between anything 'deeper' than that. Indeed, King, Keohane and Verba especially warn against including unobservable concepts that cannot be empirically operationalised into the testing of theories.[54] Observable behaviour of individuals, or individual-like actors (for example, states conceived of as unitary actors), provides the most obvious types of variables for the political sciences.

Also, we can see that causal relation is viewed as a relation between two independent sets of observations. Any 'interlinking' between variables is seen to 'contaminate' the results. Thus, a researcher must be sure that the independent and dependent variables are truly distinct and not interrelated, in the sense that they are observed 'independently'. This is an important point because of the acceptance of the Humean assumption that events need to be 'independently observed' to qualify as causes or effects: causal relations are relations between 'external' independent events/patterns; they do not involve 'internal relations'. This is a particularly Humean assumption that, as will be seen in later chapters, does not characterise many non-Humean philosophies of causation.

Furthermore, and crucially, King, Keohane and Verba do not talk about relations between things: causality, for them, is a strictly

[53] See King, Keohane and Verba (1994: 208–30).
[54] King, Keohane and Verba (1994: 109–12, 115–49).

epistemological concept and the relationship of causes and effects a logical relationship of patterns of observables, or statements pertaining to them. The very fact that definition of causal effects is expressed in formalised form makes this clear.

Also, their account is regularity-deterministic: the primary goal is, indeed, to create 'closed systems' (isolate causal variables). King, Keohane and Verba accept that excessive emphasis on parsimony can have some adverse effects and hence they do not advocate it as a principle applicable in all contexts.[55] Thus, causal complexity is allowed up to a point, in the sense that many causal variables can be studied within the same research. However, according to the empiricist logic, it is noted that too much concentration on the complex and the unique dampens the 'efficiency' of the explanation; accounting for too many contributory factors lowers the 'mean causal effect' of the key variable.[56] At the end of the day, the causal effects of a variable should be studied through artificial isolation of an independent variable, as if to create a closed system where its effects can be independently measured.

Also, prediction is seen as something associated with causal inquiry. Although predictive qualities of theories are not made a primary criterion of validity as with many 'hard' positivist approaches, it is still assumed that the better the causal argument, the better the predictions. Thus, if a study had made reasonably valid generalisations, for example, about the 'mean effect' of incumbency on electoral success, they argue that 'certainly new incumbents would wish to know the variation in the causal effect of incumbency so they can judge how closely [*sic*] their experience will be to that of previous incumbents and how much to rely on their estimated mean causal effect of incumbency from previous elections'.[57] Generalisations, or variations in general patterns, are presumed to stay relatively 'constant' and, hence, it is the generalisations that effects are derived from: given generalisation X, 'if A, then (with probability Z) B'.

King, Keohane and Verba's account is steeped in Humeanism. They argue that correlation is not causation, but accept that the search for causal relationships is defined by and limited to the search for general

55 King, Keohane and Verba (1994: 20).
56 King, Keohane and Verba (1994: 104, 182–3).
57 King, Keohane and Verba (1994: 82).

patterns between observables in empirical data. Importantly, talking about causes involves, not saying what, and how, something is 'causing' something else, but specifying the 'mean causal effect' of a variable when the test environment has been trimmed to perfection. Data need not be mere large-N data and hence they can distance themselves from classical behaviouralist positivism. Yet, they assert that the scientific logic of inquiry is the same throughout different kinds of empirical data and that this logic requires that a number of instances or empirical implications of a theory are examined. By 'disciplining' causal theorists sufficiently, we can make claims about causal relations in qualitative data.[58] The key point is that science can provide more reasonably objective and reliable knowledge of causal relations in social affairs as long as the rules of 'scientific method' are adhered to.

These types of empiricist guidelines, rationalists have pointed out, apply to the study of various 'objects', including the study of ideas. Causal analysis of ideas and beliefs is possible, then: yet only in so far as beliefs are operationalised in accordance with the logic of science. First, to be valid as a causal category ideas or beliefs must be tied to observables: one must have empirical proof of the holding of belief or of the effect of the holding of the belief (evidence can be obtained in an interview or deduced from the behaviour of actors). Second, regularities must be present: the goal of ideational causal explanation is 'to seek valid generalizations, without which no causal analysis [would] be of much value'.[59] The goal is, through careful generalisation, to isolate the causal effects of particular ideas. Goldstein and Keohane, for example, argue that particular ideas that 'individuals hold'[60] can be treated as causal 'switchmen' if we can track observable patterns on the basis of assuming the existence of these ideas.

In *Ideas and Foreign Policy* Goldstein and Keohane argue that the most obviously causal ideas are so-called 'causal beliefs' for they have direct impacts that are generalisable: the holding of the theory of penicillin, for example, has had clear generalisable impacts and, hence, a 'proven' causal role in modern medical science. Other ideas, such as principled beliefs and world-views, have a less clear-cut causal role:

58 King, Keohane and Verba (1994: 75–114).

59 Goldstein and Keohane (1993a: 29).

60 Ideas are seen as something that 'individuals hold'; they do not refer to an 'intersubjective' or 'social' category. Goldstein and Keohane (1993a: 3).

this is because their effects are not easily generalisable and deterministic (when A, then B). Rationalists recognise that, since these ideas are more difficult to observe, validate and generalise about, these ideational causal analyses are often incomplete and uncertain. However, they argue that the problems of ideational causal analysis are not inherent or insurmountable, but can be mitigated through a careful systematic empirical study.[61] At the end of the day, explanation of the causal role of ideas, emotions or perceptions, as independent causal variables, can be conducted in exactly the same way as an analysis of more 'material' factors.[62]

A note on the rational choice approaches

Another methodological ground we have to cover in understanding approaches that go under the label 'rationalist' in IR is rational choice theorising. Rational choice theorists argue that if we think of individuals, or states, as egoistic 'mini-maxers', place these individuals in different (formal) structural situations and observe, or hypothesise about, how they act, we can gain some crucial insights into how human societies/systems work. The idea of rational choice theory is that the particular structure of a 'game' defines a hypothetical causal structure within which the behaviour of actors can be predicted, given the assumption that they act rationally or in a specified 'goal-directed' way. The rational choice approach to social inquiry has become highly influential in rationalist IR. Some theorists have gone for a fully formalised rational choice approach,[63] while others have opted for a 'softer' approach, taking on board the assumptions about rational actors and utility maximisation, as well as those about the structures of games, but without explicit formalisation and mathematical calculation of probable actions.[64]

[61] Goldstein and Keohane (1993a: 8–10, 27–9).

[62] Nicholson too emphasises that ideas, emotions and perceptions can also be quantified and studied through the empiricist form of explanation. See Nicholson (1996b: 133).

[63] Which fully lays out the matrices and probability calculations for the actions to be predicted; see, for example, Bueno de Mesquita (1989).

[64] See, for example, Gilpin (1981); Grieco (1988); Mearsheimer (1995); Krasner (1991); Axelrod and Keohane (1985); Keohane (1984); Snidal (1993).

The game theoretical models are not strictly Humean in the traditional sense. First, most rational choice theorists do not perceive themselves to be engaged in causal analysis as such: rather, they are engaged in modelling possible and likely courses of action. Also, even when explanations seek to answer why-questions, the rational choice accounts do not necessarily rely on generalisations and correlations gathered through extensive empirical research in the inductive sense. Nevertheless, game theory and rational choice methods 'fit in' with the Humean assumptions very well because they share many of the assumptions that inform traditionally Humean approaches. First, game theory has equal faith in the empirical definition of 'scientific' knowledge; rational choice theorists also believe in generating clearly defined hypotheses that can be empirically tested. Equally, rational choice approaches have faith in deductive methods as a path to reliable knowledge: the emphasis is, as in Humeanism, on predicting outcomes on the basis of deductive logic. Game theory also, similar to Humean approaches, analyses the social world as if it was characterised by stable patterns of behaviour, in this case derived from the rationality models. Also, game theory is based on observable atomistic ontology, that is, ontology based on analysis of behaviour of individuals. Crucially, individuals are seen as essentially non-social rational actors in the sense that rational choice approaches have traditionally made relatively little effort to take into account the 'unobservable' social conditioning of actors through norms, rules or social structures.

With this in mind, it is important that we clarify the meaning of causal mechanisms in rational choice work. Crucially, it must be noted that references to 'causal mechanisms' in rational choice approaches are premised on Humean assumptions. The 'causal mechanisms' that rational choice theorists refer to point either to the logical structure of the game (given rationality and the structure of the game the individuals are logically deduced to act in certain ways), or to the probability distributions deduced from the choice-matrices (probabilistic causality). Both understandings of causal mechanisms are premised on logical deducibility. If the DN-model of causal explanation is premised on deducing particular events from laws and initial conditions, game theoretical models are premised on assuming 'a set of circumstances in which decision makers of a certain sort (entrepreneurs, governments, individuals or whatever) operate' and 'a set of goals which they pursue' and then seeing 'what choices and what consequences follow from this as an issue of logic'.[65] The test of the theory, then, is how well the predicted consequences match up with observed empirical data.

This section has sought to review some of the central methodological and epistemological guidelines that causal theorising in IR aims to live up to. It has been seen that Humeanism has played a crucial role in defining these methodological precepts. The next section will examine how the Humean assumptions play out in substantive 'positivist' or 'rationalist' theorising. I will also point to some of the consequences that Humeanism has for the way in which positivists or rationalists deal with world politics, consequences that, in the light of the following chapters, will be seen as problematic.

Varieties of Humeanism and their consequences

Although the methodological precepts of rationalist IR are deeply informed by Humeanism, it should be noted that Humeanism plays itself out in various different forms in the substantive research of the mainstream of 'rationalist' IR. Indeed, Humean discourse, while it forms an important underlying discursive background, interacts with some other analytical tendencies. While some theorists conduct explicitly and strongly Humean quantitative research in the vein of classical behaviourism, other theoretical frameworks are shaped by Humeanism in much more implicit forms.

Explicit and implicit Humeanism

The influence of the Humean assumptions can be identified clearly among IR theorists who follow positivist or empiricist precepts in an explicit and 'strong' form. The dominance of Humeanism has been very explicit in those theoretical frameworks that accept an unashamedly quantitative approach to causal analysis. One need not do much more than open up some of the IR journals, for example, *International Studies Quarterly*, *International Organization* or *Journal of Conflict Resolution*, to gain an appreciation of the highly influential nature of the quantitative approaches in IR. Analyses based on general statistical models, which entail tracing the associative relations between variables

[65] Nicholson (1996b: 139).

in large scale, have been utilised in studies of all aspects of international relations: from state behaviour, to trade relations, as well as recently to new areas such as the study of the role of women.[66]

One area where many examples of the use of quantitative approaches can be found is the study of liberal democratic peace: the debates in democratic peace theory have classically been firmly based on Humean assumptions. Analyses of whether democracy can be said to cause peace tend to concentrate on the examination of the statistical associations between regular patterns of observables pertaining to the democratic peace hypothesis. In the traditional democratic peace literature, democracies' propensities for peace are sought through the conduct of careful mathematical studies of statistical relations of variables in extensive statistical data drawn from the quantitative databanks.[67] Both the advocates and the proponents of democratic peace have traditionally made use of the positivist approach, specifically a quantitative positivist approach. The proponents, on the basis of their analysis, have argued that the proposition 'democracies do not go to war' is 'one of the strongest non-trivial, non-tautological generalisations that can be made about international relations': indeed, it is often considered the 'closest thing to an empirical law' in IR.[68] Critics of democratic peace have, on the other hand, pointed out that the correlational associations found by the proponents seem statistically insignificant when they are compared with the (statistical) explanatory weight of other causal variables (alliances, cultural unity, wealth).[69] Many democratic peace theorists, on either side of the argument, have firmly believed that statistical quantitative analysis of observable variables gives us reliable and valid knowledge of the truth or falsity of the democratic peace propositions. Because of the common acceptance of the quantitative approach to the object of study, the disagreements between the political realists and the liberal democratic peace theorists often come

[66] At the time of writing, various articles in recent editions of *International Organization* demonstrate the impressive range of uses to which Humean type analyses can be put. See, for example, Goldstein, Rivers and Tomz (2007); Colaresi (2007); Gray, Kittilson and Sandholtz (2006).

[67] See, for example, Russett (1993); Brown, Lynn-Jones and Miller (1999). See also numerous submissions on democratic peace in *Journal of Conflict Resolution*, *American Political Science Review*, *International Organization* and *International Studies Quarterly*. See also Rummel (1995).

[68] Russett quoted in Brown, Lynn-Jones and Miller (1999: ix).

[69] For critics of democratic peace theory see Spiro (1994); Layne (1994).

down to narrow differences in the interpretation with regard to the data (which data entries are included or excluded and on what basis) and disagreements over the particular statistical and mathematical methods of finding 'associations' between variables.[70]

In recent years, the exclusive concentration on statistical analysis has been challenged as some theorists have argued that we need to pay closer attention to historical data[71] and to explanation of the 'causal mechanisms'[72] that bring about democratic peace. However, these explanations have not escaped the Humean assumptions: for example, Russett's and Maoz's efforts to account for the 'causal mechanism' of democratic peace through structural and normative explanations, in the end, are nothing but attempts to demonstrate the 'robustness' of correlative relations between the two independent variables (pertaining to democratic norms and institutional constraints) with the dependent variable peace.[73] 'Causal mechanisms' have been conceived of and analysed as conglomerations of variables, a particularly Humean approach to the study of causal mechanisms.[74]

It is relatively easy to identify such statistical studies where Humean assumptions play a crucial role in directing analysis of general data, and hence I will not discuss them further here. However, it is also important to look at some of the rationalist theorists that do not *explicitly* espouse the strong and explicit form of Humeanism. I will now examine some key IR theorists whose theoretical outlooks are shaped by the Humean assumptions more 'implicitly' or inadvertently.

A good place to start is Waltz, whose work is one of the most foundational but also one of the most criticised in contemporary IR. Waltz is often lumped together with the 'positivists'.[75] This term would logically entail the association of Waltz with some form of Humeanism.

[70] See, for example, Rummel's critiques of other democratic peace theorists (1995).

[71] Owen (1994). [72] Maoz and Russett (1993: 624–38).

[73] Maoz and Russett (1993: 624).

[74] Democratic peace theorists more oriented towards analysis of historical case studies, such as Owen, have arguably also remained within the remit of regularity criteria. Although theorists such as Owen have put more emphasis on discussing particular historical cases and have remained more open to the possibility of locating different 'causal mechanisms' of democratic peace, the historical cases have not been used on their own merits, but as 'complements' to statistical analysis (from which the true causal explanations are seen to arise). Owen (1994). See also discussion in chapter 7.

[75] See Burchill (2001b: 88–9, 92–5).

Waltz did not, however, explicitly call for quantitative or regularity analysis of world politics, nor did his structural explanation of the causes of war derive its causal arguments from a clear-cut statistical analysis of past conflicts. Can Waltz be characterised as a Humean?

Adherence to certain key assumptions of Humeanism can, indeed, be identified in Waltz's work, although they are less explicit than in some of the more openly empiricist or positivist frameworks. First, although Waltz was never as explicit about it as the behaviourists or the quantitative theorists, the aim of Waltz's theory was to explain observed regularities. Although Waltz makes it clear that correlation is not causation, and that regularity in itself is not *sufficient* to establish causation, he implies that regularities are *necessary* for any causal account. Indeed, it is because of this assumption that he assumes that the cause of the recurrence of war must be equally as stable as the recurrence of war.[76]

Second, throughout his reflections on the philosophical underpinnings of IR theorising, Waltz displays a very Humean scepticism of the ability of theories to reflect on anything 'real' beyond the observable. For him, observability is central to science: science is about building theories that explain how patterns of observables link together as they do.[77] However, there is no need to assume the existence of any deeper 'reality' beyond observational patterns. Theories do not necessarily reflect, or need to assume, the existence of an underlying reality: theory idealises, abstracts and isolates a realm of empirical phenomena for instrumental purposes.[78] As a consequence, the structure of the international system is not 'real', but a theoretical construction that can parsimoniously account for the important observable regularities in international politics (recurrence of war). Similarly, according to Humean logic, Waltz argues that causation is only an 'assumed'

[76] Waltz (1979: 66).

[77] Importantly, theory for Waltz (1979: 1–17) is not equal to regularities (laws) but refers, rather, to conceptual models that try, as parsimoniously as possible, to account for regularities. Regularities, then, do not in themselves explain. This opens a door towards a philosophically realist conception of theory (abstraction) but is not explored by Waltz in any detail.

[78] Waltz (1979: 6–8). The link between positivism and instrumentalism becomes clear here. Waltz is an instrumentalist in the sense that for Waltz, as for many positivists, there is no truth in theorising; theories are judged on the basis of their usefulness in explaining events (that is, explaining conjunctions of regular patterns).

connection between patterns of facts, not a description of objective reality or an ontological causal connection.[79]

Third, an assumption of regularity-determinism can be seen to underlie his theory. While trying to avoid seeing the international system as logically 'necessitating' effects in the 'when A, then B' manner, Waltz finds it hard to resist deducing logical effects from the system. Arguably, this is because the microeconomic model his theory is based on works on the basis of a 'closed system' view of the social world. Given the structure of the system (anarchy) and the assumption of rational actors certain behaviour or patterns of events are logically deducible. This assumption is inherently linked to the Humean regularity model, as we have seen: it is only through accepting certain logically determinist assumptions that one can attempt to achieve 'closure', that is, one can come close to achieving the invariance required by the regularity-premised causal model. The regularity-deterministic assumption also necessitates isolation of systems (or structures), as well as the acceptance of an atomistic conception of agents. These features can also be seen to characterise Waltz's account.

Importantly, Humean assumptions create tendencies in Waltz's theorising that he, on occasion, seemed to want to avoid. It should be remembered that Waltz has always argued that anarchy is only an indirect, underlying 'permissive' cause of war. In 1986, Waltz further clarified his position by arguing that the structure of the international system only 'shapes and shoves' not only because 'unit-level and structural causes interact, but also because the shaping and shoving of structures may be successfully resisted'.[80] Crucially, however, Waltz's statements about anarchy as 'permissive cause' do not fit easily with the regularity-deterministic logic that his arguments presuppose as a result of accepting the microeconomic foundation and the regularity-deterministic logic attached to it. It could be argued that the acceptance of the key assumptions of the Humean regularity model is at least in part responsible for the tendencies his theory has towards a parsimonious and deterministic account of structural causes.

Other approaches, too, end up accepting Humean assumptions, often more as a result of the lack of clear alternatives than because of an explicit wish to follow these assumptions. Gilpin's *War and*

[79] Waltz (1979: 5, 43–6).
[80] Waltz (1986: 343). See also Waltz (1959: 134–5).

Change in World Politics starts initially from a non-Humean theoretical basis, Thucydides' so-called theory of hegemonic war. The assumption behind Thucydides' account was that he was, through careful study of 'symptoms', advancing an understanding of the disease of war between Athens and Sparta. Gilpin recognises that this kind approach arose from his Hippocratic conception of science, a conception of science very different from the 'modern study of international relations' that entails 'linking independent and dependent variables'.[81] Thucydides' account then entailed not Humean regularity analysis, but rather a structural understanding of the nature of social systems.[82] Gilpin likes Thucydides' explanation but, being embedded within a modern empiricist-positivist discourse of science, is directed to frown at its 'weaknesses' in the context of modern social science. Thucydides' explanation is, he argues, 'incomplete', for example, in that it cannot 'forecast when a hegemonic war will occur and what its consequences will be'.[83] Thucydides' 'theory [cannot] make predictions that can be tested and thereby meet rigorous scientific standards of falsifiablity'.[84] His explanation *only* helps us understand why certain wars (hegemonic types) take place.

Following the assumption of empiricist-positivist science that valid knowledge needs to be systematically empirically grounded, Gilpin considers it valuable to render Thucydides' theory testable and predictive: to study change 'we isolate and analyse the more obvious regularities and patterns associated with change'.[85] A theory, for Gilpin, must tell us something about the generalisable patterns of events we can observe, even if it cannot provide us with 'laws of change'.[86] He also wants to apply rational choice assumptions to make the 'logic' of the argument persuasive.[87] Gilpin, however, seems to acknowledge that imposing these standards on Thucydides and the study of history is somewhat arbitrary. For example, Gilpin comes across the realisation that Thucydides' theory does not easily lend itself to generalisation and prediction.[88] Despite his questions about the validity of the regularity approach, Gilpin cannot see beyond this 'modern scientific' model and method of explanation.

Schweller's more recent realist work is also Humean in the same vein. This work was initially spurred on by Schweller's unhappiness with

[81] Gilpin (1989: 18–20). [82] For discussion see, for example, McNeil (1996).
[83] Gilpin (1989: 29). [84] Gilpin (1989: 29). [85] Gilpin (1981: 3).
[86] Gilpin (1981: 3). [87] Gilpin (1981: xi). [88] Gilpin (1981: 2–3).

some of the cruder mono-causal 'variable-based' explanations of the structural conditioning of war. Schweller sought to draw on more traditional historical analysis in devising an amendment to Waltz's structural theory. He acknowledges that the causes of war are not merely structural (imbalance of power → German revisionism), or agential (say, reducible to Hitler) and, moreover, that the balance of these different types of causes can vary from one situation to another.[89] Judging the hierarchy and balance of these causes, he acknowledges, is a difficult task and a 'deterministic' (when A, then B) explanation on either structure or unit level results in a skewed understanding of war. Schweller argues that there needs to be a much closer extrapolation of the different types of structural qualities (he introduces tri-polarity) and agents (their size and positioning within the system affects their interests), and there needs to be more recognition of the uniqueness of complex historical events as all wars do not 'fall neatly into a class of events that can be studied in a systematic comparative fashion through the application of general laws in a straightforward way'.[90]

One might be tempted to think that Schweller is trying to avoid the Humean framework of thinking about causes of war. However, Schweller, in fact, turns to King, Keohane and Verba to frame his approach. Relying on *Designing Social Inquiry*, Schweller argues that the scientific approach is possible even in explaining singular case studies: 'the key is to generate as many observable implications of the theory as possible'.[91] Interestingly, the goal, in the end, is not just historical understanding but also 'to devise a systems theory that yields determinate balance-of-power predictions'.[92] The approach to explanation turns in a distinctly empiricist direction as criteria for empirical validation drawn from King, Keohane and Verba are put forward. Schweller follows the empiricists in emphasising that the formulation of observationally testable hypotheses and predictions is a key aspect in theory evaluation: 'the more predictions a theory generates, the more tests we can construct to evaluate it',[93] which in turn gives us better understanding of the reliability of a theory. Also, on recognisably empiricist lines, the study also seeks to make use of the quantitative databanks to look 'for associations between variables' that are

[89] Schweller (1998: 4–7).
[90] Quoting King, Keohane and Verba (1994). Schweller (1998: 11).
[91] Schweller (1998: 11). [92] Schweller (1998: 10). [93] Schweller (1998: 11).

'generalizable'.[94] Although Schweller claims to take into account perceptions and judgements, the emphasis is on analysis of largely observational and measurable data concerning power balances (for example, different attributes of states, power ratios derived from Correlates of War data). Although he criticises the more extreme forms of Humeanism, Schweller buys into Humean assumptions about the importance of regularities of observables, closed systems and regularity-determinism. While aiming to get away from parsimonious, regularity-obsessed and (regularity-)deterministic theories,[95] Schweller curiously, and unnecessarily, still calls on the Humean criteria drawn from King, Keohane and Verba to justify causal statements.[96]

The liberal end of IR theorising can also be seen to be informed by Humean assumptions. In contemporary IR the central liberal approach has been the so-called neoliberal institutionalism. In the 1970s Keohane and Nye made contributions to rethinking actors in the international system,[97] but in the 1980s they moved closer to structural- or neorealist assumptions by accepting the centrality of the state as 'agents' and anarchy as the 'structural' condition of world politics – in order to demonstrate, through their own framework, that the neorealist conclusions about the nature of international politics are not necessarily self-evident.[98] In so doing, however, the neoliberals came to accept some of the key assumptions of Humeanism.

Although the key figures in neoliberalism have rarely advocated the solely quantitative form of analysis of world politics, their frameworks are premised on and geared around the Humean assumptions. First, throughout the 1980s the neoliberals started emphasising their 'scientific' credentials. Emphasis was put on accepting the positivist view of science with its focus on empirical testing: the key was to show that neoliberal accounts provided better results in empirical testing and in predicting patterns of events.[99] Also, the game theoretical assumptions characteristic of the atomistic neorealist models were accepted, even though the neoliberals used rational choice models to show that certain rational strategies, such as iteration, building 'shadow of the future' and monitoring, can be used to explain co-operative patterns of behaviour.[100] From the rational choice premises it followed that,

[94] Schweller (1998: 13). [95] Schweller (1998: 4, 7, 11).
[96] Schweller (1998: 11). [97] Keohane and Nye (1977).
[98] Keohane (1984, 1989). [99] Baldwin (1993a).
[100] Axelrod and Keohane (1985).

for neoliberals, behaviour can be logically deduced from the rational choice matrices, as a question of logic, and verified in terms of the regular and predictive patterns that could be observed. Indeed, it is important to note that in the neoliberal co-operation literature, causal explanations are, in the end, justified either on the basis of the statistical correlations they can point to or in reference to the accuracy of the predictions they provide.

Indeed, the whole mainstream theoretical debate between the neorealist and neoliberal stances has been distinctly Humean. Both sides have accepted that science is characterised by the study of regularities of observables, and their associations, and that through such study we can gain more or less 'objective' knowledge of the nature of the world. Also, despite their differences, both neorealists and neoliberals agree that their accounts can be evaluated against each other, and that the criteria can be based broadly upon empiricist (or positivist) criteria: both sides accept that the more comprehensively one accounts for regularities of observable instances of state behaviour, the more plausible and powerful one's account. As Baldwin states it, 'social scientists try to develop generalisations about social phenomena' and hence the goal of the theoretical approaches is to provide better generalisations, as well as predictions, than the other approach.[101]

The acceptance of the same view of science and the same methodological, epistemological and ontological assumptions has helped the neo-neo theorists to evaluate the contributions of their respective approaches. However, arguably, it has also narrowed down the IR debates. As some critics have pointed out, the differences that remain between the theoretical approaches are very slight, and in fact, insignificant, since most neo-neo theorists now accept that the theories are both right and simply explain different contexts.[102] As Alexander Wendt puts it: 'the debate seems to come down to no more than a discussion about the frequency with which states pursue relative rather than absolute gains'.[103]

The rationalist conception of what it means to do valid social science has arguably put some fairly rigid limits on what is considered systematic social scientific causal research in IR. We will now turn to drawing out some initial observations about the kinds of consequences

[101] Baldwin (1993a: 14–15). [102] Powell (1991). [103] Wendt (1999a: 3).

that the acceptance of Humean assumptions has had on the rationalist form of IR theorising.

Consequences of Humeanism

The kinds of meta-theoretical assumptions we work with have repercussions for how we study the world around us, how we conceive of objects, how we use evidence and how we judge others' accounts.[104] Although the influences of meta-theoretical discourses have often gone unnoticed in IR by those who prioritise empirical study and consider meta-theoretical discussion with suspicion, paying attention to the underlying meta-theoretical discourses is crucial. This is because it allows us to better understand certain unacknowledged assumptions underlying empirical IR research. Arguably, many kinds of theoretical and epistemological trends are at work in the rationalist approaches, such as the tendency to reify objects of study that postpositivists have pointed to. However, amongst these trends, the Humean discourse also plays a particular role in rationalist accounts. The acceptance of Humeanism seems to give rise to particular kinds of approaches to the study of causes in world politics, ones that have certain characteristic limitations that we will now draw out.

The strength of Humeanism could be seen to be that it entails a systematic empirical study of observable aspects of social life (in the form of variables) and openness about data and methods of analysis. The Humean approaches are very specific in the formulation of hypotheses and variables under study. Also, they have traditionally been particularly precise in reporting data and the steps taken in analysis: they tend to justify their variables and report in detailed ways the manner in which the independent variables relate to dependent, control or intervening variables. Also, it should not be forgotten that the Humean tradition has been responsible for amassing a great amount of data pertaining to patterns in world politics: the Correlates of War and other projects have provided an important source of general observational data on world political patterns.

However, Humean approaches also have characteristic limitations. These characteristics fall into three main categories: Humeanism (1)

[104] For a more detailed account of the role of meta-theory in IR, see Kurki and Wight (2007).

creates tendencies towards additive and isolationist causal research; (2) it directs theorists to associate causes with regularities and regularity-determinist assumptions – even when theorists want to avoid such tendencies; and (3) it renders their ontological assumptions 'observation-dependent', making it difficult for them to develop ontological frameworks that answer *why* regularities identified take place. The Humeans' fixation on observability makes it difficult for them to deal with certain kinds of questions, notably analysis of social construction. Let's explore these limitations in detail.

First, what is meant by the claim that Humeanism gives rise to 'additive' and parsimony-driven approaches to assessing causal factors in world politics? The notion of 'additive' theorising refers to the tendency, or necessity, of theorists to treat causal factors as 'independent' variables that act 'side by side' rather than evaluate the complex interactions of various causal forces.[105] This tendency is dictated by the Humean model of causal analysis that directs theorists to 'isolate' observable regularities in order to examine their 'causal effect'. When examining the impact of the democratic institutions on state behaviour, for example, a rationalist theorist must isolate the (statistical) 'mean causal effect' of this factor (or indexed variable) from those of other factors such as alliances, economic interdependence, cultural contacts (all treated as measurable variables). Once impacts are thus isolated their significance can be compared against each other, making possible the judgements over causal weighting. However, it is difficult for Humean approaches to recognise or deal with the fact that factors which 'variables' are trying observationally to measure can be (ontologically) deeply intertwined, co-constituted and inseparable from other causal conditions.

It follows that Humeanism seems to give rise to theoretically reductionist tendencies: there is a tendency to prioritise certain causal factors 'over' others, often on the basis of their higher associative 'mean effects' for variables. In the democratic peace debates, for example, (level of) institutionalisation of democracy can be considered a more 'causal' variable than say (level of) wealth, if and when this variable has a higher statistical 'mean causal effect'. This causal ranking, however, tells us nothing about the ways in which wealth and democracy might be complexly interrelated, co-causal or mutually conditioning. The rationalist

[105] Dessler (1991).

accounts also must limit the range of variables that 'matter' because recognising complexity drives down the 'mean causal effects' of other variables. Causal complexity poses problems for Humeans. In the study of democratic peace, for example, although models and tests that allow us to capture a variety of 'variables' have been called for, since empiricist Humeanism as a philosophical discourse directs researchers to concentrate on particular narrow causal problems (associations of specific variables), all theorists can do in the end is to recognise the difficulty of finding any adequately holistic statistical models that would account for the complexity of relations between variables.[106] The possibility that there might be other, non-statistical, non-Humean ways of dealing with causal complexity is not recognised. While statistical models have developed significantly in analysis of multiple variables, perhaps exploring non-statistical answers to causal complexity opens more productive horizons.

It should be noted that the generalising and 'additive', rather than 'integrative',[107] tendencies in rationalist causal explanations are reflective *not* of rationalist theorists' disinterestedness in wider causal forces – often they acknowledge the importance of wider study of variables – but rather of particular tendencies inherent within the Humean approach to causal explanation, dependent on independent observation of the role of variables. Crucially, as will be seen in later chapters, accepting these additive assumptions is unnecessary when causal analysis is conceived of beyond the Humean discourse.

It should also be noted that besides the tendencies towards additive research amongst the rationalists, many rationalists have also tended to assume the epistemological objectivity and primacy of empirical knowledge derived from observation. Rationalist theorists, the democratic peace theorists, for example, have often, on the basis of the regularity evidence, proceeded to make objectivist and universalistic claims about the nature of democracies and their foreign policies.[108] Neo-neo contenders, too, have been accused of assuming the epistemological superiority of their rational choice based models over those interpretive approaches that have conducted research in a way that does not live up to the standards of empirical science as they define it.[109] It will be argued in later chapters that social scientific causal analysis, to be

[106] Huth and Allee (2002b: 51). [107] Dessler (1991).
[108] See, for example, Rummel (1995). [109] Baldwin (1993a: 9).

persuasive, need not conform to the prescriptions of the rationalist frameworks and that analysis of social causes can in many instances be analysed more productively through 'interpretive' means.

Second, Humeanism seems to lead theorists to associate causation with regularity criteria and regularity-determinism – and, crucially, even when they would have liked to avoid these assumptions in their theorising or more common-sensical causal statements. As we have seen Waltz's theorising was to an important extent influenced by the Humean meta-theoretical assumptions that he accepts about the nature of causation, even though his other theoretical claims are less deterministic, less Humean. Gilpin's and Schweller's frameworks, too, exemplify a similar tension: tension between the requirements of Humeanism and the more moderate and complexity-sensitive explanatory interests. There is a discrepancy in rationalist theorising, then, between some of the more 'common-sensical' (non-Humean) causal interest/claims and the more strictly defined 'scientifically justified' (Humean) causal claims. Even democratic peace theorists, on occasion, resort to 'loose' causal language – for example, in describing the kinds of processes that produce dispositions towards peaceful behaviour – yet, they are quickly drawn back to the Humean fold that maintains that all causal language must be verifiable and justifiable in accordance with the Humean assumptions.[110] Because of their inability to think outside the Humean box about the nature of causes or causal discourse, this tension within rationalist theory has remained unrecognised and unconceptualised.

Moreover, Humeanism leads to certain consequences in the framing of social ontology. These manifest themselves in many ways. First, as we have already noted, the focus of Humean study is on analysis of relations of variables in data, less on development of conceptual models of social processes that account for patterns in data. Though rationalist theorists develop 'explanatory models', which they then test against observable patterns, these models are of a particular kind: they tend to postulate relationships between specific variables but rarely entail development of in-depth ontological frameworks within which explanations of why observable variables are associated are developed.

Also, it should be noted that the Humean positivist models are often considered problematic by more interpretive or social constructivist theorists in terms of their ability to develop adequate

[110] See, for example, Maoz and Russett (1993).

conceptualisations of actors and their social context. Waltz's structural ontology, for example, assumes that the behaviour of atomistic actors can be logically deduced from the (postulated 'as if') structure of the anarchic system. Equally, the neoliberals have also bought into such assumptions: the co-operation-engendering strategies, crucially, are arrived at, and are premised on, the rational choice assumptions about the nature of individual actors (self-interested and rational). Importantly, the neorealists and the neoliberals attribute intentions to individual actors that are not necessarily the ones they possess or act according to: according unified interests and rationality to actors, and especially complex structural actors such as states, is, arguably, problematic.[111] Also, the assumption that actors are atomistic pre-social rational agents, although the key tenet of liberalism, is highly controversial and, importantly, leads to ignoring wider social determinants of social actions.

Importantly, neorealist and neoliberal approaches, because of their acceptance of the rational choice assumptions, leave unexplored questions concerning *how* the international system or institutions engender either war or co-operation: specifically, questions of 'social construction' or socialisation are not dealt with. Interestingly, Waltz accepts that processes of socialisation are important in maintaining the logic of the international system:[112] however, these processes are not studied, rather war-proneness is assumed as a question of logic. Keohane, too, acknowledges the role of socialisation or social learning in the way institutions work – as the very notion of 'shadow of future' presupposes some sort of social learning. However, he makes little attempt to theorise how this social learning works, that is, to explore the processes through which actors within institutions come to accept the common ideas, goals and strategies.[113]

[111] Indeed, the IR rationalist approaches clearly suffer from the most intractable problem of rational choice modelling: that is, the grounding of models in real motivations, beliefs and rationality of agents. If the agents do not actually hold the rational beliefs accorded to them, the formal models cannot, arguably, say much about why they do what they do. This can be seen to remain a problem even in the attempts at historically contextualised rational choice modelling, such as the Analytical Narratives models. See Bates et al. (1998). See also Elster's (2000) critique.

[112] Waltz (1979: 74–7).

[113] Goldstein and Keohane (1993a: 7) study the 'effects' of particular ideas not the 'sources of these ideas'.

It could be argued that the questions of socialisation are not dealt with by these theorists because they open up major cans of worms concerning, not just the nature of actors, but also the nature of ideas, social context and the actual processes through which observable patterns in world politics are engendered and conditioned. Exploring these issues might entail that the parsimonious explanatory systems and their regularity-deterministic statements as to the 'when A, then B' effect, would become problematic, and certainly would present difficult challenges to the criteria of observability. Hence, the neorealists and the neoliberals choose to avoid these questions through, in effect, defining them away. Instead, the issues of social construction, socialisation and the deep social role of (intersubjective) ideas and beliefs has been left for the constructivists to deal with (see next chapter).[114]

Conclusion

The rationalist approaches have been dominant in IR for decades. These approaches have assumed that the empiricist and positivist methods modelled on the natural sciences can be also utilised in IR. Methodological guidebooks, such as Nicholson's and especially King, Keohane and Verba's accounts, have solidified the grip of Humeanism as the 'norm' for causal analysis in IR. Indeed, most mainstream studies in IR have followed these epistemological and methodological precepts – either explicitly or more implicitly.

The rationalists have often been confident about the high quality of their scholarship, which requires not only ability for careful observation but also the grasp of a variety of sophisticated mathematical methods (from associative methods to game theoretical algebra).[115] While this confidence is not wholly misplaced – the rationalist and positivist accounts have provided IR with systematic, rigorous and data-rich accounts of world politics – it has arguably engendered dissatisfaction amongst those who point to limitations in the rationalist frameworks. The rationalists have often assumed that their approaches are systematic and reliable, whereas approaches that do not conform to their criteria are non-scientific, vague and scientifically untrustworthy.[116] While

[114] See, for example, Keohane and Martin (1995); Wendt (1995).

[115] Baldwin, for example, likes to emphasise that the quality of scholarship, in the case of the neo-neo debates, 'is extraordinarily high'. Baldwin (1993a: 9).

[116] Keohane (1988: 392).

the rationalist approaches have undoubtedly made certain important contributions in IR, it is not obvious that the rationalist frameworks are unproblematic. It is argued in chapter 6 that the rationalists have not adequately recognised the limitations inherent in their chosen view of science and causation. As with any philosophy of causation, Humeanism constrains and enables the way in which we do causal analysis. While it has enabled study of large-scale general patterns and careful measurement of observable facets of world politics in terms of specific causal variables, it has also tended to advocate additive research, which tends to shy away from the study of deeper and holistic connections in favour of maintaining theoretical parsimony. Humeans also tend to become confused by implicit more common-sensical (non-Humean) causal statements in their own work as well as in that of others. Also, these theorists have difficulties in dealing with theorisation of actors in a social context, or the complex role of ideas and processes of social construction in world political arenas.

As will be seen in later chapters, these characteristics of rationalist causal theorising are a part of the Humean problem-field, involving restrictive methodological, epistemological and ontological assumptions. While Humeans perceive their approach as the most scientific and systematic, it will be argued in later chapters that this approach to causal analysis should not be accepted as a self-evident or as an unproblematic discourse of causation. The goal of Part II is to give an account of causation that allows us to rethink the methodological, epistemological and ontological assumptions concerning causal analysis, thus lifting off the Humean 'straitjacket' conception of causal analysis from IR theorising. Before moving on to rethink the concept of cause, however, we must also analyse the reflectivist approaches in IR. It will be seen that, although these approaches have criticised the rationalists, they, too, have accepted certain fundamentally Humean assumptions concerning causation.

4 *Reflectivist and constructivist approaches in International Relations: more cases of Humeanism*

Since the 1980s many new theoretical approaches have come to play an increasingly important role in IR. These approaches, encompassing poststructuralism, critical theory, feminism and constructivism, are commonly referred to as 'postpositivist' or 'reflectivist'[1] because of their reluctance to endorse the mainstream rationalist conception of how to study world politics. They have sought to challenge the narrow focus of the mainstream IR debates by opening up new avenues for investigation, notably the study of the role of ideas, norms, rules and discourses, as well as the examination of processes of social construction and socialisation. The goal of this chapter is to examine the treatment of the concept of cause among the 'postpositivist' and 'reflectivist' theorists. The approaches examined here are often called 'constitutive' theoretical approaches in IR: this is because these approaches tend to reject, or at least delimit, the idea of 'causal theorising' in IR scholarship in favour of investigating how world politics is 'constituted' through ideas, rules, norms or discourses. It will be seen that even though these positions are sceptical of causal theorising and terminology, nevertheless they tend to reinforce the influence of the Humean discourse of causation in IR. This is because when they reject causal analysis, they reject it on the basis of having accepted, often inadvertently, core Humean

[1] These terms will be used here because they are widely used in IR, although they are in many senses problematic. For a more detailed examination of the terms see Kurki and Wight (2007). It should be noted that the term 'postpositivism' is confusing in a wider philosophy of science context: Popper and Lakatos, for example, described themselves, and are widely referred to, as 'postpositivists'. The term 'reflectivism' was coined by Keohane (1988) and is also far from unproblematic because the term might be taken to imply that reflectivists do not engage in empirical analyses or that their analyses are somehow 'irrational'. Hence, not all theorists charaterised here as reflectivists would necessarily accept such a categorisation. It should also be noted that this chapter will examine some constructivist theorists that do not traditionally fall within the 'reflectivist' category because of the association of reflectivism with the more 'radical' end of postpositivist theorising.

assumptions regarding the nature of causation. The inability of more radical reflectivists, as well as of most constructivists, to conceptualise causation beyond the assumptions of Humeanism has some important consequences. It leads to a paradoxical legitimisation of the Humean empiricist conception of causation in IR, as well as certain theoretically reductionist tendencies. Also, it leads to blindness towards non-Humean causal assumptions: the reflectivists and constructivists make a number of claims that seem common-sensically causal, yet cannot be understood as causal because of the dominance of the Humean conception of what it means to talk about causes.

The analysis here will proceed through a number of steps. We will first examine the basic arguments of postpositivist theorising in IR. Then, we will examine how reflectivists and constructivists come to adopt scepticism with regard to causal terminology as a result of their anti-positivistic assumptions. Finally, we will explore some of the main consequences and inconsistencies of the contemporary causality sceptics in IR.

Postpositivism in IR theory

In the mid-1980s many IR theorists came to question the guiding assumptions of the mainstream IR approaches. The neo-neo debates seemed to assume that facts just sit 'out in the world' and wait to be discovered; that facts can only be interpreted in one way; and that the de-linking of politics and morality from social scientific 'facts' and 'theories' is straightforward.[2] The central point of attack for the so-called critical and postpositivist theorists became 'the positivist mainstream' of IR: it was argued that by advocating a positivist conception of social science as the 'gold standard',[3] the mainstream was ignoring and marginalising other approaches that had important things to say about world politics, theoretically and empirically.

One of the first explicitly to attack the positivist mainstream was Robert Cox. Cox characterised mainstream IR theorising as 'problem-solving theorising': theorising that has a role in solving specific puzzles but is limited in its scope because, taking its objects of study (states, the international system) as given and stable objects, it is unable to avoid

[2] Fred Halliday quoted in Burchill (2001a: 13). See also Neufield (1993).
[3] S. Smith (1996: 13).

reifying and reproducing those structures it takes for granted. For Cox, contra the positivists,[4] theory is something that projects a particular conceptualisation of how the world hangs together and, crucially, in so doing is never neutral but inherently social and political: 'theory is always for someone and for some purpose'.[5] The implication of Cox's argument was that IR theorising, instead of assuming the unproblematic existence of objects or patterns, must remain open to the way in which social objects are reified, or naturalised, through our theories. Cox highlighted that the theoretical assumptions that underpin IR theorising must be recognised explicitly. He argued that the epistemological and ontological assumptions accepted in mainstream theorising are inherently political and, hence, implicated in the kind of 'findings' that the theories put forward. Mainstream IR, he boldly argued, is implicated in the ideological reproduction of the capitalist system and the states system.[6]

IR theorists who termed themselves constructivists also started pointing to the theoretical and empirical problems of mainstream IR. Many came to argue that the central 'variables' of rationalist IR were underpinned by much deeper, and for the positivists, unnoticeable factors and processes, notably ideational factors and socialisation processes.[7] The constructivists started emphasising the importance of ideas, rules and norms, as well as of 'shared understandings' and 'practices' that they inform, in shaping world politics, thus initiating a distinct 'cultural turn' in IR.[8] They rejected the rationalist separation of interests and ideas and the 'logical deducing' of interests from game theoretical

[4] As we have seen in the previous chapter empiricist rationalist approaches see theories as conglomerations of statements that are derived from and corroborated through observational regularities, or alternatively, as 'as if' models that can parsimoniously account for regularities. Waltz (1979: 1–17). See also Nicholson (1996a).

[5] Cox (1981). [6] Cox (1992: 173).

[7] Some of the earlier explicitly constructivist theorists were Onuf (1989) and Wendt (1987, 1992). Also, the works of Ruggie (1998) and Kratochwil (1989) became associated with constructivism early on. Other influential scholars associated with constructivism include, for example, Katzenstein (1996), Finnemore (1996), Hopf (1998), Risse-Kappen (1995a, 1995b) and Checkel (1997).

[8] Lapid and Kratochwil (1996). However, it is not clear how distinctly new this turn was: as Tim Dunne (1995) has shown, social construction had already been addressed by theorists within the English School.

matrices, arguing, instead, that the interests and identities of actors are deeply shaped by the ideational contexts of action.[9]

Importantly, the way in which ideas, norms, rules and discourses were studied by the constructivists challenged the rationalist framing of social science. Indeed, most constructivists challenged the rationalist study of ideas through the Humean 'variable' approach that emphasised regularity and observation of the behaviour of individuals.[10] Also, the constructivists challenged the framing of ideas and beliefs as 'individual mental states': ideas, for them, referred to a social 'intersubjective' category.[11] Constructivists have also tried to avoid giving limited and *a priori* roles for ideas in the rationalist vein – for example, as solvers of multiple equilibria situations – but have sought to examine the deeper and more plural roles that norms and rules play in international politics.[12] The theoretical challenge to the mainstream was also complemented on an empirical basis: a number of constructivist empirical studies emphasised that taking into account the 'social construction of international politics' allows us to explain processes and events better in world politics.[13]

The poststructuralists took the constructivists' arguments even further by arguing that many of the central analytical concepts of IR are far from unproblematic. Richard Ashley, drawing on the deconstruction methods of Derrida, pointed to the way in which the conceptual bases of IR discourse are underpinned by a discursive dualism based on the distinctly modern discourse of 'sovereign man'.[14] The concept of sovereignty was seen as 'constitutive' of the discipline of IR, in a similar sense to the way in which the notion of 'sovereign reasoning man' has been the central assumption of Enlightenment philosophy. Ashley, Walker and others came to argue that through its discursive framework, IR reproduces the notion of sovereignty and certain crucial dichotomies attached to it (inside/outside, domestic/international). These conceptual dichotomisations, they argue, are what define 'IR'

9 Ruggie (1999: 227).
10 Exemplified by Goldstein and Keohane (1993b). For criticisms see, for example, Kratochwil (1989: 100).
11 Kratochwil (1989: 101). This has also been emphasised well by Laffey and Weldes (1997).
12 Ruggie (1999: 227–8).
13 See, for example, Koslowski and Kratochwil (1995); Risse-Kappen (1995a, 1995b); Klotz (1995); Checkel (2001).
14 Ashley (1989).

as a distinct discipline and its 'legitimate' objects of study (the international system, states).[15] This critique gave the impetus to initial attempts to think through the way in which IR and its 'objects of study' are framed: many postpositivists have come to question the assumption that 'objects', such as the international system or the state, can be assumed to be pre-given and unproblematic. Instead, they highlight the role of a variety of discourses, representations and stories that give rise to social 'objects'.

The feminist IR theorists expanded the critique of positivism in a new direction.[16] The feminists came to challenge the positivist portrayal of IR as 'gender neutral'. They have argued that there are many important questions that need to be asked about how international politics works, but that these questions have not been asked owing to the dominance of the traditional IR definition of 'what matters' in IR. Through emphasising the importance of the 'personal' in construction of the 'international', the feminist approaches have emphasised the deep embeddedness of patriarchal representations and social relations in the international system, and in the academic discipline of IR.[17]

It should not be forgotten that there is much infighting between these approaches: the postpositivist theoretical perspectives vary hugely in terms of their focus and their political, theoretical and epistemological assumptions. For example, there are deep divisions within these approaches about the role of theory and its relationship to 'reality'. Critical theorists of a Gramscian and Frankfurt School mode, alongside most 'moderate' constructivists[18] and feminists, challenge the positivist methods and assumptions, but still argue that we can assume the existence of a social reality, analyse evidence (although of a broader non-quantitative variety) and construct theoretical explanations of how the world 'hangs together'.[19] However, the more 'radical constructivists' and poststructuralists are sceptical

[15] Walker (1993); Biersteker and Weber (1996).
[16] Enloe (1990); Tickner (1992); Sylvester (1994); Steans (1998); Zalewski and Parpart (1998).
[17] See, for example, Weber (1994).
[18] The distinction between 'moderate' and 'radical' constructivists has been widely accepted in recent years. See, for example, Hoph (1998); Checkel (2004).
[19] This is Ruggie's term (1999). See also Cox (1987) and Enloe (1990), for example.

about claims pertaining to the 'objective' nature of a social 'reality'. They choose to avoid talking about 'truths' or 'realities', emphasising, instead, the political implications that all, including the constructivist, claims to 'truths' about 'social reality' entail.[20] 'Reality', for them, is fundamentally constituted by interpretations, or perspectives: there is no 'one reality' or 'one truth' about world politics, but an innumerable plurality of perspectives. Crucially, different perspectives cannot be given hierarchical status over each other without taking political and power-infused decisions.[21] Emphasising that judgements between theories involve politics, and responsibility, is the primary goal of post-structuralist approaches.

For our purposes the specific disagreements between the perspectives mentioned above are not of crucial importance. Rather, what is most striking is that most, if not all, reflectivists and constructivists, irrespective of their specific theoretical orientation, criticise the positivist descriptions of international politics.

First, the postpositivist approaches largely reject the idea that regular patterns, laws or generalisations can serve, at least on their own, as a basis for studying the social world. The reflectivists and constructivists, then, critique the rationalist analyses of international politics that are seen simply to trace the correlative relations between independent and dependent variables, without adequate recognition of the complexity of meanings and intentionality in the social world. The postpositivists emphasise that the social world is not easily 'quantifiable' as human actions and patterns of behaviour are not always clearly generalisable. Analysing the social world through the search for 'laws' hides the complexity and historical nuances of social life. Parsimony, they argue, is not simply a virtue; social life is complex and theories should recognise this. The postpositivists also challenge the reduction of knowledge of the social world to observable patterns of behaviour. The emphasis on empirical knowledge, as defined by the positivists, reduces social

20 It is important to note that the poststructuralist stand, despite some assertions to the contrary, does not necessarily entail the rejection of an independent reality but rather the emphasis on the political consequences of representations of reality, which makes it justifiable, for theoretical purposes, to bracket the notion of 'reality'. For a good account of the poststructuralist take on reality see Zehfuss (2002: 256).

21 Campbell (1998a: 34; 1998c).

life to observable variables, such as patterns of behaviour, and hence leads to theoretical approaches that ignore the deeper, and much more interesting, questions about how and why these behavioural patterns come about. This critique also involves questioning the ontological primacy of individuals or individual-like actors (states) that are accorded preconceived interests and are seen to make choices according to preconceived interests: it is emphasised that individuals, or states, must always be acknowledged as positioned in social contexts, social contexts that 'constitute' them as actors.

The postpositivists also reject the 'determinism' implied by many positivist approaches: that is, the way in which the rationalists logically deduce conclusions and predictions from a 'closed systems' view of international politics (for example, the anarchical nature of the international system). The postpositivists tend to emphasise the contingencies and the openness of social life. Some, further, challenge the 'gate-keeping' tendency in rationalist IR, that is, the marginalisation of critical and 'ideational' explanations in the mainstream because of the prioritisation of the positivist empiricist view of what constitutes valid knowledge.[22] It is argued that the positivist conception of science is not the only way of delineating what is an interesting or a non-interesting, a justifiable or a non-justifiable, account of the social world.

This anti-positivist – and seemingly anti-Humean – stance is interesting in that it provides a number of ways of challenging the mainstream approaches. These criticisms, as will be seen in later chapters, can be accepted as by and large persuasive. However, the reflectivist and constructivist critiques are not unproblematic, notably when it comes to the treatment of the notion of cause.

Reflectivist aversion to causal language

It is crucial to note that the postpositivist challenge in IR has had some crucial consequences for the treatment of the concept of cause in the discipline. One of its key consequences has been that it has given rise to a powerful tendency, not just to critique positivist approaches, but also to avoid, or delimit, causal descriptions in favour of 'non-causal' or 'constitutive' terminology.[23]

[22] See especially Campbell (1998b: 207–27).

[23] This differs from early anti-positivist theorising of idealists, classical realists and the English School as these all accepted and utilised the notion of cause as

Gramscian critical theorists demonstrate well this wariness of causal theorising: Robert Cox, for example, has almost entirely dropped references to causes or causal analysis. This is because causes are associated with positivist theorising and its objectivist assumptions. Cox argues that the concept of cause is applicable strictly to the positivist framework. Causal explanation, he contends, is not applicable to his 'historicist' framework, because the historicist approach does not accept the assumption of regularity or the other assumptions of positivism. Causal explanation, which he equates with positivist Humeanism, cannot capture the complexity of the social world as the 'historical approach' can.[24] This association of causes and Humeanism, crucially, arises from the fact that the critical theorists actually accept the positivist form of causal analysis as characteristic of causation and causal analysis. The critical theorists critique Humean assumptions but, crucially, not the legitimacy of the Humean conceptualisation of causation.

A similar aversion to causal terminology can be seen to characterise the poststructuralist approaches: poststructuralists in IR have been decidedly anti-causal. Jenny Edkins, for example, argues that the poststructuralist challenge has some fundamental implications for knowledge claims about causes: because all objective readings of history can, on the basis of the poststructuralist insights, be seen as 'impregnated by the present', the notions of cause and effect have been made 'untenable'.[25] We cannot 'objectively' account for causes and effects: these judgements are already embedded in a discursive field and its power relations.

Edkins considers cause to be one of the notions that the discourse of modernity has objectified and moulded into a 'depoliticising' tool. She gives an example of how this 'technologisation' and de-politicisation through the notion of cause has had important consequences in IR:

we have seen in chapter 3. It should also be noted that some theorists do not fit this categorisation. So-called rationalist constructivists such as Finnemore and Sikkink, for example, do accept and use causal descriptions. However, it should be noted that they never clarify what they mean by their preferred term, the notion of 'causal mechanisms'. Finnemore and Sikkink (1999); Klotz (1995).

[24] Except, he notes in a footnote, in a 'trivial sense': a sense the meaning of which he does not clarify. Cox (1996: 51 fn).

[25] Edkins (1999: 15).

Processes of technologization and depoliticization can be seen in international politics itself, as well as in the discipline that studies it. One example of this is found in responses to famines, humanitarian crises, or complex political emergencies. Agencies and governments outside the crisis area do not take account of the political processes that are under way, of which the crisis is a symptom. Instead, they rely on interventions derived from abstract, technical analysis of the situation, one that looks for 'causes', not political reasons or motivations.[26]

Following a similar line of thought, David Campbell in *Writing Security* also declares causal descriptions misleading and dangerous. The purpose of his poststructuralist theorising, he argues, is not to give causal explanations: he is opposed to 'cataloging, calculating and specifying the "real causes"'.[27] Instead, Campbell maintains that his poststructuralist theory aims to inquire into the 'political consequences of adopting one mode of representation over another'.[28]

The role of representation, discourses and practices in poststructuralist theorising is often referred to through the notion of 'constitution': representations, discourses and practices, it is argued, 'constitute', rather than 'cause', identities, social meanings and practices.[29] There are a few reasons for this term being preferred. First, the notion 'constitutive' is used because it emphasises that discourses are ideational forces. Causes are often associated with 'materialist' accounts.[30] Second, avoiding causal terminology emphasises that the poststructuralists do not see the social world as characterised by 'pushing and pulling' or mechanistically necessitating forces. Since the emphasis of poststructuralism is on the fluidity of social life, identities and practices, and their 'contingent effects' on each other,[31] the notion of cause that is seen to imply fixity and determinism is sidelined in favour of the wider and more fluid notion of 'constitution'. The use of the notion of 'conditions of possibility' appeals to the same effect: poststructuralist accounts try to inquire into the way in which discourses define our relationship to the other and, thereby, provide 'the condition of possibility' for 'us' and our practices.[32] Also, poststructuralists wish to highlight that 'constitutive' theorising emphasises that the theories we hold of the world are

[26] Edkins (1999: 9–10). [27] Campbell (1998b: 4). [28] Campbell (1998b: 4).
[29] The emphasis is especially on how relations with 'the other' constitute the self and practices. See, for example, Edkins (1999: 15).
[30] Campbell (1998b: 4). [31] Ashley (1996: 253). [32] Campbell (1998a: ix).

'constitutive' of practice: academics, it is argued, are complicit in the constitution of realities they merely claim to describe.[33]

Again, it is important to note that the rejection of causal accounts seems to arise from the association of such accounts with the Humean assumptions, its 'laws' and 'determinism'. Indeed, poststructuralists have seen causal accounts as accounts that assume the existence of laws and as accounts informed by 'images of billiard balls colliding in a Newtonian universe'.[34] Because poststructuralists reject such images in accounting for the social world, they have also come to reject causes – although interestingly and significantly, in his recent work David Campbell has opened the door to the potential that conditions of possibility might in fact entail some kind of causal relations.[35]

It is not only the critical theorists and the poststructuralists who reject causal descriptions in IR: many feminists in the discipline, too, have been sceptical of causal terminology. Many feminists in IR argue that notions of masculinity and femininity do not 'cause' actions but are 'constitutive' of practice and other discourses. As a result, reviews of feminism in IR invariably conceive of feminism as part of the 'broad category of constitutive theory'.[36] Although an anti-causal stance is not characteristic of feminism in general,[37] it can be understood to be a consequence of the association of feminism with the interpretive strands of thought in social theory. Also, the fact that in the past many 'scientific' accounts of gender roles, such as the biological theories of social hierarchies, have been averse to feminist ideas, has made feminists wary of the causal claims of science.[38]

The notion of 'constitutive' theorising is also utilised by the constructivist theorists. The constructivists are, arguably, slightly less forceful in their rejection of causal descriptions than are the critical theorists, poststructuralists and feminists. Wendt, for example, explicitly advocates causal accounts in IR. I will discuss Wendt in more detail in the next chapter owing to the fact that he draws on a distinctly non-Humean philosophically realist account of causation. The focus here is on those constructivists who have held an 'oscillating' position on causation.

[33] See, for example, Ashley (1989); Campbell (1998a: 14).

[34] Walker (1993: 96).

[35] Campbell (2007: 224–5).

[36] True (2001: 247); S. Smith (1995: 27).

[37] MacKinnon (1989), for example, retains causal terminology although she is critical of positivist causal descriptions.

[38] Steans (1998: 13). See also Harding (1986).

As a consequence of their unwillingness to specify what they mean by cause, many constructivists have come to oscillate between causal and constitutive logics and inadvertently to reinforce acceptance of a Humean understanding of causation in IR.

Nicholas Onuf is one theorist whom we might characterise as someone who oscillates between causal and constitutive descriptions. The focus of Onuf's work is on how people construct social reality and how agents are 'constituted' by the social arrangements around them. Onuf rejects the positivist notion of explanation centred on material resources and predictable behaviour, and argues that we need to pay more attention to rules and social arrangements as the key ingredients of social life. Rules are crucial because they provide context for action, conditions of speech and basis for other sets of rules.[39] Importantly, when it comes to causation Onuf accepts that the notion of cause may not be entirely redundant in social science: he accepts that rule-following 'presupposes a category of causality'.[40] However, despite addressing the issue of causation and accepting the causal qualities of norms, he does not advance a clear understanding of what he comprehends by the notion of cause. Also, following the anti-causal post-positivists, he ends up resisting causal descriptions. Onuf wants to give a special meaning to intentionality, rules and the 'constitution' of social action, meaning that cannot be understood through the category of causality. Also, he seems to prefer the 'constitutive' terminology in his more substantive work: in talking about the role of rules in shaping social reality, he constantly avoids talking about causes, in favour of the 'constitutive' description of the role of rules. At the end of the day, causal language is avoided because Onuf seems to be drawn to associating causes with accounts that imply straightforward 'when A, then B' relations and, indeed, relations that imply some sort of regularity.[41] Humean assumptions still retain their presence in Onuf's thinking and direct him to adopt the 'constitutive' terminology over causal descriptions.

A similar tendency can be detected in the work of other constructivists such as Friedrich Kratochwil. Kratochwil rejects the rationalist

[39] Onuf (1998b: 61).
[40] Onuf (1989: 49). Onuf also interestingly discusses Bhaskar's critiques of Winch at length (1989: 49–52).
[41] Gould (1998: 81).

emphasis on laws and determinism.[42] Specifically, he rejects the rationalist assumption that rules can be treated through the Humean regularity approach.[43] Kratochwil explicitly attacked the mainstream approaches for being 'wedded to a particular and mostly inappropriate concept of causality'.[44] This 'inappropriate concept of causality', it seems, refers to the Humean approach built into the mainstream theories, that is, the regularity-based, observation-tied, closed system analysis of causation characteristic of the positivist frameworks. The Humean approach cannot, for Kratochwil, deal with rules, especially the way in which they condition speech, constitute other rules, as well as guide action. We make reference to rules when we say and do things, but these rules do not cause us to do what we do; rather they constitute the context of our practice.[45]

Despite the rejection of outright Humeanism, what the alternative 'appropriate' assumptions about causation entail remains unclear. Because causes are not theorised beyond the rejection of Humeanism, Kratochwil is unable to give a clear account of what causes mean and how they can be applied in constructivist theorising. Given the uncertainty about what causes mean, Kratochwil decides to avoid using causal descriptions: despite explicitly rejecting only a particular form of causal analysis – the Humean approach – causes disappear from his theorising. He avoids talking about rules as causal, preferring instead to talk of 'constitutive rules' that 'mould decisions' and 'constitute practice'.[46] This is because, in the end, Kratochwil has no 'positive' alternative to Humeanism in conceptualising causation. Although he knows what he rejects, he has no clear idea about what it is that he would accept about causation. Because of his unwillingness to theorise causation, Kratochwil inadvertently ends up reproducing Humeanism as the only viable account of causation.[47] The same could be said to be the case with Karin Fierke, who is also sceptical of the idea of cause in favour of a more constitutive form of inquiry.[48]

[42] Koslowski and Kratochwil (1995: 128).
[43] Kratochwil (1989: 100).
[44] Koslowski and Kratochwil (1995: 136).
[45] Kratochwil (1989: 6–12). [46] Kratochwil (1989: 4–8).
[47] Jamie Morgan has demonstrated that Kratochwil's account is steeped in Humeanism as he ends up attaching Humean biases – such as 'determinism' and 'materiality' – to causal descriptions. Morgan (2002: 106–8).
[48] See Fierke (2005: 1–18).

Another interesting constructivist theorist is John Ruggie. He accepts, more explicitly than Onuf, Kratochwil or Fierke, the legitimacy of causation in constructivist analysis. For example, he explicitly acknowledges his belief in 'ideational causation'.[49] Yet, Ruggie finds it extremely difficult to conceptualise what this might mean. Confusingly, he always discusses causation alongside the DN-model explanation: he has not made an effort to think about causation any more deeply than is the convention in the mainstream of the discipline. The fact that he accepts a traditionally Humean account of causation means that causation has a rather limited role in his constructivist analyses. Indeed, Ruggie continually contrasts causal explanations with the so-called constitutive 'non-causal explanations'.[50] For Ruggie, such things as beliefs, agents and meanings fall into the category of 'reasons for action' that should be distinguished from 'causes of action'.[51] Specifically, he is of the opinion that ideas cannot be causal in the same way as brute facts and that categories of intentionality ('aspirations', for example) should be separated conceptually from causes of action.[52]

The aversion to causal language and the resulting dichotomisation of causal and non-causal theories and categories has, as we have seen, played a crucial role in postpositivist theorising. Reflectivist and constructivist approaches in IR have avoided, or marginalised, causal framings in favour of constitutive terminology. Constitutive approaches and questions have been seen as 'non-causal' because they do not make 'deterministic' claims about ideas, rules, norms, discourses, theories: ideas do not 'push or pull' but rather 'make/define/constitute something'. The crucial thing to note is that the delineation of causal and non-causal factors has been fundamentally tied to the Humean assumptions: causes are implied to involve regularities and deterministic relations, while the 'constitutive' aspects of social life are considered non-causal because they do not entail these things. This aversion to causation on Humean grounds has some important implications that we must now address.

Consequences of inadvertent Humeanism

The acceptance of Humeanism has some important consequences for how reflectivists and constructivists conduct their theorising. First,

[49] Ruggie (1999: 226). [50] Ruggie (1998: 34).
[51] Ruggie (1999: 229). [52] Ruggie (1999: 229).

because of their aversion to causality, the reflectivist and constructivist approaches have treated causation on an overly simplistic Humean basis, without showing much interest in exploring alternative conceptualisations of the concept of cause. Neither the radically anti-causal reflectivists, nor the more moderately sceptical constructivists, have engaged with non-Humean philosophies of causation: they have been content simply to do away with the concept of cause or limit the influence of causal language through the use of constitutive language. The unwillingness to explore wider meanings of the concept of cause is not only curious considering that these theoretical approaches have been otherwise very interested in reconceptualising the theoretical premises of IR research, but also problematic because it has, arguably, reproduced simplistic and dichotomous lines of discussion in IR debates on causation and constitution.

Indeed, if the rationalists have had undue confidence in scientific method and have been restricted in specific ways in their causal theorising (see chapter 3), many reflectivists and constructivists have also adopted rather dichotomous and restrictive terms of debate because of the acceptance of Humean assumptions concerning causation. Since causal analysis has been associated with positivism, science and materialist explanations, which the postpositivists do not endorse, they have come to assume that their theorising is somehow very different from causal theorising. Not only have they come to accept that it is illegitimate to evaluate constitutive approaches on the basis of the positivist causal criteria, but also it is assumed that non-causal theorising is somehow incommensurable with, or at least not reducible to, a causal approach to the social world.[53] Crucially, the theoretical and conceptual systems of these theorists tend to become focused on 'reflection' over the 'non-causal' role of 'ideas', 'discourses' and 'intersubjective understandings' in shaping meanings in social life and, as a result, the most crucial explanatory factors are seen to be 'normative' or 'discursive'.[54] This not only goes towards divorcing the concerns of these theorists from the concerns of mainstream IR, but also results in a tendency towards theoretical and conceptual reductionism (towards the ideational, normative or discursive) that is not necessary or desirable.

[53] Koslowski and Kratochwil (1995: 137–8).

[54] See, for example, Koslowski and Kratochwil (1995: 134–59); Campbell (1998a).

Besides the problem of dichotomisation that the rejection of causation gives rise to, there is an even more fundamental problem with the unwillingness to reflect on the meaning of the term cause. Despite the explicit anti- and non-causal lines of argumentation, the reflectivist and constructivist approaches do also seem to utilise implicit causal descriptions: causal descriptions, however, that have not been recognised as causal by themselves, owing to their association of causal descriptions with Humean criteria.

Humeanism has associated causes with regularities and mechanistic 'when A, then B' type relations. However, in our everyday language we use the notion of cause in a much wider sense: we deem ourselves to have put our finger on the cause of something when we say that 'Andy hit Alex because he stole his girlfriend' or that 'Labour won the elections because of Tony Blair's charming qualities'. We also say that various 'forces' and 'factors', for example, media representations, capitalist structures or political ideologies, 'have consequences' in world politics. We also, arguably, imply causal connections when we talk of things, ideas or people as 'influencing', 'producing', 'constraining', 'enabling' or 'shaping' courses of events. The Humean model of causal analysis does not allow us to understand this more 'common-sensical' everyday terminology as causal because of the association of empiricist requirements with making causal statements (causal claims must be based on observational regularities). However, as will be seen, in the light of non-Humean conceptualisations of causes explored in later chapters, these implicit causal descriptions can be understood as causal. The goal of the remainder of this section, in preparation for the discussions to follow, is to demonstrate that common-sensical everyday causal language can be considered to characterise supposedly anti-causal reflectivist approaches in IR.

Despite his anti-causal arguments, Cox's account, for example, is characterised by terminology that can in fact be seen as implicitly causal. His account is based on a careful outlining of structural 'forces' – material, ideational and institutional – that form the essence of the historical developments that he tries to explain. Cox describes the layered and interacting 'forces' in world politics, not as causes but as 'pressures and constraints'.[55] Other critical theorists convey similar implicit causal assumptions: Linklater, too, conceives the world as

[55] Cox and Sinclair (1996: 95).

consisting of certain structures, processes and ways of thinking that 'shape' the world we live in (capitalism, racism, sexism). Even in his more explicitly normative work Linklater recognises the importance of identifying (through sociological inquiry) how the present social structures are historically and socially 'formed' and how they 'affect' world politics.[56] Arguably, countering these oppressive social structures and processes that 'bring about' the boundedness of political identification, disenfranchisement and oppression is precisely one of the key aims of critical theory.

It is hard to see how the critical theory analyses of world politics are not causal, if we start recognising more implicit terminology as causal. Indeed, it becomes difficult to understand why the critical theorists would even talk about these social structures and processes if they were not causal in some sense. For example, why does capitalism matter as a 'force' in world politics for these theorists? Because capitalism, as a structure of social relations, is seen as in some sense causal over individuals: capitalism has the (causal) power to constrain the human flourishing of some, while enabling others to possess wealth and opportunities (for a more detailed discussion, see chapter 7). Both Cox and Linklater associate causation with positivism and its covering-law theorising, the deterministic assumptions of which they then seek to criticise. As a result, they avoid talking about causation in their theories – while having a deep (implicit) interest in what seem to be 'causal' forces that shape the modern world.

These 'common-sensical' causal descriptions can also be seen to characterise poststructuralist accounts. As we saw in the previous section, Edkins voiced some powerful criticisms concerning the failures of the discipline of IR to tackle problems in world politics, such as famine. Edkins blamed 'causal analyses' for this failure. Causal analyses, she argued, 'do not take account of the political processes that are under way, of which the crisis is a symptom' and do not look for 'political reasons or motivations'.[57] If we pay attention to the more common-sensical causal terminology, we can see that the notion of cause becomes unfairly implicated. This is because Edkins fails adequately to delineate what she means by the term cause. Arguably, she accepts the Humean model of causal analysis as characteristic of the form of causal analysis that she criticises: causal analysis, for her purposes, is about abstract

[56] Linklater (1998: 3; 1990). [57] Edkins (1999: 10).

scientific generalisation beyond context. In equating causation with regularity-based Humean causation, Edkins fails to see how her own assessments depend on causal understandings: presumably the 'political processes' of which a crisis is a 'symptom' are, in fact, some sort of 'causes'.

Edkins returns to this issue later on by discussing the debate over whether famine relief should be considered, in some cases, as the cause rather than the solution to famine. She argues that 'the impact of relief is to be measured and analyzed more carefully'. Yet, Edkins follows this statement by saying that 'to regard famine relief as the cause rather than the solution of famine is merely to invert the oppositions inherent in the approach that seeks, in a logo-centric manner, for solutions in terms of cause and effect'.[58] What is needed, she argues, is 'to make the move that treats relief as the undecidable – and hence political'.[59] Presumably, it is through this that we can 'repoliticise' the issue of famine relief. The problem is, however, that Edkins seems to assume that causal analysis cannot be complexity-sensitive, that it necessarily entails claims about 'ultimate causes' and that it must be apolitical. This, it will be shown in the rest of this book, is a crucial mistake, a mistake, again, deriving from a Humean, positivist understanding of causation.

David Campbell, as we have observed, has also been known for his rejection of the idea of causation. However, Campbell's work, too, is full of references to how particular conceptual resolutions and discourses produce effects in the practices of people by constraining, making, encouraging, enabling, reproducing, reifying ranges of action. Indeed, representations and discourses matter because they, as Campbell puts it, have certain 'political consequences'.[60] For example, in *National Deconstruction* Campbell argues that the 'ontopology' binding together territoriality, statism and mono-culturalism in Western liberal discourses had some crucial implications for how the West viewed and dealt with the situation in Bosnia: 'historical representations have political consequences. One of the principal effects of the historical fatalism associated with the ontopolitical rendering of the Bosnian war has been to disenable calls for political or military action . . . Through the violence of conceptual determination, the international community legitimized, replicated, and extended the violence

[58] Edkins (1999: 80). [59] Edkins (1999: 80). [60] Campbell (1998b: 4).

of ethnic cleansing.'[61] This claim is not a-causal, if causes are not understood exclusively through the Humean model: Campbell is arguing that the way in which Western discourse frames political community and international processes has important consequences for the kinds of actions that agents, informed by these discourses, can take.

Despite the self-proclaimed a-causality of the postmodern turn in IR there are many causal-sounding claims being made within these supposedly a-causal theories. The claims do not refer to deterministic or mechanistic ('when A, then B') forces or connections, yet it seems that even the poststructuralists talk of discourses and representations precisely because they have 'consequences' for identities or practices. It could be argued, then, that the poststructuralists' rejection of causation does not necessarily constitute a rejection of the principle of causation, but rather, arises from their acceptance of a Humean conception of causation. Interestingly, recently Campbell himself has come to recognise this causality in his work and, indeed, has opened the door towards investigation of the causal nature of 'conditions of possibility' through utilisation of alternative conceptions of causality developed by Connolly.[62] This is a positive move and provides important room for advancement of non-positivist conceptions of cause, such as advanced here in chapters 5 and 6.

Feminists, as we have seen, have also been averse to making causal claims, owing to the association of causal language with 'male-stream' gender-blind scientific IR. However, feminists have clearly made a number of claims, not just about the gendered nature of society, but about the reasons for the *production* of particular gendered assumptions and gendered world political realities. Feminists have noted that women are unequally represented in world politics as well as, perhaps more deeply, that they are affected differently by events and processes in world politics (for example, economic liberalisation, technologisation, environmental degradation, militarisation). Why do feminists highlight the gendered norms, discourses or social practices in explaining these differences in experience between men and women? Presumably because the gendered social norms and structures have real effects on women's lives, even if sometimes indirectly, or unintentionally – they are causal, if not in a deterministic or mono-causal manner. Arguably, the very

[61] Campbell (1998a: 84, 225). [62] Campbell (2007: 224–5).

project of feminism depends on making some causal claims about the nature of patriarchal societies and global structures.

The fact that some sort of causal analysis is central to feminism has, interestingly, been noted by Enloe.

> It's a mistake to portray feminist analysis as merely about impacts – for example, revealing the effects of war on women, or of international debt on women. That, in fact, is significant to reveal. But most feminist analyses reveal *more* than impacts. For instance, *Bananas* tries to show why the colonial project occurred the way it did. *Bananas* and *Maneuvers* both seek to show why states are so needful of ideas about masculinity and femininity. That's making a theoretical argument about causality.[63]

Arguably, in recognising the causal role and conditions of gender in world politics, Enloe has tried to escape from the Humean conception of causation, even if this has not been conceptualised explicitly or coherently.

It seems that the role of these inadvertent causal statements has not been understood within these approaches precisely because many reflectivists and constructivists have been wedded to a Humean understanding of causation and have not been aware of alternative non-Humean framings of the concept of cause. The purpose of Part II of this book is to explore alternative philosophical framings of causation: ones that allow IR theorists to move beyond the conceptual muddles reproduced by the acceptance of, or the simple rejection of, the Humean model of causal analysis. When the concept of cause is rethought the supposedly anti-causal theorists in IR will be seen as far from anti-causal.

Conclusion

Postpositivists in contemporary IR have advanced some powerful criticisms of the positivist mainstream: their conception of social science methods (quantification), epistemology (empiricist objectivism) and ontology (with emphasis on observables). As will be seen, the

[63] Enloe in an interview with *Review of International Studies* (2001: 656); emphasised also at a talk given at University of Wales, Aberystwyth on 10 May 2001.

arguments advanced here are largely in agreement with the post-positivist criticisms of the positivist mainstream informed by a Humean empiricist view of causal analysis. However, I have argued that many reflectivists and constructivists actually work within certain Humean assumptions concerning the idea of causation. In their anxiety to challenge the mainstream, the reflectivists have dismissed the notion of cause too promptly, and, crucially, on a Humean basis.

As a result, the postpositivist challenge to the mainstream has been an unnecessarily 'anti-causal' project. Buying into the Humean discourse on causation has meant that causes and causal analyses have been associated with 'determinism', 'materialism', 'depoliticisation' and 'reification'. The reflectivists and constructivists have not noticed that their criticisms of causes and causal analysis are targeted at the Humean model of causal analysis, rather than at causal approaches more widely. This has given rise to two problems. First, because there has been no willingness to think about causation in any deeper sense, the reflectivists and constructivists have not really challenged Humeanism; they have simply conceived themselves to be engaging in a different, 'anti-causal' project. This has meant that the Humean model of causal analysis has retained its role as the 'only game in town' when it comes to causal analysis. It has also entailed that reflectivists have developed some isolationist or theoretically reductionist tendencies: the constitutive theorising they conduct is seen as non-scientific (primacy on interpretation), non-causal (primacy on constitution of meanings), non-deterministic (primacy on contingency) and non-material (primacy on ideas). This has entailed the narrowing down of theoretical and conceptual horizons.

Second, dominance of Humean assumptions has meant that IR approaches have had no way of understanding more 'common-sensically' causal claims and assumptions. Indeed, as was seen in the previous chapter, it is far from clear, when we pay attention to more common-sensical causal terminology, that postpositivism is non-causal. As we have seen, implicit causal terminology can be detected in all reflectivist theories. Indeed, paradoxically, their own accounts of concrete processes, and their normative projects, rely on certain 'vaguely' causal claims about the state of the world: they consider their accounts to 'matter' for IR and the practice of international politics because the 'ways of thinking', discourses, representations, norms and rules that they point to can be shown to have important consequences in world politics. We will now move on to consider what these 'vague' 'common-sensical' causal statements might mean and in what sense they can be considered causal. Also, their relationship to the notion of 'constitutive theorising' will be clarified. This is necessary in order to elucidate a way forward from what is seen here as the Humean problem-field in IR theory and research.

PART II

Rethinking the concept of cause

5 *Attempts to move beyond Humeanism: strengths and weaknesses*

Part I of this book has argued that so-called Humean assumptions, which reduce causal analysis to regularity analysis of observables and entail the assumptions of regularity-determinism (given regularities, we can make 'when A, then B' statements about causal relations and have a basis for prediction) and efficient causality (given regularities, causes should be thought of as 'pushing and pulling forces'), have been overwhelmingly dominant in twentieth-century philosophy of science and philosophy of social science. It has been seen that contemporary IR theorising has also been deeply informed by these assumptions, which has given rise to particular kinds of understandings of the nature of causes and of causal analysis in the recent disciplinary debates. We have seen that rationalists, in their efforts to conform to prescriptions of the Humean conception of causal analysis, have conducted causal research that has tendencies towards 'additive' and regularity-deterministic analysis and that has found it difficult to engage with unobservable aspects of the social world, notably with processes of 'social construction'. On the other hand, the reflectivists who have analysed these aspects of the social world have tended to reject causal analysis, with the hope of thereby avoiding the deterministic connotations of the Humean approaches. Constructivists have often retained some reference to causation but have in most cases been unable to think outside the Humean box when it comes to causal assumptions. Because the reflectivists and the constructivists in IR have failed to engage with non-Humean philosophies of causation, they have not recognised that some of their own supposedly non-causal claims might be considered causal.

Part II seeks a response to the Humean framing of causal analysis in IR through a philosophical reframing of the concept of cause. The aim is to put forward a conceptualisation of causation that uncovers the richer meanings of the concept of cause, meanings that have been hidden by the Humean discourse of causation. The rethinking of the concept of cause, it will be seen, allows a reframing of the Humean problematique that informs both the rationalist, the reflectivist and most constructivist approaches in IR. Chapter 5 will introduce and evaluate two key philosophical alternatives to Humeanism: pragmatism and philosophical realism.[1] The aim here is to gain a sense of what alternative philosophies of causation argue and to evaluate some of the strengths and weaknesses of these alternatives to Humeanism. Moreover, we will also examine how these alternative philosophical stances have been drawn on by some theorists in IR in order to escape the limitations that the influence of Humeanism has propagated in the discipline of IR.

It will be seen that the pragmatist and the philosophically realist approaches, in general and in IR specifically, raise important arguments against Humeanism, and in fact provide important alternative discourses to the dominant positivist theory of science. However, it will also be seen that they have not always challenged the Humean discourse of causation comprehensively. This is the case especially with pragmatist approaches, but also partially with the philosophical realists. Pragmatist approaches have been characterised by certain anti-realist and relativist assumptions and still, as do the Humeans, prioritise an epistemological engagement with causation. Philosophical realism interestingly presents an alternative that focuses on the ontological aspect of causation and thereby radically challenges the core assumptions characteristic of modern philosophical accounts of causation. While generally persuasive, this approach continues to reproduce language of causal mechanisms and efficient causation, which is unnecessary and in certain respects unhelpful. Chapter 6 will propose a philosophical alternative to the Humean conceptualisation of causal analysis that will overcome some of the aspects that remain problematic with the existing accounts of causation in IR. This account will build on philosophical realism but seeks to complement it through a broader Aristotelian conception of cause.

[1] There are other philosophical accounts of causation that confront aspects of Humeanism, notably the singularity account, Cartwright's account of laws (1983, 1989, 1999) and Salmon's causal mark approaches (1984, 1998; see also Dowe 1992). These accounts will not be discussed here for the sake of space and focus.

Pragmatism

Pragmatist philosophical arguments as defined here are premised on the idea that knowledge of the world around us is based on what is pragmatically workable or useful. Instead of accepting a correspondence theory of truth (characteristic of many empiricist-positivist approaches) where truth is linked to observation of certain states of events or facts, pragmatism emphasises that truth is that which is pragmatic as a way of belief. In terms of causation, pragmatism refers to a broad category of approaches that see causal explanations as specific kinds of answers to our specific kinds of 'pragmatic' inquiries. When we define causation, pragmatists argue that we need to define it in relation, not to meta-physical realities, but to the pragmatic ways in which people utilise the concept. Causes and causal explanations, the pragmatists argue, are tied to our wishes to make the world 'controllable' or 'intelligible' for us. Pragmatism will for the purposes of this chapter be divided into three main strands: (1) the American tradition of pragmatism of Dewey, James, Peirce and Rorty; (2) the so-called manipulability theory pragmatism of figures such as Collingwood and Dray; and (3) the 'causation as an explanatory relation' approach associated with the work of Michael Scriven. There are significant differences between the traditions when it comes to the notion of causation, and more widely, and also the traditions do not have explicit links between them. However, they are treated together here since they all share an interest in defining causality, not as linked to regularities alone, but as something linked to our interests in knowing or doing.

American pragmatism

William James and John Dewey were the first pragmatists to make a mark in American intellectual life. Their point was to emphasise 'humanism' in the study of the world, that is, the notion that all knowledge is tied to human interests and activities. The central contention was that knowledge is not something 'absolute' that can be formulated outside the practicalities of human life. Thus 'truth' is defined as 'whatever proves itself to be good in the way of belief, and good . . . for definite assignable reasons'.[2] 'Reality' as a distinct and 'deep' philosophical

[2] James quoted in Thayer (1975: xxxvi).

concept recedes to the background. For the pragmatists practical actions have primacy in generation of knowledge: '[t]hought is a practical organ of adaptation to environment... knowledge is a tool to encompass this adaptation, rather than a picture of reality'.[3] The target of the attack is 'objectivism', science that works without the recognition of human activity. The classical pragmatist philosophy associated with Dewey and James was revived in the 1980s, perhaps most influentially in the writings of Richard Rorty, who united the pragmatist insights with the Wittgensteinian philosophy of language. Rorty argues that language is a crucial 'practical' element in social life and that truth cannot exist beyond language. Hence truth is not the 'mirror of nature' but part of our language games and hence contingent. According to Rorty we should avoid vocabulary and language games that presume the primacy of objective truths and essences. Instead we would be better off if we learnt to accept that all we can have is, as Nietzsche puts it, 'a mobile army of metaphors' that we manipulate for practical purposes.[4]

What does the tradition of American pragmatism have to say about causation? James seems to have something to say about pragmatism's import for aetiological concerns. Pragmatism, he argues, encourages us to '[look] away from first things, principles, "categories", supposed necessities; and [look] towards last things, fruits, consequences, facts'.[5] Pragmatism then turns on its head the traditional hierarchy of cause and effect (like in Nietzsche's deconstruction of causality[6]): the effects are more important than the causes.

The notion of cause does not disappear from pragmatist writings, however. Nor do many common-sensical causal assumptions like belief in the world consisting of a multiplicity of causes. Rorty himself acknowledges that 'most things in space and time are the effects of causes which do not include human mental states'.[7] But pragmatism of the American variety seems somewhat unclear as to what causes should mean, especially with regard to human activity and language. James summarises the pragmatist problem with causation:

> We have no definite idea of what we mean by cause, or of what causality consists in. But the principle expresses a demand for *some* deeper sort of inward

[3] Dewey quoted in Pettegrew (2000: 4). [4] Rorty (1989: 17).
[5] James (1995: 57). [6] Culler (1982: 87). [7] Rorty (1989: 5).

connection between phenomena than their merely habitual time sequence seems to us to be. The word 'cause' is, in short, an altar to an unknown god; an empty pedestal still marking the place of a hoped-for statue.[8]

There are close connections between early pragmatism and radical empiricism, which makes Ayer suspect that James deduces causation down to 'certain sorts of phenomena [that] are regularly correlated'.[9] Indeed, James does state that pragmatism helps reduce abstruse concepts to simple ones and that this includes 'cause' being given the meaning 'you may expect certain sequences'.[10] This sounds strikingly Humean. However, pragmatists argue also that the causal claims that arise from regularities are accepted, not because empiricist method provides us with knowledge of the truths about causal forces, but because the statements this knowledge of regularities generates are useful, they are pragmatic as ways of belief. To quote Peirce '"in the long run" we can be as certain of the methodological validity of inductive verification of causal laws as we can be of our increasing ability to master nature in practical and technical manner'.[11]

The American pragmatist conception of causality is Humean in certain important respects – indeed most pragmatists do not challenge the empiricist avenue for understanding causation as such, merely the premises on the basis of which it is justified in our knowledge constructions. It is important to note this connection between American pragmatism and Humean regularity theories of causation, as it is to recognise the fact that many positivists and Humeans are not adverse to this pragmatist line of thought. Indeed, many positivists precisely adopt pragmatic instrumentalist bases within their empiricist-positivist frameworks. For them, statements about laws and the relations of regularly observed events can be said to be plausible precisely because these claims are useful. In this sense then, at least going by the logic of James's thinking, there seem to be some close interconnections between Humean and the American pragmatist logics and indeed, they seem to be complementary in important ways, not least in the wish to avoid treating causation as something with a definite existence in a metaphysical sense outside pragmatic human experience.

[8] James quoted in Ayer (1968: 208).
[9] James quoted in Ayer (1968: 208–9).
[10] James quoted in Ayer (1968: 201).
[11] Peirce quoted in Apel (1984: 89).

More radically anti-Humean pragmatist currents of thought on causation, however, are evident in Collingwood's manipulability theory of causation as well as in the causation as an explanatory relation approach.

Manipulability theory

The manipulability theory of causation, developed in Collingwood's and also von Wright's writings,[12] provides an interesting alternative to Humeanism. The manipulability account challenges the Humean assumption that causes and causal explanation are dependent on regularities of observables. Rather, the manipulability theorists argue that causes should quite simply be seen as those things that we assign as causes. But how do we assign something as a cause? Manipulability theorists emphasise that we often term causes those things that we can control or manipulate for our pragmatic ends. The term 'cause', in manipulability theorists' view, refers to whatever event, process, thing, power, condition, which human agents can control in order to produce or prevent another state of affairs (their 'effect'). As Collingwood puts it, a cause of a given event is 'the handle, so to speak, by which human beings can manipulate it'.[13]

Since 'for any given person, the cause . . . of a given thing is that one of its conditions which he is able to produce or prevent',[14] there is no way we can speak of causes except from a particular perspective and informed by our interest in 'producing or preventing a certain kind of event'.[15] Thus, against Hume, 'for a mere spectator there are no causes'.[16] Collingwood invites us to consider an example:

[12] This is not to say that von Wright's (1971, 1974) and Apel's (1984) accounts are not interesting in their own regard.

[13] Collingwood (1940: 296). Collingwood distinguishes between three senses of cause of which the manipulability account of cause is the second. The first refers to the use of causes in history, that is, accounts of how actors were 'afforded' certain motives. Sense III, the use of causation in the theoretical sciences, is understood on the lines of counterfactual Humean theories of cause. Collingwood (1940: 296–312). Collingwood's philosophy of history (1948) focuses on the motives of actors.

[14] Collingwood quoted in Dray (1964: 45).

[15] Collingwood (1940: 307).

[16] Collingwood (1940: 307).

> A car skids while cornering at a certain point, strikes the kerb, and turns turtle. From the car-driver's point of view the cause of the accident was cornering too fast, and the lesson is that one must drive more carefully. From the county surveyor's point of view the cause was a defect in the surface or camber of the road, and the lesson is that greater care must be taken to make roads skid-proof. From the motor-manufacturer's point of view the cause was a defective design in the car, and the lesson is that one must place the centre of gravity lower.[17]

The manipulability theorists thus stress that our accounts of causes always put emphasis on different factors, depending on our differing 'manipulability' interests. Douglas Gasking, following Collingwood, emphasises the way in which scientific accounts use this manipulability logic. Gasking argues that a statement such as 'a rise in temperature of iron causes it to glow', in fact means the same as 'by applying to iron the general technique for making things hot you will also make it glow'.[18]

The manipulability theory of causation is interesting in that it challenges the Humean notion that regularities are the most crucial ingredient of causal explanation, and it does so more directly than the American pragmatist tradition. However, the manipulability account is not entirely incompatible with Humean accounts either: indeed, many causal accounts that work on the basis of regular observations and aim at prediction can also emphasise the importance of 'control' interests.[19]

Causation as an explanatory relation

An interesting, and quite a different kind of broadly pragmatist position, is Michael Scriven's 'causes as an explanatory relation' approach. This position could be said to build on the manipulability approach to causation, but in a way that avoids accepting the assumption of physical control in such a strong way. Scriven argues that we should understand causes, not as regularities or as 'what we control', but as

[17] Collingwood quoted in Beauchamp (1974a: 116).

[18] Gasking quoted in Beauchamp (1974a: 117). See also Gasking (1974).

[19] In Judea Pearl's (2000) causal modelling, for example, interventions are seen as an essential part of establishing causality. Also, many IR accounts can be seen to emphasise 'control' interests. See, for example, Waltz (1979: 8).

fundamentally 'explanatory': causes are those things that make the world intelligible for us.[20] Causal accounts, he contends, 'can only be understood or explicated by reference to a number of contextual parameters'.[21] For example, to say 'heat caused a heart attack' is to say that 'accounting for heart attack by reference to heat' allows us to explain the occurrence of a heart attack in a given explanatory context. Causes, Scriven argues, cannot be reduced to any simple definitional criteria: they can be all kinds of things or factors that make something intelligible to us by advancing an explanation to a specific 'causal puzzle'. This is an interesting account in the sense that it transfers the idea of pragmatic interest from manipulability to the idea of explanation. Arguably, Hidemi Suganami's account of causes of war in IR could be seen to develop a line of thought similar to that of Scriven: the focus of causal analysis becomes the kind of explanation that makes something intelligible for us in a given context, rather than unearthing the real causes in the world *per se*.

It should be noted that the pragmatist reconceptualisations of causation, especially those of Collingwood and Scriven, have an important impact on how causes can be talked about in social science, and on the framing of social science debates. Notably, their assumption that we can only say what a 'cause' is from our subjective 'inquisitive' point of view, has had a great deal of resonance in the philosophy of history. Drawing on Collingwood, William Dray has sought to clarify the meaning of the pragmatist framing of causation for the social sciences, notably history.

Dray and historical explanation

Dray's focus was on challenging the Humean and, thereby, the dichotomous positivist vs. hermeneutic framing of historical inquiry. Dray argues that regularities and supposed laws of behaviour are neither *possible* nor *necessary* in causal explanations in the social world.[22] For him, in explaining historical events, it is more important to show that a condition X (say, Hitler as the leader of Germany) was a necessary condition for an event Y (Second World War) than to demonstrate a regularity connection of X and Y type observables (Hitler-like

[20] Scriven (1975). [21] Scriven (1975: 4). [22] See Dray (1975: 86–9).

leaders and wars).[23] Causal language of various kinds, he recognises, is constantly used in our claims about the world. However, following pragmatism, causes are seen as those things that allow us to explain the world around us in a *pragmatic* way.

Dray's idea of explanation and causation has a particular solution to offer for the reasons–causes debate. He argues that the difference between stating reasons for action and the causes of it 'is one of approach, or point of view, or kind of inquiry'.[24] There is no fundamental philosophical gulf between the reasons and causes accounts for Dray as there was for most hermeneutic interpretive theorists; their status is defined simply by the pragmatics of a given inquiry.

Limitations of pragmatism

While in many ways useful in challenging the dominance of the regularity accounts, and the dichotomisations they have upheld in the social sciences, the pragmatist approaches are not entirely unproblematic in terms of providing an alternative or a challenge to Humeanism. The pragmatist approaches have not escaped the Humean 'anti-realist' framing of the problem of causation.

Pragmatists, as Humeans, prioritise epistemology (how we derive knowledge, that is, observe/think) over ontology (what is). In so doing, they reject the claim that our causal accounts are of something 'real'. As far as they are concerned, we can never know what the 'causes out there really are': all we have are many competing causal accounts, none of which should be given priority as a 'true' description of 'real' causal relations: '[i]t is true that in the explanatory statement... one or a few conditions are picked out as "the cause". But this does not... confer upon the causal condition any mysterious ontological priority.'[25]

In the pragmatist approaches the independent existence of a reality beyond 'our accounts' is effectively denied: all there is to causation is, literally, 'our accounts'. The pragmatist critiques are premised on prioritising human knowledge and interests: they are epistemological and inherently anthropocentric. Because these approaches sidestep, just as do the Humeans, the ontological problem of causation (are there

[23] Dray (1964: 41–7). See also Dray (1975: 112).
[24] Dray (1975: 154). [25] Dray (1975: 114).

causes beyond 'our accounts'?), the pragmatist accounts also come to accept certain relativist assumptions. Collingwood, for example, puts forward a relativist account of causes: he argues that people often use the notion of cause to assign blame and, hence, their accounts are always from a subjective perspective reflecting our interests and interpretation of contexts.[26] Scriven, too, sees causal accounts as fundamentally linked to 'our interests', not to the nature of the world or its 'real causes': causal accounts are seen as 'intersubjectively corroborated'.[27] The pragmatists find it difficult to give grounds for justifying how we might make judgements between causal accounts: if there are no 'real' causes, our accounts can never account for 'something' in 'better' or 'worse' ways. All accounts are in this sense accepted as 'equal': the only difference between them is that some engender more 'control' or that some happen to be 'intersubjectively' more acceptable than others.

However, this raises a crucial question: where does the ability to 'control', or, indeed, the 'intersubjective corroboration' arise from? Arguably, the pragmatists have not succeeded in answering the crucial question: why do some schemas about the world work better than others? Why can some things be controlled through certain 'handles' and why are some explanations more easily 'intersubjectively corroborated' than others? The 'intersubjective consensus' on the inability of humans to fly (unaided), for example, is strong, and such knowledge seems to have important instrumental (control) uses too. But is the consensus strong merely because of a pragmatic acceptance that humans cannot fly or because certain causal forces in the world 'really' limit what humans can and cannot do? Are there ontological 'real causes' in the world that our accounts either manage or fail to account for? Are pragmatic explanations, in fact, premised on some 'real causes'? Are some explanations accepted because they grasp the real causes in the world better than others do?[28] The pragmatist approaches, while useful in some respects, are haunted by some important questions: questions that their frameworks cannot persuasively grapple with because the pragmatists are unwilling to delve into the ontological aspect of the problem of causation.

[26] Collingwood (1940: 303–4). [27] See, for example, Scriven (1975: 12).
[28] Some pragmatists build links to philosophical realism. See, for example, Hacking (1995: 243); Margolis (1986).

Pragmatism in IR: Hidemi Suganami

These questions are present in Hidemi Suganami's interesting and groundbreaking study of causes of war in IR. *On the Causes of War* is one of the first comprehensive works trying to grapple with the complex conceptual problems in theorising causation in IR. Suganami argues that in IR the causes of war have been unhelpfully left for the 'empirical' scientists to study. Because of the empirical scientists' aversion to conceptual study, he contends, empirical engagements with the causes of war in IR have remained confused.[29] Suganami wants to clarify some of the conceptual issues relating to the debates on the causes of war. He argues that, to avoid confusion, we should start distinguishing between three distinct types of questions concerning the causes of war: questions concerning 'prerequisites', or 'necessary conditions', of war, questions concerning circumstances of likelihood of war, and questions concerning causes of particular wars. The different goals of these types of causal questions, he believes, have not been adequately addressed in IR.[30]

For our purposes, the main import of Suganami's theorisation is his critique of the Humean regularity approach to causation. Suganami argues that the Humean correlational studies in IR have yielded certain limited insights in answering questions about the circumstances in which wars are frequent. However, he maintains that correlational studies cannot 'explain' the causes of war, especially the causes of particular wars.[31] Moreover, he asserts that the correlational approaches are not adequately attuned to the possibility that wars, or democratic peace for that matter, might be caused by many different mechanisms or causes in different historical periods.[32]

Suganami proposes a radically different way of framing causal explanation in IR. He draws on the pragmatist notion of cause, more specifically the 'causation as an explanatory relation' approach. Suganami argues that the aim of causal explanation is, not to correlate regular patterns, but to render events or patterns intelligible.[33] He contends that neither regularity, nor counterfactual theories of cause, can give an adequate account of what causal explanation involves. Causal explanations, he believes, are stories that, by linking together various events

[29] Suganami (1996: 2). [30] Suganami (1996: 11–47).
[31] Suganami (1996: 111). [32] Suganami (1996: 104, 107).
[33] Suganami (1996: 134–8).

or patterns, render a given causal puzzle 'intelligible' for us. To state a cause of an event, he asserts,

> is to explain its occurrence. To explain the occurrence of an event is to render the occurrence more intelligible than before. To do this we show the sequence of relevant events, leading to the event in question, in such a way that a specific puzzle or puzzles we have about the occurrence of the event concerned can be solved.[34]

Suganami stresses that a theorist, or a historian, looking to give an account of causes must, in order to 'explain' something, devise a narrative account through which (s)he can explicate how various events or processes brought about a given phenomenon. The point of a narrative account of causes of war is that it 'renders the outbreak of the war more intelligible to us than before, *the sequence of events thus narrated* constituting the cause of the war'.[35]

Importantly, Suganami emphasises the importance of accepting a multi-causal and complexity-sensitive approach to causal analysis. The kind of causal factors any explanatory account of causes of war must deal with are manifold but can, according to Suganami, be categorised into four main areas: relevant background conditions, chance coincidences, mechanistic processes and actions/inactions by key individuals.[36]

Suganami builds a powerful critique of the regularity approach to causal analysis in IR. By opening up the notion of cause, he radically opens up the IR discourse on causation and causal analysis. Through this approach we can see that, contra positivists, causal theorising does not require analysis of regularities: in fact, historical and qualitative data play the most crucial role in many causal explanations.[37] Also, it highlights the need for more holistic explanations and narratives that explain how various conditions or events coming together bring about certain phenomena. Importantly, Suganami also reminds us that causal conditions are not necessarily of the 'same kind' either, as sometimes misleadingly implied in philosophical and social science accounts that lay out the logic of multi-causal analysis in a manner that simply lists causal conditions (C1, C2, C3, … Cn).[38] Suganami's reframing of

[34] Suganami (1996: 139). [35] Suganami (1996: 139–40). Original italics.
[36] Suganami (1996: 143–4). [37] Suganami (1996: 109).
[38] Suganami (1996: 138).

causal explanation also allows us to challenge the conventional division of IR into explanatory (causal) and understanding (non-causal) approaches: causal analysis that gives an account of something both 'explains' and allows us to 'understand'.[39] Suganami's account allows us to see various, including reflectivist, accounts in IR as 'causal' in that they provide 'narrative accounts' that make the world more intelligible. Because of the acceptance of the narrative view of causes, it can be accepted that various words, such as the implicit references to 'origins', 'conditions', 'forces', 'consequences' and so on, are, in fact, causal: they are crucial linguistic devices through which causal narratives 'intelligibilify'.

As with the other pragmatist accounts, Suganami's avoids according ontological status to causes. In Suganami's view, we have no safe grounds to assume the 'real existence' of objects of science or of social science, or to accept their 'real' causality: what matters in social inquiry is our representations, or stories, of what is postulated to exist.[40] Thus, such things as social structures, for example, should not be simply accepted as real: 'it is *as if* they existed, which is categorically different from saying that they *really* do'.[41] It follows that Suganami rejects any possibility of inquiring into 'real causes': 'any claim to know what *really* caused a given war is simply a claim to *know* what caused that war; nothing is added by the adjective "really"'.[42]

For Suganami, because of his sceptical stance on our ability to know 'real' ontological causes, no distinction is drawn between what is causal (ontologically) and what we think is causal (epistemologically). The acceptance of this reduction of 'what is' to 'what we think' has some important implications. It leads to important questions concerning the ontological status of causes: do causal narratives refer to something outside our narratives or do our causal narratives exhaust the meaning of causation? For Suganami, it seems, causes are literally defined by 'our stories': our stories of the causes of war '[constitute] the causes of war'.[43] In making no distinction between 'our accounts' and their (ontological) 'referents', Suganami advocates an anti-realist stance on causes: although important in making things intelligible, causes have no ontological status.[44] Causation, in the end, is nothing more than an

[39] Suganami (1999: 372). [40] Suganami (1999: 376–9).
[41] Suganami (1999: 378). [42] Suganami (1996: 208–9). Original italics.
[43] Suganami (1996: 140).
[44] As pointed out also by Patomäki and Wight (2000: 229).

epistemological and (as for Hume) an 'imagined' relation, not something that characterises the world outside our stories.

This position, while logical within the pragmatist philosophical framework, leads to some difficult questions regarding the evaluation of causal explanations. If causes do not exist independently of our narrations of them, how can we make judgements between causal accounts? Suganami, like the other pragmatists, leans towards relativism and implies that the weighting of different causal factors is, indeed, relative to our 'intelligibilifying' interests and stories[45] – although he also points out that 'there is still room for intersubjective agreement as to the relative merits of one type of (normatively embedded) depiction compared to another'.[46]

However, it could be questioned whether causes are merely an epistemological category, or 'imagined' – and whether the evaluation of our stories is just relative to our 'intersubjective' context. If our causal stories have no referents, and nothing but intersubjective constraints on them, our stories can be 'innumerable', as Suganami argues.[47] However, it seems that we do not talk of the world in 'any' possible way: our accounts of the world, although multifarious, are not 'innumerable'. It is conceivable that this is the case, not just because of the 'intersubjective constraints' on our stories, but because something outside our stories puts constraints on them. Is it not possible that a causal story – and, indeed, intersubjective consensus on whether it is plausible – is shaped by something outside language: by the ontologically 'real' referent with which the story is trying to grapple?

The analysis of causes of war, for example, involves contestation and can be explained in many ways, through various narratives concentrating on different factors or processes. However, the intersubjective consensus that causes of war involve factors such as the interests of states, their interactions or their conditions in the international system (rather than, say, the migratory patterns of rabbit populations or variation in agricultural traditions) is not necessarily random but has conceivably arisen because there is some 'real' referent to our explanations, even if complex and difficult to grasp (and, hence, contested). It follows that perhaps all accounts of the causes of war are not 'equal', or merely 'intersubjectively corroborated' in different ways; maybe some fail to

[45] See, for example, Suganami (1996: 140, 149). See also Suganami (1999: 372).
[46] Suganami (1999: 380). [47] Suganami (1999: 379).

account for evidence or to give a plausible account of the 'real' processes involved in war causation, and that is why they are not accepted.

Suganami, while providing an excellent critique of Humean regularity analysis of causation, is not interested in delving into the ontological questions that underlie causal analysis.[48] For a pragmatist, ontological questions are literally collapsed into the epistemological problem of causation. However, dealing with the ontological aspect of causation is not impossible and, in fact, can provide important new avenues in analysis of causation. The ontological aspect of causation has been dealt with explicitly by the philosophical realists, to whom our focus now turns.

Philosophical realism

The philosophical realists, just like the pragmatists, aim to build a critique of the Humean conception of causation. However, they seek to invert all the traditions of modern philosophy and take the ontological questions, not the epistemological issues, as their starting point. In this section the basic premises of philosophical realism will be examined, with regard to the nature of reality, truth, science and causation, as well as with regard to the nature of social objects and social science. The latter part of this section will evaluate how philosophical realism has been applied in IR, that is, the contributions of theorists such as Alexander Wendt, David Dessler and Heikki Patomäki. Philosophical realism discusses the ontological problem of causation in a broadly persuasive manner and has advanced many important insights that allow us to address the Humean problem-field in modern philosophy. Indeed, because good reasons are seen to exist for the acceptance of causal realism suggested by these theorists, chapter 6 will defend some of the key tenets of philosophical realism on causation, while also seeking to develop it in new directions.

Philosophical realism, science and causation

To put it simply, philosophical realism is a position that argues that there is such a thing as reality, and this reality, contra both empiricist

[48] Although it seems that Suganami, just as Scriven, implicitly accepts that causal stories have some sort of real referents. For Scriven's acceptance of realist assumptions see Scriven (1991: 306–9).

and idealist philosophical traditions, exists independently of human minds that theorise it. Philosophical realism has a long history in philosophy of science: realism was the guiding assumption behind Aristotelian, Scholastic and early modern science.[49] However, during recent centuries, especially the twentieth century, philosophically realist assumptions have been under fierce attack from various anti-realist philosophers who have perceived any acceptance of realist assumptions as 'metaphysical'. The 1970s saw the return of philosophical realism, as philosophers such as Rom Harré , Mario Bunge and Roy Bhaskar started to (re)develop a realist approach to the philosophy of science. We will concentrate here on examining Bhaskar's philosophical realism, especially in its early form.[50]

Bhaskar argues that, instead of prioritising epistemological questions, such as 'how do we provide scientific knowledge?', we should start our philosophical inquiries into the nature of science from the analysis of the practice of science and from asking the ontological question 'what must the world be like for our knowledge of it to be possible?'[51] Bhaskar asserts that much of modern philosophy, having prioritised epistemology, has conflated the question 'what is?' (ontology) with the question 'how do we know?' (epistemology). As a consequence, the idealist tradition has reduced reality to 'what we think', while the empiricists have reduced reality to 'what is perceived'.[52] Bhaskar claims that both traditions portray the nature of reality in misleading ways and, as a consequence, fail to understand the nature of scientific inquiry.

Bhaskar argues that, for the practice of science to be possible, we must presuppose (1) the existence of mind-independent reality and (2) a deep and 'stratified' conception of reality. Scientific theories, he maintains, are *of* something, and that something they are *of* is quite independent from our observations and theories: while we observe effects and theorise about objects, objects of science do not depend for their

[49] For a comprehensive account see Wallace (1972a, 1972b).

[50] As developed in *Realist Theory of Science* (1978) and *Possibility of Naturalism* (1979), and later elaborated in *Reclaiming Reality* (1989) and the *Philosophy and the Idea of Freedom* (1991). Key writings also available in Archer et al. (1998). I will not deal with the so-called dialectic turn (Bhaskar 1993, 1994), or Bhaskar's later work on 'meta-reality' (2000, 2002). Other interesting realist formulations include, for example, Tooley (1987, 1997, 1999) and Bunge (1959, 1979, 1996).

[51] Bhaskar (1978: 23).

[52] Bhaskar (1978: 26).

existence on our observations or theories.[53] Men do not 'create' scientific objects or laws: indeed, 'if men ceased to exist sound would continue to travel and heavy bodies fall to the earth'.[54] The fundamental problem of modern philosophy of science, Bhaskar argues, has been the avoidance of dealing with ontology and the resultant conflation of reality (intransitive mind-independent reality) and how we talk of that reality (through concepts and descriptions). Bhaskar accepts that we talk of 'reality' always under certain socially embedded descriptions. Science is always 'dependent upon the antecedent knowledge and the efficient activity of men'[55] and has to use 'transitive' tools to study anything, that is, pre-existing socially engendered theories, paradigms, models and linguistic conventions. Scientific knowledge, then, is 'a social product, actively produced by means of antecedent social products'; yet, it is a social product that is shaped 'on the basis of continual engagement, or interaction, with its (intransitive) object'.[56] Although our descriptions are socially embedded, this does not deny the 'real' that our descriptions are of. We must separate the 'intransitive real' from our descriptions, for any of our descriptions to make sense.

Bhaskar argues that the practice of science, and the intelligibility of its experimental methods, presume that 'real structures exist independently of and are often out of phase with the actual patterns of events'.[57] Ruth Groff aptly summarises Bhaskar's critique of the empiricist tradition where observed regularities are not distinguished from the independent 'real' causal laws of nature:

> Scientific experiments, Bhaskar reminds us, consist of the artificial generation of regularities. The idea is that by bringing about a particular constant conjunction of events in an artificial environment – one in which the number of causal variables is limited – we will find out something about what the world is like outside such an environment. This belief, however – that experiments can tell us something about what the world is like outside the experimental setting – presupposes that while scientists do (and in general must) actively induce regularities, they do not thereby produce the *causes* of such regularities.[58]

Bhaskar proposes that we must recognise three distinct levels of reality: the level of the 'empirical', consisting of our empirical experiences;

[53] Bhaskar (1978: 22–3). [54] Bhaskar (1978: 21). [55] Bhaskar (1978: 24).
[56] Patomäki and Wight (2000: 224). [57] Bhaskar (1978: 13).
[58] Groff (2004: 12). Original italics.

the level of the 'actual', consisting of events and actual states of affairs; and the level of the 'real', consisting of the unobservable real structures and mechanisms that, in interaction with other real structures and mechanisms, bring about states of affairs and make empirical observation possible.[59] Scientific theories, Bhaskar argues, far from merely stacking up empirical regularities, aim to grasp and theorise this deeper unobservable level of reality.

Empiricism, Bhaskar points out, is 'realist' about something: about the observable. He argues that empiricists are 'empirically realist': for the empiricists, 'the real entity' with which science is concerned is 'some particular object of perception'.[60] In contrast, for a philosophical realist, the object of science is 'some general feature or property of the world'.[61] Bhaskar maintains that because the empiricists have 'flattened' scientific reality to perceptual reality, they have based their view of science on an 'atomistic' conception of facts and objects of science. He argues that the practice of science presumes that scientific objects exist beyond their empirical facets, and that they are 'structured' in certain ways, giving them the powers to act the way they do in experimental conditions.[62] Scientific objects, moreover, are considered 'emergent', that is, it is emphasised that often the 'conjunction of two or more aspects gives rise to new phenomena – which have properties irreducible to those of constituents'.[63] Thus, water and its properties, although based on hydrogen and oxygen atoms and their properties, cannot be reduced to them.

Philosophical realists recognise that we have no direct access to 'truths' about the world. It follows that the theory of truth that underlies philosophical realism is not the 'correspondence theory of truth', whereby scientific models are seen to 'reflect' an unproblematically accessed reality. Instead, science is seen as characterised by 'transitive' truths, but also by 'alethic truths'.

The philosophical realists in the Bhaskarian vein accept that the meanings of our concepts are not constituted through simple reference to an object but through a web of meanings: words and concepts are given meanings through their relations with other words and concepts. However, the relationship between the 'signifier' and the 'signified' is not entirely discursive and unstable. This is because the interplay of

[59] Bhaskar (1978: 13). [60] Bhaskar (1978: 26). [61] Bhaskar (1978: 26).
[62] Bhaskar (1978: 33–6). [63] A. Sayer (2000: 12–13).

meanings, for the philosophical realists, is not just a question of 'difference', as the poststructuralists would have it.[64] Rather, philosophical realists see meaning as constituted through triangular relations of signification between the signifier, the signified and a referent ('that which we speak or write about, be it something physical or a discursive object such as a story'[65]). Meaning is still constituted through difference but, contra the poststructuralists, not *only* through difference.[66]

It follows that scientific theories do not simply 'reflect' the world, they 'suggest a resemblance' between the transitive concepts and the intransitive objects of study through the use of various metaphors or analogies (that are rooted in the social intersubjective understandings or metaphorical structures).[67] Scientific theories, through concepts and metaphors, build a descriptive picture, or interpretation, 'of a possible world, a possible causal complex, which is presumed to be responsible for producing the phenomena we are interested in explaining'.[68] Scientific accounts 'are interpretative and based on implicit and explicit conventions of language', but these 'conventions are also *projective*, the model describes and posits existential hypotheses about entities and their relations'.[69]

Philosophical realists also argue that beyond our pragmatic and conventional 'metaphorical' truth claims, an independent reality must be presumed to exist. Since science does not simply 'create' the intransitive world through its models and theories, it must be accepted that there are also intransitive truths (alethic truths) in objects, and between them, that pre-exist our accounts – although we can never have direct access to these truths (*our* truth claims are always transitive and metaphorical).[70] It is pointed out that intransitive reality, and its alethic truths, are impossible to escape, even for those who deny their existence. Indeed, although we can 'say' and 'think' whatever we want about the state of the world, the intransitive world resists our thoughts, or at least our actions, from being 'whatever': although I can say that I can fly, the world will teach me otherwise. There are some constraints on our transitive, or 'metaphorical' truths, set by the nature of the intransitive ontological reality beyond our descriptions.

[64] Derrida (1978). [65] A. Sayer (2000: 36).
[66] For a more detailed discussion see A. Sayer (2000: 35–40).
[67] Patomäki (2002: 149). [68] Patomäki (2002: 78–9). Italics removed.
[69] Patomäki (2002: 79). Original italics. [70] Bhaskar (1989: 152).

It follows that, for the philosophical realists, explanatory accounts are not 'relative' in the sense that they are for the pragmatists, for example. Because science is conceived as a human practice of trying to devise 'depth explanations' of the intransitive world, it is still possible in principle to provide justifiable grounds for preferring one theory over another. Despite recognising the transitivity of science, philosophical realism maintains the hope in the principle of 'judgemental rationalism', that is, the assumption we have some basis for making rational judgements between theoretical accounts. Not all accounts are equal, either because evidence in no way holds up with some accounts or because the existential claims made in accounts are simply not plausible. The criteria for plausible explanations are different, however, from the empiricist accounts: ontological plausibility, scope of evidential support (across kinds of data), self-reflexivity are all taken into account along with methodological precision.

This account of the nature of reality, truth and scientific theories has important consequences for how we think about causes. The philosophical realist accounts of cause challenge Humeanism on a fundamental level: they challenge the regularity assumption, the basing of science on the observable as well as the logical necessity assumption.

The emphasis of the philosophical realist accounts is on making an ontological distinction between causes and events as the empirical facets of causes: 'the Humean account depends upon a misidentification of causal laws with their empirical grounds'.[71] For realists what is important in tracking causal connections is not identification of law-like regularities of empirical observables but, rather, the description of the real properties, structures and generative mechanisms that underlie the actualisation of events and their empirical observations.

Also, central to the philosophical realist accounts is the reinstatement of the notion of *natural necessity* between causes and effects.[72] Causes, for the philosophical realists, are real ontological entities that ontologically necessitate their effects: causal necessity is not 'logical' but 'natural'. Causes are seen as 'naturally necessitating' because, crucially, causes are conceived to consist of, and carry, 'causal powers' to bring about effects. These causal powers arise from the internal constitution, or the ontological structure, of objects.

[71] Bhaskar (1989: 16). [72] Harré and Madden (1975).

The philosophical realist 'causal powers' account presupposes a 'deep ontological' conception of the nature of causation, which is very different from the Humeans' 'flat ontology'. Harré and Madden argue:

> We conceive our world to be an interacting system of powerful particulars. The patterns of events and ensembles of properties which they produce in their interaction upon one another give rise to the multitudinous phenomena of the world we experience ... [O]ur differences with the Humean or positivist tradition are deep ... [W]hen we think of causality and action we look to such images as springtime plant forcing its way upwards towards the light, as the pulsing, surging movement of the protoplasm within an amoeba, of a flash of radiation as a positron and electron meet, of the enormous flux of electromagnetic radiation from a star, of the mobility and imaginative control of his own actions exercised by a human being, of the potent configuration of a magnetic field. For us, a billiard ball table is relevant to philosophy only in so far as it is conceived of as surrounded by the players, and embedded within a gravitational field.[73]

Importantly, just because the causal powers and structures (behind observed events) that Harré and Madden point to are often unobservable, sometimes unexercised, or exercised unrealised, this does not, for a philosophical realist, entail the rejection of their reality or causal necessity. Bhaskar argues, on the basis of the notion of different ontological levels (real, actual and empirical), that the absence of empirical regularity does not mean the non-existence of real or necessary causes on the deeper ontological level. Causation is not tied to regularities, or observability, neither is the reality of objects: 'to be [and to cause] is not to be perceived, but ... to be able to do'.[74] Importantly, within the philosophically realist framework, causation is tied to the reality of objects. What justifies the reality of objects is not perceptual criteria, but rather the 'causal criterion'. It is argued that something is real if it has the capacity to make a difference in states of affairs: what can be conceptualised to cause, can be conceived as real.[75]

Also, philosophical realists make a distinction between open and closed systems. It is accepted that in experimental environments we can sometimes isolate the effects of single causal mechanisms and, hence,

[73] Harré and Madden (1975: 7). [74] Bhaskar (1998: 12).

[75] Importantly neither perceptual nor causal criteria are met by fictional objects. Bhaskar (1991: 122).

achieve the 'closed systems' invariance presupposed by the Humeans (making absolute 'logical deduction' and prediction possible). However, the philosophical realists emphasise that causal laws do not refer to mere regularities of observables, or the logical relations between statements pertaining to them, but rather to the real causal structures and powers that make things happen. Also, it is noted that the empirical world consists of the complex coming together of all kinds of real causal laws (or powers), and that, hence, the world outside experimental closure is 'open'. The lack of regularity and (logical) closure does not entail the lack of causally necessary relations since '[l]aws do not describe the patterns or legitimate the predictions of kinds of events. Rather they must be conceived . . . as situating limits and imposing constraints on the types of action possible for a given kind of entity.'[76] Philosophical realists argue that although laws (or powers) of nature are naturally necessitating, they are not (pre)determining, nor regularity-deterministic, that is, perfectly predictable on the event level.[77]

Critical realism and the social sciences

Critical realism, the social science version of Bhaskar's philosophical realism, is based firmly on the wider philosophically realist assumptions.[78] Critical realists argue that social science, just as natural science, is based on the study of the causal powers or properties of objects: the social sciences try to gain an understanding of the causal powers of agents and of their social context, and through such understanding, be able to account for the complex concrete processes in the social world. This approach echoes Marx in that he, too, believed that empirical observation cannot be the only aim of science – for 'all science would be superfluous if the form of appearance of things directly coincided with their essence'.[79] Marx too emphasised that social sciences should study, not merely the patterns of behaviour of people, but the underlying structures of 'social relations' that shape social life and as a result, contrary to popular belief that he was a positivist, Marx could be said to be an important example of a philosophical realist thinker: he did

[76] Bhaskar (1978: 65). [77] Bhaskar (1978: 105).

[78] Initially referred to as 'critical naturalism' as Bhaskar accepts naturalism but on anti-positivist grounds. See Bhaskar (1979: 3).

[79] Farr (1991: 114).

not see laws as regularities or 'when A, then B' forces, but rather he believed in the ontologically real nature of society, its complexity and the importance of studying its 'inner mechanisms'.[80]

Bhaskar argues that the social sciences can be studied scientifically, although because of the ontological differences between the fields, not exactly in the same manner as the natural sciences.[81] However, this 'pro-science' view is premised on a firm rejection of a dominant positivist view of the nature and methods of science. We have seen in chapter 2 that the empiricist-positivist Humean view of science and of causation has played a crucial role in shaping twentieth-century philosophy of social science, giving rise to reasons–causes, and constitutive–causal theory, dichotomies. Because critical realism challenges the Humean account of cause, it can also challenge the dichotomies that this view of causation has given rise to in the social sciences.

Critical realists argue that causes in the social world, as well as in the natural world, must be accepted as real. The social world can also be seen as constituted by various ontological objects (though not necessarily 'things') that have powers to bring about change. Crucially, social causes, for critical realism, always exist within 'open systems': the social world can be seen to consist of open systems in which 'multiple generating mechanisms operate simultaneously on various levels' and 'are in constant flux'.[82] Critical realists argue that we should not assume the existence of Humean 'closed system' causal relations in the social world:[83] to assume the existence of invariant regularities and the possibility of predictive success is to misunderstand the nature of the social world. Critical realists, however, can deal with the difficulties of obtaining invariant regularities and with the complexity of social causation because, for them, the lack of regularity and closure does not mean the lack of causally necessary relations. This is because prediction is not necessary for causal accounts, nor are regularities a necessary or a sufficient condition of causation.[84]

[80] For accounts that emphasise Marx's philosophical realism see Meikle (1985). Pike (1999) traces the Aristotelian leanings in his work. It should be noted, however, that just because Marx was a philosophical realist, this does not make philosophical realism Marxist, as Brown, for example, has argued (2007).

[81] Bhaskar (1979: 26–7). [82] Porpora (1987: 7).

[83] Nor in the natural world where they do not exist in open systems but are merely generated by scientists in specifically conditioned closed system environments.

[84] Bhaskar (1978: 12).

Owing to the stratified conception of reality adopted from the wider philosophically realist framework, critical realists can, crucially, deal with unobservables as causes. For a critical realist, a cause does not need to be actualised on the 'event' or 'empirical' level of reality to be 'real'. This separation of real causes from their empirical facets allows the critical realists to escape the distinctly Humean problem of studying mere observables, which has severely limited the appeal of causal explanation in the social sciences. With the help of the philosophically realist account of causation, the critical realists can learn to recognise the causal role of unobservables – such as ideas, rules and discourses – that social sciences have tended to frame as non-causal. Indeed, critical realism allows us to criticise empiricism for being, as Collier puts it, 'irretrievably actualist in its account of causation'.[85]

Contra hermeneutic theorists, the critical realists also reframe the reasons–causes problem. If the regularity account of causation with its assumptions of lawfulness, observability and regularity-determinism is rejected, we can recognise reasons as causal in the sense that they 'produce' outcomes, that is, they are the 'because' of which purposive actions happen. For critical realists, reasons are causes because 'the agent's reasons are a necessary condition for the bodily movements that occurred, in the straightforward sense that had the agent not possessed them they would not have occurred'.[86] It is because reasons are causes that an interpretive hermeneutic approach to the social world is adopted by the critical realists. However, it should be noted that while critical realists see interpretive methods as central to their analyses, they are also sceptical of those interpretive and hermeneutic approaches that assume that actors' perceptions or quoted reasons are the sole and a trustworthy source of analysis. Critical realists emphasise that interpretation of reasons and motives should always take place in the context of conceptual systems that provide an understanding of why actors might also lie or be mistaken about what the real reasons for their actions might be.

Bhaskar's critical realism also involves rethinking the causal nature of the social context of agents. Bhaskar's model of the social world, the Transformational Model of Social Action (TMSA), is, like Marx's system, based on accepting the social context of human action as causal

[85] Collier (1994: 75). [86] Bhaskar (1979: 113–14).

and, hence, as ontologically real.[87] The social world is not reducible to agents or their behaviour – agents, Bhaskar argues, live in social conditions that pre-exist them. These social conditions, for Bhaskar, are captured by the notion of social structures. Bhaskar argues that social structures (1) unlike natural structures, do not exist independently of the activities they govern, (2) do not exist independently of agents' conceptions of what they are doing, and are only (3) relatively enduring.[88] Nevertheless, they are real and form an ontologically emergent level of reality. Bhaskar argues that social structures and agents always work in relation to each other, but that there is an 'ontological hiatus' between them, that is, they are different kinds of 'things'.[89]

Crucially, Bhaskar conceives of social structures as causal. But causal in what sense? Although Bhaskar has at times drawn an analogy between social structures and electromagnetic fields as a type of cause,[90] an analogy that arguably raises mechanistic pushing and pulling images of causation, it is crucial to note that he also recognises that social structures should not really be considered causal in the sense of 'pushing and pulling' (efficient cause) or as 'deterministic' in the regularity-deterministic, 'when A, then B' sense. Nor are they to be seen as 'external' to agents: they are seen as the necessary conditions of social agency that condition the range of agents' actions. Two key causal concepts specifically are invoked to describe the nature of the causal conditioning that social structures have over human agents. At times social structures are seen as the *INUS-conditions* of social action: social structure is a 'necessary condition' among other (insufficient conditions) in bringing about an effect.[91] At other times, an Aristotelian *material cause* analogy is drawn on. Bhaskar argues that his Transformational Model of Social Activity 'suggests a radically different conception of social activity . . . an essentially Aristotelian one: the paradigm being that of a sculptor at work, fashioning a product out of the material and tools available to him or her . . . to use the Aristotelian terms, then, in every process of productive activity a material as well as efficient cause is necessary'.[92] Both of these conceptualisations

[87] As Marx puts it: 'men make history but not in the conditions of their own choosing'. Marx (1975: 115). For TMSA see Bhaskar (1979: 42–3).
[88] Bhaskar (1979: 48–9).
[89] Bhaskar (1998: 37).
[90] Bhaskar and Harré (2001: 34).
[91] Bhaskar (1979: 165, 207); Patomäki (2002: 76–7).
[92] Bhaskar (1989: 77–8).

are useful in moving beyond classical 'when A, then B' conceptions of causality and as a result critical realism is able to deal with the causal role of social structures in a more useful manner: through distancing *ubiquity causal determinist* arguments (everything has a cause) from the Humean *regularity-deterministic causal* accounts (when A, then B).

The critical realist conception of social science is ontological, yet it is not 'objectivist'. It is accepted that the social sciences are characterised by 'double hermeneutic' relations with objects of study and that the social and political context of all social accounts matters. Critical realism also accepts epistemological relativism, that is, the assumption that there are many ways to study the social world and that all social accounts are socially contextual and fallible.[93] Moreover, methodologically, it is emphasised that the empiricist observational methods alone do not give us causal explanations, but importantly, neither are they useless. We can use both qualitative and interpretive data, and quantitative and statistical methods, for both can give us useful insights. As Sayer explains, 'intensive' and 'extensive' methods do different things but both have the capacity to bring to light social causes.[94] Most critical realists accord priority to qualitative data and interpretive methods in getting at causal relations as qualitative data and interpretive methods often help more directly in detailing the workings of causal processes in the social world, but this does not mean that other methodological approaches, including quantitative methods, are rejected.[95] Critical realism is committed to methodological pluralism.

But what should a causal account of a social object look like, according to critical realism? Bhaskar has put forward the so-called RRRE pattern of explanation. An explanation starts with Resolution, that is, the analysis of the various possible causal components of an object of study. Then, the researcher goes through the step of Redescription, that is, (s)he redescribes the various mechanisms identified through the theory (s)he holds/tests. Next, the researcher Retrodicts the causes of the components of his/her explanation, thus widening the sphere of explanation. The process of explanation will, in open systems, also include the crucial process of Elimination: there may be any number of causes that could have co-determined an event but that can be eliminated. What we end up with is an account in form close to an everyday explanation where causal connections are described in terms of transitive

[93] Patomäki (2002: 9). [94] Sayer (1992). [95] Patomäki (2002: 135–6).

verbs: a causal explanation is 'a historical narrative in which a multiplicity of transitive verbs maps a complex causal sequence'.[96] This process of explanation is strikingly different from the Humean way of approaching causation. It is, in some ways, similar to the pragmatist conception of causal narratives (emphasis on pragmatic complexity-sensitive causal stories) but, in contrast to pragmatism, it is ontologically grounded and maintains a belief in judgemental rationalism, that is, the idea that we can have good reasons to accept the plausibility of one account of a social process over another.

Limitations of philosophical and critical realism on causation

The philosophical realist framing of science and social science is interesting in that it provides a radically different understanding of reality, and of causation, than most modern philosophical accounts. Although philosophical realism has been a red flag to the anti-realist traditions in modern philosophy, from radical empiricists to pragmatists and conventionalists, its arguments have been considered increasingly persuasive by many philosophers of science with regard to causation. While it would of course be difficult to prove conclusively the correctness of any philosophy of causation, it is accepted here that philosophical realism provides good reasons for accepting the ontological reality of causes, their ontologically deep nature and the legitimacy of their study by scientists, in both natural science and social inquiry. Chapter 6 seeks to summarise and defend the basic insights of the realist philosophy of causation: it will be argued that we should accept the philosophical realist framing of causation because it allows us to 'deepen' our understanding of causes and causal analysis in three important ways. However, philosophical realism, like no philosophy of causation, is self-evidently unproblematic. Not only is it possible for empiricists and pragmatists to attack the idea of reality in general, although these arguments will not be rehearsed again here,[97] but also a number of 'internal' limitations could be seen to characterise a philosophically realist challenge to the Humean discourse of causation. Among the philosophical realists, there is, arguably, some lack of clarity with regard to

[96] Collier (1994: 122).

[97] For sophisticated defences of empiricism see, for example, Bas Van Fraassen's account (1980) and for a pragmatist anti-realist account see Rorty (1980).

the definition of causation, whether it can be characterised as efficient causation, as well as with regard to the notions of 'mechanism' and 'condition' frequently used by the philosophically realist accounts.

The philosophically realist notion of cause is much wider and more 'common-sensical' than that most philosophers and social scientists are used to because of the influence of Humeanism. For philosophical realists causes are seen as those things, forces, powers, mechanisms or sets of relations that make things happen or 'trigger' events.[98] Nevertheless, in my view the connotations attached to the notion of cause have not been given adequate thought by the philosophical realists. As a result, they have predominantly conceptualised causes through the efficient cause metaphor – what is considered here an unnecessarily narrow and mechanistic conceptual frame.

The non-Bhaskarian philosophical realists are especially tied to the efficient cause notion. Harré and Madden, for example, define causation and causal powers squarely through the metaphor of efficient cause as Paul Lewis has perceptively pointed out.[99] For them, 'causation always involves a material particular which produces or generates something', that is, '[powerful] particulars are to be conceived as causal agents'.[100] The causal powers metaphor refers only to the powers of particulars to 'act' as 'moving causes', that is, to 'push and pull'.[101] Crucially, this reduction of causes to efficient causes is behind the refusal of philosophical realists such as Harré and Varela to conceptualise non-agent-like factors as causal. For them, social structural causation is not considered causal because social structures' 'causal powers' are not equitable with the agency of powerful particulars: social structures are not 'sources of change' in an efficient way – for they are not powerful particulars that, by virtue of their own nature, produce changes in the material world. The only 'powerful particulars', the 'sources of activity' and, hence, the only causes in the social world, for Harré and Varela, are individual agents.[102]

Efficient causes have also been important in Bhaskar's critical realism: they have referred, much like for Harré and Varela, to those things that through their action precipitate change. In the social world, for example, human agents have been seen as efficient causes, as the 'only

[98] These triggers can also be internal to the objects. Bhaskar (1978: 83).
[99] P. Lewis (2000). See also Ruth Groff's discussion (2004: 107–9)
[100] Harré and Madden (1975: 5). [101] Harré and Madden (1975: 6).
[102] P. Lewis (2000: 255–7).

moving forces in history'.[103] However, the Bhaskarian critical realist treatment of causation cannot be reduced to the idea of efficient causation in the same sense as causation has been in many modern mechanistic accounts. First, it should be noted that the notion of efficient cause has carried an unusually broad meaning in critical realist frameworks. The notion of efficient causes has not referred to merely the agents, or their actions, but also their reasons for action, and even the ideas or discourses that have informed their actions. It could be argued that the reason for the unusually wide notion of efficient cause is that the category of efficient cause in critical realism has, in fact, subsumed three different categories of cause: what in Aristotelian terms can be seen as efficient, final and formal causes. In order to clarify the critical realist treatment of causation, chapter 6 seeks to 'open up' this unusually broad category of efficient cause.

It should also be noted, moreover, that Bhaskar has rejected the Harré and Varela argument with regard to the nature of social structures: crucially, through expanding the meaning of the notion of cause. Indeed, Bhaskarian critical realism has sought explicitly to open up the meaning of the notion of cause beyond the (unusually broad) efficient cause category by, interestingly, drawing on the Aristotelian notion of material cause. The Aristotelian definition of material cause, some critical realists argue, provides us with a useful way to frame the causal nature of social structures.[104] Aristotle's material cause refers, as we have seen in chapter 1, to 'that out of which something comes to be'.[105] Critical realists have been attracted to the Aristotelian notion because it exemplifies well the causal powers of context or, if you like, 'passive' conditioning causation. The material cause analogy helps critical realists to define the 'way' in which social structures are causal: they are not 'pushing and pulling' efficient causes but, rather, provide a causal context for efficient moving causes (agents). As Paul Lewis argues:

> Just as a sculptor fashions a product out of the raw materials and tools available to him, so social actors produce their actions out of pre-existing social structure. Like the medium in which the sculptor works, pre-existing

[103] Bhaskar quoted in Groff (2004: 102). However, it remains a contested matter whether individuals are the only moving forces. Some critical realists have attacked the individualist premise that this argument presupposes. See, for example, Benton (1998).

[104] Bhaskar (1989: 77–8); P. Lewis (2002: 20–1).

[105] Aristotle (1998: 115).

> social structure lacks the capacity to initiate activity and make things of its own accord – social actors are the only efficient causes or prime movers in society – but it does affect the course of events in the social world by influencing the actions that people choose to undertake . . . And by influencing the behaviour of social actors, pre-existing social structure makes a difference to and hence exerts a (material) causal influence over social life.[106]

This argument concerning the material causality of social structures, importantly, is the main claim behind the critical realist insistence on the causal powers of social structures.

While such an expansion of the meaning of the concept of cause – something that is supported in chapter 6 – Bhaskar's account of social structures has, arguably, acquired some problematic characteristics through the use of the material cause analogy. Because Bhaskar uses the notion of material cause for two different purposes, matter as 'material cause' and social structures as 'material cause', the meaning of the notion 'material cause' has become confused. Bhaskar, in fact, ends up not being able to make conceptual distinctions between material and social structural causes. In his 1996 reply to Harré, for example, Bhaskar draws on the notion of material cause in two senses, material causes as material resources and material causes as social structural causes, and gets the two confused.[107] Bhaskar's treatment of material causes is not only conceptually unclear but seems to lead to a conflation of the two types of material causes. Indeed, on occasion Bhaskar ends up, misleadingly, referring to social structures as literally akin to material 'things'.[108]

It could be argued that, although Bhaskar is right to rethink the concept of cause and, indeed, the way in which social structures are causal, the material cause analogy is not necessarily a coherent one by which to understand social structural causation.[109] It could be argued that to treat social structural causes as 'material causes' is, arguably, to narrow down the causal nature of social structures unnecessarily. This analogy should be rethought. This is what chapter 6 seeks to do by advancing a clearer and more pluralistic understanding of causes and their role in social structural causation.

There are also problems with the philosophically realist notion of causal mechanisms. The philosophical and critical realists have avoided

[106] P. Lewis (2002: 20–1). [107] Bhaskar and Harré (2001: 29)
[108] Bhaskar and Harré (2001: 34).
[109] As Ruth Groff has also argued (2004: 109).

the mechanistic and regularity-dependent definitions of causal mechanisms characteristic of many empiricist accounts,[110] by seeing causal mechanisms as ontological and as dynamic rather than as 'mechanistic'. However, it is not by any means obvious what the concept of mechanism refers to in philosophical and critical realist frameworks. Specifically, the equation of the concept of cause with the notion of causal mechanism, it could be argued, is far from straightforward. This is important to recognise especially as it is precisely the association of causal descriptions with mechanistic analogies that has turned off many interpretive scholars from philosophical and critical realism. The relationship of causes and mechanisms is not a self-evident one: and has not been clarified well enough within the realist philosophical tradition.

There are issues also with the notion of 'condition'. Bhaskar makes a distinction between causes and conditions but it is not clear what this distinction entails. Does Bhaskar want to argue that conditions are not (ontological) causes?[111] Clarifying the concept of condition is important but has not been dealt with consistently enough by Bhaskar or the critical realist tradition. This is an important weakness, not least in that lack of clarity on the causal nature of conditions has enabled many anti-causal social theorists and IR theorists to continue to treat conditions, such as discursive conditions of possibility, as non-causal, despite the implicit causal implications of this term.

Chapter 6 argues that a three-fold ontological 'deepening' of the concept of cause is crucial in giving an adequate account of causation. In so doing, it is accepted that philosophical realism and critical realism are highly insightful. However, while these approaches are drawn on, the weaknesses of the philosophical and critical realist accounts of cause will also have to be addressed. In chapter 6, this is attempted through 'broadening', as well as deepening, the meaning of the notion of cause.

Philosophical and critical realism in IR: Wendt, Dessler, Wight and Patomäki

Philosophical realism is not new to IR: it has been drawn upon by a small selection of IR theorists, notably by Alexander Wendt, David

110 In the social sciences see, for example, Elster (1989) and Hedström and Swedberg (1998).
111 See Collier (1994: 125–7).

Dessler, Colin Wight and Heikki Patomäki.[112] These theorists make some important contributions to rethinking causation in IR. However, it is also noted that these theorists do not always apply the philosophically realist conception of causation consistently or fully and that, hence, room remains for a clearer and more comprehensive realist account of causal analysis to be developed for the purposes of IR theorising.

Alexander Wendt was one of the first IR theorists to draw on the philosophically realist approach. Wendt's initial aim was to challenge the Waltzian model of explanation through challenging the conception of agency and structure that underlay Waltz's theorising.[113] Wendt challenged the neorealist conception of the international system on the basis of drawing from philosophically realist meta-theory in combination with Giddens's 'structuration theory'.[114] By emphasising that structure is made up through the process of social interaction between agents, Wendt argued that 'anarchy' in international politics is not 'immutable', but 'socially constructed' through historical patterns of social interaction.[115] In his *Social Theory of International Politics*, the focus of the discussion here, Wendt also wanted to challenge the rationalist–reflectivist divide in IR through reconceptualising the notion of cause.

Drawing on philosophical realism, Wendt proposed a 'philosophically principled middle way' between rationalism and reflectivism in IR.[116] Wendt wanted to show that it is by no means necessary to portray the rationalist and reflectivist approaches in IR as oppositional 'zero-sum' approaches, but that, instead, it is possible to see them as complementary.[117] He has drawn on Bhaskar's realist conceptualisation of science and of causation to ground his synthesis of rationalist and reflectivist theorising. Thus, he argues that science is not simply about observing empirical regularities and about predicting 'closed system' outcomes. Nor is causal explanation, for him, defined through regularities but, rather, it refers to the inquiry into 'why', in reference

[112] Although their work has often been misunderstood in the discipline. Kurki (2007).

[113] Wendt (1987).

[114] Giddens (1984) sees social as constituted by 'mutually constituting' relations of agents and structures. Structures make social action possible while social action constitutes structures.

[115] Wendt (1992). [116] Wendt (1999a: 2). [117] Wendt (1999b: 102).

to generative mechanisms, something occurs.[118] He asserts, against the rationalists, that 'causation is a relation in nature, not in logic' and, against the reflectivists, that ideas do not preclude causal effects.[119] He also argues that all IR theories can do causal theorising: there is no basis for apartheid separation of causal and constitutive theorising.[120] Wendt, then, has challenged the traditional Humean framing of causation in IR and has, thereby, pointed to the weakness of the rationalist–reflectivist dichotomisation.

However, Wendt also introduces some curiously Humean aspects into his account of causation. It follows that his treatment of the causal–constitutive theorising dichotomy actually ends up reproducing the very divisionary logic that he, through philosophical realism, tried to transcend.

Wendt asserts that a relation between things is causal when cause 'X is necessary for effect Y', and 'when X is prior to and independent of Y'.[121] These criteria for causal analysis are curiously reminiscent of the Humean approach to causation. The notion of 'independence' of causes and effects, for example, arises from the Humean philosophy of causation. Humeans need to argue that causes and effects have to be 'independent' because they need to be 'observed' independently. However, for the philosophical realists 'independence' of causes and effects means little; for them science looks for how things are *linked* on the deeper ontological levels:

> The apparent independence of events upon which Hume's arguments and indeed the whole positivist tradition ultimately rests is . . . an illusion which has been fostered by the undoubted fact that events which are identified as cause and effect are capable of independent identification and thus *a fortiori* of independent description. But the descriptions under which they are independent do not include their causal efficacy or their origin. Considered as causes and effects they are not independent for they are related through the generating mechanisms upon which they operate and through which they are produced.[122]

Causes, for philosophical realists, are *ontologically* related to the effects and, hence, I argue in agreement with Harré and Madden that emphasising the 'independence' of causes and effects is an unnecessary

[118] Wendt (1999a: 77). [119] Wendt (1999a: 81). [120] Wendt (1999a: 165–6).
[121] Wendt (1999a: 79). [122] Harré and Madden (1975: 130).

criterion for causation. To maintain such a criterion means, as we will see, that one may come to assign as non-causal relations that should in fact be interpreted within a causal framework (for example, constitutive norms).

Temporal priority, too, seems to have Humean connotations. Temporal priority was the only way for Hume to distinguish causes from effects: causes were those events/particulars *observed* prior to effects. Philosophically realist accounts have not drawn on such a criterion, as causes have not been defined by their observational status, but in terms of 'depth ontology'. Acceptance of such a criterion is, arguably, not just unnecessary for a philosophical realist, but also has adverse side-effects: it leads to a misleading understanding of the nature of some causes. It is conceivable that certain causes, while they pre-exist effects, do not pre-exist them in the mechanistic 'first A, then B' manner that Wendt seems to imply, but rather cause 'simultaneously' (through 'conditioning').[123] When it comes to these kinds of causes, the requirement of temporal priority of the form 'X must be prior to Y' confuses more than it clarifies.

Moreover, and crucially, Wendt endorses a rather narrow understanding of 'constitutive' theorising. Initially, Wendt defines constitutive theorising as something that accounts for 'the properties of things by reference to the structures in virtue of which they exist', how a thing, whether a natural or social object, is constituted.[124] While such a definition is compatible with philosophical and critical realism, Wendt narrows down the meaning of constitutive theorising to so-called 'conceptual relations'. He argues that, while causal questions ask about how 'independently existing X produced an independently existing Y', constitutive how-possible and what-questions ask about 'conceptually necessitating' relations.[125] Wendt talks of various things as 'constitutive' conceptually necessitating relations. Thus, 'treaty violations' are conceptually related to the discourse that defines promises, while 'terrorism' is conceptually dependent on the discourse that delegitimates non-state violence. Also, rules, discourses and social structures are, for Wendt, 'conceptually constitutive' of objects, agents or actions.[126]

Given his background in philosophical realism this 'conceptual' treatment of 'constitution' of social life is curious. Wendt does not

[123] For interesting discussion of time and causation see, for example, Faye (1989).
[124] Wendt (1999b: 107–12). [125] Wendt (1999a: 83, 84).
[126] Wendt (1999a: 84).

adequately highlight the fact that, for philosophical realists, conceptual relations matter, not just as conceptual relations, but in that they give rise to ontologically necessitating social relations and practices.[127] It is important to note that the constitution of the social world is, for the philosophical realists, not just conceptual but also ontological, that is, conceptual relations that define meanings play themselves out in the (materially embodied) world outside of language. Constitutive theorising, then, is not just about inquiring into conceptual relations (meanings) but about inquiring into how they play themselves out in the social world, giving rise to certain practices and social relations. For example, while the discourse of diplomacy constitutes (or defines) – conceptually – the meaning of 'interstate bargaining', philosophical realists would point out that the same discourse (along with other factors) causes – in a naturally necessitating way (ontologically but not in a 'when A, then B' manner) – processes of interstate bargaining, that is, it conditions the intentional actions of agents. Wendt's definition of constitutive relations as conceptually necessary leads him to obfuscate this meaning of constitution that is central to philosophical realism.

The combination of the curiously Humean criteria for causation and the narrow treatment of constitutive theorising gives rise to an unnecessary dichotomisation of causal and constitutive theorising in Wendt's conceptual framework. Despite emphasising that most IR theorists do both causal and constitutive forms of theorising, Wendt accepts some of the guiding thoughts of the traditional causal–constitutive division in IR. The 'reasons account', for example, often becomes equated with constitutive theorising in the anti-causal reflectivist sense.[128] He sees constitutive theorising/reasons accounts as, at least potentially, a separable 'non-causal' form of inquiry that is an important end in itself.[129] His account of causation is also characterised by repeated resort to empiricist/positivist terminology about causal relations: he makes repeated references to causal inquiry being about analysing 'independent and dependent variables', and even refers to himself as a positivist.[130] While Wendt's account has taken some important steps in introducing philosophical realism to IR, it could be argued that,

[127] This is especially curious since he seems to accept the naturally necessitating nature of internal relations in the natural world. Wendt (1999a: 83).

[128] See, for example, discussion on Campbell. Wendt (1999a: 56). On confusing statements on reasons and causes see Wendt (2000: 170).

[129] Wendt (1999a: 86).

[130] Wendt (1999a: 85, 39).

in his effort to please both rationalists and reflectivists, Wendt does not distinguish clearly enough the non-Humean philosophically realist account from the (philosophically very different) positivist Humean accounts that dominate the rationalist mainstream in IR. I agree with Colin Wight that Wendt has not made adequately clear that 'consistent scientific realism must eventually lead to a wholesale rejection of positivism'.[131]

Wendt, in the end, largely seems to accept the Hollis and Smith dichotomy, although this dichotomy is based on a Humean notion of causation.[132] The problem with Wendt's account of causal and constitutive theorising is not that he treats constitutive theorising as an adjunct to causal analysis, as the postpositivists argue,[133] but, rather, that he could take his arguments about causation further. As will be seen in the next chapter, Wendt's criteria for distinguishing causal and constitutive theorising can be rejected. To do so chapter 6, paradoxically, takes a cue from Wendt's later work on the world state[134] to initiate an inquiry into the contributions that the Aristotelian conceptions of causation can make to IR.

David Dessler has also drawn on philosophical realism. He has engaged in the agency-structure debates, critiquing Wendt's 'intersubjective' Giddensian conceptualisation of social structure on critical realist lines.[135] However, more importantly for the purposes of this book, he has also critiqued the mainstream positivist understanding of science and causation in IR. Drawing on realist philosophy, Dessler has tried to show that while laws and regularity-based knowledge claims have a role to play in IR, there are other kinds of knowledge claims that we can take as equally 'scientific'.[136] Particularising or interpretive inquiries, he argues, can equally tell us important things: they can fill in the gaps left by the Humean covering-law theorising.[137]

With regard to causation, Dessler has pointed out that the positivist causal theories have led to the adoption of certain problematic tendencies in causal analyses in IR. Specifically, Dessler has argued that because the variable-based inquiries have been prioritised, IR theory has been lacking 'integrative' causal theories, for example, of the causes

131 Wight (2006: 15). 132 See Hollis and Smith (1990: 3).
133 S. Smith (2000). 134 Wendt (2003).
135 That is, his reduction of structure to intersubjective understandings. See Dessler (1989). For more detail see chapter 6.
136 Dessler (1999). 137 Dessler (1999: 136–7).

of war.[138] Because of the dominance of the positivist model of causal analysis, he argues, there have been too few efforts to tie together explanatory factors (the hows and whys) within coherent holistic conceptual frameworks. Rather positivists have favoured assessing the impact of variables 'additively', side by side.[139]

Drawing on philosophical realism, Dessler argues that causal theorising involves not correlating variables, nor locating conditions under which X type of events happen, but, rather, explaining why things happen through accounting for the various causal mechanisms and processes at play in the bringing about of a given event. In giving accounts of causal mechanisms, he contends, we must draw on qualitative and particularised empirical investigation, not just rely on quantification. Dessler argues that our efforts to understand something might start with studying regularities, but that we must move beyond regularities to construct models that actually explain the structures and processes at work. This is the only way we can start distinguishing between causal and accidental sequences and start generating more integrative knowledge claims about the causes of wars.[140]

While helpful in challenging the 'norm' of causal analysis in mainstream IR, Dessler's work also demonstrates some confusion on causation. First, Dessler seems to work on the basis of a confusingly wide conception of positivism and seems to equate a great deal of 'particularising' work with the 'generalising' (Humean) tradition.[141] Occasionally, it seems as if, like King, Keohane and Verba, he wants to show that historical and reconstructive work actually assumes the logic of generalisation and predictability.[142] This is disturbing considering that philosophical realism, as it is understood here (in accordance with Bhaskar), is distinctly anti-positivist and anti-Humean. Dessler, like Wendt, leaves uncertain the relationship between positivism and the realist philosophies of science: he does not discuss how the metatheoretical differences of these approaches translate to differences in how theorists see causation. It follows that despite his potentially

[138] Dessler (1991). [139] Dessler (1991: 339–40). [140] Dessler (1991: 343–5).

[141] He states, for example, that 'positivism is rooted in a realist epistemology'. Dessler (1999: 28). By this he means that positivists believe in a reality independent of the mind and in seeking of truths through our inquiries (Dessler 1999: 24–5). It is hard to see, on the definition of positivism adopted here, how positivism can work on the basis of what seem to be realist ontological assumptions.

[142] Dessler (1999: 30).

ground-breaking philosophical premises, Dessler makes very modest claims about the scope and role of his alternative model of causal theorising.

Also, Dessler does not account for how the philosophically or critically realist conception of causation impacts on reflectivist theorising: he argues that causal explanation is only one tool in social science.[143] However, he fails to explain what the 'other tools' might be and what their relationship to causal theorising is. As a result, the relationship between causal and 'constitutive' theorising is not addressed adequately.

It seems that in order to appease the mainstream, Dessler is content merely to 'tweak' the traditional frameworks in IR – even though his meta-theoretical groundings would give him the opportunity to attack the meta-theoretical premises of IR theorising much more radically. It is the aim of the following chapter to advance a more radical critique of mainstream causal theorising, than that which Dessler has settled for.

The work of Heikki Patomäki and Colin Wight has gone further than that of Wendt and Dessler in challenging the disciplinary framework of IR. Patomäki and Wight have pointed out that IR has been built on a Humean–Kantian philosophical 'problem-field' that needs to be challenged on a fundamental meta-theoretical basis.[144] Drawing on the critical realism of Bhaskar, Patomäki and Wight argue that one of the main reasons for the contemporary disciplinary divide in IR is the acceptance, on all sides of the debate, of an anti-realist approach to social science. If we start from ontology, they assert, we can transcend much of the epistemological infighting in IR between the positivists and the postpositivists. Patomäki and Wight's work has been important in that it has been one of the first consistent and comprehensive challenges to the empiricist positivist conception of science in IR. As will be seen, the argument of chapter 6 will follow similar lines of thought to theirs. However, the aim of this work is to elaborate on the implications of rethinking the meta-theoretical grounds of IR for the issue of causation and causal analysis. This issue, although it has been raised by Patomäki and Wight, has not been dealt with by them in a sufficiently comprehensive manner, certainly in the context of IR debates.

[143] Dessler (1991: 347). [144] Patomäki and Wight (2000).

Patomäki, out of the two, has developed a more distinct account of causation and hence will be discussed in more detail.[145] Patomäki has argued that, on the basis of philosophical and critical realism, we can challenge Humeanism in a fundamental way. Patomäki has sought to follow through with a critical realist naturally necessitating, all-encompassing but non-regularity-deterministic conception of causation.[146] His aim has been to demonstrate that causal accounts are 'of' something, even though they are socially and pragmatically bounded. He has argued – contra positivists, reflectivists and pragmatists – that causes refer to real ontological features of the world. Patomäki admits that interpretation is involved in weighing causal theories against each other. Yet, he argues that dialogue between interpretations is possible, as Patomäki does not deny the ontological existential status of causes beyond our accounts of them.[147]

Importantly, Patomäki has rejected the reduction of causal accounts to regularities, emphasising, instead, that causal accounts in the social world require analysis of 'unobservables', such as reasons, rules, norms and discourses. Contrary to many constructivist and poststructuralist theorists, Patomäki argues that discourses, beliefs, reasons and the historical constitution of actors – all conventionally 'non-causal' in IR – matter precisely because they play crucial causal roles in shaping world politics. It is because the constitution of objects, actors and relations is causal, and because reasons are causes, that hermeneutic and discursive methods are so important for social scientific inquiry.[148]

Patomäki has also emphasised the complexity of causes, and hence the fact that causal accounts in IR need to be complexity-sensitive rather than parsimony-driven and 'variable-based'. He argues that in the social world causes are always complex, exist in complexes of conditions and, hence, that there are never single causes at work.[149] He suggests that causal explanation entails that we account for so-called 'causal complexes'. Causal complexes comprise, according to Patomäki, five necessary elements of social being: 'historically constructed corporeal actors; meaningful, historically structured action; regulative and constitutive rules implicated in every action and the

[145] For Colin Wight's reflections see sections on causal analysis in *Agents, Structures and International Relations* (2006: 21–2, 29–32, 272–9).

[146] Patomäki (1996; 2002: 70–95).

[147] Patomäki (1996); Patomäki and Wight (2000: 225–7).

[148] Patomäki (2002: 89–91).

[149] Patomäki (2002: 118).

constitution of actors; resources as competences and facilities; and relational and positional practices'.[150] These factors – including regulative and constitutive rules – can all be considered as causal. He argues that we can usefully understand different parts of causal complexes as INUS-conditions: they each form a part of the causal complex, they are the 'necessary' but 'insufficient' parts of a causal complex that brings about certain concrete processes or patterns. Crucially, to introduce a consistent philosophically realist premise to Mackie's account of cause,[151] Patomäki redefines the INUS-condition account as follows: a cause for Patomäki is an '**I**nsufficient but **N**on-redundant element of a complex that is itself **U**nnecessary but **S**ufficient for the *production* of a result'.[152] By emphasising that complexes of causes produce results, Patomäki demonstrates that the INUS-condition account can be useful in social sciences but should be combined with a framework that recognises the reality of the complexes of causes. Patomäki also utilises the metaphor of 'material cause' in describing the way in which contextual causes (social structures) are causal: they provide the material out of which social action arises.[153]

As will be seen the arguments of this work move on similar lines to those of Patomäki: this work, too, accepts the ontological reality of causes, also in the social world, and emphasises multi-causality. However, chapter 6 seeks to develop an account that goes beyond that of Patomäki in two key respects. First, the goal is to clarify the consequences that the philosophical realist reframing of causation has for the theoretical debates and disciplinary divisions in IR. Patomäki has not drawn confusing lines of division between causal and constitutive theorising, as Wendt has. Yet, Patomäki does not discuss in any detail the implications that the acceptance of critical realism has for the causal–constitutive divide in IR. Also, besides 'deepening' the notion of cause, chapter 6 seeks consistently to 'broaden' it, thus enabling us to recognise that causes can cause in different ways. The argument advanced

150 Patomäki (2002: 78).

151 Bhaskar notes (1979: 207, fn 23), if somewhat vaguely, that Mackie's definition 'First, by omitting crucial notions of necessity, generation and power . . . is susceptible to well-known paradoxes. Second, in as much as the concept of an INUS condition presupposes the possibility of Humean causal laws, as talk of sufficient conditions and causal regularities indicates, it must be rejected.'

152 Patomäki (2002: 76). Original bold and italics.

153 Patomäki (2002: 119).

here agrees with Patomäki's emphasis on multi-causality, but seeks to take this argument further by elaborating on *how* different factors in a causal complex can be considered causal in different ways. Chapter 6 will argue that especially the material cause analogy dominant in many critical realist frameworks should be and can be rethought.

Conclusion

This chapter has sought to demonstrate that the Humean framing of causation, and the analytical leanings it has given rise to in the philosophy of science, social science and the discipline of IR, can be challenged. The pragmatists have argued that the notion of cause should be considered a pragmatic metaphor that allows us to 'explain', or 'make intelligible'. The key insight of the pragmatists is that our causal explanations always take place in an explanatory context and that the aim of causal explanations is to make the world intelligible. They have also problematised the rationalist belief in the 'objective' nature of causal accounts, and have aimed to do away with the reasons–causes divisionary logic that has been appealed to by many in the social sciences and IR. Furthermore, they have emphasised the multiple ways in which we can talk of causes. However, in emphasising the pragmatic role of causal explanations in human inquiries, these accounts, including Suganami's explanation of causes of war, have denied that causes exist, not only in our narratives but also in the world outside our accounts. This has also entailed the adoption of a relativist stance on causal explanation: what matters is what 'we think' causes are, not what causes 'really' are. Through their acceptance of anti-realist assumptions, the insistence on prioritising epistemological concerns (our knowledge) over ontological ones (what is), it could be argued, the pragmatists are, along with the Humeans, tied to an unnecessary anti-realist philosophical problem-field.

Realist philosophy has sought to challenge the anti-realist trends in modern philosophy by seeking to ground science and causation on an ontological understanding of the nature of the world. Philosophical realism argues that all scientific, and everyday, accounts of the world require the assumption of realism. Philosophical realism challenges the empiricist conception of science that the positivists advocate. It also fundamentally challenges the validity of the Humean framing of causation, both in the natural and in the social sciences. However, much of philosophical realism is still embedded within the efficient cause understanding of causation. Also, the framing of the causal nature of such 'conditioning' causes as social structures has been confusing even when the more 'passive' notion of material causes has been drawn on. Moreover, there have been definitional issues with the notions of mechanism and conditions – philosophical realists have failed to give consistent accounts of what these notions mean and what their relationships to the idea of cause are. Besides the general philosophical problems of philosophical realism, the application of the philosophically realist approach in IR has left certain aspects of the issue of causation unclear. Wendt, for example, seems to have reproduced, rather than transcended, the causal–constitutive division in IR. More remains to be done. Importantly, we must clarify what a coherent philosophically realist conceptualisation of causes entails and what it means for theoretical divisions in IR. Moreover, as will be seen, the 'deepening' of the concept of cause should be tied to the 'broadening out' of that same concept. The next chapter seeks to build a coherent alternative philosophical framework for thinking about causes in IR, a framework that can claim to address some of the central problems of Humean causal analysis in IR, as well as the weaknesses of the previous rethinkers' approaches that have been examined in this chapter.

6 *Rethinking causation: towards a deeper and broader concept of cause*

The previous chapters have sought to demonstrate that contemporary International Relations theorising has been informed by a rather narrow Humean discourse of causal analysis that has been closely entwined with the empiricist and positivist currents of thought in twentieth-century philosophy of science and social science. Chapter 5 has examined some of the alternatives to Humeanism by discussing the pragmatist and the philosophically realist frameworks. These frameworks have sought to challenge the basic precepts of the Humean philosophy of causation, and a handful of IR theorists, Suganami, Wendt, Dessler, Wight and Patomäki, drawing on them, have taken some steps towards rethinking causal analysis in IR. This chapter seeks to build on, but also to go beyond, the previous attempts to reconfigure the nature of causal analysis in IR. It seeks to develop a coherent non-Humean account of cause that both 'deepens' and 'broadens' the meaning of the term 'cause' and that, thereby, enables us to address some of the central theoretical problems that the rationalists and the reflectivists as well as the rethinkers have had with causation in IR.

The first section of this chapter will draw out the nature and implications of the so-called Humean problem-field in IR theorising by summarising the main problems of causal analysis amongst the different theoretical traditions in IR. We will, then, tackle the problems that characterise different IR theoretical approaches through advancing a two-pronged argument. First, drawing on the philosophical realism of Roy Bhaskar, I argue that we should give causation 'deep ontological' meaning. This allows us to deepen our understanding of the types of causal forces that fall within the remit of IR as a social science and provides a more methodologically open set of tools for social scientific causal analysis. Second, drawing on Aristotle's four causes account, I argue that we should broaden the meaning of the notion of cause beyond the 'pushing and pulling' efficient cause metaphor. Through complementing the deeper notion of cause with a broader conceptualisation of how different kinds of causes 'cause', we can clarify how to transcend the causal–constitutive theory divide in IR, as well as elucidate how to avoid the problems of theoretical reductionism in the discipline. The rethought conceptualisation of causation provides a more holistic and pluralistic ontological, methodological and epistemological basis for engagement with causation in IR, thus in part directing IR theoretical frameworks towards new ways of dealing with questions and debates about world politics. The focus in this chapter is on resolving philosophical and theoretical issues. Illustration of how this rethought notion of cause impacts on substantive IR research into world politics will be left for chapter 7.

Causal analysis in IR: the Humean problem-field

It was argued in Part I that the discipline of IR has framed its debates on causation drawing on the Humean conception of causation. The acceptance of Humean assumptions has had some crucial consequences in contemporary IR theorising: it has given rise to a so-called Humean problem-field.[1] What does this mean? It means that IR theoretical treatments of causal analysis have been constrained – albeit in a variety of different ways – by having been informed by the Humean discourse of causation. This section seeks to integrate the key aspects of the analysis so far and to build a coherent overall picture of the Humean problem-field to be tackled in IR.

Rationalism in the Humean problem-field

The rationalists in IR have most systematically and openly sought to follow the precepts of the Humean assumptions in IR causal analysis. Most rationalists have explicitly accepted the Humean regularity criteria, although some have adopted the Humean assumptions in implicit and unsystematic form. In chapter 3 we observed that the rationalists go about their inquiries into world politics in a particular fashion owing to the acceptance of the Humean conception of causal analysis. Three observations were made about the kinds of consequences that the Humean assumptions have had on rationalist causal analysis in IR.

[1] This is a term also utilised to powerful effect by Patomäki and Wight (2000: 215) in their description of anti-realist tendencies in IR theory.

First, the rationalists tend to advocate generalising and 'additive' causal analysis; second, they attach regularity-deterministic 'when A, then B' logics to causal descriptions; and, third, they have difficulties in exploring causal explanation through conceptualisation of unobservable aspects of the social world, such as processes of social construction. While amongst those who have accepted the Humean framework as a given these characteristics have not been seen as particularly unproblematic – arguably they have been seen as natural limitations of causal research in general – the positivist approaches have been much criticised as a result of these leanings. These characteristics it is argued here are *particularly* Humean. International Relations theorising has suffered from unnecessarily restrictive *methodological*, *epistemological* and *ontological* assumptions as a result of the taken-for-granted influence of the Humean discourse of causation.

The rationalists are, first, *methodologically* hindered in that, because of the empiricist grounding of knowledge on the perceived, their causal analyses cannot draw on certain important interpretive types of methods of analysis and are unable to use and evaluate certain important types of evidence. Hermeneutic interpretation of reasons and motives of action, and their meaningful context, for example, is largely ignored by the positivist causal analysts: interpretive study of meanings, motives and reasons is not deemed important, and if so, only to the extent that reasons, motives and meanings can be shown to have 'stable' observable outcomes.[2] Also, methods of and approaches to discourse analysis are not engaged with, outside of quantifiable strands of linguistic analysis exemplified by content analysis. This is because, in failing to conform to Humean criteria, the methods of discourse analysis, in Foucauldian or poststructuralist senses, for example, are considered unsystematic and unscientific.[3] Even qualitative or historical evidence is used in a narrow sense by the rationalists: when qualitative or historical data are used, they are made to conform to a form of 'localised' regularity analysis; we look for general patterns in interviews or historical data.[4] While these methodological restrictions on how we use and analyse data are unproblematic within the Humean

[2] See, for example, Goldstein and Keohane (1993b: 3–33).
[3] Keohane (1988).
[4] The democratic peace debates demonstrate this well. See chapter 3 and also chapter 7.

discourse – these kinds of uses are the only ones that conform to the criteria of scientific inquiry according to empiricist epistemological prescriptions – such an empiricist bias in causal analysis in IR is not necessary. The Humean empiricist discourse directs the mainstream rationalists to use data and methods in a way that could be considered unnecessarily narrow: when examined through an alternative philosophy of causation we can recognise that qualitative, interpretive, historical and discursive forms of analysis are also able to provide us with causal accounts of world politics.

The rationalists are also *epistemologically* restricted in that they imply that the empiricist form of gaining knowledge through observational testing has epistemological superiority in explaining world politics. The positivists presume that empirical knowledge has priority over other ways of knowing and that the strict criteria for scientific knowledge advanced by the likes of King, Keohane and Verba can provide the social sciences with better, and more reliable, knowledge of world politics.[5] In so doing, however, the rationalists miss out on the crucial importance of other epistemological approaches and, crucially, fail adequately to recognise the problems involved in acquiring knowledge simply through systematic empirical observation of patterns of events. Indeed, the postpositivists have powerfully criticised the epistemological prioritisation of observational knowledge that characterises rationalism: the positivists, they argue, not only unjustifiably ignore other ways of gaining knowledge, but also can remain blind to the way in which their own assumptions are informed by the social and the political context of inquiry. It is not necessary that causal analysis entails epistemological objectivism, certainly of an empiricist kind.

Humeanism has also entailed the adoption of unnecessarily 'flat' *ontological* assumptions. Many postpositivists have argued that the social ontologies adopted by the rationalists tend to be individualistic and atomistic in nature. This is partly owing to the fact that the assumption of observability plays such a crucial role in the empiricist knowledge claims: because of the demand for observability of objects of knowledge, world political inquiry often becomes reduced to analysis of behavioural patterns of atomistic actors (whether they be states or individual leaders) or quantification of observable material resources. If structures or systems are conceptualised, these tend to be seen as

[5] King, Keohane and Verba (1994).

deterministic 'closed systems' from which the behaviour of individual actors can be deduced (for example, Waltz). The rationalists avoid forming 'deep ontological' conceptual systems concerning the social structures or powers in world politics. Even when theories make claims about 'deeper' causal forces at work in world politics, these claims are cushioned in 'as if' terminology that allows the positivists to avoid the accusation that they are making deep ontological claims.[6] Crucially, these 'as ifs' are considered to matter only to the extent that they can be shown to have regular observable effects. The inability to theorise these deeper and complex causal forces is problematic, not just theoretically, but ultimately because it means that these theorists run the risk of not identifying the role of certain deeper causal forces in world politics, such as structures of capitalist social relations, ideological power or discursive conditions.

Reflectivists and constructivists in the Humean problem-field

As we have seen in chapter 4, many reflectivist and constructivist theorists in IR have attacked the ability of positivist analysis to account for social affairs. These theorists themselves, however, have not avoided getting tangled up in the Humean discourse on causation. The problem reflectivism has with causation is that most reflectivists are unable to think of causation beyond the Humean criteria. Because of their association of causation with positivism, the reflectivists have either rejected, or at least have avoided using, the notion of cause. Reflectivists, rather than exploring non-Humean philosophies of causation, have been content to argue that they are engaging in a completely different kind of analysis of social affairs: a non-causal, or so-called constitutive, form of analysis.[7] Inability to escape Humean assumptions has also characterised many constructivist accounts, which also tend to separate causal and constitutive forms of inquiry. By not questioning the legitimacy of the Humean account as a model of causal analysis, the reflectivists and constructivists *have inadvertently reinforced Humeanism* 'as the only game in town' with regard to causal analysis.

[6] Neorealists, such as Waltz, argue, for example, that it is not that the structure of the international system 'really' is anarchic, but that the international system can usefully be thought of 'as if' it were anarchic. Waltz (1979: 6–8). See also chapter 3.

[7] See, for example, Campbell (1998b: 4).

The inadvertent acceptance of Humeanism by the reflectivists and constructivists has given rise to a powerful dichotomisation of causal and constitutive approaches in IR. The reflectivist and constructivist IR theorists have failed to notice that this dichotomy arises from their acceptance of a largely Humean conception of cause as their 'benchmark' for evaluating causal approaches. Moreover, as a result of their inability to theorise causation beyond Humeanism, the reflectivists and constructivists have not noticed that *many of their own 'constitutive' claims seem causal*, if not causal in the Humean sense: most reflectivists and constructivists, as we have seen, do make claims about 'forces', 'influences', 'constraints' or 'consequences'. Recognising that these references refer to causal forces is important in directing reflectivists and constructivists towards more constructive engagement with wider causal explanations and, indeed, other IR theorists.

Theoretical reductionism

In addition it should be noted that the Humean discourse of causation in IR has also led to theoretically 'reductionist' tendencies in IR – on all sides of the theoretical divisions.On the rationalist side the acceptance of Humean variable-based study of the social world has led to emphasis being put on parsimonious explanations that 'isolate' causal variables. The empiricist variable-based study of the social world has led to the treatment of causal factors as the 'causal effects' of 'independent' variables that have been measured 'against' each other on the basis of measures of statistical significance. This has led to 'additive' rather than 'integrative' analysis of causal factors.[8] The neo-neo debates, for example, have revolved around measuring the 'average' effects of absolute and relative gains 'against' each other, rather than examining how both considerations can be explained holistically (how different motivations arise in different contexts).[9]

The reflectivists, too, tend towards reductionist framings of world politics – arguably because of their anxiousness to avoid the deterministic and 'materialistic' connotations associated with mainstream causal analyses. Reflectivists and constructivists have often come to concentrate their analyses on the 'ideational' aspects in social life: they inquire into the rules, norms and discourses that inform particular events or

[8] Dessler (1991). [9] Powell (1991).

processes. In so doing, it is often argued that ideas matter because they are the most 'crucial' determinants of social life: the material world and its objects are seen to have no 'determining power' outside their ideational, normative or discursive contexts.[10] It is also often assumed that ideas, norms and discourses are somehow 'independent' of material forces (emphasised by political realists in IR), even when some sort of 'rump materialism' is accepted.[11] This kind of terminology that separates the 'ideational' (or conceptual/normative/discursive) from the wider social context, arguably, reproduces the logic of isolating factors from each other: it leads to the tendency to weigh 'ideational' factors 'against' other factors. It follows that important questions concerning the material out-folding and conditioning of ideas, rules, discourses or motivations are often sidelined and more holistic understandings of the social world are impeded.[12]

The treatment of causal analysis in IR, as we have seen, is characterised by a set of problems on all sides of the theoretical divides. The dominance of Humean discourse of causation has, arguably, played an overwhelming role in giving rise to these various problems. The aim of the following sections is to deal with the many problems and inconsistencies embedded in the contemporary accounts of causal analysis in IR. The goal is to rethink the problem-field that characterises IR accounts of cause. I also aim to deal with the limitations identified in the rethinkers' frameworks (chapter 5), such as Suganami's issues with causal ontology[13] and philosophical realists' inability to overcome the influence of partially Humean assumptions.[14]

The aim here is to build a consistent philosophical account of causation through, first, clarifying the philosophically or critically realist framing of causation: this framing allows us to deepen our understandings of causation and causal analysis in three important ways. This 'deeper' account of cause is complemented by an Aristotelian 'broadening out' of the idea of cause. The deepening and the broadening of

[10] See, for example, Hopf (1998: 173–7); Kratochwil (2000).

[11] See, for example, Koslowski and Kratochwil (1995: 134).

[12] Indeed, Kratochwil and Koslowski (1995: 137) explicitly bracket out these questions.

[13] Suganami (1996).

[14] Bhaskar (1978); Harré and Madden (1975); Wendt (1999b); Dessler (1991). Patomäki (1996, 2002) has taken the realist critique furthest but has not comprehensively developed the implications of philosophical realism within IR.

the concept of cause provides us with the philosophical and conceptual tools to provide an alternative to the Humean model of causal analysis. While it by no means entails that Humean research or reflectivist theories should be thrown out as inadequate, it offers an important alternative framework for the treatment and study of causes in world politics, an alternative that provides certain desperately needed correctives to IR discourse on causation.

Deeper concept of cause

The philosophically realist framing of causation, examined in chapter 5, provides a number of good reasons to avoid the anti-realist traps that have characterised twentieth-century philosophers of science and social science when it comes to causation. The insights of philosophical realism will be defended here as the basis for a 'deeper' ontological account of causation in the social sciences. I argue here that philosophical realism allows us to 'deepen' our understanding of causes in three important ways. First, it gives the concept of cause a general ontological grounding, an important assumption in challenging the Humean model of causal analysis as the 'hand-maiden' of social scientific inquiry. Second, through accounting for the causal role of unobservables, such as ideas, reasons and discourses, critical realism allows us to lift the empiricist-positivist 'straitjacket' from the social sciences, ontologically, epistemologically and methodologically – as well as allowing us to avoid the anti-realist and relativist claims of the poststructuralists. Third, the philosophically realist conceptualisation of causation allows us to deepen further our understanding of social scientific causal analysis by emphasising that it involves, not just the study of behaviour or understandings, but also the study of *structures of social relations*. Below, each of these points is elaborated on and defended: despite the risk of some repetition this discussion is necessary in order to clarify the often misunderstood contributions of philosophical and critical realism in IR.[15]

[15] Powerful criticisms of philosophical realism in IR have been presented by Kratochwil and Chernoff for example. Kratochwil (2000); Chernoff (2002). Yet, these can be considered problematic too in important respects. See, for example, Wight (2006, 2007); Kurki (2007).

Deep ontological understanding of the concept of cause and scientific practice

One of the central aims of philosophical realism has been to challenge the Humean empiricist account of causation. As we have seen in chapter 5, the philosophically realist approach, especially a Bhaskarian one, challenges the applicability of the regularity, observability and regularity-determinism assumptions when it comes to causation. It does so through reviving the notions of 'causal powers' and 'natural necessity'. The ontological grounding of the concept of cause through these concepts is important because it allows us radically to rethink what 'scientific causal analysis' involves.

The notion of cause, philosophical realists argue, is not just a concept referring to a logical or conceptual relation between patterns of events, or statements pertaining to them, but is a notion that refers to the real ontological structures, forces or relations that generate and bring about events. Although the concept of cause is a human concept and applied in a transitive social context, it is a concept that has referents not just in observed facts as for the Humeans, but in real underlying ontological aspects of the world. Central in understanding causation in a philosophically realist manner is the notion of causal powers, developed famously by Harré and Madden.[16] Underlying changes and events, they argue, there are 'things' in the world that have certain real properties and causal powers by virtue of their composition: for philosophical realists 'the world consists ultimately of things [or objects] that have their causal powers essentially that determine what they can, must, or cannot do in relation to other things'.[17] The importance of the idea of causal powers is that it deeply challenges the Humean account of cause as consisting in constant conjunctions of observations. Instead of regularities, the world is conceived to be constituted by a plurality of causal powers, the nature and role of which scientific inquiries seek to track. The philosophically realist challenge to the empiricist idea of scientific causal analysis has three key characteristics. First, on the basis of the causal powers account, regularities can be considered *neither sufficient, nor necessary* for establishing a causal relation.[18] Although the philosophical realists accept that statistical investigation of frequency, spread, covariance and so forth can be extremely useful when applied

[16] Harré and Madden (1975). [17] Ellis (2001: 5). [18] Bhaskar (1978: 12).

in the right context, crucially, philosophical realism gives us grounds to argue that statistical regularities themselves are not causation, nor do they in themselves provide a 'causal explanation'.[19] Causes, for philosophical realists, are not equated with regularities but can be seen to refer to real ontological features of the world. Scientific causal explanation, then, is not equated with analysis of observable regularities, but is seen to arise from the construction of conceptual models that try to grasp the nature of objects through making existential claims about their constituting structures and causal powers, thereby enabling explanations of various 'actual' or empirical processes and tendencies. Regularities are of interest to science because they allow us to test theories regarding causal powers in artificial closed system environments. Yet, observed regularities do not constitute causality: causality exists in the *underlying* causal powers and causal explanation in accounting for these underlying causal powers.

Second, philosophical realism challenges the observability assumption to which empiricists give primacy. Empiricists have reduced the objects of science to what can be observed, and as a result, have been unable to conceptualise the deeper ontological nature of scientific objects. The stratified philosophically realist ontology entails that reality can be seen to exist on three different levels: the real (unobservable), the actual (events) and the empirical (observed).[20] This means that causation does not simply refer to relations of observables, nor to relations of events, but can be identified and conceptualised to exist on a deeper unobservable level of reality. 'Deep ontological causes', such as the structures or constitution of objects, can be conceptualised as causal because neither causation nor science is tied to the empiricist assumption of observability.

Third, the assumption of 'logical necessity', and the regularity-determinism of Humeanism, can be rejected and as a result causation is distanced from the particular type of deterministic prejudices attached to it by the positivists. Regularity determinism is considered valid only in closed systems, which can be obtained only in laboratory conditions but are not characteristic of real world open systems. In contrast to regularity-determinism (given regularities we can make 'when A, then B' statements), 'ubiquity determinism', which characterises philosophically realist frameworks, is not 'deterministic' in the traditional sense:

[19] Danermark (2002: 54). [20] Bhaskar (1978: 13).

causes can be considered to 'determine' effects but this refers merely to the way in which causes, in combination with many other causes, contribute to changes in the world.[21]

It follows that predictability cannot be the primary aim of science. Prediction cannot be considered enough for scientific explanation because:

> Being able to predict things or to describe them, however accurately, is not at all the same thing as understanding them . . . [I]magine that an extraterrestrial scientist has visited the Earth and given us an ultra-high-technology 'oracle' which can predict the outcome of any possible experiment, but provides no explanations. According to the [positivist] instrumentalists, once we had that oracle we should have no further use for scientific theories, except as a means of entertaining ourselves. But is that true? How could the oracle be used in practice? In some sense it would contain the knowledge necessary to build, say, an interstellar spaceship. But how exactly would that help us to build one . . . ? . . . The oracle only predicts the outcomes of experiments. Therefore, in order to use it at all we must first know what experiments to ask it about. If we gave it a design of a spaceship, and the details of a proposed test flight, it could tell us how the spaceship would perform on such a flight. But it could not design the spaceship for us in the first place. And even if it predicted that the spaceship we had designed would explode on take-off, it could not tell us how to prevent such an explosion . . . [B]efore we could even begin to improve the design in any way, we should have to *understand*, among other things, how the spaceship was supposed to work. Only then would we have any chance of discovering what might cause an explosion on take-off. Prediction – even perfect, universal prediction – is simply no substitute for explanation . . . The oracle would be very useful in many situations, but its usefulness would always depend on people's ability to solve scientific problems in just the way they have now.[22]

In philosophically realist accounts prediction is not symmetrically related to 'causal relations' and 'explanation', as in the empiricist positivist accounts.

Philosophical realism provides a coherent non-positivist view of science and its causal explanation. Scientific causal explanation is not defined by rigid epistemological and methodological criteria relating to what constitutes systematic observation or testing – an assumption characteristic of all positivist/empiricist approaches even when

[21] Bhaskar (1978: 70–1). [22] Deutsch (1998:2, 4–5).

they disagree about what should constitute the criteria of a 'scientific method'.[23] Instead, for philosophical realists science is defined, more broadly, as a 'refinement and extension of what we do in practical functioning of everyday life'.[24] Scientific explanation is about providing deep understanding of the processes and objects around us, it is about going beyond everyday accounts through exploration of evidence and careful conceptualisation. One way to gain scientific knowledge, one step on the way towards deep understanding, involves empirical testing and tracing of patterns, but this does not mean that we should equate this potential mode of identification[25] of constant conjunctions with the definition of what constitutes science. Much more than mere perception of patterns is involved in scientific practice, including, importantly, the development of understandings and conceptualisations of the nature and powers of objects, the reality of which scientists then can proceed to test. Thus, though empirical study is crucial to science it does not exhaust science: scientific realism avoids 'reducing scientific practice to nothing but an exercise in empirical data gathering'.[26]

It should be noted that the empiricist positivists vehemently criticise this challenge to the idea of science: for them, philosophy of science need not and must not accept the reality of objects that cannot be observationally proved to exist. Such a move increases the possibility of unfalsifiable and potentially unsubstantiated knowledge claims in science.[27] Positivist critics also argue that explaining the world through the notion of causal powers is tautological. When a physician explains the sleep-inducing tendencies of a powder through its 'dormitive power', he is said to have committed the classic mistake of advancing a meaningless tautological answer to the inquiry and has, hence, failed to account for the cause of drowsiness. While these criticisms are important, philosophical realists also have answers to them.

In reply philosophical realists would emphasise that their alternative understanding of science cannot endanger science because scientific inquiries are already premised on their ontologically grounded assumptions: sciences study the structure of things – or rather objects, since scientific objects, for Bhaskar, do not need to be 'thing-like' to be

[23] Wight (2006: 19). [24] Lopez and Potter (2001a: 9).
[25] Wight (2006: 46). [26] Wight (2006: 35).
[27] See, for example, Fred Chernoff's criticisms of scientific realism. Chernoff (2002: 189–207; 2007: 399–407).

real[28] – by which they have particular causal powers. Scientific practice presumes that it is the underlying causal powers of objects that allow them to generate certain 'actual' processes in particular conditions – conditions which remain 'contingent'.[29] The philosophical realists then argue that acceptance of unobservables provides a condition of the very practice of science and empiricist observation of regularities. Also, philosophical realists would argue that the dormitive power argument is a misleading criticism. While reference to 'dormitive power' might not answer this particular causal puzzle, the analogy of power is not tautological if a theorist explains what it is *about* the structure of something that gives it these powers.[30] For the philosophical realists, the notion of causal powers captures the idea that things or forces in the world consist of, or are structured through, sets of 'internal relations', which give them properties for acting in certain ways. Philosophical realists argue that science focuses on accounting for these internal relations that explain what it is *about* something that brings about change/effects, for example, what it is about the structure and constitution of 'dormitive powder' that brings about sleepiness.

Of course, it is important to recognise that an account of unobservable powers made by scientists is not the final truth about reality: it is but a transitive truth claim, advanced on the basis of evidential knowledge and conceptual knowledge available to scientists. Contrary to many empiricists and poststructuralists then, scientific knowledge claims about powers are not infallible for philosophical realists: on the contrary, they are considered to be inherently fallible and to await refutation. Science, for philosophical realists as much as for empiricists, can of course be wrong about its objects: it is precisely this fallibility that drives science on.[31]

It is not my aim to revisit the entire debate between empiricist positivism and philosophical realism, yet it seems fair to say that the philosophically realist arguments for a causal powers account can provide some good reasons for the acceptance of an ontological account of cause. Notably, it seems that this account is presupposed in the practice

[28] Lòpez and Potter (2001a: 11).

[29] Sayer makes a useful distinction between necessary internal relations and contingent external relations. The former refer to relations within structures, while the latter refer to the conditions within which internal relations act out. See, for example, Sayer (2000: 16).

[30] Sayer (1992: 106). [31] Wight (2006: 38).

of science: the philosophical realist account does not necessitate doing away with the idea of science, rather it explains it in a new way. In fact, as Hilary Putnam has put it, it is the only account of science that does not make the success of science a miracle.[32] Not only is this account of science theoretically plausible but also empirical evidence from scientific practice can be provided to sustain the plausibility of a philosophically realist framework of thought.[33] Indeed, in philosophy of science, philosophical or scientific realism is now a widely accepted position, even though this seems to have eluded many scholars in IR.

'Very well,' a critic might say, 'but what are we to think in regard to the social sciences?' Many theorists might accept that the objects of natural sciences are real and even causal but still maintain that the objects of social sciences cannot be accorded reality, or a causal role.

Causes in the social world: rethinking ideas, reasons and concept-dependence

Can we accept the reality of the social world, the reality of social objects and can we accept that there are ontological real causes in the social world? The answer here is yes, and again philosophically realist – or rather specifically critical realist[34] – reasoning can be seen as broadly persuasive on this account. In exploring the nature of social reality the critical realists start from the ontological question: 'what must the social world be like, for our efforts to explain it to make sense?'[35] The positivists' empirical realist reduction of reality to the observable is rejected as a result of the fact that it unnecessarily limits the world and its objects to the observable and, thus, gives a very narrow and atomistic account of 'social reality'. Empiricist 'actualist' explanations focused on observable patterns of behaviour fail to account for, and conceptualise, the role of meanings, concepts, rules, discourses and social construction in social life. Critical realists allow room for engagement with these social causes and accept that these

[32] Putnam (1975: 73). For Putnam's particular version of realism see also Putnam (1987, 1990).

[33] See, for example, Psillos (1999).

[34] This term refers to positions that draw on Roy Bhaskar's critical naturalist philosophy of social science. See chapter 5.

[35] 'It is the nature of objects that determines their cognitive possibilities for us.' Bhaskar (1998: 25).

objects cannot simply be observed but are often captured best through interpretive means.

What about the other extreme, that is, the poststructuralist argument that reality is constituted in its entirety by our concepts and language, hence making references to reality or causality of social objects inherently relative? Critical realism argues that this stance results in the acceptance of unnecessarily relativist conclusions and, indeed, a self-contradictory logic. Critical realists point out that if 'descriptions' of the social world are not separated from the 'reality' of the social world we have no basis for theoretical debate or assessing the validity of our statements or discourses. Our debates and discourses have to be seen as literally self-referential:

> If discourses construct the objects to which discourses refer, then the discourse itself can never be wrong about the existence of its objects ... nor can an alternative discourse possibly critique another discourse, since the objects of a given discourse exist if the discourse says they exist. External criticism of existential claims of discourses seems impossible.[36]

On the basis of critical realism, the absolutely discursive understanding of social reality can be seen as a misleading exaggeration. It hides the fact that those who deny the existence of real objects and forces beyond our discourses/narratives/stories/perspectives, arguably, do end up making some assumptions and claims (existential hypotheses) about external social reality, if nothing else, about the reality of discourses or stories. Critical realists persuasively point to the fact that most of our everyday life and communication is premised on the acceptance of some 'realities', even if discursive ones, and this extends even to the poststructuralists.[37] Indeed, if there was no reality to which our different accounts referred, the disagreements between our accounts would not be comprehensible.[38]

An example from IR can be used to clarify this issue. In discussing Bosnia and the Bosnian crisis, David Campbell denies that he is giving a 'true' account of a 'fixed' reality of the Bosnian war. This is because patterns of events or 'facts', he argues, can be plotted along various lines and it is the stories we tell (how we pick 'facts' and link them) that

[36] Patomäki and Wight (2000: 217). [37] Sayer (2000: 69).
[38] For a treatment of incommensurability see Wight (1996; 2006: 40–5).

'narrate reality': historical or social realities cannot be assumed to pre-exist our representations.[39] Even so, to deny the extra-linguistic reality of Bosnia, or rather its discursive construction *in reality* through a variety of discourses, is not possible for Campbell. Indeed, he proceeds to make various claims about the discursive 'realities' in Bosnia. He argues, for example, that a 'territorial discourse', among others, was involved in framing Bosnia, the Bosnian crisis and the responses to it. Arguably, it is precisely because the discourses that made Bosnia, and framed the 'crisis', are real in some sense that Campbell thinks it is important that we recognise their role in 'constituting' the crisis and responses to it. The very fact that he ends up arguing that his account points to something important that mainstream theorists have ignored, and that he can give a better account of how the Bosnian crisis took the shape it did,[40] implies that his theorisation does have a referent, even if a primarily discursive, non-deterministic and complex one. This referent is engaged with through historical data that can of course be interpreted in a plurality of ways; however, arguably, not in 'any' way.[41]

It is also important that we recognise that although our conceptualisations and accounts are socially embedded and can have influence in the social world, social theorists do not 'create' the social world. We do not need a social scientist to conceptualise social life before it can exist: it has a reality outside social scientists' descriptions, although these can come to have some impact back on social reality.[42]

Critical realism allows us to accept the reality of social objects, but also to emphasise that the social world is complex and dynamic: it is composed of complex interactions of various real objects. For the critical realists the social world is characterised by 'open systems'. Contra positivists, the social world is not seen as a closed system where we can isolate behaviour or conduct experiments on a 'when A, then B' basis. Because open systems characterise the nature of the social world, efforts to equate success of a social causal explanation with the predictive power of the account are misleading.[43]

[39] Campbell (1998a: 34–6). [40] Campbell (1998a: 3).

[41] Indeed, Colin Wight (1999a) has pointed out that despite his rejection of 'historical record', Campbell cannot avoid resorting to some sort of a historical record. Thus, although there is 'continual contestation' between accounts it is not as if 'any' account is as good as another.

[42] Bhaskar (1989: 5). [43] Bhaskar (1979: 27).

Importantly, the complexity of the social world and the lack of regularity and closed systems that would allow successful prediction do not make the social world a-causal. If we follow critical realist insights, the social world can be seen as causal, just as can the natural world: just like in the natural world, 'nothing in the social world comes from nothing'. Crucially, unlike the Humeans, the critical realists work on the basis of an unusually open definition of causation: causes are things or forces that make things happen, that bring about effects. The social causes are ontological, that is, they are existing (real) rather than 'imagined', even though causes in the social world, as in the natural world, are unobservable (exist on the level of the real rather than the empirical). The unobservability of causes is not a problem for the critical realists as causes, for them, simply refer to those things that make things happen, whether observable or not, and are almost always 'got at' through conceptualisation (abstraction) rather than direct perception.

Through its ontologically grounded and complexity-sensitive account of causation and social ontology, critical realism shows us the importance of reassessing some of the central debates in the philosophy of social science. Importantly, as was noted in chapter 5, critical realism advances an interesting solution to the reasons and causes controversy that has raged between the positivist and the hermeneutic theorists. Critical realism argues that the hermeneutic 'reasons account' that denies the applicability of causality in the social world is predicated on a narrow conception of causation: reasons are thought to apply in the social world because the Humean causal model 'when X, then Y' does not seem to work. If causation is not seen as co-terminous with regularity (which brings with it regularity-determinism) and 'cause' is conceptualised more 'common-sensically' as that which 'so tip[s] the balance of events as to produce a known outcome',[44] causal explanations can be seen to reach much more deeply into social life than typical reasons accounts allow. Bhaskar argues that the reasons we hold are causal on our actions. Our reasons must be causes of our action because, as Bhaskar puts it, 'the agent's reasons are a necessary condition for the bodily movements that occurred, in the straightforward sense that had the agent not possessed them ... they would not have occurred'.[45] To give a 'reasons account', then, is to explicate those reasons that are causally efficacious in motivating agents' actions. It can be

[44] M. Scriven quoted in Bhaskar (1998: 83). [45] Bhaskar (1979: 113–14).

accepted that agents are often mistaken about their reasons for actions (rationalisations); however, this does not challenge the assumption that the agent's reason (though not necessarily the one cited by the agent) was the cause of the action.

> [A] person may possess a reason R for doing A, do A and R may not be the reason why s/he does it. It is only if X does A because of R that we are justified in citing R as the reason for A. And there would seem no way of explicating 'because' save in terms of causality ... Unless a reason could function as a cause there would be no sense in a person evaluating different beliefs in order to decide how to act. For either a reason will make a difference to his/her behaviour or it will not. In the former case it counts as a cause.[46]

Importantly, critical realism allows us also to accept that meanings, ideas and beliefs are central to social science and its causal explanation, despite not being directly observable or regularity-deterministic. Because meanings, ideas and beliefs give people reasons for acting, they form a crucial part of any causal explanation of the social world. Indeed, critical realists argue that it is only through recognising the causal importance of ideas that the poststructuralist claims, for example, make sense.[47] To use Campbell as an example again, if the territorial representation of Bosnia that he points to did not have an effect on how the situation developed in Bosnia, why is Campbell talking about it? Surely, his account is referring to something (a certain kind of discourse) that has real effects: hence his frequent references to its 'consequences'.[48] The critical realists allow us to understand ideas and representations as causal, even when their role is not deterministic or simple, while Campbell himself lacks the conceptual apparatus to conceptualise causation beyond deterministic (Humean) assumptions. However, the critical realist conceptual apparatus for understanding *how* reasons and 'ideational' frameworks are causal needs to be clarified. Arguably, the idea of efficient cause, which most critical realists resort to in understanding the role of reasons and ideas in the social world, is not ideally equipped to deal with causes such as those that Campbell and other poststructuralists deal with. The latter part of the chapter will aim to develop such a conceptual apparatus for engaging with normative or discursive causes.

[46] Bhaskar (1979: 115). Italics removed. [47] Sayer (1992: 111).
[48] Campbell (1998b: 4).

Despite some of the conceptual inadequacies of the critical realist framework, the critical realist emphasis on social causes, such as reasons and ideas, is important because, contra positivism, it allows us to accept the use of hermeneutic and discursive methods in the social sciences. As Patomäki argues, hermeneutic methods, for example, are necessary for any causal analysis, precisely because reasons are causes.[49] The same applies for discourse analysis. The difference between a critical realist and an interpretive approach is that the critical realists situate interpretation in real practical contexts: interpretive understanding is seen as a 'normal and indispensable part of everyday practice, indeed social life depends on its being reasonably successful for much of the time'.[50] Contra poststructuralists, critical realists accept that there is a degree of stability of meaning, which everyday life and discourse depend upon.[51] Interpretation is also seen as non-relativist in that even the most contestable meanings in social life – identities, for example – are not seen as 'simply matters of discursive construction or the play of difference within discourse. Rather they relate to determinate characteristics and acts, to what actors, groups and societies have done. These acts are of course open to differing interpretations, but the [interpretations] have some things in common – the interpretandum – over which they differ.'[52]

Critical realism allows us to reject the epistemological 'feelings of superiority' of the empiricists in favour of the principle of epistemological relativism: all knowledge is socially situated and contextual, and there is no one certain way to come to know 'what is'. However, we need not accept judgemental relativism, that is, give up on the principle that some accounts can be better than others. Often the justification for the relativist stance is drawn from the concept-dependent and 'theory-determined' nature of our accounts. This can be seen as an exaggerated position. Just because social life and our accounts are premised on previous conceptual and theoretical constructions, this does not make our accounts entirely 'theory-determined'. Although the accounts and concepts we advance to explain the social world arise and exist within a social context, it is important to recognise that the referents of our accounts may exist outside our discourse. Indeed, it is because

[49] Patomäki (1996: 108). [50] Sayer (2000: 46).
[51] Sayer (2000: 93). [52] Sayer (2000: 46).

'discourse and knowledge are not merely self-referential – that is why they are fallible'.[53]

For example, even highly 'incommensurable' accounts – neoliberal and Marxist accounts of the world economy, for example – are not 'relative' because they share, at least partly, a common referent (global economic processes). If they did not, there could be no debate between them – since they would have nothing to disagree about.[54] Evaluating the plausibility of such accounts against each other is, of course, a complex process. However, we do constantly evaluate theories against the state of the world and against each other and, importantly, although evaluations do not have simple and non-political outcomes, it is not as if 'anything goes' in interpreting accounts. Thus, although the neoliberal and Marxist accounts of the world economy have very different terminologies and methodologies, and they point to very different kinds of causal connections and relations, it is not as if 'anything' can be plausibly asserted by these accounts.

Evaluating the explanatory adequacy of theories is difficult partly because there are no fixed universal criteria to draw on in doing so. Also, evaluations are complicated by the fact that they are not a-political. However, it is not as if the ontological assumptions advanced can be 'whatever' or that evidence can be interpreted in 'any' way. Concerns such as internal coherence, ontological plausibility, scope and strength of evidential support (of various kinds) come into play in the way we assess theories and accounts against each other. The critical realists remind us that the 'ambiguousness' of the process of assessing social scientific theories is unavoidable, but not necessarily an insurmountable problem. It is accepted that the ambiguousness and incompleteness, as well as the socially and politically embedded nature of our accounts of the social world, are characteristics that arise from the ontological nature of the objects of social sciences. Indeed, as Sayer puts it 'we should not expect more precision than the object allows. We should not expect something like cultural values to be unambiguous and determinate any more than we should expect a lump of granite to be malleable and indeterminate.'[55]

Arguably, the danger in the political/ideological nature of social science is that, when theorists are not reflexive about the political

[53] Sayer (2000: 62). Italics removed.

[54] Sayer (2000: 47).

[55] Sayer (2000: 45).

assumptions at work in their theorising and the biases they might generate, they can come to make ontologically and empirically implausible judgements about the nature of the world.[56] While social and political embeddedness of theories is unavoidable, showing the fallibility of some of these accounts is not. Crucially, a critical realist can argue against racism and fascism, for example, not just on 'normative' grounds but also because 'they can be shown to have inferior cognitive status – they are based on misleading accounts and explanations of human society, ones which are inferior to non-racist theories'.[57] Social science always runs the risk, not just of political theorising, but of politically motivated unreflective and implausible theorising. This is why reflexivity is essential: theorists must remain aware of how their assumptions can result in making unsustainable ontological and evidential claims. They must also remain critical of other people's accounts of their own reasons and beliefs: interpretation, while advocated, should always be critically reflective and premised on a conceptual analysis of the people's context of action. People's accounts of their own beliefs and actions, it should be remembered, are not always trustworthy because not only can people lie but they can also misunderstand their own reasons for actions.

The critical realist notion of cause, and scientific causal explanation, gives us a good place to start in allowing us to accept the reality and the causal nature of the social world, including the causal role of reasons and ideas. It helps us lift off the positivist straitjacket on social analysis as well as allowing us to avoid the exaggerations of poststructuralist accounts. It allows us to avoid the positivist concentration on the 'superficial' level of empirical observation and generalisation and, also, permits us to reject the overly swift attempts to throw away reality, causation and science. However, it is crucial that we do not leave things here but also note that there is another sense in which the critical realist account of social science provides a 'deeper' approach to causal analysis of the social world: it emphasises the importance of analysing *social relations*.

[56] Sayer (2000: 53).

[57] Sayer (2000: 77). Importantly, critical realists acknowledge the connection between explanatory and normative claims. This is not to say that normative claims cannot be made but that they too are often based on explanatory understandings. For realist normative theory see, for example, Sayer (2000: 155–88).

Causal analysis and structures of social relations

Contra positivists, the philosophical realists frame the world in relational terms, that is, science is seen to be about inquiring into the 'internal relations' that make up objects. Importantly, this applies also in the social world and gives rise to the adoption of conceptual tools that both the empiricist Humeans and the interpretivist (anti-causal) Humeans tend to ignore. Empiricists tend to see social life in terms of patterns of regular behaviour of individual agents. Interpretivists, on the other hand, tend to emphasise 'meanings', 'concept-dependence', 'rules' and 'intersubjective understandings' in making up the social world. Critical realists argue that the goal of social science should be not merely the study of individual or group behaviour, or understanding the shared intersubjective ideas and norms that give meaning to social life (interpretivists), but, beyond them, also the study of *structures of social relations*.

The notion of social structure is a controversial one in the social sciences. Many empiricists adopt 'closed system' deterministic framings of the concept of structure as we have seen. Poststructuralists, interpretivists as well as some philosophical realists, on the other hand, argue that we should avoid the notion of social structures or, at most, adopt a 'minimal' definition of social structures, that is, see them as referring to shared rules or intersubjective understandings that inform social life.[58] Accepting social structures as 'ontologically autonomous', 'real' and 'causal', the sceptics argue, hides the fact that social forms are fundamentally dependent on agents and their intentionality and, hence, runs the risk of reifying social forms. However, it is my view that Bhaskar's argument for the utility of the notion of social structures is broadly persuasive.

Critical realists accept that social life is meaningful, concept-dependent and rule-governed. However, they argue that concepts, meanings and rules also give rise to materially unfolding *structures of social relations*, that is, they give rise to materially embodied 'internal relations' between agents, and it is the study of these relations that

[58] King (1999). See also Harré and Varela (1996). Giddens also leans towards a limited definition of social structures, which critical realists reject. Social structures for Giddens are, at the end of the day, 'virtual' (while influencing some material factors) rather than real material social relations. For criticisms of Giddens see Archer (1995).

social science should focus on. The tenant–landlord relation, for example, is seen not just as a 'conceptual relation' (words define each other's meaning), a 'shared understanding' (actors understand themselves and their actions according to some rules) or a pattern of behaviour (landlords tend to behave in X, tenants in Y ways), but as a material social relation that defines the social roles and positions of the agents locked into it. The tenant–landlord relation forms a 'structure' of 'social relations' because it 'internally relates' agents to each other (tenants, landlords), thus shaping their practices (paying rent) and defining their relations to material objects (house).[59] Social structures, just as do other 'structures', 'internally relate' aspects of the world to each other. However, Bhaskar accepts that social structures, (1) unlike natural structures, do not exist independently of the activities they govern, (2) do not exist independently of agents' conceptions of what they are doing and are only (3) relatively enduring.[60]

Bhaskar's notion of social structure is useful in that it captures the sense in which agents in the social world are not 'independent' but deeply related through their social context. It allows us to recognise that, through their intentional and rule-governed action, agents give rise to social relations that have 'emergent properties' beyond them.[61] It allows us to recognise that society and its social relations 'pre-exist' individual actors and their particular conceptions of the social world. The notion of social structures also emphasises that social positions and roles defined by structures of social relations are materially as well as 'ideationally' embodied.[62]

To use an example, the social structure of the British state is dependent on the actions of individual intentional agents and their adoption of certain 'ways of thinking'. However, these ways of thinking give rise to certain social roles and positions (for example, 'citizen', 'Prime Minister', 'policeman') that condition (and, indeed, enable) the thoughts and actions of agents within these structures. Importantly,

[59] Sayer (1992: 92). [60] Bhaskar (1979: 48–9).

[61] Bhaskar (1979: 124–5). I agree with Bhaskar in seeing social structures as an ontological, not just as an 'analytical' category. This is because social structures can be seen to be ontologically causal on individual actors (both materially and formally, see next section), even if they are also ontologically inseparable from agents that make them up. For a contrasting position see, for example, Hay (2002).

[62] For a more detailed discussion of structures and the structure and agency issue from a broadly critical realist perspective, see Wight (2006).

even if you do not share a belief in the 'state' (say, you are an anarchist) the structure of social relations still constrains you: because it pre-exists you, is irreducible to individual actors, and is materially unfolding. Against those social constructivists that reduce social life or social structures to 'ways of thinking' (conceptual-dependencies, rules, norms, discourses), the critical realists emphasise the 'pre-existence' and the material embodiment and properties of social relations. Also, critical realists, crucially, emphasise that people are often not aware of the social structures around them, how they are informed by them, and how they reproduce them. Critical realism emphasises that intentional action can have unintentional consequences that reproduce structures of social relations. As Bhaskar puts it: 'people do not marry to reproduce the nuclear family or work to reproduce the capitalist economy'.[63]

Social structures, it should be noted, can be of many kinds, as social structures can be conceived to exist on different 'strata of depth': they can be more concrete, taking the form of a particular institution (family), or be more abstract (nuclear family, state, capitalism). Also, they can vary in their durability. However, Bhaskar points out that, although social life is dynamic and social structures are reproduced by intentional actors, the 'internal relations' that characterise social life can be, and often are, surprisingly enduring. Further, importantly, when social structures change they change through transformation: agents reproduce and transform pre-existing social relations; they do not 'create' or 'destroy' them at will.[64]

Bhaskar importantly argues that social structures have impacts and, hence, should be considered causal. Social structures are causal, for Bhaskar, because they are a *necessary condition* for any intentional act of agents.[65] Sometimes critical realists specify this definition further by arguing that social structures are an INUS-condition or a 'material cause' of agency. As we have seen these conceptualisations, especially that of material cause, are not unproblematic. Because of the unclear causal nature of social structures, the issue of social structural causation will be further clarified in the next section. However, even if lacking in conceptual clarity, Bhaskar's acceptance of the causal nature of social structures is important, because it opens up the treatment of social causation further than other branches of social science have. It allows us to give a real causal role to the social context of action, something

[63] Bhaskar (1979: 44). [64] Bhaskar (1979: 42–3). [65] Bhaskar (1979: 46).

that many empiricist individualists, as well as many 'interpretivists', have avoided.

Causal analysis: abstract and concrete

A brief note should be made concerning the type of research process that this deeper social relations centred approach to social scientific causal analysis entails. Social research as conceptualised here is seen to involve two stages: abstraction and the study of the concrete.[66] The study of the concrete can be understood as the study of the events and actualities concerning the object of explanation. In explaining the causes of terrorism, for example, one might look into the terrorist agents, or terrorist groups, their actions and capabilities. In order to grasp the nature of the concrete, critical realists accept that we can taxonomise events and observables and try to see what kind of regular patterns characterise the concrete objects. We could, for example, construct observable variables about the capabilities, behavioural patterns, or even quoted motivations expressed by terrorists and try to find whether regularities that could associate specific variables with, say, the tendency to attack particular kinds of targets, could be found. However, a critical realist explanation of the causes of terrorism would have to go beyond such taxonomical study of concrete observables: it would have to involve careful conceptualisation, or abstraction, concerning the social relations within which the concrete patterns/actors are embedded.

The process of abstraction takes the concrete as its starting point, but develops a deeper understanding of the level of the 'actual' through conceptualising (making existential hypotheses about) the underlying structures that give rise to actual observables, that is, through embedding the concrete objects/actors/actions/measurables in various sets of social relations. Through abstraction a researcher aims to understand the deeper sets of social relations within which concrete actors or processes are embedded and that, hence, allow us to explain the concrete event-level in 'deeper' ways.[67]

[66] See, for example, Sayer (1992: 85–8, 138–43).

[67] Sayer (1992: 9). Arguably, the more layered (in abstraction) and the more complexity-sensitive (in the analysis of the unfolding of complex sets of social relations in concrete situations) explanations are, the more explanatorily adequate they tend to be. See also van Bouwel and Weber (2002).

Finding or developing suitable conceptual frameworks, or 'redescription' of social objects, is crucial in the process of abstraction. Also, it should be noted that the interpretation[68] of qualitative and historical data plays a crucial role in coming up with good abstractions: through these we can penetrate deeper into the hidden relations that link together agents or aspects of the social world, as well as gain a better understanding of the processes through which these (complex) relations unfold in concrete contexts.

It follows that a theorist of terrorism, for example, needs to conceptualise how actors, their thinking and their capabilities are embedded in various social relations. (S)he could ask questions about the social relations within the group (its hierarchies, its ideological precepts, etc.), the local economic positioning of agents and possible political grievances within state structures. To uncover how social relations have causal roles, the researcher would conduct an intensive (qualitative and historical) study of the groups and their social contexts. The 'intensive' methods help him/her to come up with more nuanced conceptualisations of social relations as well as allowing him/her to understand how these social relations give rise to particular concrete processes (for example, how agents develop particular motivations or take particular actions in particular conditions). Besides the more 'local' social relations, a researcher would ideally also seek to develop an understanding of more global social relations, such as the structures of the world economy or the social relations within and between global religions, and embed local social relations (and actors within them) within these deeper sets of social relations. Thus, an explanation of the causes of terrorism should not concentrate merely on the individuals but necessitates embedding them within complex local and global conditioning social relations.[69]

It is important to note that the study of the concrete and the conceptualisation (abstraction) of social relations form two sides of the same coin. We cannot reduce social analysis to the analysis of the concrete because if we do so, we may miss many of the crucial 'whys' and 'hows'

[68] Patomäki (2002: 136) emphasises that qualitative data are always interpreted through 'fusion of horizons' – there is no 'objective' interpretation. However, data can still be evaluated: one must be reflexive about one's assumptions and models in the light of the data.

[69] This is what the more sophisticated terrorism theorists have, indeed, recognised. See, for example, Crenshaw (1995); Reich (1998).

that shape concrete contexts. On the other hand, mere abstraction on its own is also dangerous in that, if applied in isolation, it may lead to misleading conclusions about the concrete objects: we can come to see the concrete through the 'parsimonious' abstract, that is, derive the content of the concrete (complex) from the abstract (we may end up deriving the causes of particular terrorists' actions from the world economic system, hence ignoring the particularities of the concrete context). Also, through excessive abstraction (which is synchronic) we may miss the dynamic (diachronic) actions, interactions and processes that give rise to changes in structures of social relations.

Questions relating to social relations, especially abstract structural relations, are often difficult to settle. Since the social world makes up an 'open system', where various kinds of social structures, concrete and abstract, global and local, constantly impinge on actors and interact and counteract in complex ways, the task of social science is not an easy one. Critical realism allows us to accept this but does not give up on the aim of seeking more nuanced explanations of the social world. It is recognised that social scientific explanations remain 'incomplete' for epistemological reasons (knowledge is always fallible and revisable) but also for ontological reasons (the nature of social objects is dynamic and they are embedded in complex and varying conditions).[70] It is accepted here that it is often difficult to make sense of the messy nature of the social world. However, through a careful study of the concrete and through a careful process of abstraction (that is, through conceptualising the nature of social objects and their relations) social sciences can, arguably, improve or deepen 'everyday' accounts of social relations and processes.[71]

The deepening of the concept of cause and the problems of causation in IR

The philosophically realist critique of the positivist conception of scientific causal analysis and the critical realist framing of social ontology allow us to deepen our conceptions of scientific causal analysis, our understandings of social causation and our conceptual and methodological tools in analysing the social world. In so doing the philosophically realist approaches can solve some of the intractable problems

[70] Sayer (1992: 234). [71] Sayer (2000: 19–20).

that the rationalists and the reflectivists have had with causation and causal analysis in IR.

The philosophical/critical realist framing allows us to challenge the rationalist mode of causal analysis in IR: methodologically, epistemologically and ontologically. First, the rationalist methodological criteria for causal analysis can be shown to be overly restrictive. The essence of causal explanation is not the gathering of regularities but conceptual explanation of the forces that bring about these regularities of observable effects. Causal explanations in IR, then, cannot rely on a fixed conception of 'a scientific method' that can 'deliver' objective scientific causal knowledge of a lawful kind. Rather, explanations have to advance plausible theoretical (existential) claims about the nature of ontological objects and be able, thereby, to account for concrete processes and interactions. These claims can, and in the social world should, draw on a variety of types of evidence, including hermeneutic, qualitative, historical and even discursive. Because the essence of social explanation is dealing with the complexity of causal forces and relations, it is misleading to highlight the virtues of strictly parsimonious explanations. Notably, it is not productive for social analysis simply to focus on looking for the role of singular causal forces just because through them we can provide general parsimonious explanations. It follows that causal analyses are not 'true' because they correctly predict outcomes. Some estimates can be made of what might happen in the future, but these, crucially, are based on understanding the social structural environment and its complexity; predictions cannot simply be 'logically deduced'.

Philosophical realism also allows us to challenge the epistemological confidence of rationalism in the superior objectivity of observational methods. The claims to give 'objective' accounts of world politics can, indeed, be considered problematic, as the postpositivists have noted. All scientific accounts, the philosophical realists recognise, are 'transitive', that is socially and politically embedded. This is crucial in the social world, for accounts of the social world have important social and political implications. The rationalists in IR have tended to ignore this because of their (often unquestioned) belief in the accuracy of a broadly empiricist view of science. This has meant that they have not paid adequate attention to the fact that their own accounts of world politics are socially constructed and carry within them politically loaded and consequential assumptions.

The critical realist framing is also important because it challenges the ontological framings of the social world advanced by the rationalists. For critical realists observability is not the only, or even a useful, criterion for 'what matters' in IR. As the reflectivists have pointed out, only so much can be explained through the study of 'measurable variables' and their statistical associations. Instead, it can be accepted that unobservables are real and causal. Reasons and motivations as well as rules, norms and discourses can be conceptualised as 'real' and as 'causal', and can be accepted as legitimate objects of social science, even if they are not directly observable or 'stable' in terms of empirical outcomes. Also, the critical realist framing of the agency–structure problem directs IR away from the methodologically individualistic 'ontologically flat' accounts that characterise many Humean approaches in IR and forces IR theorists to adopt more nuanced and complexity-sensitive structurally embedded conceptualisations of agency.[72]

Philosophical/critical realism allows us to challenge, not just rationalism, but also reflectivism. It emphasises that when the Humean criteria for causal explanation are rejected, causes can be seen as an important part of most social scientific explanations: accounts of reasons, motivations or rules are not non-causal just because they do not resemble Humean accounts. The deeper conception of causation allows us to understand that, as was implied in chapter 4, the reflectivists are, indeed, involved in making a number of causal claims. The reflectivist and constructivist accounts concentrate on tracing the influence of rules, norms and discourses in world politics. Philosophical realism allows us to recognise that these accounts are, in fact, causal. However, arguably, the *way* in which these accounts are causal needs some further elaboration and will be discussed further in the next section.

The accounts of the 'rethinkers' of causation can also be challenged. The philosophically realist framing allows us to accept Suganami's emphasis on the pragmatics of explanation and his multi-causal approach to causal story-telling, while being able to emphasise that causes are also 'real' beyond our accounts. As a consequence, we can also accept that, in principle, we can make judgements, although complex and fallible ones, between causal accounts and their ability to explain 'the world'. In contrast to the arguments of Wendt and Dessler, in my view philosophical realism has the potential powerfully

[72] Wight (2006); Patomäki (2002).

and comprehensively to transcend the Humean problem-field in IR. Thus, Wendt's and Dessler's accounts of causation can be critiqued for being overly attached to the conventional disciplinary categories.

However, we also need a more detailed understanding of how these theorists go wrong with regard to the causal–constitutive dichotomy. Indeed, it should be noted that the mere 'deepening' of the notion of cause does not answer all of the problems of causal analysis in IR. First, it does not address the causal–constitutive division with enough depth. Through showing that this division is based on Humeanism, and through avoiding making such a distinction, critical realism has taken important steps towards doing away with it. However, arguably, more could be done to clarify the way in which traditionally non-causal factors, such as reasons, ideas, rules, norms and discourses, are causal, which in turn would allow us to clarify how exactly the causal–constitutive divide can be transcended. Also, we need to deal with the problem of theoretical reductionism in more depth. While critical realism has emphasised that causal contexts and, hence, causal explanations are always complex and that reductionism (materialist, ideational, agential, structural) should be avoided, more clarity could be achieved on how theoretical reductionism can be evaded in IR. Answering these concerns requires that we complement the 'deepening' of the notion of cause with 'broadening' it.

Broadening the concept of cause: Aristotle revisited

It was argued in the previous chapter that Alexander Wendt's treatment of causation in IR was problematic in certain respects, even though his work has generated a plurality of important new avenues for IR theorising in other areas. While this critique stands, it is important to note that since his *Social Theory of International Politics* Wendt has added an interesting new angle into causal analysis – an angle that we now seek to elaborate on. In his article 'Why the World State is Inevitable', Alexander Wendt turned to the Aristotelian notion of cause in order to elucidate a 'teleological' logic for the development of the world state.[73] In the article concerned Wendt focused specifically on developing the notion of final cause in order to build his theoretical argument. However, while this was his focus, he also pointed out that other Aristotelian

[73] Wendt (2003).

categories might be useful in thinking through causation. Interestingly, he argued that parallels can be drawn between constitutive analyses in IR and the Aristotelian causal categories of formal and material causation.[74] Thus, Wendt opened up the possibility of broadening out the notion of cause for the purposes of IR theorising.

This section takes as its cue Wendt's initial explorations of wider concepts of cause: it aims to examine how causes can be conceived of in a wider sense beyond the 'pushing and pulling' efficient cause metaphor that has dominated many theorists' engagements with causation. Broadening the meaning of the notion of cause allows us to specify the way in which different aspects of the social world – agents, normative and discursive context, reasons as well as social structures – can be seen as causal. Giving our causal accounts further direction through the Aristotelian conceptual system, an argument recently also explored by Ruth Groff, albeit on slightly different lines,[75] helps to bring light to some of the crucial issues that have remained problematic for philosophical realists (that is, their inability coherently to escape the efficient cause notion, see chapter 5) and for many IR theorists (that is, their inability to conceive of causes as anything but pushing and pulling). It should be noted that the objective here is not to revive, or to draw directly on, the Aristotelian philosophical system as a whole. Rather the goal is simply to make use of the rich four-fold typology of causes as a useful conceptual approach to further directing the ways in which we can conceptualise social causes.

Aristotle's four causes account

As was seen in chapter 1, the concept of cause in the modern philosophy of causation has predominantly been understood through the notion of 'efficient cause': causes, since Descartes, have referred to 'pushing and pulling' forces, those things that through their action or movement precipitate change. The efficient cause assumption has characterised the Humean approaches but also, as has been seen in chapter 5, has dominated some of the philosophically realist engagements with causation.[76] The Aristotelian system provides grounds for overcoming the modern tendency to collapse the concept of cause with the 'singular monolithic'

[74] Wendt (2003: 495). [75] Groff (2004: 99–134).
[76] Harré and Madden (1975: 5).

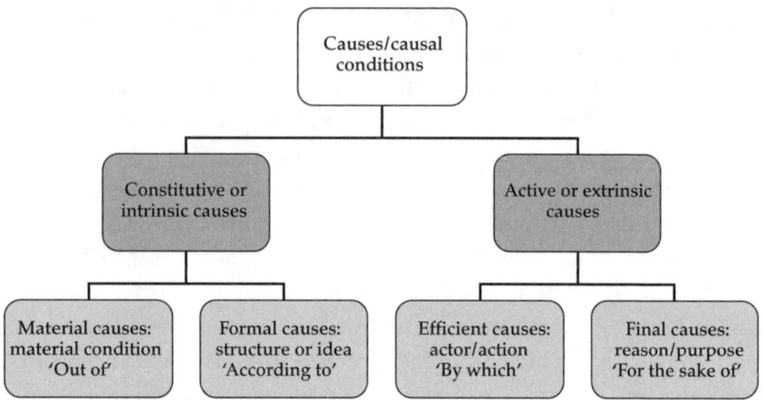

Fig. 1 Aristotelian causes

idea of cause.[77] The Aristotelian meaning of the word cause, the Greek word *aition* (plural *aitia*), did not have a precise meaning in the sense that modern philosophy has tried to establish. An *aition* was anything that contributes in any way to the producing or maintaining of a certain reality. Through his reflections, Aristotle came to the realisation that causes work in different ways, for there are many ways in which things can be brought about. He categorised causes into four basic types of constituents: material, formal, efficient and final causes.[78]

These four Aristotelian causes cause in different ways. Crucially, they do not just 'move' things: they also 'constitute' or 'condition' things. In understanding Aristotelian causation we must understand the distinctions between intrinsic, or constitutive, and extrinsic, or active, causes. An intrinsic cause is that which is within the thing being caused, that which continues to be present in a thing through constituting it.[79] An extrinsic cause is that which is not within the being, but which lends an influence or activity to the producing of something. In the Aristotelian four causes model material and formal causes, as the basic constituents of being, are the intrinsic causes and efficient and final causes, as movers, are the extrinsic causes.[80]

77 This singular monolithic idea of cause has also been powerfully criticised recently by Cartwright (2004).
78 Aristotle (1970b: 4–5).
79 Waterlow (1982: 11).
80 See also Dolhenty (2007).

Material causes, for Aristotle, have ontological primacy in the world in the sense that nothing in the world can exist without materiality.[81] This means that all explanations of the state of the world will have to inquire into the material basis from which things arise. Aristotle's material cause does not refer to just anything 'out of which' something comes to be, as often interpreted in critical realism, but, rather, to the passive potentiality of matter or material substances. However, Aristotelian material causes are not reductionist but work at different 'levels' or 'steps'.[82] So-called prime matter, the substantial principle found in all bodies or substances, can be seen as the material cause of the physical existence of any object. However, so-called secondary matter, that is, an existing bodily substance with a form (such as wood or a gun), can also, in a given context, be understood as a material cause (that is, cause of a table or cause of a killing).[83] Pre-formed things can be material causes, because they are the material potentiality 'out of which' things come to be.[84] The material potentialities of substances are shaped by their internal structure (form), often on multiple levels. A gun, for example, has certain material powers in relation to how it has been shaped (its form) as well as arising from the substance out of which it is shaped (a wooden gun has different properties from a silver one).

Although material causes are ontologically primary and, hence, crucial in any explanation, Aristotle argues that to make sense of the world, and indeed of matter, another basic constitutive element must always be grasped. *Formal causes* refer to what Aristotle conceptualised as that which shapes or defines matter. Forms define the forms of matter, that is, the intelligibility of matter. A formal cause is the 'according to which' something is made or constructed. Forms, too, work on different levels: while we can refer to the form of a substance (e.g. the constitution of marble), we can also refer to the structure of an object as formal cause (e.g. the form of a house). Crucially, formal causes were, for Aristotle, intrinsic or 'constitutive' rather than active causes in that they constitute things by defining meanings and relations, rather than by acting as moving sources of change.

[81] Something that critical realism too seems to accept. See Collier (1994: 46).

[82] See Frank Lewis's (2001: 248) account of 'relation of thing and its matter' in Aristotle's framework of thought.

[83] Ross (1960: 167–8).

[84] Aristotle (1970b: 5).

Strictly speaking, the only active 'actualisers', for Aristotle, are efficient causes. The Aristotelian notion of *efficient cause* refers to the primary movers, or sources of change. Aristotelian efficient causes are extrinsic causes in that efficient causes do not exist within the given substance they go towards producing, like formal and material causes. Efficient causes refer quite simply to the setting in motion of the *potentia* of a patient.[85] Efficient causes do not 'guide' things (this comes from potentiality (material and formal) and final causality); they simply actualise things through activating interactions of form and matter. Nevertheless, Aristotelian efficient causality is not the same as the modern understanding of efficient causality as a purely mechanical type of cause (when A, then B); efficient causality is fundamentally embedded within and in relation to other types of causes and cannot in itself explain anything. In fact, Aristotle's efficient causes are inconceivable without relationships to other causes, for efficient causes themselves are substances, bodies or things constituted by the other causes.

For Aristotle, *final causes* – the ends and purposes 'for the sake of which a thing is'[86] – are closely associated with efficient causes. Yet, they refer to an irreducible type of cause.[87] For Aristotle, final causality was a crucial element in explaining changes or things holistically: so-called 'mechanical' explanations, popular with Democritus and Empedocles, were considered to be, although not 'wrong', lacking a crucial part of what makes a 'holistic' explanation, that is the 'final causes', the purposive goals that direct 'mechanistic' processes.[88]

Crucially, although these four causes were separable as types of causes, Aristotle conceived of them as always working in relation to each other, not in isolation. Hence, in inquiring into any change or thing, he argues, we must always ask many different kinds of why-questions: inquiring merely into singular causes tells us little since causes never exist in isolation from other types of causes.[89] The key to understanding and using Aristotelian concepts is that they are flexible and multifaceted and apply to various different situations in various different ways, indeed, 'their varieties are numerous'.[90] The Aristotelian categories remind us that there are always multiple cycles of multiple causes at work in the world and that causal explanation is about inquiring into and making sense of these various causes and their interactions.

[85] Des Chene (1996: 179). [86] Aristotle (1970b: 4). [87] Gilson (1984: 5).
[88] Gilson (1984: 105). [89] Aristotle (1970b: 4). [90] Aristotle (1970b: 5).

Multifaceted social ontology, pluralistic causal powers

How can we understand the social world through the Aristotelian conceptual system, and what added value does this have? The Aristotelian conceptual system allows us to conceptualise the ontological parameters of social inquiry in a useful way: it directs us towards a multifaceted understanding of causal powers in the social world.

First, if we accept the Aristotelian understanding of material causes, we can recognise that material causes are fundamental in any explanation: without accounting for material potentiality and conditionality, any account of the world, including the social world, is limited. Materiality is a basic ontological condition of all existence. However, the Aristotelian notion of material cause allows us to use material causes as a flexible category referring to a wide range of material substances, things and resources and, importantly, allows us to conceptualise these material resources as 'limiting' and 'enabling', or 'conditioning', causes. The Aristotelian framing of material causes is useful in that it directs us away from the complete rejection of material factors, as well as allowing us to avoid attaching deterministic overtones to materially based explanations of the social world.[91]

Second, if we accept the notion of formal causes, this, arguably, provides us with a useful way of framing the causal role of ideas, rules, norms and discourses in the social world. What are ideas, rules, norms and discourses and how are these formal causes? Arguably, all the categories above refer to various 'ways of conceiving' or 'defining meanings'. Contra positivists, ideas, rules, norms and discourses should not be conceived as individual 'mental states'. Rather, it could be argued, on social constructivist lines, that we gain a better understanding of the 'ideational' context of social life if we see ideas, rules, norms and discourses as inherently social, relational and intersubjective ways of conceiving or defining meaning that 'make possible the articulation and circulation of other sets of meanings'.[92] The crucial thing to note is that intersubjective frameworks that give meaning to social life do not just constitute 'conceptual relations', that is, relate

[91] Marxist explanations are often accused of deterministic materialist explanations. It should be noted, however, that Marxist explanations do not necessarily entail deterministic logic but have been accorded it through the transposing of empiricist closed system (law-based) logic on Marxist frameworks. Engels was, arguably, one of the first to give such deterministic connotations to Marx's system. See, for example, Thomas (1991).

[92] Laffey and Weldes (1997: 209–10)

concepts to other concepts, but also define or constitute meanings to objects, agents or practices by defining them in relation to other concepts, objects, agents or practices. The 'meanings' or 'ways of conceiving' that are dominant come to inform the intentions and the actions of agents, that is, the meanings that constitute social life 'condition' agents' intentions and actions. Ideas, rules, norms and discourses have impacts in the world, that is, by virtue of the coming together of certain concepts and the intersubjective legitimisation of such conceptual relations, some actions are made possible and other actions are precluded.[93]

The 'conditioning' role that ideational causes play can be understood through the notion of formal cause.[94] Ideas, rules, norms, or generally 'ways of thinking', can be understood as the 'according to which' social life is made. As formal causes, ideas, rules, norms and discourses can be seen as causal shapers of social life: they are the 'according to which' agents form their identities, intentions, decisions and actions. To give an example, the rules of chess provide a set of meanings and rules that define the meaning of the game chess. However, understood as formal causes we can see that the rules of chess do not merely form conceptual relations (define conceptual dependencies that define the pieces, the board, the meaning of the game), but also can be considered the causes of the game of chess, in that these rules, by giving the game meaning, come to define the non-conceptual relations, that is the materially unfolding relations, between pieces, board and players. The rules of chess are the 'according to which' identities, intentionality and social action of agents become 'formed'. Ideas, norms and rules as formal causes define and structure social life by relating agents to each other, material contexts, their social roles and meanings of their practices.

In social life there are, of course, many forms at play at any one time, which can 'form' intentions or actions and these compete and interact in dynamic ways. However, ideas, beliefs, rules, norms and discourses do have relatively stable meaning structures. This is made possible by the fact that often certain ideas, beliefs, rules, norms and discourses are constructed so as to 'fit together' into coherent wholes.[95]

[93] Laffey and Weldes (1997: 210).
[94] The account differs here from Ruth Groff's (2004) in that she sees formal causality as social structural causality, an interpretation not adopted here.
[95] Laffey and Weldes (1997: 203).

Crucially, the category of formal cause gives us a radically different way of thinking about the causal role of ideas, rules, norms and discourses: Aristotle's conception of formal cause can be seen as a 'constraining and enabling' type of cause, not a 'pushing and pulling' active cause. What I mean by this is that formal causes 'condition' as contextual causes rather than actively bringing about their effects. Thus, while the rules of chess provide a causal condition of the game of chess, it is not that these rules 'push and pull' agents; rather they 'constrain and enable' their thoughts and actions, that is, they provide a conditioning context within which agents make decisions.

The Aristotelian understanding of efficient cause is important in understanding agency in the social world. Most accounts of agents follow the efficient cause framing in accepting that in the social world the most obvious efficient causes are agents or their actions that 'cause' through inciting a change. However, the Aristotelian model reminds us that efficient causality of agents' actions is always embedded in a causal context. If the Aristotelian conception of efficient causes is accepted, efficient causes, and hence agency, must always be linked to the material form of causality in the sense that agents' movements and actions are taken within a material environment and are based on the material base of human mind and body. The actions also take place drawing on the formal environment around the agents, and the agents' intentionality is formed in relation to that environment. Accounts of the social world that assume away the social context of action are limited in their explanations of the social world.

What about the role of final causes? Many would doubt the applicability of 'teleology' in the natural sciences. However, it is much harder to dismiss final causes in the social world where intentionality is in many ways the most obvious form of causality.[96] Most social theoretical approaches recognise that human agents and their actions are purposeful and intentional, even when actions are spontaneous and not 'planned'. However, most social theorists, including the critical realists who see intentionality as fundamental in the social world,[97] have avoided using the notion of final cause. Indeed, even von Wright, one of the most open advocates of teleological intentional explanations as a specific characteristic of the sciences of man, refrains from recognising fully the causal origins of intentionality in the Aristotelian logic that he

[96] Gilson (1984: 8). [97] Porpora (1983).

seeks to revive (against what he terms the Galilean regularity-bound and mechanistic cause approach). Instead, he contrasts causal tradition of a Galilean kind with a hermeneutic intentional form of explanation.[98] He does so explicitly because he wants to restrict causal terminology, but recognises that there is the possibility that one might reject his characterisation of certain explanations as quasi-causal through the expansion of the notion of cause and through an attack on the experimentalist idea of causation.[99]

The aim here is to do exactly what von Wright tentatively opens the door for: that is, recognise the causality of intentionality as a very different non-mechanistic non-regularity bound causal force. In my view accepting the notion of final cause, and distinguishing it from the notion of efficient cause, is important for two reasons. If we accept final causes we can, first, give intentionality the fundamental role that it deserves in social explanation: it can be recognised that social life cannot be explained without reference to intentions and motivations, the 'purposes' that drive agents' actions. Furthermore, we can recognise that intentions are a type of cause, but also a type of cause that is not reducible to efficient causality. Accepting final causes emphasises the different way in which intentions are causes. Intentions, and reasons, are 'active' causes; yet they are not physical 'powerful particulars' in the efficient cause sense.[100] They refer to a different kind of causal category, that is, the particular intentional powers of agents, reference to which allows us to explain the efficient actions of agents (in a particular context).[101]

Importantly, through the Aristotelian conceptual system, we can get rid of some of the prejudices against final causes. We can recognise that final causes, too, are only a part of the complex social world and of social explanation.[102] Also, it must be accepted, against common misconceptions, that the notion of final causality does not downgrade other types of causes but works within, or in relation to, them.

[98] Von Wright (1971: 2–3). [99] Von Wright (1971: 86, viii).

[100] For a similar argument regarding final causes see Groff (2004: 124–5).

[101] Groff (2004: 124).

[102] The role of intentionality within social context is, arguably, characterised well by the so-called 'strategic-selectivity' approach to the structure-agency debate, where agency is always seen as strategic (intentional), yet within 'strategically selective' structured social context. Jessop (1990); Hay (1995).

It should additionally be noted that, following Aristotle, we can also come to recognise the close relationship between types of causes, especially between efficient, final and formal causes. For example, we can often treat an agent's actions (efficient cause) and his/her intentions (final cause) as a closely knit 'causal pair' in explanation. This does not mean, however, that efficient cause exhausts the notion of final cause. Also, the relationship of final causes with formal causes is important. A good example of a case when the categories overlap is with regard to 'reasons'. In certain situations a (causal) reason for action would be described in terms of final causes: Andy went to the shop because he wanted an ice-cream. In certain situations the reason would, however, be more closely associated with formal causes: jealousy, for example, is a social form linked to many other socially engendered patterns of thinking. When cited as a reason (Andy wanted to kill Alex because he was jealous of his success) the final cause needs to be framed within the formal social context. 'Reasons' explanations, then, often draw on both categories and must be dealt with in relation to each other, not in isolation from each other. The Aristotelian categories, although separable, are very flexible in explaining events and processes.

As we have seen the four basic constituents that Aristotle outlined can be used to grasp the make-up of the social world in a pluralistic and holistic way, allowing us to talk of various different aspects of the social world as causal – although as causal in different ways. However, something is missing from this account of social ontology, certainly from the point of view of critical realism: what about structures of social relations?

The critical realist definition of social structures is useful, as we have seen, for it accepts the reality and causal role of structures of social relations, while accepting their social construction and dynamism. However, we need to be more precise about how their causal powers should be conceptualised. Some critical realists argue, as we have seen, that the type of causality to be associated with social structures is the 'Aristotelian material causality': social structures have been conceived to shape social action as the underlying 'material' that defines the scope and means of social agency. Others have seen social structures as an INUS-condition cause, as an in itself insufficient but nevertheless necessary causal condition of social action. Both these analogies can be clarified by understanding social structures through the Aristotelian four-fold categorisation of causes.

On the basis of the Aristotelian categories, we can understand social structures as carriers of various causal powers. It could be argued that social structures are caused by intentional agency in the sense that intentional agency gives rise to social structures. We can understand this agency through the efficient and final cause notions, as we have seen. However, arguably, social structures are also causal on agents. How can we conceptualise the causal role of social structures?

Social structures as material social relations 'carry' both material and formal causal powers on agents: they form 'related wholes' within which intentional agents act and, thereby, reproduce or transform the social conditions (material and formal) of their own activity.[103] Crucial in making up social structures are people's understandings and ways of thinking: these define how people see themselves, others, objects, their roles and their practices. Formal causes, we have seen, capture the sense in which agents are constrained and enabled by ideas, rules, norms and discourses (ways of thinking). Formal causes, then, are crucial in understanding social structures and their causal powers. However, critical realists have emphasised the fact that social structures are materially unfolding and give rise to material properties. These properties have a materially causal role in directing agents. As we have seen, we can view material causes as those materials 'out of which' something emerges, or through the use of which an action takes place (e.g. wood, gun). However, we can also see material causal powers within the material properties and resources carried within social structural contexts (e.g. social positions, rent, money). It follows that the causal role of social structures cannot be reduced to the formal causal powers but must be acknowledged to carry also material causal powers that condition action.

On the basis of the Aristotelian conceptual system we can conceptualise agents as existing within structural conditions in which both formal and material causal powers form a singular simultaneous causal conditioner of agency.

Think of the social structure of capitalism. The internal relations between capital and wage labour depend on shared understandings of meanings. They also depend on rules that define how agents should act

[103] Scaltsas (2001: 111–13) emphasises that so-called related wholes refer to such objects that are not 'substances' in the traditional sense, nor are they reducible to the components. This, arguably, fits the notion of social structures well.

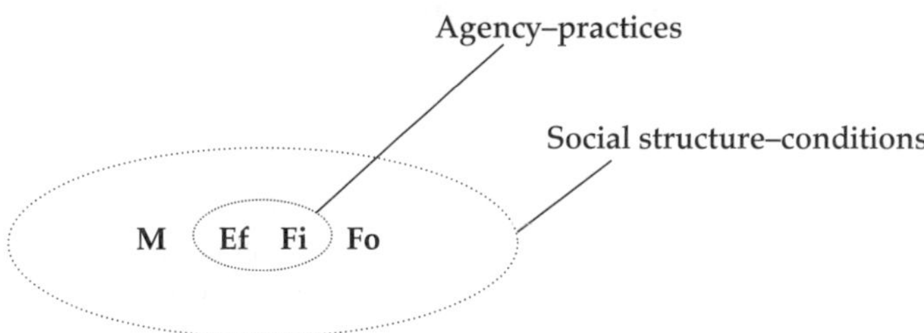

Fig. 2 Aristotelian causes and social structures (M = material causes, Fo = formal causes, Ef = efficient causes, Fi = final causes)

and rule-following practices of agents. However, the shared meanings and rules give rise to material social relations and, crucially, to material constraints and enablements on agents within structures (for example, minimum wages, capital/property ownership, distribution of profit). These material properties act as 'constraining and enabling' material causes on agents in particular social positions within the structure: a worker by virtue of his position in the structure has different material resources at his disposal than the property-owning capitalist. The social structure of capitalism and the social roles and positions it defines are, then, not reducible to the 'rule-following' or the 'practices' of individuals but also carry material causal powers in the form of material structural properties.

Material causes, as causal powers embedded within social structures, can be seen to play a role also in less obviously materially determining social structures. Consider the structure of a family, for example. The rules that define agents' identities and roles (mother, father, children), positions (for example, of hierarchy) and practices (respect, obeying, telling off, etc.) in their material unfolding give rise to material properties which constrain and enable agents in the family in different ways: as my father's daughter it is not just that I have come to obey the rules of social interaction but that, as a result of my role and position in the family, I am also materially constrained in a way that my father is conversely enabled (as possessing the authority position he can legitimately correct me, as owner of the family home and provider of food and finances he has material resources I am dependent on). Indeed, it is important to note that 'social (structural) positions' are not just 'ideational understandings' that agents possess, but real material positions that carry material as well as formal 'constraints and enablements'.

It is useful to view social structures as carrying two types of causal powers: both formal and material. Social structures constrain and enable agents – simultaneously – both through the 'understandings' or rules (whether consciously or routinely followed) embedded in social structures, and also through the material constraints the internal relations of agents have given rise to and that pre-exist the individual agent. As Paul Lewis argues, there are two senses in which social structures are limiting/enabling: 'both the social rules and the distribution of interests and resources laid down by historically given social structures . . . exert an influence on social affairs'.[104] Importantly, the Aristotelian framing of social structural causal powers also allows us to see material and formal causes embodied in structures of social relations as causal in a conditioning sense: they enable and delimit human actions by defining the context of action. Thus, contra Durkheimians, social structures are not simply agent-like entities that have intentions or that can undertake efficient actions; they are in a basic sense 'relations' that, by setting the material and ideational context of human agency, condition human action.[105]

Conceptual clarifications: conditions and mechanism

In the light of the Aristotelian model, we can clarify some of the conceptual inconsistencies and confusions that have plagued many Humean, but also philosophically realist, framings of the notions 'condition' and 'mechanism'.

First, the relationship of the notions 'cause' and 'condition' can be usefully clarified on the basis of the Aristotelian model. Often social theorists have been uncertain about the relations of the notions of cause and condition. Conditions have been understood as a non-deterministic way of referring to the world, whereas causes have been associated with deterministic accounts. Indeed, those that have been sceptical of the notion of cause because of its deterministic and mechanistic

[104] P. Lewis (2002: 20).

[105] Collier (1994: 147). Collier (1989: 89) and Groff (2004: 111) take this to mean that social structures should be understood as formal causes. This view of social structures is not adopted here although it can be seen as closely related to the conceptualisation here.

connotations have often preferred to utilise the notion of condition. The poststructuralists, for example, have wielded the notion of 'conditions of possibility' and have predominantly interpreted this as non-causal terminology.

Even critical realists have, at times, been unsure whether there is an ontological difference between causes and conditions. Bhaskar, for example, has been unsure of the ontological status of conditions, of whether they should be considered a real naturally necessitating cause or not.[106] In the light of the causal model advanced here, we can see that what we call conditions are, in fact, a type of cause, and an ontological type of cause.[107] Conditions can be understood through the material and formal cause notions: they refer to causal powers that 'condition' or 'constrain and enable' the context of social agency. The terminological distinction between causes and conditions, then, can be seen as a conceptual distinction between different types of causes, not as a divide between naturally necessitating causes and non-necessitating non-causal conditions. Indeed, as Collier also argues, 'aside from our forensic or other practical concerns, there is nothing that is "the *cause*", only causes. And these include "conditions".'[108]

What should we make of the fact that conditions are always plural? Indeed, any act, or change can be seen to have almost an infinite number of conditions. Here explanatory pragmatism is seen as a way of dealing with the plurality of conditions. The fact that any act or change has many causal conditions is not considered problematic here because it is recognised that, in a given pragmatic context of inquiry, some conditions, even though causal, do not need to be referred to since many conditioning causes are already presupposed in our accounts, making it unnecessary to refer to them.[109] Crucially, what we assign as 'causally important' depends on how we ask causal questions, as the pragmatists have also argued.

Consider the example of explaining the processes that led to the formulation of the European Convention. If we asked 'why did the

[106] For a critique of Bhaskar's confusions on causes and conditions see Collier (1994: 125–7).

[107] Counterfactual conditions of an INUS-condition account need to be ontologically, not logically, grounded. Counterfactual accounts, to be truly explanatory, require accounts of why the particular condition was counterfactually causal. Patomäki (2002: 76).

[108] Collier (1994: 125).

[109] Sayer (1992: 235).

European Convention come about?' we would proceed to examine various causes and conditions that brought this about. We would ask questions about the people involved and about their aspirations for European unity. We would also, arguably, examine the structural environment for these decisions, including the institutional structures of the European Union as well as the wider global structural context of the Union. In this context of inquiry, the 'rules of diplomacy' would not count as an important causal conditioner of the process and we would probably not consider including this causal factor in our account. However, if the same process was inquired into differently, if, for example, we were interested in inquiring why certain decision-makers (state leaders and bureaucracies rather than people on the street) were involved in making the Convention, we would probably cite the 'rules of diplomacy' and their embeddedness in international structures and processes as an important causal conditioner. In both cases the rules of diplomacy are an (ontological, naturally necessitating) causal conditioner of the process; the difference in the causal importance of this ontological cause is that it is not pragmatically as important in certain explanatory contexts as in others.

It should be noted that in analysis of conditions, and in causal analysis in general, postulations of counterfactuals can be useful, postulation such as, had diplomatic conventions entailed that men only can attend diplomatic negotiations in the European Union, the processes and outcomes might have differed in such and such ways. Crucially, however, these kinds of counterfactual causal arguments involve, as Patomäki has emphasised, the postulation of causal powers and properties in complex causal conditions: they do not involve, as counterfactual hypotheses have for many empiricists, analysis of *logical relations of events* (often in reference to predictive laws, see chapter 1). Instead of analysing the mere logical structure of events ('had Suzy not thrown the rock the bottle would not have broken', or 'had Gorbachev not engaged in negotiation with US leaders, the Cold War would not have ended'), counterfactual analysis as adopted here is premised on analysis of causal powers, structures and interactions that underlie such events (the causal powers of Suzy's rock, Suzy and bottle; the causal powers of Gorbachev, causal forces at work in his context and the Cold War environment). Also, counterfactual analysis as seen here does not entail predictive regularities: even if Gorbachev can be seen as an important counterfactual condition of the end of the Cold War, this does not entail a law or generalisation to the effect 'when Gorbachev-type actors, end of hostile confrontations'. Counterfactuality, contra positivists, is not taken to imply laws or regularities: it is instead tied to arguments made about causal powers.

Besides clarifying the issue of conditions, the concept of (causal) mechanism can also be reframed through the Aristotelian categories. The concept of mechanism has been deeply problematic for many social theorists. The notion has often been understood 'mechanistically': a mechanism has been understood as an object made up by individual parts (whether atoms in molecules or individuals in society) that 'push and pull' each other along.[110] The Humeans have also often understood the notion 'non-ontologically', according to the Humean logic, as 'intervening variables that explain why a correlation exists between an independent and a dependent variable'.[111] The philosophically realist theorists have sought to give mechanisms a 'deep' ontological meaning and to avoid the 'mechanistic' view of mechanisms. However, among the philosophical realists the notion of mechanism, arguably, lacks a clear definition. Moreover, the relationship of the concept of cause and that of mechanism has remained unclear: Bhaskar, for example, seems to see the two as interchangeable.[112]

The Aristotelian schema allows us to avoid these conceptual problems. We can follow the philosophical realists in arguing that mechanisms are rooted ontologically, they do not refer to mere 'intervening variables' conceived of as regularities (as for many positivists). However, instead of seeking to define mechanisms in a fixed way, or shying away from defining them, we gain a better understanding of the rather vague metaphor 'mechanism', if we define it, quite simply, as 'complexes of causes'. In the light of the Aristotelian plural conception of ontology and causal powers, it could be argued that mechanisms are usefully thought of as the particular kinds of, often relatively stable, interactions that take place between certain types of causal forces. Mechanism explanations, then, can be seen as accounts of the processes of interaction between different elements that bring about given events or processes.[113] On such a definition we can refer to various

[110] See, for example, Hedström and Swedberg (1998); Elster (1989).
[111] Mahoney (2001: 578).
[112] See Bhaskar's early work, especially, for example, Bhaskar (1978: 14–20, 46).
[113] In this sense Suganami's (1996: 164–8) understanding of mechanisms as narratives that make a given phenomenon intelligible can be seen as

causal interactions or processes as mechanisms: from market mechanisms (not seen as a logically necessary system but made up of various socially embedded and positioned agents and structures coming together in certain ways[114]) to mechanisms of discursive reproduction (for example, variously socially positioned and shaped strategies of media representations).

This definition of mechanisms provides us with an open definition for an already vague term, but also allows us to separate causes from mechanisms. Indeed, contra philosophical realists who have defined the notion of cause through the notion of causal mechanism, we can argue that causes are not defined by mechanisms. Importantly, because the notion of mechanism is not given ontological priority here, it can be accepted that the notion of mechanism is *not* necessary for a causal account. The model here does not presume mechanism-accounts, but accounts of the interaction of causes. Since critical realism has at times been accused of the use of concepts such as mechanisms,[115] this interpretation leaves room for the interpretation that other concepts, for example the notion of 'causal process', may often better convey causal interactions in the social world.[116]

Implications of broadening the concept of cause in IR

The pluralistic conception of causal powers advanced here has some important implications for clarifying problems of causation in IR. It provides us with (1) a better way of dealing with the causal–constitutive divide as well as (2) a way of tackling the problems of theoretical reductionism in IR.

First, when causation is opened up to the formal cause meaning, we can recognise the causal nature of many reflectivist explanations. Ideas, rules, norms and discourses are studied by the reflectivists because these aspects of social life are the 'according to which' agents form their

somewhat similar to the account here. However, mechanism explanations are here understood to have real referents, nor do they need to be 'mechanistic' (non-purposive), although they are often used to refer to relatively 'routinised' or enduring causal processes.

114 For a critical realist critique of orthodox economics see Lawson (1997).

115 Peacock (2000: 319–23).

116 Heikki Patomäki (2002: 130) is also sceptical of the use of the mechanism metaphor.

intentions, identities and undertake their actions. The reflectivists do not do Humean causal analysis, nor do they trace active efficient causes in social life. However, this does not mean that their accounts are non-causal. Arguably, these theorists track the 'conditioning' causes that delimit and enable agents by constituting the framework of meanings (and social relations) around them.[117] Thus, when the constructivists talk of the 'constitutive' norms and rules 'because' of which shifts happen in world politics, they are engaging in causal analysis in that they are contextualising the agents' actions within a formal context, a formal context which shapes the agents' perceptions and thinking processes. Feminists, on the other hand, analyse forms of gendered norms and discourses, not just to uncover meanings and rules, but because these meanings and rules causally condition the way in which men and women act and give rise to social structural conditions that asymmetrically constrain and enable men and women. Equally, when poststructuralists, such as Campbell, highlight discourse or theories in 'constituting' social life, they think them important because these discourses or theories, through constituting agents' perceptions and reasoning, have 'consequences' for how agents perceive the world, themselves, others and, hence, their actions.[118] Poststructuralists highlight causal conditions of agency and action, especially the background conditions that often go unnoticed in mainstream analyses.

It follows that separating causal and constitutive forms of inquiry is misleading: we would be better placed to deal with the social world and its complex causes and causal conditioning if we saw constitutive theorising as an inseparable part of causal theorising. We can, of course, ask non-causal questions of meaning (for example, 'what does X mean?). However, when accounting for the social world our

[117] Regulative and constituting rules have the same role in this regard, even though varying in strength, not decidedly different ones (one causal, one not) as Wendt (1999a: 165) would have it. The difference is that constitutive rules, since they refer to internal relations, have a more persevering nature, that is, they 'retain their identity under regulative rule violation' and often make regulative rules make sense (condition them), as Patomäki (2002: 102) argues. Thus, the regulative rule 'do not cross the road when the light is red' is causal upon us by 'constraining and enabling' our behaviour, just as the constitutive rule 'green means go, red means stop' does. (Why did you not cross the road? Because I should not go when the light is red. Why should you not go when the light is red? Because it means stop, cars are coming.) The latter has a deeper meaning that the causal powers of the regulative rule depend upon.

[118] Koslowski and Kratochwil (1995: 127); Campbell (1998a: 84).

inquiries are not limited to (non-causal) understanding of meanings: most theorists, including poststructuralists, also want to account for how those meanings were made, reproduced or reified and how they shape, influence, provide a conditioner of social life. It is important that we recognise that inquiring into the latter questions is far from non-causal. We should accept that accounts of 'constitutive' meanings, in most contexts, are essentially inseparable from causal claims. To make statements about the 'constitutive' role of conceptual relations and structures of social meaning (say, a particular discourse) entails, in fact, that these conceptual relations have effects (and determinants) that are not just conceptual. Conceptual relations are played out in the world (ontologically) and the way they play themselves out is causal: this is because conceptual relations form the meanings 'according to which' agents form their intentions and actions.

In reflectivist IR theorising the metaphor of 'constitution' has been applied in such a way as to hide the causal nature and importance of social constructions.[119] The conceptualisation of causation advanced here opens up the causal role of constitutive factors. Seeing rules, norms and discourses as formal causes means that it is hard for theorists to deny the causal role of rules, norms and discourses – even if 'constitutive' terminology is favoured. Recognising constitutive rules, norms and discourses as causal is important, not only because it allows us to see and treat these causal factors as just as causal as other factors (although in a different *way* to other factors), but also because this insight deeply challenges the self-image of many 'constitutive' theorists in IR.

Second, the Aristotelian conceptualisation also gives us tools to battle theoretical reductionism in IR by emphasising that social ontology is always pluralistic and we must try to ask a plurality of different types of questions concerning their causal roles. The model here recognises that social explanation is always pragmatic in the sense that it aims to answer particular sorts of questions one is interested in explaining. We can use the Aristotelian categories in various ways, depending on the context of inquiry. For example, in inquiring into the processes that bring about particular rules or norms one might study how these have come about through the speech acts of certain key individuals. This rule

[119] For a discussion of the misleading nature of the metaphors of 'construction' and 'constitution' see Sayer (2000: 45).

springing from speech acts, on the other hand, can be treated as a formal cause in another context, that is, as a 'constraining and enabling' socialising principle that pre-exists agents and their actions.[120] However, explanatory pragmatism is here tempered by conceptual pluralism and ontologically open horizons. Even if one is interested in particular speech acts or a formal cause in a specific context, crucially, the wider context (formal, material and structural) of these factors should not be ignored, certainly as a matter of theoretical '*a priorism*'. Often such a priori judgements have been made on an epistemological basis: here we can recognise that epistemological approaches should not become dogmatic constraints on the kinds of ontological forces we deal with and, moreover, we can see that explanations should remain open to holistic ontological causal horizons. Which kind of causes have emphasis in concrete explanation remains an empirical issue, but our empirical studies should not be predetermined by overly narrow conceptual and epistemological bases. One type of cause, be it material, agential, final or formal, even if empirically shown to be dominant, forms only one part of any explanation and, thus, should not be assumed to exist, or be examined, in isolation from other types of causes.

Indeed, contra many reflectivists, we have to recognise that rules, norms and discourses do not, on their own, provide holistic explanations: we must understand also the complex structural context within which these rules and norms arise, operate and die. Contra many constructivists and poststructuralists in IR, it can be argued that these contexts carry also material causes. Of course, material resources emerge from previous social structuring and practices and derive their meanings from social structures and practices: yet, they must be accepted as real in the sense that these material resources and potentialities pre-exist individual agents and causally condition the ranges of action they can take. Thus, for example, the fact that guns were available in Bosnia (and that they were there for structurally embedded reasons, for example, because of the structures of the world economy and its trade processes) provides an important condition for the war or attacks that took place. It is not that the availability of guns alone determined

[120] The same applies for efficient causes. Many social actors are, in fact, social structures. Yet, they can be treated as agents for pragmatic purposes in different explanatory contexts. However, as will be seen in the next chapter, accepting that structures can be agents requires the recognition of important ontological caveats involving the conditions in which agents act as agents.

what happened but it cannot be ignored that guns have a real material potentiality and real material existence.

Also, the way in which material causes condition social life is vital for understanding the dominance of certain social structures and discourses, and specific actions, in world politics for it is often the norms and discourses with (pre-constituted) material power behind them that 'win out'. To accept that norms of neoliberal economics, for example, have simply become accepted in world institutions through a variety of speech acts is to ignore the structural power (material and formal) behind these norms. Ideas and 'intersubjectivity' are crucial shapers of the social world – but ideas do not exist in a vacuum: they structure material contexts and, indeed, arise from and are constrained and enabled by a pre-existing social structural context, which is also materially determining.

Material reductionism, characteristic of some neorealist framings, is also highly problematic. Material resources and constraints, in and of themselves, have only passive causal powers. Of course material resources matter, for they condition much of international politics, but not only are material resources not to be understood in a mere military sense but also material resources must be recognised as constituted through social processes involving social actors and socialising principles (formal causes) and, indeed, lend their influence differently in the light of different formal causes or social structural contexts. Neorealists in IR, because of the 'pushing and pulling' connotations that they attach to causation, are often inhibited in their ability to think through and examine how material resources are determining of outcomes (for example, how they condition or give rise to ideas, rules and norms or motivations). This, arguably, is an important reason for why these materialist explanations of the causes of particular wars, and of wars in general, have been considered somewhat problematic both theoretically and empirically (see chapter 7 for a more detailed discussion).

Moreover, the notion of social structures is useful in framing how various factors come together to form relatively enduring sets of social relations. Many postpositivists in IR have rejected the notion of structure. This has partly to do with the fact that the notion of structure has often been associated with the Waltzian image of logically determining closed system types of structure. However, it has also had to do with the wide acceptance of an ontologically narrow framing of social life among the constructivists: many constructivist theorists have seen social life as simply emerging from 'social norms' and the 'practices' they give rise to.

The notion of structure is accepted here as crucial in social explanation. However, because of the rejection of Humeanism, the Waltzian closed system view of structure is rejected. Also, the limited 'intersubjectivity' focused meaning of social structures, characteristic of some constructivist frameworks, can be seen as inadequate. Social life cannot simply be reduced to activities or practices of agents, nor their rule context. Social structures cannot be treated as mere intersubjective understandings and practices, but should be seen as social relations that define social roles and positions of agents in relation to each other. As such, they are real, pre-existing individual agents and carry material as well as formal causal powers to constrain and enable agency. Most feminists, for example, would accept that it is not simply that gendered norms inform people's practices but that the world is deeply structured by these norms and practices, that is, the gendered norms give rise to structural conditions that define women's (as well as men's) roles in a very real material sense, that is, social positions, roles and resources are materially as well as formally conditioning.

The acceptance of the notion of social structures is important in our analysis of IR, as will be seen in chapter 7, for it highlights the role of pre-existing and relatively stable (materially embodied) social relations in structuring world politics. These relations, of course, are complex owing to the open system nature of social life where, in concrete contexts, various social structures, more global and more local, constantly interact with and counteract each other in complex ways. The challenge for IR as a discipline is to develop a complexity-sensitive ontological framework, which allows us to conceptualise world politics, its structures of social relations and the complex concrete processes they give rise to, in more nuanced ways. This, as will be seen in chapter 7, can be achieved through careful ontologically guided abstraction, and through the epistemologically and methodologically pluralistic study of concrete social life.

Conclusion

This chapter has built a philosophical account of causation that 'deepens' our understanding of cause beyond the Humean assumptions through drawing on insights of philosophical realism, and 'broadens' the meaning of notion of cause beyond the efficient cause understanding of causes through drawing on Aristotle's conceptual system. Causes can be conceived to have real 'naturally necessitating' ontological existence outside of our stories or observations, and it has been seen that the goal of causal explanation is to build conceptual systems that provide accounts of the various kinds of ontological causal forces in the world, accounts that are fallible, yet of a kind that provide evidential and conceptual reasons for their adoption. Further, the Aristotelian conceptual system helps direct the way in which we conceptualise these various kinds of causal forces. We can conceptualise causes as 'constraining and enabling' rather than just as 'pushing and pulling' forces and recognise that the social world is made up by the complex interaction of various different types of causes. Notably, it has been demonstrated here that there is 'no reason to collapse the concept of causality into that of efficient cause'.[121]

The deeper and broader conceptualisation of causation provides *an alternative interpretive horizon* to the dominant Humean causal discourse. This deeper and broader account of cause, arguably, answers many crucial questions that IR theorists have not managed to deal with within their traditional frameworks, informed by Humeanism and the efficient conception of causation. Instead of insisting on regularity analysis, the model of causation advanced here emphasises methodological pluralism. Instead of maintaining epistemological confidence in mere observational knowledge, the account here accepts epistemological relativity and emphasises the importance of qualitative and historical data, but also interpretive approaches to analysis of such data. Instead of concentration on the observable, individualistic and atomistic ontological assumptions, the account here emphasises 'deep ontology' and ontological pluralism. Instead of a singular idea of cause, this account advances a variegated plural account of the meaning of the term cause. For those troubled by the limitations imposed on research by the Humean discourse, this conception of cause provides an alternative framework.

Although sympathetic to many interpretivist concerns, the account of causation here also challenges the reflectivist denial of causal analysis and science in social life. Ideas and reasons are causal: that is why they matter for social scientific analysis. The Aristotelian broadening of the

[121] Groff (2004: 112)

concept of cause has clarified how exactly ideas, rules and norms should be considered causal. It has been argued that the notion of formal cause can provide a useful way of conceptualising their 'constraining and enabling' causal powers on agents. This has allowed us to transcend the causal–constitutive divide in IR: 'constitutive' accounts, it has been seen, make causal claims, even if only about the 'conditioning' powers of ideas, rules or discourses. Moreover, the broadening of the categories of cause, and embedding them in relation to each other, has directed us away from the theoretical reductionism that has characterised both rationalist and reflectivist theorising.

The emphasis of this chapter has been on the conceptual and philosophical issues: the aim has been to provide a more conceptually adequate solution to the problem of causation which can answer some of the theoretical problems identified within IR schools of thought. Many empirical scientists in IR are often demeaning of such conceptual and philosophical examinations: 'what difference', they ask, 'does such conceptual rethinking of causation make in explaining world politics?' As chapter 7 will show, the rethinking of causation does have some important implications for how IR researchers should go about explaining and debating world politics.

PART III

Reconfiguring causal analysis of world politics

7 Expanding horizons in world political causal inquiry

The previous chapter argued that by 'deepening' and 'broadening' the meaning of the concept of cause we gain a radically different understanding of causation in comparison with the approach followed by the Humeans. Against sceptics that deny the reality of causes, causes are here conceived to have real ontological existence, in both the natural and the social worlds, and the goal of causal explanation, in both realms, is seen to consist in constructing conceptual models that provide understandings of the nature of and interaction between various kinds of causal forces. The Aristotelian conceptual system, I have argued, can direct the ways in which we conceptualise different kinds of causal powers: causes can be conceptualised to range from material resources to normative frameworks, from agent's intentions and actions to social structural relations, and each factor can be seen as causal in a distinct manner. By opening up the issue of causation in IR ontologically, methodologically and epistemologically, the reconceptualised notion of cause can help us deal with some of the theoretical problems that characterise existing treatments of causation in IR. It allows us to reinterpret some divisive theoretical issues that IR scholars have grappled with recently, notably the causal–constitutive theory divide and the tendency towards theoretical reductionism.

The point of this book is to make a philosophical and theoretical case for an alternative conception of causation in IR scholarship: the goals of this work thus differ significantly from those studies in IR that seek to engage in the concrete empirical study of world political processes. However, since meta-theoretical systems, as we have seen, are not without consequences – they influence our conceptual choices, how and which kind of data we use and the kind of knowledge claims we make – it is likely that the meta-theoretical reframing of causation advanced in the previous chapter has some consequences for the concrete study of world politics. It is the aim of this chapter to examine some of the implications that reframing causal analysis has for the practice of world political inquiry. In accordance with the overall aims of the book, the point here is not to give new explanations of world political processes – this is a task for experts in the empirical areas concerned. Rather the aim here is to demonstrate that with a revised conceptualisation of causal analysis in hand, we can consider some new avenues and tools in analysis of causal puzzles in world politics. The revised conception of cause expands the kind of world political causal analysis we conduct: it directs us away from observational regularities towards more conceptually focused and interpretive forms of analysis. Also, it opens up multi-causal explanatory horizons for those approaches so far attracted to reductionist mono-causal arguments.

This chapter seeks to elucidate the implications of rethinking the notion of cause in three steps. First, some reflections will be made on the ontological field of world politics: this is important in that it sets the context, or an 'interpretive horizon', within which we can conduct deeper and broader world political causal analysis. Then, two specific theoretical debates in IR will be examined: the democratic peace debates and the debates over the end of the Cold War. I will seek to analyse some of the limitations that have characterised causal analyses in these areas and provide openings for post-Humean avenues in world political causal research.

Reconceptualising the social ontology of world politics

Philosophical realists argue that ontology matters in the study of International Relations: as Colin Wight has put it, 'politics is the terrain of competing ontologies'.[1] Philosophical realists recognise that ontological assumptions are fundamental in directing how we analyse the world; they create 'interpretive horizons' through which to engage with the empirical world. Dealing with ontological matters then is important: 'putting ontological matters at the heart of analysis reverses a long-standing dogma of traditional IR scholarship',[2] where positivist and interpretive infighting over epistemological matters has been privileged over questions of ontology.

Because of the lack of attention ontological assumptions have received, many conceptual frameworks in the social sciences have been inadequately reflective about the fact that they have drawn on

[1] See, for example, Wight (2006: 2). [2] Wight (2006: 2).

empiricist assumptions, and as a result have been premised on certain peculiarly 'flat' and 'atomistic' ontological assumptions.[3] This section aims to examine the problems of the traditional ontological conceptualisations in IR and advance some suggestions towards a better ontological conceptualisation of the field. It should be noted that the ontological reflections made here do not seek to build a 'new theory of international politics', nor should the ontological framework set out here be considered the only ontological framework within which the deeper and broader account can be applied. Since a discourse of causation does *not* fully determine the content of one's specific theoretical ontology, this chapter seeks but to provide some broad outlines of the kind of social ontology that is more suited to work as a context for the post-Humean conception of causal analysis advocated here.

The traditional conceptual framing of IR: the international system and the state

The central lynchpins of IR 'ontology' have been the notions *international system* and *state*. The most influential account of the 'international system' has been that of Kenneth Waltz. In *Theory of International Politics* Waltz aimed to give a precise definition of the international system and its role in shaping world politics. Waltz argued that in engaging with international political life states act within a specific structural context: within an 'anarchic' international system. In contrast to domestic order where social hierarchies are in place, the 'international system', Waltz argued, has no 'Leviathan' to order relations between actors (states). It is because of the anarchic nature of their context of action that 'rational' states within the international system remain constantly fearful of the motivations of other states, and it is because of this constant 'security dilemma' that the distribution of material resources has a crucial role in shaping the patterns of international politics.[4]

This definition of system is deeply embedded in the empiricist assumptions consistent with Humean premises as we have seen in

[3] This has been pointed out in various disciplines. See, for example, Bhaskar (1979); Collier (1994); Sayer (2000); Lawson (1997); Hay (2002). In IR, Patomäki (2002), Wendt (1999a) and Wight (2006) have powerfully made this point.

[4] Waltz (1979).

chapter 3. Waltz treats the structure of the international system as a 'closed system' from which the behaviour of ontologically flat agents (undifferentiated states) can be 'logically deduced'. Despite his later efforts to emphasise that the international system merely 'shapes and shoves',[5] Waltz, owing to his acceptance of microeconomic theory with its regularity-deterministic assumptions, was directed to consider the international system as a 'closed system' (regularity-deterministic) structure (see chapter 3). Meanwhile, following empiricist anti-realist assumptions, this structure, he argues, is not 'real', that is, it does not aim to postulate an existing reality as such. Rather, the 'structure' for Waltz is but a theoretical construction, a model that, for instrumental purposes, isolates and theorises a hypothetical structure 'as if' it existed.[6]

This definition of the international system, even if not Waltz's specific conclusion, has been accepted by many scholars in the discipline of IR. The international system has been seen as an isolated 'international political realm' with its functionally defined 'logic of anarchy'. This theorisation of the international system is characteristic not just of the realist and neorealist frameworks, but also of the neoliberal institutionalist approaches, even though they emphasise that anarchy in the international system can be mitigated through creating and fostering the right incentives and strategies.[7] Crucially, even when Waltz's particular conceptualisation of the international system has not been adhered to, the assumption that the 'international' constitutes a discrete 'level of analysis' separable from the domestic realm has been widely accepted. This assumption has, in fact, provided the justification for a separate field of study called 'International Relations'.

Interestingly, the English School, with its emphasis on the sharing of common values in international *society*, has also separated the international from the domestic,[8] as have arguably some constructivists.[9] In the classical canon of Anglo-American IR, the 'international', even international society, has been understood as a relatively '"thin" space of strategic interaction, populated by diplomats, soldiers, and capitalists',[10] whereas the domestic has been seen as the site of

[5] Waltz (1986: 343). [6] Waltz (1979: 6–7).
[7] Axelrod and Keohane (1985); Keohane (1984).
[8] See, for example, M. Wight (1966); Bull (1977).
[9] Wendt (1999a: 193–245).
[10] Barkawi and Laffey (2002: 110) paraphrasing Raymond Aron.

interpersonal social relations.[11] The international system, or international society, have been defined as separate, distinctly 'international', largely 'political' spheres of interaction that can (and should) be studied in separation from the rest of social phenomena.

A crucial part of the traditional definition of 'IR' has also been played by the theorisation of the role of the state. The state enjoys a hegemonic position in the conceptual system of IR in the sense that most IR theories, from realism, to liberalism, to the English school and many sectors of constructivism, see states as the sole units, or agents, that IR theory should be concerned with. 'Statism' in this sense has been the 'flip side' of the acceptance of the particularly narrow view of the 'international': if IR is defined by the existence of an 'international system/society', this international system/society has been defined by the interaction of states. However, the assumption of 'statism', it must be noted, has not resulted in states having been theorised in any great depth in IR. Indeed, as Hobson has argued, despite the central role of statist assumptions in mainstream IR, most mainstream IR theorists have no sophisticated theory of the state.[12]

States in IR have predominantly been conceptualised through a set of empiricist assumptions, Colin Wight has argued.[13] Wight points out that although states have been accepted as the central units in IR, many rationalists have not even accepted the state as a 'real' structure or actor. This is because empiricism has de-legitimised any ascription of reality to unobservable entities such as the state. Some rationalists have made their empiricist commitments explicit by declaring that the state simply 'does not really exist'.[14] Others have treated the state merely as a 'useful abstraction' that can be assumed to exist under 'as if' descriptions: when we say the state exists, we are simply saying that it is useful to talk about it 'as if' it existed. The 'as if' descriptions have provided the positivists with a useful way of avoiding 'metaphysical' discussions concerning the 'real' nature of the state.[15] Importantly, states have been treated not only as 'as if' units, but importantly as 'as if' units

[11] Arguably, Martin Wight's characterisation of the domestic as the site of the good life implies this distinct separation of international (anarchic) and domestic (societal). M. Wight (1966: 33). Even if the international can be seen as 'societal', as in Bull's works, it is seen as a society of states, not of people.

[12] Hobson (2000: 3–4).

[13] Wight (2004: 269–73). See also Wight (2006: 216–17).

[14] See, for example, Gilpin (1986: 318).

[15] See, for example, Wight (2004: 269–73).

that are unitary 'person-like' actors. This has powerfully reproduced the empiricist assumption of flat ontology. States have been seen as those ('as if') units that matter to the extent that they have observable effects, or 'behave' in such ways that we can generalise about them.

Recently many IR theorists have started criticising the traditional understandings of the international system and of the state. It has become very attractive to study and theorise the linkages between 'domestic' and 'international'. Many rationalists[16] as well as constructivists[17] have started to doubt the 'black-boxing' of the state and have tried to incorporate analysis of domestic politics into their accounts. Yet, these frameworks have not escaped the influence of 'flat' ontological assumptions. First, the focus of these approaches has not been on rethinking ontology, that is, conceptualising the ontological relationship of the international and the domestic social relations; rather it has been on drawing out the effects of one level of analysis on the other, by adding domestic or international 'variables' into explanations. Crucially, most rationalists and constructivists have not seen the domestic and the international as fundamentally connected, or as ontologically intertwined; rather they have sought (observation and regularity-based) associations between domestic and international 'variables', precisely because they see them as clearly (observationally) separable levels of analysis in international politics.[18] Also, the focus has still been mostly on the political variables, conceived as separable from other 'variables'. Although some economic or cultural variables have been discussed, they have only been conceived of as 'intervening variables' in 'political' interaction. Statism has also been accepted: even the constructivists have tended to raise the issue of identity on the level of states and/or their interaction and, hence, perpetuate the separation between the domestic and the international.[19]

Some approaches have sought to get beyond this 'level of analysis' thinking in IR. The poststructuralists, for example, have opened up the issue area through questioning the 'discourse of sovereignty'. They have pointed out that the level of analysis that IR is focused on studying, the 'international system', is not a natural level of analysis or a system but, in fact, a discursively constructed one. The principle of sovereignty,

[16] Bueno de Mesquita (2002: 1–10); Milner (1997); Keohane and Milner (1996).
[17] Katzenstein (1996); Risse-Kappen (1995b). [18] Clark (1999: 27–8).
[19] Wendt (1999a: 13). One might imply this separation even from Onuf's sophisticated discussion of necessity of levels. Onuf (1998a: 218).

they argue, has served as the crucial linguistic device through which IR and its 'object of analysis' are constructed. The poststructuralists have argued that the notion of the international system is based on a particular modern normative conception of 'order', of security and of the nature of political community[20] and that by taking these notions for granted IR as a discipline hides and reproduces, rather than elucidates, how world politics is (discursively) constructed.[21]

The poststructuralist approaches not only criticise traditional framings of world politics in IR but are also sceptical about putting forward an alternative conceptualisation of the key ontological objects of world politics. This is because the poststructuralists see all conceptual systems as power-infused and reproductive of the 'objects' they claim to study. Although poststructuralist are justifiably critical of the traditional IR framings of world politics and are right to highlight the need for reflectivity in conceptualising world politics (since notions we use can reify social reality), it is not self-evident that all conceptualisations of international or world political realities are *equally* problematic. Neither is it obvious that we should do away with the concepts 'state' and 'international system' just because these aspects of the social world are socially and discursively constructed. Perhaps the better option is radically to reconceptualise the underlying premises of IR: that is, to redefine the content of concepts such as the state and the international system in ways that allow us to understand how the social relations or discourses that they refer to are constructed and reproduced.

Sørensen has taken some steps towards a better theorisation of the linkage between domestic and international by seeing the two concepts as interlinked. He argues that the 'international' shapes the domestic structure of the state, which, in turn, affects the types of international system in the world. He sees the domestic and international as part of a 'whole' rather than as two separable 'variables'.[22] He also conceives of 'domestic' and 'international' as constituted by economic and normative relations as well as political-military relations.[23] Also, Ian Clark, drawing on structurationist social theory, has sought to emphasise the mutual constitution of the international system and the state through discussing the debates on the effects of globalisation. He argues

[20] Biersteker and Weber (1996); Walker (1993).
[21] Ashley (1989); Walker (1993). [22] Sørensen (2001: 5).
[23] Sørensen (2001: 5–23).

that we cannot conceive of the state and the globalisation process as two separate things, or tendencies that work 'over' each other (as if they were two separate spheres): we need to see the two as fundamentally part of the same process. They refer to social relations that 'each adapts to changes in the other'.[24] It follows that 'a theory of the global is itself an integral dimension of a more plausible theory of the state'.[25]

These insights are useful in that they have aimed to reframe the ontological nature of the state–international relationship. However, even more holistic reconceptualisations of the social ontology of world politics are possible. Heikki Patomäki's challenge to the level of analysis thinking has made an important contribution to rethinking the ontological objects in IR, as has Colin Wight's work on structure and agency.[26] Through utilising the conceptual apparatuses of critical realism, as Patomäki and Wight have done, and through reinterpreting some of the more traditional IR concepts, I will now seek to advance a conceptualisation of world politics as a scene made up of complexly embedded sets of social relations. This view of world politics will provide a more appropriate ontological interpretive horizon for world political causal analysis, as understood here.

Reconceptualising the social ontology of world politics

In reframing IR ontology it is useful to start with thinking through the ontology of the state. As we have seen, the positivists in IR, because of their avoidance of ontological debate and acceptance of flat ontology, fail to give a nuanced sociological account of the nature of the state. Reflectivists, also, tend to avoid dealing with the social form of the state: they tend to deny the ontological reality of the state and hence the issue of theorising the state is sidestepped. It is assumed that if the state is socially constructed, it is not 'real' but rather 'metaphorical'.[27] The school of philosophical realism drawn on here, critical realism, directs us to recognise that the state is not *just* a useful abstraction, or a metaphor, but that the concept has a referent: a real and a causal social structure.

In chapter 6, it was argued that social structures refer to relatively enduring internal social relations that are given rise to by relatively

[24] Clark (1999: 173). [25] Clark (1999: 18).
[26] Patomäki (1996, 2002); Patomäki and Wight (2000); Wight (2006).
[27] See, for example, Neumann (2004: 259–67).

enduring nexuses of rules through their material unfolding in the intentional actions of agents. Structures of social relations materially and formally condition actors through defining their social roles, positions and resources. On the basis of this definition, the state[28] should be seen as a real and a causal social structure. It is real and causal in the sense that, although it is reproduced through our actions and, hence, is dynamic, it also pre-exists individual agents (materially and formally) and, hence, causally conditions (constrains and enables) the activities of agents, in their roles, identities, positions and practices.[29]

States as social structures can be seen to have certain common 'functions' or 'roles'. States as social structures have the right to take actions in the 'international system', including decisions on war and peace. States as social structures also monopolise legitimate violence and coercion within their borders and 'govern' people(s) within their borders.[30] States also have roles in the economic life of a state: they control and manage the resources of production, they protect private property and employers' rights, as well as mediating the grievances between the workforce and the capital. In the twentieth century states also taxed and (re)distributed resources and services.[31] These roles of states, contrary to what the 'state of nature' theorists posit, are not a-historically pre-given; rather they should be seen as functions that these structures have taken on in specific historical conditions, that is, because of their embeddedness in particular sets of structural conditions (that is, the international system built on sovereignty relations and the economic system built on property and wage relations, see below).[32] States are social forms that exist in, and by virtue of, certain international, global as well as local (domestic) structures of social relations. These, as will be seen, deeply condition (or 'constitute' as postpositivists might have it) states as social structures.

[28] State as an abstract social relation, as well as specific concrete forms of state.

[29] See Wight (2004: 270–3).

[30] See, for example, Giddens (1985).

[31] Contra some Marxists, we do not have to see the state as a social structure fully determined by, or a puppet of, capital; yet, it is important to emphasise that states as social structures (in structuring constitutive norms and resources and in upholding laws and the right to coercive actions) provide the key preconditions for capital accumulation and relations of production. See Jessop (2002).

[32] For historically nuanced accounts see, for example, Mann (1988, 1993); Tilley (1975, 1990); Evans, Rueschemeyer and Skopcol (1985).

What should we make of the assumption that the state can be treated as the primary and, indeed, a unitary person-like actor in international politics? IR theorists from various camps have assumed the 'personhood' of states: under 'as if' descriptions this was unproblematic since it did not involve any ontological baggage. It was not until Alexander Wendt explicitly argued that 'states are people too' that this assumption has come under serious debate. Wendt argued that we can think of states as 'people' owing to the fact that states can also be attributed intentionality and, hence, agency. Wendt contends that if we avoid individualism and the notion that only physical human minds can have intentionality, it is essentially unproblematic to accept social groups as 'cognisant' and, indeed, as 'persons'.[33]

Wendt is justified in arguing that social structures, such as states, can in certain contexts be talked about as agents. Given that the rules of the international system and the conventions of international law and diplomacy define states as agents it is not unreasonable to refer to them as agents in those contexts. Wendt also has a point in arguing that there is no need to reduce the concept of agency simply to individual human agency. However, it should be noted that although states can be referred to as agents in certain contexts, they are, in fact, corporate agents and do not possess the same causal powers as individuals. As Colin Wight has argued, there is an 'ontological wall' between state agency and individual human agency:[34] states' 'person-like corporate agency' is built upon an institutional setting (centralisation of decision-making) and ideological grounds (the 'idea of the state as person') rather than arising from the natural causal powers of the mind as with individuals. This means that corporate agents are not the same (ontologically) as people, even if corporate agency can be attributed to them. Arguably, anthropomorphising the state runs the risk of misunderstanding the ontological nature of states – as complex internally and externally structured social structures.[35]

Also, we should problematise the way in which states as agents have been conceptualised as akin to 'individualistic' agents. Wendt's account, for example, seems to veer towards the assumption that states are not just 'like agents', but like abstract independent individualistic agents. Although Wendt's states have intentions and identities, these

[33] Wendt (1999a: 215–43). [34] Wight (2004: 279).
[35] States can be seen as what Collier calls 'structuratum'. Collier (1989: 85–90).

are formed only in interaction with other states, not as a consequence of deep external and internal social structural conditioning. It is perhaps preferable to avoid simplifying the nature of states and explicitly recognise the deep structural conditioning of all social agency, individuals and states, within the world system.

Moreover, there are normative grounds for rejecting 'anthropomorphic' states. The 'statist' discourse in IR, as many postpositivists have argued, is a discourse that reifies states, and in so doing is not a neutral theory of international politics, but a discourse that serves the purposes of certain agents and structures within the global system. It follows that for ethico-political as well as explanatory reasons, it might be important to avoid treating social structures simplistically as anthropomorphic agents. Indeed, framing the state as a harmonious and unitary entity (which contrasts with the anarchical and threatening 'international system') masks the more complex nature of the state, as well as the deep external constitution of the state. We must remember that, as feminists and poststructuralists have argued, states are often based on various violent and oppressive structures and practices that are hidden away by the statist discourse. These 'internal' 'non-interesting' processes (for traditional IR purposes) can, also, often be connected to wider global relations and processes (global gender relations, territorial order). Although it can be said that 'the state acts', this begs far more crucial and deeper questions. What allows the state to act as it does? Why does the state act as it does? Whose interests does the state action serve? To reify the state as a unitary actor and a 'convenient' level of analysis is to refuse to move to deeper levels of social explanation.[36]

We have argued so far that we should treat states as open and changing social structures embedded within wider structural conditions. Let's now turn to discuss this wider structural environment and how it might be conceptualised. Arguably, it is best captured, not through application of singular ontological/conceptual frameworks, but through the simultaneous use of a variety of concepts capturing different aspects and levels of the complex social ontology underlying international and world political processes.

One way of capturing this wider context is through the notion of the 'international system'; however, defined differently from Waltz's

[36] Patomäki (2002: 87).

conceptualisation. The account here seeks to avoid the Waltzian conceptualisation of structure, which assumes pre-existing units and deduces their behaviour from a 'closed system' logic. However, it is not necessarily useful simply to throw away the 'international system' as a concept. The international system I argue constitutes a part of the structural environment of world politics: an environment that conceptually constitutes, as well as causally conditions, albeit not in a singular mono-causal manner, states and other actors. The international system is taken here to refer to the social relations of the 'state system', social relations that parcel the world into certain socially and legally 'legitimate' units called states and direct their behaviour by carrying conceptions of how they interact. The international system as it is understood here is actually very close to what is often referred to as rules of international society.[37] The social relations of the international system are, importantly, given rise to by a variety of rules, norms and discourses that define states, their roles and their relations. The rules of the international system can be seen to refer to the norms or discourses of international law, such as 'sovereignty of territorially defined states', or 'non-intervention'. The social relations of the international system also carry within them various conceptions, or socialising principles, concerning how states should interact. These socialising principles guide acceptable or routine behaviour in world politics. The norms of diplomacy or, indeed, the norms of balance of power politics can be seen as such socialising principles. The rules, discourses and socialising principles of the international system are embodied and played out in organisations such as the UN and NATO that codify, and to a more limited extent, enforce these basic rules of the international system.

These rules, discourses and socialising principles define conceptual relations but, crucially, also give rise to materially embodied practices and social relations, that is, they act as formal causes in world politics and thereby come to define material social relations between agents. They are causal conditioners of world politics in that these rules, discourses and socialising principles 'constrain and enable' the identities, positions and actions of agents (corporate and individual). On the

[37] Indeed, the English School can be seen to have a better social ontology for the purposes of IR, even though it is distinctly lacking in wider, especially economic, social ontology. See, for example, Patomäki's critique (2002: 79). Here, however, the 'pre-societal' conception of the international system of the English School theorists is not advocated.

basis of the definition accepted here, the 'international system' can be referred to as a social structure, because it defines sets of 'internal social relations'. Arguably, the international system is a less concretely institutionalised structure than the state. Yet, it is nevertheless a real social object, relatively enduring, and has real conditioning causal powers over corporate and individual agents.

It should additionally be noted that international organisations and states can also promote other more 'solidarist' social rules that go beyond the maintenance of the idea of a state system and traditional state relations, such as human rights norms or democracy promotion. These rules and discourses are perhaps best conceptualised as international or global norms that instead of maintaining international systemic social relations, go beyond them to make prescriptions about the nature of societal and inter-human life within states in the international system. These rules can also have important consequences for building social relations between states that go beyond international systemic relations: close cultural and normatively bound social relations can, for example, be noted between states in the 'Western cultural sphere' in the international system, although it seems that it is not only the fact that these countries share certain democratic and human rights norms that explain their social relations. International and global norms are one set of factors that go beyond classical state system logic. These have been much emphasised by many constructivists and liberals, but perhaps somewhat excessively at times and perhaps in too much isolation from wider structural forces within world politics.

One way to start taking into account this wider conditioning of world politics is by giving some room for what is often referred to as the notion of the 'world system'. The concept of the world system was initially developed by Immanuel Wallerstein. He developed this notion to emphasise the world economy as a structural feature of modern world politics. As opposed to the 'political' logic of anarchy advocated by the neorealists, Wallerstein's world-systems theory emphasises the determining logic of the world economy of capitalism on world politics. For Wallerstein, the world system is a real determining structure in world politics and, hence, the state and the state system, for him, are considered as secondary, and indeed, the structural effects (or 'carriers') of the wider structure of the world economic system.[38] The reductionist

[38] Wallerstein (1984).

tendencies in Wallerstein's argument are rejected here: the interstate system cannot be simply reduced to an effect of economic structures according to a deterministic base–superstructure logic. Arguably, the domestic (more concrete localised) class relations cannot be ignored, nor should the relationship between world systems and the interstate system be considered merely mono-causal or functional.[39] Wallerstein's approach has a-historicist and mono-causal connotations, and because of his concentration on the 'abstract' structure of capitalism, does not necessarily provide nuanced explanations of specific contexts. However, the notion of the world system is still important because it emphasises that there is a global capitalist social structure at work in structuring world politics. Indeed, the social relations of the world economic system (in terms of both norms/discourses as well as the distribution of material resources it gives rise to) 'frame' or condition the international (interstate) system. IR research must be aware of the complex ways in which the social relations of the interstate system are embedded in wider global social relations defined overwhelmingly by capitalist principles, even if they take a variety of local (concrete) forms.

Through the idea of the world system we can provide a politico-economic horizon to the ontological field. However, why should our framing of the structural conditioning of world politics stop at the analysis of the international system, society and the world economic structure? We should also open our analyses to other forms of social relations. It is important to notice other discourses and social relations, which are even less institutionally concrete than the international or the world systems, but embedded within these structures, such as patterns of patriarchal and racial relations. Arguably, gendered, 'civilisational' and race-related nexuses of rules and socialising principles, and the material properties and social relations that they give rise to, are also deeply embedded in the international system, the world system and the states and, indeed, provide the framework for the operation of the 'international system' and states within it. Gender and postcolonial perspectives have made important contributions to deeper understandings of the ways in which international political and economic relations have been structured through gendered and race-related social norms and relations.[40]

[39] Hobson (2000: 138–40).

[40] For gender perspectives see, for example, Enloe (1990); Marchand and Runyan (2000). For postcolonial perspectives see, for example, Grovogui (1996); Nair and Chowdhry (2002).

What does this redefinition of social ontology mean for reframing traditional IR analysis of international politics? It does not provide us with a specific theory of international relations but it allows us to challenge the empiricist, ontologically flat, deterministic and mono-causal overtones in IR theorising. It means that the traditional framing of the 'international system' in terms of black-box 'billiard ball' states is highly misleading. States can be accepted as real social structures; but as complex ones. They are structured through complex internal and external sets of social relations. Also, the international system cannot be thought of as anything resembling a 'closed system' from which state behaviour can be deduced. It follows that we cannot understand world politics through the narrowly defined notions of state and international system as suggested by many rationalists and methodological individualists in IR. Not only does the traditional framing assume atomistic ontology, but it facilitates suggestions that international politics can be talked about in mechanistic, or regularity-deterministic ways: when X, then Y (e.g. structure → behaviour).

The approach here is opposed to the simplistic determinist structural frameworks of the neorealists. Contra traditional neorealists in IR, it is the *socialisation* of states to the historically embedded rules and structural context that reproduces the presumed pre-given 'logic' of the international system. The main failing of the neorealists is that they fail to see the 'logic of anarchy' as a discourse or a socialising principle and also, crucially, fail to embed this formal cause within the wider structural and historical context (and, hence, take the logic as pre-given and a-historical).[41] In the light of the conceptual system advanced here, we cannot understand 'the logic of anarchy' in world politics, unless we embed the development of this form of thinking within the context of the global socio-economic structuring of the world.[42]

The approach here opens up ontological horizons away from rigid ontological assumptions that hide the complex social conditioning of social action and social relations in world politics. However, against the poststructuralist attempts to ignore the 'international', it is argued here that we are better off trying to understand how the international system/society is engendered and how it works rather than refusing to

[41] Ruggie (1998). [42] See J. Rosenberg (1994: 147–51).

conceptualise it and, hence, running the risk of ignoring or misunderstanding its impact on world politics.[43]

Instead of working on the basis of the traditional narrow framing of the international system in terms of ('surface-level') interactions of states, or ignoring the fact that social and discursive constructions are relatively enduring and causal, we should examine the historical development of world politics through embedding states, and different forms of state and state interactions, within wider social structural contexts – economic, political, military and cultural. It is important that IR research conceptualises global and international structures of social relations that condition the more concrete structures (states, local markets) and processes (war, trade) of world politics. Global social relations, while they can be considered as real and causal (through abstraction), must always be examined in local and historical contexts where many types of global and local sets of social relations interact with and counteract each other in complex ways.

Are there examples of ontological framings of world politics that come anywhere near the kinds of arguments made here? There are. The complex working of the world system, the international system, and states within them, is something that has been elucidated in complexity-sensitive and holistic terms by Robert Cox. He has traced the historical rise of the modern forms of state and international system by embedding them within the historical development of forms of production.[44] Cox has accounted for historical processes and developments through careful conceptualisation (abstraction) of the nature of various global social relations and (concrete) study of their complex interactions within specific historical contexts. Despite his aversion to causal terminology and lack of engagement with philosophically realist philosophy, his studies can be seen as largely commensurate with the view of social ontology advanced here. His conception of social ontology is 'deep', complexity-sensitive and holistic.

Another example of a broader ontologically variegated and complexity-sensitive approach to studying world politics can be taken from feminist research. Gender analysis, as Cynthia Enloe conceives of it, is about looking into the gendered nature of various global and local social relations, that is, about tracing how gendered social relations are at work within various global and local processes. While the global

[43] A similar point has been made by J. Rosenberg (2000: 53–61).
[44] Cox (1987).

structures of gendered social relations can be seen to be embedded, for example, in the processes of international trade and production, these global gender relations can be seen to work through the local social conditions which co-determine the actual social relations the global gender relations take. Conceptualising these complex processes is a challenging exercise, yet this conceptual work is necessary to gain an understanding of the multifarious processes at work in world politics:

> It takes a lot of information gathering, a lot of thinking, a lot of trial and error, and a lot of emotionally draining work to understand how notions about femininity and masculinity create and sustain global inequalities and oppressions in just one of [the sectors of international and domestic politics]... Yet a truly effective international feminism requires us to make sense of how patriarchal ideas and practices link all of these sectors to each other – and to other relationships whose gendered dynamics we have scarcely begun to fathom.[45]

This complexity of social explanation, that is, of drawing the holistic links between various embedded, interacting and counteracting social structures (and the ideas, rules and discourses and material resources and positions that give rise to or carry them) is, in the light of this work, considered to be the very essence of social scientific exercise.

Because of the empiricist assumptions built into the traditional ontological framework of IR, the study of world politics has been missing ontological depth and complexity-sensitivity. The social ontology of international politics should be conceptualised as complex and multifaceted, which in turn means that the causal powers within the world political arena are conceived of as multifaceted. Analysing world politics with more 'ontological depth' and plurality has, arguably, the capability to 'powerfully subvert any understanding drawn straightforwardly from observation of the surface appearance'.[46] The recasting of social ontology in IR facilitates a set of new avenues for investigation, notably the historical and dynamic nature of 'objects' of IR and the deep structuring of these objects through a variety of global and local social and economic relations. Such an opening up of ontological assumptions, alongside the revision of the nature of causal analysis, has, as will be seen, certain notable effects for the study of specific causal puzzles in world politics.

[45] Enloe (1990: 18). [46] Rosenberg (1994: 159).

Expanding understandings of democratic peace

Having reframed some core assumptions of IR ontology, we need now to appreciate how causal research itself is impacted by the reframed idea of causal analysis. This section seeks to show that the dominance of Humean assumptions in the study of processes such as democratic peace has meant that IR as a social science has been characterised by certain methodological, epistemological and ontological limitations, which have shut off from inquiry certain alternative, and potentially very fruitful, avenues of causal analysis. While the Humean approaches have contributed a great deal of general data to the analysis of democratic peace, there is some evidence to suggest that perhaps what is needed is not more data, or better statistical tools, but rather exploration of new conceptual and methodological avenues in the study of the causal relations involved. It will be argued here that if causal analysis is developed in the directions indicated by the revised conception of causal analysis advocated here, specifically the 'deeper' conception of causation, certain potentially productive, methodologically pluralist, historical, self-reflective and ontologically holistic avenues can be explored in democratic peace inquiry. Opening up these avenues might just pave the way towards more nuanced understandings of the complex relations of democracy and peace.

Humeanism and democratic peace theory

The aim of democratic peace (DP) theory is to study 'claims about the international conflict behaviour of both democratic and non-democratic states and to test such claims against the historical record of military conflict in the international system involving either type of state'.[47] The DP theorists do not form a united or uniform camp, however. To start with, some DP theorists are ardent advocates of the democratic peace proposition, while others are fervently against it. Also, the proposition that the DP theorists study is not uniform: some theorists concentrate on the monadic proposition (democratic states are less violent towards all other states), others on the dyadic one (democratic states are less violent towards other democratic states).[48] As for their causal analyses: some seek to explain DP in terms of the

[47] Huth and Allee (2002b: 32).

[48] For a good summary see Özkeçeci-Taner (2002).

structural/institutional model (constitutional checks and balances limit war-mongering), others in terms of the normative model (democratic norms and values encourage peaceful options), while some others still prefer to assess both 'causal mechanisms'.[49] However, some overarching similarities can be detected. As has already been noted in chapter 3, a deep-seated Humeanism is one of them.

Democratic peace has classically been analysed overwhelmingly through evaluation of patterns of observed regularities: it is the identification of the regular association of democracy (variously defined) with peaceful state interaction (variously defined) that underlies the study of democratic peace. By its advocates, the democratic peace proposition has been maintained because it has been considered 'one of the strongest nontrivial, non-tautological generalisations that can be made about international relations'.[50] Some scholars go as far as to argue that the 'absence of war between democratic states comes as close as anything we have to an empirical law in international relations'.[51] It is because of the general regularity-confirmed nature of the democratic peace hypotheses that some have argued that democratic peace studies provide perhaps the best example of cumulative knowledge that indicates progress in the field.[52]

By its critics, the democratic peace proposition is often treated in an equally Humean manner, however: it is rejected because the generalisations advanced by advocates are seen to be based on curious interpretations of data entries and statistically insignificant correlations.[53] Critics have argued that there are many other 'independent variables' (international organisations, alliances, trade links and wealth) that explain the regular association of democracy and peace in the Western 'zone of peace'. Interesting responses to the critics' claims have been provided by democratic peace theorists and, indeed, something of a cottage industry has developed, assessing the claims of liberals and realists against patterns of data.[54]

[49] Maoz and Russett (1993).
[50] Russett, quoted in Brown, Lynn-Jones and Miller (1999: ix).
[51] Levy, quoted in Gleditsch (1992: 370). Chan also agrees (1997: 60).
[52] Chernoff (2004).
[53] Spiro (1994); Layne (1994); Farber and Gowa (1995). See also Henderson (2002).
[54] See Russett (1993); Russett, Layne, Spiro and Doyle (1995); Maoz (1997); Chan (1997); Huth and Allee (2002a); Gleditsch (1992); Brown, Lynn-Jones and Miller (1999); Cox, Ikenberry and Inoguchi (2000).

It is important to note that as a result of the critical commentaries, and increasing debate on the democratic peace proposition, in recent years there have been interesting methodological developments in the democratic peace debates. Some theorists have sought to perfect the statistical models for the study of democracy and conflict,[55] while others, interestingly, have turned away from statistical analysis towards more qualitative and historical analysis and analysis of the 'causal mechanisms' that link democracy to peace.[56] However, Humean regularity assumptions are still present in many of these analyses, or have not been explicitly questioned. They are more manifestly present in the correlational statistical analyses, but, interestingly, also play a role in the more qualitative inquiries. Historical case studies, for example, are often treated as mere supplements to the real 'scientific causal analysis' conceived to consist of study of general patterns.[57] Case studies are seen as useful in looking at exceptional cases, and in deciding whether to include a particular country in the data, but testing of the general validity of the thesis, the social scientific *causal* logic, is associated with the study of the plausibility of the associations found in general data.[58]

The uncritical acceptance of the Humean background assumptions is aptly demonstrated in summaries of democratic peace theory literature. Answering the question 'does democracy cause peace?' seems to demand a theory that can be backed up by a statistically significant relationship between observable variables (mostly involving level of democracy and war-proneness variously defined, although other possible explanatory variables are also controlled for).[59] Crucially, because questions of causation are only considered within the empiricist-positivist philosophy of causation, the possibility that causal logics involved in democratic peace could be reframed and studied

[55] See, for example, Maoz and Russett (1993); Rummel (1995). See also the exchange between Beck, King and Zeng (2004) and de Marchi, Gelpi and Grynaviski (2004).

[56] Owen (1994). [57] Owen (1994: 92).

[58] This attitude seems a fair interpretation of Doyle's discussion of the role of statistics and case studies. See Doyle in Russett, Layne, Spiro and Doyle (1995: 182–3); Maoz (1997: 163). Empiricist assumptions also seem to characterise Rosato's (2003) interesting contribution to the debate on causal logics of democratic peace. Although his focus is on investigating causal mechanisms, the plausibility of causal explanations is still also related to correlational support (Rosato 2003: 585–6).

[59] Ray (1998).

through 'intensive' and interpretive methods has received surprisingly little explicit attention despite the partial turn away from 'hard positivist' methods by some scholars. Interestingly, the Humean starting point is strangely rarely challenged even by those critics who do not explicitly follow the empiricist regularity logic. For example, although Christopher Layne makes the important point that the democratic peace theorists' causal logics seem to falter because they offer no explanation of why democracies do not fight, the deeper meta-theoretical problem of the *kind* of model of causal analysis that is applied in the literature is not picked up.[60] There is an apparent unwillingness to challenge the dominant discourse on causation. In the view of the reconceptualised concept of cause, IR theorists should not be afraid to challenge the dominant account of causation that informs this debate and research area. With a more confident challenge to the self-evidence of Humean causal theorising we can come to recognise some key methodological, ontological and epistemological limitations of existing Humean causal theories of democratic peace.

Humean problem-field in the study of democratic peace

In the light of the deeper approach to causation advocated here we can see that Humeanism provides just one way to access and theorise the causal relations of democratic peace, and is an approach that has certain characteristic limitations. First, Humean DP theorising is *methodologically* hindered in that it tends to base its theorisations exclusively on observational generalising methods. Although there are methodological debates among democratic peace theorists, these seem to pertain to how best to analyse regularities or how to pick cases, not to the possibility of looking for radically different kinds of non-regularity based qualitative, interpretive and historical data and forms of analysis.[61] Although there are plenty of theoretical models too, these seem to amount primarily to statements of associations between particular variables, which are tested against observational data. Although various explanations or 'theoretical models', such as interdependence, international organisations, liberal institutions or liberal cultural assumptions,

[60] Spiro's argument especially is focused on analysis of the statistical insignificance of the regularities associated with democratic peace. For Layne's comments on causation see Russett, Layne, Spiro and Doyle (1995: 176).

[61] See, for example, Rummel's (1995) critiques of his colleagues.

are tested in the literature, it is somewhat problematic that these theories come down to hypothesis testing of statements such as 'when x (say liberal democratic institutions) are present, then y (say peace) tends to follow', even if each hypothesis is meticulously measured. This is because the analyses of the role of independent variables, and additive theorising in general, do not seem to generate knowledge about *how* different variables are causal and how causal forces interact (say liberal democratic cultural assumptions arise from and sustain liberal economics or international organisations are outgrowths of the Western cultural sphere). Rather than additive testing, perhaps more emphasis should be put on generating conceptually nuanced complexity-sensitive understandings that explain *why* and *how* democracies act like they do in their social contexts, that is, *what it is about* social structures or cultural assumptions of democracy, and perhaps their causally conditioning environment, that engenders peaceful interactions. Although scholars emphasise that explanations referring to different causal variables are not mutually exclusive, the question remains 'how do different causal conditions and actors come together in particular ways to bring about certain results or a set of results?' Increased observational data and honed statistical methods only go so far, as Starr argues: 'Although many of the questions of [democratic peace] literature return to the different meanings, operationalizations and indicators of "democracy", the key problem is not one of measurement. The central problem of research design and theoretical cumulation seems to involve failures in conceptual clarification.'[62] Because Humeanism sets the parameters of how causal knowledge is provided, emphasis in improving analyses is put on better measurement and mathematic data analysis at the expense of focusing on interpretive analyses and conceptual and theoretical reformulations.

Also, within the Humean straitjacket, there has been little basis on which to criticise the regularity-deterministic assumption built into DP methodology. Many DP theorists, even if inadvertently, come to assume that, given regularities between variables have been observed, we can assume a 'when A, then B' type relation between types of events involved: that is, given that democracies (as specified) have not fought in the past, they will not do so in the future. This assumption and the predictive logic it entails (when democracy, then peace) gives the DP

[62] Starr, quoted in Chan (1997: 85).

debates questionably deterministic overtones, which many critics and even advocates reject, but the meta-theoretical origins of these types of claims are not recognised.

Second, on the basis of the alternative approach to causation advocated here, it could also be argued that DP debates have been characterised by certain 'objectivist' *epistemological* assumptions about the nature of democracy and the level of certainty provided by statistical evidence.[63] Owing to the acceptance of a Humean framing of scientific research, which accords observation-based knowledge supremacy, the DP theorists have often assumed that adopting an open scientific attitude and methods ensures that their studies are relatively trustworthy and unbiased.[64] While the critics point to subjectivity of definitions or methods, the Humeans re-emphasise that the knowledge claims about democratic peace should be measured by their 'logical soundness and the empirical validity',[65] a reply that arguably fails to engage with the deeper postpositivist claims that no empirical study is simply objective. This emphasis on scientific validity has arguably served to de-legitimise other epistemological approaches to democratic peace, notably interpretive frameworks. Moreover, the acceptance of the epistemological supremacy of observational methods, and confidence in their ability to siphon off value-biases, has led to many DP theorists remaining blind to the way in which their own studies might be premised on certain politically embedded and politically consequential assumptions. This is what many critics have pointed to as a deeply problematic aspect of this particular section of IR as a social science. As Rupert has argued, 'to the extent that practitioners of this newest liberalism bestow upon themselves the status of objective observers – inhabitants of an extraterrestrial realm of scientific value neutrality – they effectively absolve themselves from responsibility for the political consequences of their representation of the world'.[66]

Moreover, in the light of the causal horizons set here, the *ontological* assumptions that inform DP theorising can be seen as somewhat problematic. First, as mentioned before, because of the focus on

[63] See, for example, criticisms posed in Oren (1995).

[64] In reply to Oren's criticism that conceptions of democracy are subjective, Maoz, for example, states, following the empiricist logic, that 'clear definitions of concepts and explicit measures allow inspection of biases – if such exist'. Maoz (1997: 183).

[65] Maoz (1997: 163).

[66] Rupert (2001: 159).

associating variables, there is little engagement with deeper causal ontology, that is, conceptualisation of the normative frameworks, discourses, structures and relations that go towards *explaining* how patterns of regular observations come about. Also, for the same reasons, the DP theorists often accept flat ontological assumptions about objects of study: democracies, for example, are 'measured' in terms of quantifiables – they are indexed according to observable characteristics – rather than understood sociologically or structurally. This is considered necessary because without clear observable indices according to which democracy and war can be measured, no systematic study of their relationship can be provided.[67] This assumption is particularly empiricist and entails a 'flat ontological' treatment of objects of explanation.

The DP theorists also come to view the world through isolated 'variables', that is variables are measured against each other statistically rather than conceptualised holistically. There is little interest in engagement with the deep ontological nature and context of democratic peace, or with the complexity of the causal conditioning of the interaction of democratic states, although in this regard moves towards recognising the interlinkage between liberal market economy and democratic peace are an important development.[68]

The lack of ontological reflection also contributes to the fact that the DP theorists can rather uncritically accept ontological premises that are not self-evident, or a-political. Thus, most DP theorists uncritically accept statist and liberal premises concerning democracies. 'Liberal democracies' are understood as ordered and liberating societies void of fear, oppression and danger. Democratic regimes are seen as 'enlightened' societies with 'political will' and are often treated as political systems isolated from the structural conditions (e.g. economic) underlying them.[69] DP theorists are distinctly unable to see how these assumptions are informed by a particular liberal political discourse which tends to see social life through behaviour and choices of 'free' individuals,

[67] See, for example, the discussion in Ray (1998). See also Maoz's reply to Oren (1997: 187).

[68] For an interesting discussion of this relation see Mousseau (2003). This study still seems to draw on Humean assumptions in using statistics to study independent variables and in aiming for predictable modelling, rather than exploring the interesting ontological openings presented.

[69] De Vree (1999: 41–9). See also Oren (1995).

and thereby obscures the deep social conditioning of agents by their social context.[70]

Rethinking democratic peace

How can research into the democratic peace proposition be reframed in the light of the reconceived model of causal analysis? Methodologically, the approach to causal analysis taken here directs us to accord generalising methods a more modest role and would advocate a more serious engagement with qualitative data, and especially more historical and interpretive methods, or approaches. According to the conception of causal analysis advanced here, although some 'demi-regularities' can be useful in identifying the effects of deeper causal relations,[71] they do not explain why and how a causal process takes place. Thus, while some associations between democracies and war can be found in large-scale data, as well as those between wealth and democracy, and alliances and democracy, the correlations and statistical significances themselves explain little. Analysis of democratic peace, then, should not proceed merely on the basis of observation and statistics but should analyse *why* and *how* such concrete events and patterns have come about. To gain a deeper understanding of the causal processes involved, for example, to explain what it is about the institutional structure or cultural norms that causes democratic states to act in certain ways, the model of causation advanced here directs us to engage with other kinds of evidence, notably qualitative and historical data about the nature and influence of democratic institutions or norms. In the light of the revised form of causal analysis, it is these qualitative and historical data analysed in an interpretive manner that point us towards the underlying processes and structures that *explain* regularities of observables and importantly, these data must also be 'interpreted', not merely 'measured'.

Constructivists such as Risse-Kappen have taken some steps in the direction of more nuanced qualitative and hermeneutic analysis of

[70] Behind DP research lies, arguably, the assumption that individuals make decisions on the basis of their needs and construct social reality on the basis of those decisions. Society is but an aggregation of individuals, and the means of fulfilling individual needs. Buying into such abstract individualism means that theorists who use liberal assumptions tend to ignore the influence of pre-existing social conditions and relations on actors. Rupert (2001: 153).

[71] Lawson (1997: 204–13).

democratic peace. Risse-Kappen argues through a constructivist logic that we should study how democracies create their friends and enemies by inferring either defensive or aggressive motives from the domestic structures of their counterparts. The constructivists' goal has been to get away from regularity analysis in favour of analysing the perceptions and identities of agents.[72] This is a useful and progressive step in expanding horizons in the study of causes of democratic peace. However, we should note that although constructivism has provided a useful opening in these debates, we should also be wary of the tendency that constructivists can have to take the interpretation of actors' motives and perceptions as the most important and a relatively unproblematic source of information about the social world. For reasons discussed in chapter 6, hermeneutic interpretation, as conceived here, should be applied in conjunction with clear conceptual frameworks that can warn us of possible intentionally misleading statements made by actors whose actions and thoughts we interpret. Also, it should be noted that we should not just study the perceptions of actors, as some constructivists have, but also conceptualise the 'situational' factors within which perceptions arise. For example, in the context of analysing democratic peace, we should be aware of the fact that state leaders, in explaining why they did not attack a country, might misleadingly justify their actions in reference to democratic perceptions, and perhaps remain silent on other reasons they might have for avoiding war (such as economic interest).

Indeed, one important guiding light of causal analysis as conceptualised here is that we can see that crucial in causal analysis is having an attuned conceptual system for dealing with a variety of evidence. Data analysis, in the light of this work, is intertwined with constant (re)conceptualisation of objects of explanation. This is because it is recognised that data do not simply 'yield' their insights objectively, for an empiricist or an interpretivist; rather it is accepted that the conceptual models we have direct how we treat the data and that in so doing some conceptual models are better than others (that is, they allow us to understand the data better and more comprehensively, while others leave many issues and data unaddressed).

The approach advanced here highlights different aspects of the social world compared with the Humean approach which starts from

[72] Risse-Kappen (1995a).

observational methodological prescriptions. In the case of democratic peace debates, we can see that questions such as 'does democracy cause peace?', which we then expect to be either confirmed or disconfirmed in relation to observable patterns, do not provide the only, or necessarily unproblematic, angles into causal inquiry. According to the model here, we have first to ask complex questions about objects of explanation. To start with, we have to ask detailed questions about how democracies work institutionally, socially and historically. The ontological framework advanced here directs us to treat democracies as complex and dynamic social structures embedded in multifaceted structural contexts. Thus, contra traditional DP theorising, the concept of democracy should not just be 'indexed' (understood taxonomically) through a checklist of quantifiable characteristics (as having elections, X amount of 'free' newspapers, etc.). Nor should it be 'read back' in history: we should not assume that democracies are the same (structurally or in their 'actions') through time (even if quantifiables remain the same). The ontology here directs us to conceptualise how democracies are structured in complex ways through various economic, cultural and social relations and to analyse how they work historically in different social contexts. If framed in such a way, many often unasked questions become important in understanding the relationship of democracy and war. What are modern democracies like and how have they developed? What material bases as well as discourses have they been/are they based on? Are liberal democracies just political systems or are they also embedded by many other social relations (capitalist economic relations, Western cultural relations, hierarchical gender relations)? How do democracies structure social relations within states: what is the role of violence within as well as without liberal democratic states?

In terms of causal explanations, according to the ontology here democracies have to be framed within a wider context, that is, we need to conceptualise not just democracies, but also their embeddedness in complex global contexts. We should ask abstract and concrete questions (see chapter 6) about the social relations of the capitalist mode of production, the global forms of militarisation or even global gender discourses, the framework of the discourse of the 'international system' as well as about their more local filtering through various local economic, political and cultural environments (complex concrete unfolding of abstract social relations). Through such an approach many global processes often ignored by mainstream 'generalisers' can be seen as relevant. Thus, for example, structural violence within democracies and their embeddedness within particular sets of global social relations, such as capitalist economic structures, should not be ignored. Also, the proxy wars waged by the USA during and after the Cold War can be included in, rather than excluded from, explanations – through linking them, for example, to the capitalist relations of production inherently linked to the USA as a particular form of a democratic state.[73]

The kinds of questions advocated here, although not exclusive of Humean kinds of efforts to measure democracy and study regular associations of variables, allow us to reach beyond regularities and independent variables, and engage with historical and qualitative knowledge and interpretation as part of the study of the causal field of democratic peace. According to the approach here, to study the causal complexities involved there is no need to settle for democracy indices in the need to operationalise variables and to derive causal explanations from associational regularity analyses. Although the generalising efforts of course are not without their uses in providing a general descriptive picture of causal factors possibly involved, to capture the nature and complexity of the causal powers of democratic norms and systems on state behaviour, the approach to causation advocated here proposes that we also try asking questions that seek more sociologically and historically grounded conceptual and interpretive analysis of the causal relations involved – and not as a supplement to generalisation about regular patterns but as the core activity of causal analysis.

The more methodologically open and ontologically deeper framing of democratic peace cautions us to the possibility that 'zones of peace are not separate and discrete phenomena explained by the presence or absence of liberal institutions within states but the effects of mutually constitutive [or embedded] international political, social and economic relations',[74] and that in understanding democratic peace we should aim to understand the '*multiple* relations among democracy, liberalism and the use of force'.[75] Indeed,

> none of the terms that enable the democratic peace proposition can be taken for granted. Instead analysis must question the primacy of sovereign

[73] As Chomsky and others have argued, the proxy wars can be understood as part of capitalist core–periphery relations and motivated by access to capital as well as countering communism. See Laffey (2003).

[74] Barkawi and Laffey (2001a: 2).

[75] Barkawi and Laffey (2001a: 2).

boundaries and historicize rather than stipulate the meaning of democracy, liberalism and war. Instead of fetishizing liberal democratic norms and institutions, it must attend to the multiple meanings of liberalism and its relations with other social processes. And instead of assuming that democracy and liberalism are forces for peace, analysis must attend to the ways in which they promote the use of force.[76]

Importantly, in the research process the researcher should remain reflexive concerning his or her assumptions about the object of study. The framework of causal analysis advocated here reminds us that our accounts of the world are social, historical and political and that claims to universality and neutrality are questionable. Our analysis can be, and inevitably will be, influenced by our social conditioning and will reflect values. The fact that our views or conceptual frameworks are pre-shaped does not mean that we should give up on analysing the way in which the world works: this is because epistemological relativism cannot be reduced to ontological relativism. Since the referent of theories cannot be done away with, even if they are difficult to access and conceptualise, it is accepted that some theories can still be conceived to be getting at the world better than others, and hence, we can still make some judgements on the explanatory adequacy of theories on the basis of the evidence put before us. While the research into democratic peace is unavoidably filtered through socially and politically embedded theoretical ascriptions and descriptions, through 'changing hats' and asking critical questions about the assumptions we work with, a theorist can try to evaluate the viability of these propositions – and come to redescribe them in more nuanced ways.

It should be pointed out that one interesting engagement with democratic peace that works on the broad lines of thought advanced here has been put forward by some figures outside the mainstream of democratic peace debates: such as Tarak Barkawi and Mark Laffey. Their approach challenges the positivist scientific methodology, criticises the individualistic social ontology of the mainstream and fundamentally rejects the objectivist assumptions of mainstream democratic peace 'science'. Barkawi and Laffey, and the other contributors to the volume *Democracy, Liberalism and War: Rethinking the Democratic Peace Debate*, emphasise that we must understand international relations in

[76] Barkawi and Laffey (2001a: 19).

a deeper way than the traditional IR conceptual systems allow. We should see international politics as constituted by 'thick' sets of social, political, economic, cultural and military relations.[77] This approach emphasises the need to grasp the complex and multiple social relations tying together global processes: both the 'material and ideational conditions that underpin and make possible the historically specific couplings of democracy and peace'.[78] Drawing on a variety of evidence, they build conceptual frameworks that allow us to connect various, for mainstream DP theorists, disparate developments and processes in world politics. While a strictly Humean approach might frown at their efforts because of its open methodological and holistic ontological approach, in the light of the rethought notion of cause their explanations of the democratic peace proposition are theoretically and conceptually nuanced, evidentially systematic, self-reflective and, arguably, in certain senses explanatorily more plausible than those advanced by the positivist Humean theorists.

Interestingly, although the analyses in the Barkawi and Laffey collection are more in line with the meta-theoretical suggestions of this work than those of the Humeans, it should be noted that, paradoxically, many of these scholars, drawing on reflectivist anti-causal discourse, fail to recognise the implicitly non-Humean nature of their own causal language. Their explanations of democratic peace are sometimes still prefaced with what seems a typically 'anti-causal' reflectivist argument calling for the study of 'constitutive' rather than 'causal' questions.[79] This, in the light of the analysis of causation advanced here, is unnecessary; these theorists should openly recognise that they are investigating what is here understood as the causal conditioning of world politics. Indeed, the authors call for the study of 'the historical and systemic contexts that provide both the meaning and conditions of possibility for the empirical pattern, as well as to the multiple and complex other ways in which liberalism, democracy, war and peace are interrelated and co-determined'.[80] If causation is understood in the multifarious and dynamic way suggested here, the arguments of Barkawi and Laffey can be understood in causal terms, without throwing away any of the insightful arguments that they have advanced – as they themselves

[77] Barkawi and Laffey (2001a: 16); Barkawi and Laffey (2002: 112).
[78] Weldes and Duvall (2001: 203). [79] Weldes and Duvall (2001).
[80] Weldes and Duvall (2001: 196).

seem to fear. Arguably, when armed with an anti-positivist philosophy of science and of causation, these theorists could confront the empiricist mainstream with stronger cards in hand – as they could challenge them not just on their substantive explanations but, more fundamentally, on the limitations of their philosophy of science and causation.

While Humean causal analyses have their uses, more expansive causal horizons should be opened up in IR research. This can be done through going beyond the Humean causal assumptions and accepting the social scientific validity of deeper and broader analyses of the normative, discursive and social structural parameters of state behaviour. The approach here arguably opens up new avenues and questions in this regard and hence calls into question the self-evident superiority of a Humean approach to causal analysis of democratic peace. While asking about statistical associational relations between independent variables can be useful in obtaining knowledge about patterns or trends, causal analysis of a deeper kind involves engaging in interpretive and conceptual analysis and holistic analysis of data. In analysis of democratic peace, this approach opens up some new research avenues previously not explored fully owing to the dominance of the Humean discourse in the definition of what social scientific causal analysis involves. In sum, it presents an opening to reclaim wider sets of methodological, epistemological and ontological tools for world political causal analysis.

Explaining the end of the Cold War

The sudden end of the Cold War confounded most IR theorists, notably the political realists, and led to the emergence of a new theoretical force, constructivism. While the predominant emphasis in the previous section was on readdressing some of the misleading avenues of the rationalist approaches, this section seeks critically to examine and address the problems of a constructivist explanation of the end of the Cold War.[81] The reconceptualised deeper and broader notion of cause, and the view of social ontology advanced here, remind us that instead of seeking parsimonious 'material' or 'normative' explanations, our explanations should always aim to discuss causal factors holistically,

[81] The focus here is on Koslowski and Kratochwil's account (1995). For wider discussions one can refer, for example, to many excellent collections, such as Lebow and Risse-Kappen (1995b); Herrmann and Lebow (2004b); Westad (2000b).

something that has been forgotten by some constructivist theorisation of the end of the Cold War. The analysis advanced here reinforces the importance of engaging in multi-causal and process-sensitive forms of causal analysis, an argument in certain respects similar to that advocated recently in Herrmann and Lebow's collection *Ending the Cold War: Interpretations, Causation and the Study of International Relations*.[82]

Debating the end of the Cold War

The IR theory debates on the end of the Cold War have created dichotomous combat lines between theoretical approaches and a substantial amount of debate between theorists. Yet 'the end of the Cold War remains poorly understood'.[83] The neorealists and political realists, who have been influential in the field of IR, have emphasised that the fall of the Soviet Union, and, hence, the apparent end of a stable bipolar system, has not, in fact, changed the fundamentals of world politics.[84] They argue that the end of the Cold War was a result of the inherent weakness of the Soviet system and its consequent declining standing in the international system. The end of the Cold War is seen as just another event that proves that material capabilities are what matter. In political realist and neorealist eyes the Soviet Union sought reconciliation because it had to: in an anarchic international system a militarily and economically[85] weakening superpower has no other option but to look for accommodation: '[t]he root cause of the Cold War and its demise was the rise and fall of the Soviet Union as a global power'.[86]

Importantly, the political realists argue that Gorbachev's New Political Thinking was, if not incidental to the change in world politics, at least not fundamental to it. It is emphasised that Gorbachev's thinking took the avenues it did because of the weakening material capabilities resulting from the failing domestic economy and especially the 'imperial overreach' in the Third World. As Brooks and Wohlforth argue,

[82] Herrmann and Lebow (2004b).

[83] Herrmann and Lebow (2004a: 1).

[84] Mearsheimer (1990).

[85] The argument about the economic structure of the Soviet Union as a cause of the end of the Cold War is an important one in that it opens up political realism to influences of classical realism (away from strict concentration on the military characteristics central to neorealism). Brooks and Wohlforth (2000: 19).

[86] Herrman and Lebow (2004a: 7). See also p. 23 for a summary of recent political realist literature.

ideas were 'largely a reflection of changing material environment'[87] and, hence, changes in material forces were the most fundamental cause of change in the system.[88] Crucially, it has seemed that, for the political realists, the importance of material resources has been derived from the logic of a 'closed system' view of international politics (in an anarchic international system, balance of material resources is what matters), and empirical evidence is given a particular realism-confirming twist: '[e]nhanced feelings of trust or changing assessments of Soviet intentions play little or no role in realist accounts . . . Changing Soviet foreign policies were a function of changes in capabilities, not preferences.'[89] Political realists have not been particularly interested in explaining *how* the agents and their normative frameworks were directed by the material concerns: the focus is on emphasising 'the fact' that they did, which then 'confirms' empirically the realist explanatory logic.

The goal of constructivist approaches has been to argue against the politically realist 'structural', or 'functional', explanations of the end of the Cold War: these explanations, it is argued, 'cannot account for either the specific content of the change in Soviet foreign policy or the Western response to it'.[90] Constructivists have tried to construct explanations that avoid functionalist predetermining frameworks of explanation and, thereby, are able to provide fuller and richer explanations of the process of the end of the Cold War. In so doing, constructivism has used the end of the Cold War debate as a crucial 'jumping board' to mainstream IR theory.[91]

The constructivists have raised a number of objections to the political realist explanations. They argue that because of their narrow concentration on material distribution the political realists failed to look at factors that can bring about change in world politics. These factors, the constructivists argue, have to do with the 'normative' environment of world politics. Constructivists such as Koslowski and Kratochwil, taken as the central focus here, contend that the end of the Cold War cannot be seen as a question of mere distribution of material resources: an explanation of this event must include an account of the role of changing rules and norms in the international system. As Koslowski and Kratochwil put it, the end of the Cold War came about because '[t]he revolutions of 1989 transformed the international

[87] Brooks and Wohlforth (2000: 8). [88] As pointed out by English (2002: 90).
[89] Haas (2007: 151). [90] Risse-Kappen (1995b: 188). [91] Wendt (1999a: 4).

system by changing the rules governing superpower conflict and thereby the norms underpinning the international system'.[92]

The constructivist normative explanation of change has sought to challenge political realism on the issue of what is the most crucial explanatory factor in world politics. The end of the Cold War is seen as the proof of the importance of norms and ideas in international politics.[93] Constructivists would not deny that the economic woes and overstretched material resources of the Soviet Union provided a 'condition' in which Gorbachev's foreign policy played out, but they reject that material resources 'ultimately determined' the course of events. They argue that ideas play the most crucial role in determining how events in the social world pan out. This is because, as Koslowski and Kratochwil put it, '[f]undamental change of the international system occurs when actors, through their practices, change the rules and norms constitutive of international interaction'.[94] The emphasis of such constructivist explanations is on exploring how the changes in the ideational environment came about and initiated other changes.

The normative explanations challenge political realism in IR on the issue of contingency and determinism. It is assumed that the end of the Cold War raises some fundamentally disturbing questions about the notions of determinism and contingency in the international system. The political realist framework, based on 'immutable structures', is seen as too 'deterministic' to account for the 'contingent' role of norms.[95] It should be noted, in this context, that determinism is often equated in the constructivist camp with the idea of causal analysis.

Interestingly, although the constructivist explanations have criticised the political realists for mono-causal 'last fundament' explanations,[96] the constructivist explanations seem to have reproduced certain theoretically reductionist assumptions. Where the political realists have argued that material causes (conceived in a deterministic and mechanistic way) provide the 'ultimate cause' of the event, the constructivists have argued that ideas provide the most crucial explanatory factor of

[92] Koslowski and Kratochwil (1995: 127).
[93] Koslowski and Kratochwil (1995: 134); Risse-Kappen (1995b: 188).
[94] Koslowski and Kratochwil (1995: 128).
[95] Koslowski and Kratochwil (1995: 128).
[96] Koslowski and Kratochwil (1995: 136–7).

change. The constructivists, then, just as the political realists, have been drawn to reducing the explanation of the historical event – or rather the historical process – to one (set of) factor(s), thus verging towards theoretical reductionism, an unhelpful trend that commentators such as Westad and Gaddis have pointed out.[97]

The constructivists have contributed to the maintenance of an unproductive 'zero-sum paradigm rivalry' in IR: the normative approach has been seen as an incommensurable opposite to the political realist 'materialist' explanations. As a result, just as in the political realist camp, evidence has been 'shoe-horned'[98] to fit the established conceptual horizons of the theoretical approach, and real motivations and causal factors have remained poorly theorised. Some IR theorists, and especially international historians, have called for more holistic approaches that overcome the dichotomisation of normative and material approaches,[99] yet non-dichotomous conceptual frameworks have been slow to emerge. One such framework, and a fruitful one, has recently been provided by Herrmann and Lebow's collection *Ending the Cold War: Interpretations, lausation and the Study of International Relations*: this collection explicitly insists that contributors consider their accounts in the context of multiple causal factors. It is the contention here that we can reinforce holistic multi-causal explanations in IR when we apply the broader and pluralistic Aristotelian conceptual system developed in the previous chapter.

Reconceptualising the end of the Cold War

On the basis of the reconceptualisation of causation advanced here many aspects of the constructivist critiques can be seen to be misleading, and should be reframed to permit a more attuned conceptual framework for dealing with the end of the Cold War. To start with, the treatment of the contingency–determinism debate by the constructivists needs to be overhauled as it misleads more than it assists in communication between perspectives. In the light of the theory of causation advanced here, portraying 'contingency' and 'determinism' as polar opposites is misleading in that it tends to be based on inadequate theorisations of these concepts. The social ontology advocated

[97] Westad (2000a: 9); Gaddis (2000). [98] Wohlforth (2000: 138).
[99] Westad (2000a: 18).

here accepts that causes can be structural and agential, material or ideational, but argues, further, that causes in all those senses are both 'contingent' (in that many causes always come together in complex 'non-predetermined' ways) as well as determining (causes are real and have real causal powers). Conceptions of contingency and determinism, as applied by constructivist IR theorists, do not describe the complex interactions of causes well and, hence, confuse more than clarify the theorisation of the end of the Cold War.

However, the most crucial problem with the constructivist approaches can be seen to be the problem of theoretical reductionism, as well as the (related) tendency to reproduce the causal–constitutive theory divide. The problem of theoretical reductionism in IR, as we have seen in chapter 6, is intimately bound up with the Humean tendency to think about the world through isolating 'independent' explanatory factors. When we examine the end of the Cold War debates, it is striking how both sides still continue to talk in terms of the 'independent effect' of either material or ideational factors. Political realists, in accordance with the closed system logic, emphasise the 'endogeneity' of ideas within the causally independent (material) structures.[100] However, this logic pervades also the idea-ist side. The emphasis, contra political realists, is on assessing the 'contribution of ideas as well as the important extent to which they developed and operated independent of material resources'.[101]

The key to providing better explanations of the end of the Cold War and to initiating more constructive debate between theoretical schools is, arguably, abandoning the idea of causal (or explanatory) independence, since this is one of the key contributors to theoretical miscommunication: it prevents theorists from seeing historical processes as complex and various causal factors as interacting, as historian John Lewis Gaddis has pointed out too.[102] On the basis of the pluralistic causal ontology advanced here, we must accept that we should not treat causal forces as 'separable' and 'independent' but must always relate different kinds of causes to others. The key question becomes, not *which* factor matters more than another 'independently', but *how* and *why* the factors are interlinked.

[100] Brooks and Wohlforth (2000: 8).
[101] English (2002: 83). See also English (2000).
[102] Gaddis (2000: 29).

Herrmann and Lebow, and Lebow and Stein within their volume, take some steps towards what I am suggesting here. These authors also argue that in the case of the end of the Cold War we need to search for 'compound explanations' and to get away from the idea that explanations that emphasise different causal factors (material, ideational, structural, agential) should be conceived as in competition with each other.[103] They also emphasise the importance of analysing the complex historical situation as a process consisting of a number of turning points, which can all be explained by multiple factors, rather than seeing it as a single event with a single 'parsimonious cause'. What Herrmann and Lebow are getting at, much in the same way as the Aristotelian multi-causal framework, is that analyses that take as their starting point the examination of single variables and measure their effects, without consideration of the causal contexts of these factors, are bound to provide unnecessarily narrow accounts that cannot be sustained by the evidence.[104] World political processes such as the end of the Cold War have multiple causes and hence the search for parsimony is problematic in this case. Through their emphasis on multicausality, Herrmann and Lebow have managed to find a way to bridge approaches to the end of the Cold War in a more constructive manner: while differences of emphasis still exist – political realists still maintain that material capabilities explain more than ideas and idea-ists that material factors provide but a context for the process – there is more ready acceptance, on both sides, of the way in which ideas or material resources are conditioned by other causes.[105]

A multi-causal framing proposed here, and the kind pointed to by Herrmann and Lebow, is interesting because it raises some new types of questions for students of the end of the Cold War. It raises new questions, first, for the political realists. How exactly are material resources causal? How are the 'material' structures influential on agents and how do they go towards framing their motivations? Why are certain meanings ascribed to the material structural determinants in a given context?

[103] Herrmann and Lebow (2000a: 14). Although they suggest that parsimonious explanations are problematic only in certain situations, not in general, and continue to talk in terms of independent causes that are additive and interacting, rather than more fundamentally enmeshed as suggested here (2004a: 14). Lebow and Stein (2004: 196–7, 204).

[104] Lebow and Stein (2004: 204).

[105] See review of contributors in Lebow and Stein (2004: 191–2).

As Lebow and Stein point out, there has been only limited exploration of evidence that could support the view that the responses by the Soviet government were motivated by the desire to preserve Soviet power.[106] Multi-causality also raises questions for the constructivists. How do the ideas/norms that are studied come about? What is the structural (material and social relational) context of norms and their emergence? Why did certain norms become so dominant? How and why were these ideas transmitted and accepted by the agents? Indeed, these types of questions about how different types of accounts bridge to other causal accounts become far more important in advancing and debating causal explanations in a more sophisticated way, rather than simply deciding on which parsimonious explanatory factor should be prioritised.[107] As Herrmann and Lebow put it, explanations that emphasise ideas, material forces, domestic structures or leadership 'do not constitute distinct alternatives as much as they do different starting points for a complex and multilayered explanation'.[108] While we may of course focus our interests on analysis of the role of ideas, the aim of many constructivists, this pragmatic interest in the role of ideas does not entail that ideas act somehow independently of other causal forces and, hence, that constructivist analyses have nothing to share (ontologically, conceptually, methodologically) with other theoretical approaches.

Having an *a priori* preference for one or the other type of causal factor tends to lead IR theorists to ignore these crucial 'deeper' causal questions and, hence, leads them towards reductionist frameworks and one-sided evaluation of the evidence. Koslowski and Kratochwil's constructivist account, for example, fails to explore the more holistic causal questions as well as could be hoped. They argue that a 'fundamental type of change takes place when the practices and constitutive conventions of a social system are altered'.[109] Following this formula, the end of the Cold War is explained simply through the change in international norms of interaction initiated by Gorbachev, while the origins of the Cold War are simply reduced to the actions of Stalin in changing the

[106] Specifically in Davis and Wohlforth's contribution to *Ending the Cold War*. Davis and Wohlforth (2004). Lebow and Stein (2004: 195).

[107] Herrmann and Lebow (2004a: 14–15).

[108] Herrmann and Lebow (2004a: 16).

[109] Koslowski and Kratochwil (1995: 134).

international norms of conduct.[110] Arguably, such accounts, although not entirely wrong, are too simplistic to be explanatorily adequate. They lack crucial parts of the explanation: inquiry into where norms arise from, why they are rejected, reciprocated or modified, why some norms die out. Answers to these questions require inquiry into the deeper and complex materially based social relational context in which norms emerge and die. Although explicitly addressing the wider material contexts of action beyond norms can be something of a challenge within constructivist frameworks where norms play such a predominant role, other constructivists in IR have taken some steps to address the wider causal concerns.[111]

Another, partly related, problem with Koslowski and Kratochwil's constructivist explanation is the tendency to divide 'causal' and 'constitutive' theorising. Koslowski and Kratochwil are clearly focused on exploring the 'constitutive' role of norms and this form of analysis is distinguished from the causal explanations of the political realists. This divisionary framing, then, is used to shield the constructivists from 'unreasonable' attacks from the political realists. The wielding of 'mutually exclusive' causal vs. constitutive theory terminology, in the light of this work, is seen as misleading. When a different conception of causation is brought to bear on the debate, the terms of the discussion change in crucial ways. If we follow the model advanced here, which sees material causes in a non-Humean, non-deterministic manner as underlying 'constitutive causes', we could argue that there is nothing inherently problematic in accepting the causal nature of material resources, as many constructivists assume. Moreover, we can also argue that the constitutive theorising of the constructivists is causal theorising: constitutive theorising is getting at the formal causes of social life. When Kratochwil and Koslowski, for example, trace the changes in the constitutive norms of the international system, their analysis is not 'non-causal'. Indeed, as their own terminology portrays, changes

110 Koslowski and Kratochwil (1995: 128, 140–4).

111 Thomas Risse-Kappen's (1995b) account of the end of the Cold War, for example, traces much better the role of material and structural constraints on actors, while still concentrating on the processes of exchange and transmission of norms. Jeffrey Checkel's (1997) account also refuses to reduce explanation of idea change to ideational factors and goes for a more openly multi-causal and complexity-sensitive explanation.

in norms matter and are worthy of investigation because they bring about changes in the international system.[112] Arguably, the 'constitutive norms' do not merely 'constitute' concepts or meanings: 'constitutive norms' matter because they have causal power over (that is they constrain and enable) the practices of actors in world politics. Rejecting the causal–constitutive theory divide, advocated in chapter 6, allows us to overcome the dichotomous conceptual premises that have haunted the end of the Cold War debates. It also makes it difficult for the constructivists to avoid answering important explanatory questions through deflecting questions probing the causes of norms, as unreasonable approaches that seek 'some incontrovertible last fundament'.[113]

The agency–structure debate, too, can be clarified through reframing IR's causal ontology. Despite their emphasis on 'intersubjective rules', which are seen as irreducible to agents' beliefs, most constructivists have had a tendency to emphasise agents and the 'practices' of agents as more important than structure. Koslowski and Kratochwil, for example, are very 'critical of the analytical utility of any conception of structure'.[114] This is largely the case because the concept is associated with neorealist structural explanations. Because of their aversion to structures, Koslowski and Kratochwil have emphasised the role of Gorbachev and his 'normative' context in bringing about the end of the Cold War. However, while it is important not to ignore the agency and personal psychology of Gorbachev and Reagan[115] in the events leading up to the end of the Cold War, it should be noted that the context of Gorbachev's actions cannot be sidelined and this context cannot simply be reduced to 'ideational' context either. Koslowski and Kratochwil, although they reject structures, seem to try to capture some sort of contextual factors through the notion of 'institutions', which they define as 'settled or routinized practices established and regulated by norms'.[116] This notion, while getting at the formal causes, arguably reduces social explanation to the study of shared understandings and the practices

[112] See, for example, Koslowski and Kratochwil (1995: 128).
[113] Koslowski and Kratochwil (1995: 137).
[114] Lebow and Risse-Kappen (1995a: 15).
[115] For a nice discussion of the role of personal psychology see, for example, Lebow and Stein (2004: 209–12).
[116] Koslowski and Kratochwil (1995: 134).

they give rise to. As was seen in chapter 6, this conceptualisation is lacking in depth in that it ignores the notion of social relations: that is, forms of (material) social relations that rules and norms give rise to. In chapter 6 the notion of structure has been deemed important in that it allows us to conceptualise these social relations. Social structures, as defined here, capture the sense in which social life is not merely conceptual or 'ideational' but consists of real material relations that define agents' social roles, positions and resources. Social life, then, is not reducible to shared understandings or practices but gives rise to social relations that carry and transmit material and formal causal powers (constraining and enabling conditions) on agents. In the case of the end of the Cold War, we should position agents, such as Gorbachev, within structures (with material and formal causal powers) that pre-exist him (Soviet state, Soviet economy, Soviet think-tanks, etc.). Gorbachev and the Soviet state elite did not make their decisions and calculations in a vacuum but in a complex structural context. This context cannot simply be seen as ideational: it defines formal as well as material constraints, which causal narratives need to bring to light. Nor should the context be seen as merely domestic. Explanations should also embed these structures within the wider international and global political and economic context (structures of world economy, etc.). Research into the end of the Cold War, in the light of the argument advanced here, would adopt a pluralistic ontological and methodological approach. A researcher is encouraged to ask questions about various sorts of causal factors and conditioners. (S)he is encouraged to provide a narrative explaining how these factors, material, agential, ideational or structural, came together and conditioned the process referred to as the end of the Cold War. The different aspects of the object of study can be studied through different methods. Thus, the state of the Soviet economy and the global economy, as well as developments in military capabilities, could be highlighted through statistical data. However, the study of concrete causal connections would also have to involve interpretive and historical analysis: that is, the study of historical contexts that condition processes as well as agents' conceptions of their context and options available to them.

Crucially, methodological pluralism should be complemented by a willingness and openness to construct new types of structurally embedded conceptualisations that can capture the data and processes involved in more nuanced ways. Also, it is accepted here that Herrmann and Lebow's suggestion of thinking about counterfactual possibilities, in reference to different structural and causal factors, is a useful suggestion in avoiding the tendencies towards 'certainty of hindsight bias', which they accurately identify as a key problem in many social scientific accounts that come to accord, in hindsight, some sort of inevitability to developments such as the end of the Cold War.[117]

The kinds of causal narratives advocated here would place agents in their context accounting for the pressures on them, and for the ways in which their actions came to shape that context. When no evidence can be gathered to support an explanation, or it is deemed implausible (for example, that Gorbachev was forced to surrender to the West at gun point), we could eliminate causal explanations. However, we should not be surprised if there are many causes and conditions in the making of the end of the Cold War. Instead of seeking 'a fundamental cause', IR theorists should seek to understand the historical causal process in a holistic way, that is, concentrate on accounting for the complex interactions of various causes in specific historical contexts. In constructing a causal story that seeks to make sense of the end of the Cold War, we must not reduce our view *a priori* by adopting a rigid ontological or conceptual framework that impedes our ontological horizons and, hence, restricts the use of plurality of evidence.[118] Giving up on having to put forward an 'ultimate cause' allows us to keep an open mind towards, and to make better sense of, the multiplicity of evidence there is about this complex process, as Herrmann and Lebow's collection has successfully shown.

It must be recognised that any explanation of a historical social process always involves a balance of judgement and that balances of judgement will remain contested. There are important ontological and empirical differences between accounts of world political processes; and it is not likely that these will simply disappear. However, it seems that epistemologically, methodologically and ontologically reductionist and parsimonious frameworks tend to oversimplify and, hence, fail

[117] Herrmann and Lebow (2004a: 17).

[118] For an interesting discussion of the origins of such rigidities in thinking, that is, the ways in which ideological theory-driven 'belief systems work against learning' see discussion in Herrmann (2004: 219–20).

to explain; for this reason adoption of a deeper and broader conception of cause can be useful in providing a reminder of the importance of keeping causal horizons open to many different types of causes.

Conclusion

This chapter has sought to demonstrate that the philosophical and conceptual deepening and broadening of the concept of cause is not inconsequential for how we examine concrete causal puzzles in IR. It has been seen that the acceptance of a pluralistic conception of social ontology and the adoption of methodological pluralism have some significant impacts on how world politics and its many processes can be tackled. The first section sought to lay out the social ontology of world politics, through emphasising a holistic, socially, historically and structurally embedded conceptual approach to world politics. It has also been seen that starting from more open ontological assumptions, and accepting methodologically and epistemologically pluralist assumptions for causal research, allows for slightly different types of causal analysis in IR. It does not solve all disputes among IR scholars: debates are bound to continue over how exactly to explain empirical processes and over which types of causal forces should be considered the most crucial causal factors. However, it allows IR theorists not to get caught up in the ontological, methodological and epistemological limitations of the Humean frameworks but to develop causal questions in new directions. It also allows us to study multiple causes simultaneously, rather than seeking reductionist explanations. It follows that the alternative discourse of causal analysis put forward here, although it does not claim to solve all problems of causal analysis in IR or even lead us to particular explanations of world political events, allows IR theorists certain alternative avenues for causal research and importantly the tools to avoid getting entangled in unconstructive debates over 'incommensurable' frameworks or terminologies characteristic of some explanatory frameworks in the field.

It must be noted, however, that the reframing of causal categories in the manner suggested here does not entail any particular substantial conclusions about world politics, nor does it say what a good IR theory exactly looks like. However, it has been seen that some studies, and indeed some of the more persuasive ones, in IR already work on the basis of a multi-causal, methodologically pluralist and epistemologically relativist approach, even if the approaches have lacked an explicit and coherent philosophically realist understanding of causation or of social ontology. This suggests that it is possible and desirable for IR theorising to move beyond the Humean problem-field it has inherited from the twentieth-century philosophy of science and social science. It is hoped that the approach advanced here, by making explicit the need for more open causal horizons in IR towards post-Humean directions, will contribute towards more constructive study of and debate on world political processes.

8 *Reconceptualising causes, reframing the divided discipline*

The discipline of IR has, throughout its history, been something of a 'divided discipline'.[1] During recent decades it has become widely accepted that one of the fundamental dividing lines in the discipline runs between those who do 'causal' and those who do 'non-causal', or constitutive, theorising.[2] As the disciplinary politics in IR have become deeply informed by this divisionary logic, the debates between the positivists and interpretivists, the rationalists and the reflectivists, have become highly emotionally charged.

There is no better illustration of the animosity between the causal and the non-causal theorists than that evident in Keohane's dismissal of reflectivist theorising in his Presidential Address to the International Studies Association in 1988 and David Campbell's reply to such dismissals in the epilogue of the second edition of *Writing Security*. While Keohane dismissed the reflectivists for lacking a systematic scientific approach to IR and a clear research programme,[3] Campbell argued that IR as a discipline is defined by a game of 'border politics', where the gatekeepers of the mainstream have sought to police the disciplinary field so as to render forms of inquiry either legitimate or illegitimate.[4] While rationalists have tended to dismiss the reflectivist approaches as unscientific,[5] Campbell attacked ferociously the parochial and imperialist nature of mainstream IR and its efforts to suppress critical work, either by denouncing it as anti-scientific or by co-opting identity issues within mainstream variable-based 'causal analysis'.[6] Crucially, the questions of causation have been important for both Keohane and Campbell. While Keohane has argued that he cannot understand the utility of non-causal approaches, Campbell has conceived the rationalist 'scientific' conception of causal analysis, and the efforts to extend

[1] Holsti (1985); Hollis and Smith (1990). [2] S. Smith (1995: 26–7).
[3] Keohane (1988: 392). [4] Campbell (1998b: 207–27).
[5] See also King, Keohane and Verba (1994). [6] Campbell (1998b: 217–18).

this form of inquiry to all questions in IR, to be at the heart of the problems of the discipline of IR.

Keohane's and Campbell's assessments of the centrality of the concept of cause in the contemporary divided discipline have of course been correct in certain important respects. However, neither Keohane nor Campbell has theorised the issue of causation in IR in a manner that would involve a coherent reframing of causal assumptions outside of the Humean framework. While Keohane has stressed the importance of causal analysis in IR, he has rather uncritically advanced a Humean view of causal analysis. On the other hand, while Campbell rightly identified the rationalist conception of causal analysis as a key problem in the divided discipline, and has recently shown some interest in developing causal language,[7] by not providing an alternative to the empiricist/rationalist conception of causal analysis, he has, paradoxically, legitimated the Humean view of causal analysis and, thereby, perpetuated the disciplinary dichotomies.

The aim of this book has been to provide an understanding of the origins of the recent controversy over causal analysis in IR and to look for a way out from this predicament through reclaiming an alternative conception of causation for the purposes of world political analysis. It has been argued that the framing of the concept of cause and, hence, the debates over the legitimacy of causal analysis in IR, have been informed by a particular, by no means self-evident or unproblematic, understanding of the concept of cause and of causal analysis. Both Keohane and Campbell have been wrapped up in the same 'problem-field' in IR: what has been identified here as the Humean problem-field.[8] Although the rationalist and the reflectivist theoretical 'camps' have considered themselves fundamentally opposed over the issue of causation, they have in fact been united by a great mass of common assumptions concerning the nature of causation. It is argued here that the empiricist/rationalist mainstream can be critiqued, but not through simply rejecting mainstream causal analysis and opting for a supposedly non-causal form of theorising. A more comprehensive critique of mainstream causal theorising is attained through critiquing the wider

[7] Interestingly, in his recent work Campbell (2007: 224–5) has pointed towards post-empiricist possibilities in causal analysis through reference to Connolly's idea of emergent causality.

[8] The fact that these positions share a common anti-realist 'problem-field' has been highlighted by Patomäki and Wight (2000: 215).

meta-theoretical groundings in IR, in which the Humean conception of causality plays a crucial role.

The aim of this concluding chapter is, first, to bring together the central arguments advanced in the preceding chapters and, second, to reflect on the implications that the rethinking of causation has for IR as a discipline. Finally, some possible objections to the framework advocated here are considered.

Humeanism in philosophy of science, social science and IR

Part I of this book has provided an account of the role of the Humean discourse or philosophy of causation in IR. To understand the debates on causation in IR we have had first to understand the origins of the Humean philosophy of causation and the effects it has had, not just in IR but, more widely, in the philosophy of science and social science. To this effect, chapter 1 traces the way in which the meaning of the notion of cause became 'narrowed down' and 'emptied out' from its previous deeper and broader meanings during the seventeenth and eighteenth centuries, and how these scepticist Humean assumptions became widely accepted in the nineteenth- and twentieth-century philosophical debates. The Humean assumptions have been summarised as follows:

1. Causal relations have been reduced to regularity-relations of observables and causal analysis has been tied to analysis of patterns of *regularities*.
2. Causal relations have been seen as relations of patterns of *observables*. Causation has been assigned no 'deep' ontological meaning.
3. Causal relations have been seen as characterised by *regularity-determinism*. It has been assumed that, given certain observed regularities, when A type of events take place, then B type of events can be assumed logically to follow. This 'closed system' view of causation has given grounds for equating causal analysis with prediction.
4. Causes, since Descartes, have been understood through the metaphor of 'efficient causes', implying that causes refer to 'pushing and pulling' moving forces.

These assumptions, it has been seen in chapter 1, are deeply embedded in the twentieth-century philosophy of science, albeit in various different forms.

Chapter 2 sought to elucidate how the philosophy of social science, too, has been deeply informed by these Humean assumptions. The chapter argues that the acceptance of the Humean framing of causation and causal analysis has initiated a deep dichotomisation of the social sciences between positivist and hermeneutic approaches. It claims that the twentieth-century positivists in the social sciences have advanced a Humean regularity understanding of causal analysis, while the hermeneutic theorists, having accepted the positivist account of causation as characteristic of causal analysis, have come to reject the concept of cause altogether in favour of inquiry into the meanings of and 'reasons for' action.

Chapters 3 and 4, then, examined the treatment of causation in IR. The discipline of IR, it was noted, has also been deeply informed by the Humean framing of the concept of cause. This has had some important impacts for how both the empiricists/rationalists and the reflectivists go about their theorising. Chapter 3 has shown that the scientific mainstream has accepted the empiricist Humean view of causal analysis, either explicitly or more implicitly. The dominance of the Humean discourse of causation has meant that the self-appointed causal analysts in IR have avoided talking about 'causes' outside the Humean epistemological and methodological criteria; they have conceived of 'legitimate' causal analysis as one backed up by some generalisation about observed patterns of effects.[9] As a consequence, they have conducted 'generalising', 'additive' and regularity-deterministic research, and have had problems in framing agents in the context of unobservable causes such as ideas, rules, norms and social structures.

The reflectivists, on the other hand, have followed the hermeneutic tradition in the philosophy of social science: most 'postpositivists' in IR have rejected causal approaches as 'deterministic' and 'objectivist'. Because their accounts, contra rationalists, focus on the role of ideas, rules, norms and discourses as 'non-deterministic' (regularity analysis and the 'when A, then B' model not applicable) shapers of world politics, they conceive themselves to be working on the basis of a non-causal approach to world politics.[10] However, it has been seen in chapter 4 that, although the reflectivists in IR question the applicability of causation to the social sciences, they do not really challenge the

[9] Nicholson (1996a); King, Keohane and Verba (1994).
[10] For a classic statement of this see, for example, Campbell (1998b: 4).

legitimacy of the particular conception of causation with which mainstream IR is working. Some constructivists have tried to challenge aspects of the positivist Humean form of causal analysis but, in doing so, they have oscillated between causal and constitutive accounts without a clear definition of the meaning of either term,[11] or they have simply been confused about the *kind* of causal analysis that should replace the mainstream form of causal inquiry.[12] Lacking in-depth knowledge of alternative conceptions of causation most reflectivist and constructivist theorists in the discipline have found it hard to think outside the Humean discourse when it comes to causation. This has meant that they have been incapable of accepting that some of their own terminology might, in fact, be 'implicitly' causal (in a non-Humean sense).

Moreover, it has been seen that both rationalist and reflectivist frameworks have been troubled by tendencies towards theoretical reductionism. The rationalist analysts have engaged in reductionist 'additive' analysis in that they have focused on weighing up 'independent variables' against each other, normally on the basis of statistical methods.[13] In their concentration on the role of 'ideational', 'normative' or 'discursive' factors in world politics, the reflectivists and the constructivists, on the other hand, have often ended up arguing that these factors are the most crucial explanatory factors in world politics. In so doing, they often fail to account for how norms, discourses and ideas come about in contexts that are not reducible to 'ideational' factors. Theoretical approaches in the disciplinary debates in IR have not been able to conceive of social ontology and social causes as plural and complex.

Causation and causal analysis reconceptualised

Part II has sought to address the problems that the Humean discourse of causation has given rise to in IR by building a deeper and broader account of cause. To this end, chapter 5 reviewed the strengths and the weaknesses of some of the possible philosophical attempts to escape Humean assumptions. It was seen that pragmatist and philosophically realist approaches have managed, at least partially, to avoid the Humean framing of causation and the problems that arise from it.

[11] Onuf (1989); Koslowski and Kratochwil (1995).
[12] Ruggie (1999); Wendt (1999b).
[13] As pointed out by Dessler (1991).

Despite advancing some important insights, these approaches, however, were not considered entirely unproblematic.

The pragmatist philosophy has rejected the Humean regularity-bound definition of causation. Causes, the pragmatists argue, are those things we can manipulate, or those things accounting for which makes something intelligible for us.[14] The pragmatists' approach is useful in that it has emphasised that causal explanation is, indeed, a pragmatic human activity and is always embedded in a social context of inquiry. However, although the pragmatists provide a way out of the rigid empiricist assumptions, they do not avoid the assumption most deeply embedded in modern philosophy of causation and science, that is, putting 'what we think' before 'what is' (epistemology over ontology). Suganami's approach to causation in IR[15] is characterised by this prioritisation of epistemology. Because of the unwillingness to recognise the ontological nature of causation, his account has accepted certain anti-realist and relativist conclusions about causes and causal analysis.

The philosophically realist approach, on the other hand, has avoided the pragmatist anthropocentrism by giving priority to ontology. Our causal accounts, even if pragmatic and socially embedded, are *of* something, also in the social sciences where causes are unobservable objects such as ideas or reasons.[16] The philosophical realists reject the Humean regularity criteria, observability assumption and regularity-determinism, thereby opening up the meaning of the notion of cause. However, some problems have characterised previous philosophically realist attempts to rethink causation in the social sciences and IR. Previous attempts have had problems in defining mechanisms and conditions and they have tended to prioritise the efficient cause metaphor in thinking about causation. Some steps have been taken to open up the meaning of causation through the material cause analogy but the treatment of social structural causation through this analogy has generated confusions. In IR, Wendt, Dessler and Patomäki have drawn on the philosophically realist approach and have, thereby, rejected the rationalist focus on regularities and the observable.[17] Although they have attempted to 'deepen' the notion of cause, there are some problems with the existing philosophical realist accounts. Wendt and Dessler,

[14] Collingwood (1940: 296–312); Dray (1975). [15] Suganami (1996).
[16] Bhaskar (1978, 1998); Harré and Madden (1975).
[17] Wendt (1999a); Dessler (1991); Patomäki (1996, 2002).

for example, have not challenged the conventional positivist account of causation deeply enough, considering the potential of their philosophically realist premises.

The goal of chapter 6 was to build a consistent non-Humean account of causation that can transcend the problems and limitations, not just of rationalist and reflectivist treatments of causation, but also of the previous attempts to overcome Humeanism. Drawing on philosophical realism, chapter 6 seeks to 'deepen' the notion of cause, while also seeking to 'broaden' the concept through revisiting the Aristotelian 'four causes' account.

The model of causation advanced in chapter 6 maintains that we can avoid a number of the problems of Humeanism by asserting the importance of causal ontology, notably 'deep ontology'. Causes, following the philosophical realists, are seen as real non-conceptual 'naturally necessitating' ontological entities, structures, relations, conditions or forces that produce outcomes or processes. Drawing on philosophical realism, I argue that causal analysis should be focused on producing conceptual frameworks through which the world and its unobservable ontological causes can be understood. The natural necessity of causes, it is argued, applies in the social sciences as well as in the natural. In the social world causes are real and ubiquitous; however, they are also complex and in themselves under-determining because social causes always exist in 'open systems' where many causal forces interact with and counteract each other in complex ways. Reasons should be seen as causes, but crucially, in a non-Humean manner. Ideas, aspirations, representations and discourses, too, are seen as causal, which is why a variety of 'intensive' qualitative, hermeneutic, historical and discursive methods and approaches are seen as crucial to social scientific inquiry.

Also, the notions of social relations and social structure have been given validity in social scientific inquiry.[18] The focus on structures of social relations, rather than mere behaviour or intersubjective understandings, gives social inquiry adequate recognition of the material reality of social life. It also emphasises that individual agents live in a social context that, although it may be reproduced by them, also preexists them and, hence, acts as a causal conditioner of their thoughts, identities, roles, intentionality and actions. Since structures of social

[18] The approach here follows, although also elaborates on, Bhaskar's account of social structures. See Bhaskar (1979).

relations are seen as causal, the notion of abstraction is given a central role in social inquiry: social science proceeds through conceptualisation of the deep social structural causes and conditions, in combination with the study of the 'concrete' social forms.[19]

Through accepting some of the philosophically realist assumptions, we can get away from some of the key problems that the Humean criteria have engendered in IR theorising. We can challenge the rationalists on methodological, epistemological and ontological levels: we can uphold ontological depth and complexity and accept assumptions of methodological pluralism and epistemological relativism. However, we can also challenge the reflectivist rejection of causes and argue that rules, norms and discourses are causal. Also, Suganami's approach can be criticised for lack of ontological grounding. When causes are seen as ontologically real, we can accept that judgements can be made on the plausibility of causal accounts: although our judgements are made in a transitive context, we can accept that in principle not all accounts are equally valid, since some can be seen to account for ontological relations as well as perceptual or interpretive evidence inadequately. Further, Wendt's and Dessler's engagements with causation have been surprisingly moderate in challenging Humean framings: philosophical realism gives us grounds not just to 'tweak' conceptions of causal theorising in IR, as they have done, but to challenge it fundamentally.

Beyond deepening the notion of cause, chapter 6 has also sought to broaden the meaning of the notion. This is because it is recognised that philosophically realist conceptual systems need to be augmented and clarified so that we can better counter the problems with causation in IR, notably the causal–constitutive theory dichotomy and problems of theoretical reductionism. The Aristotelian definition of cause accounts for many different ways in which causes 'cause' by outlining four different types of causes: material, formal, efficient and final.[20] Importantly, Aristotelian categories remind us that these different causes are deeply intertwined. The Aristotelian system allows us to conceptualise the ontological parameters of social inquiry in a pluralistic and holistic way and directs us to conceive of the different ways in which causes can be seen to cause. There is no need to conceptualise causes through the limited mechanistic metaphor of efficient cause. The active powers of agents (efficient causes) must always be related to final causes

[19] Sayer (1992). [20] Aristotle (1998: 115).

(purposes, intentionality) and, crucially, be contextualised within the 'constitutive' conditioning causal powers of rules and norms (formal causes) as well as material conditions (material causes).

The Aristotelian framework allows us to transcend the causal–constitutive divide in IR. We are better placed to deal with world politics and its complex causes if we see constitutive theorising as an inseparable part of causal theorising. Constitutive theorists in IR are, in fact, far from non-causal: their theoretical claims about the constitution of social objects inevitably entail causal claims concerning the 'constraining and enabling' role of ideational, normative or discursive 'formal causes'. The reconceptualisation of causes advanced here does not deny the role of theory in constituting the world – or in 'reifying' it. However, to deny the principle of causation does not help one to counter theoretical reification: on the contrary, making people think otherwise depends on exerting causal influence on people (through other formal causes), allowing them to form alternative (causal) reasons for their behaviour.

The Aristotelian framework also allows us to avoid theoretically reductionist efforts to explain world politics. Although settling which types of causes play the most prominent role in which causal processes in world politics is of course a matter of empirical inquiry, and although debates over the hierarchical relationships of causes are bound to continue, this approach allows us to avoid *a priori* tendencies towards mono-causal accounts by emphasising that causes cause in different ways and are always deeply intertwined with other causes. In the light of Aristotelian categories, reductionist analyses of world politics, whether focused on analysing agents' behaviour (positivists), material resources (realists) or ideational context (constructivists) as 'independent causal factors', should be reframed in favour of more holistic studies that trace the complex ways in which different causal factors interact in various historical contexts. The concept of structures of social relations also allows us to avoid theoretical reductionism of social structures to either efficient-type pushing-and-pulling causes or material causes: structures of social relations must be conceived of as 'carriers' of both material and formal causal powers.

Chapter 7 sought to illustrate that the philosophical reframing of causation has certain important consequences for substantive research of world politics. First, the social ontology of IR was reframed in order to facilitate post-Humean causal research. Parsimonious framings of world politics were rejected as world politics was conceptualised as a complex web of interacting and counteracting causal powers and (structures of) social relations. The ontological reframing of IR is important because ontological systems, it is recognised, play a crucial role in how concrete causal analyses of world political processes unfold: they shape the kinds of questions theorists ask and the kinds of data, methods and epistemological assumptions that are used. The ontological framing here seeks to keep doors open for the study of various different types of causal forces and various different types of methods and epistemologies.

This deeper and more complex conception of social ontology of world politics was drawn on in examining two illustrations of concrete causal puzzles. It was seen that the democratic peace debates have been unnecessarily narrowly focused on the Humean type of causal analysis focused on exploration of patterns of regularities. It was shown that the democratic peace debates can be redirected in crucial ways through drawing on the reconceptualised notion of cause, the rethought causal ontology and the reframed understanding of causal analysis. Chapter 7 also dealt with the debates on the end of the Cold War. It was argued that while the political realist framings of this complex historical process have been misleading, the constructivist explanations have also been theoretically reductionist. With the help of the deeper and broader understanding of causation, we can reinforce the importance of multi-causal explanatory models of world political processes.

Despite the ability of the model of causation advanced here to guide IR theorising and research in new directions, it is accepted that this model does not make causal theorising easy or uncontested. On the contrary, it is emphasised that causal theorising is always a complex, messy and contested process because of the dynamic and complex ontological nature of social objects. It follows that this work cannot hope to solve all problems with causal analysis in IR. Nor does it advance clear-cut guidelines for how exactly to conduct causal analysis: in fact, it argues that existing strict criteria should be subjected to radical reformulation. This will undoubtedly disappoint many social scientists who think fixed guidelines and methods are necessary. However, it is important to recognise that fixed and rigid criteria are not necessarily what a good scientific approach necessitates: the wish to have 'hard' clear-cut methods and criteria for social science is an inclination engendered by the dominance of a particular empiricist-positivist model of science. On the basis of the understanding of science advanced here, science does not consist of simply following prescribed methodological and logical guidelines, but rather is constituted by careful weighing of the pros and cons of a variety of social science methods and, importantly, in possessing an informed awareness of the need for self-reflection, both analytical and normative-political, in developing theoretical explanations and conceptual systems of the social world.

Implications for the divided discipline

The reconceptualisation of causation as it stands here has some crucial implications for the discipline of IR. First, by emphasising that causal analysis need not follow the rationalist Humean lines but can, instead, entail adoption of non-Humean methodological, epistemological and ontological premises, the approach here opens up for re-evaluation the 'social scientific' validity and hierarchisation of theoretical approaches in IR. Also, the reconceptualisation of causation advanced here fundamentally challenges the framing of the discipline of IR. Not only does the presently advocated 'self-image' of the discipline become highly untenable, but also it emerges that the relationship of IR with other social science disciplines can be rethought.

The most direct implication of the rethinking of the concept of cause is that it gives us grounds for critiquing the 'positivist' or 'rationalist' approach to causal analysis in IR: these approaches are not the only way of doing social scientific causal analysis and can in fact be seen to be characterised by distinctive limitations. The Humean accounts, especially when rigidly Humean, can be unnecessarily narrow and also, arguably, go towards hiding important sets of causal social relations in world politics that cannot be captured through regularity analysis and traditional observational methods. The approach adopted here supports the arguments of many reflectivists. Indeed, the approach here recognises that the poststructuralist, feminist, constructivist and critical theory accounts in IR tend often to fare better with their analyses of world politics, in that they recognise the complexity and unpredictability of social life, accept methods that allow us to capture the role of ideas, meanings and reasons, and in that these approaches emphasise that all accounts of the social world are embedded in the researcher's social environment and are politically motivated in one way or another.

However, it has been pointed out that, although the postpositivist approaches tend to 'dig deeper' in analysing world politics, they still often draw on the Humean problem-field. The goal here is to provide a more consistent and comprehensive framework for critiquing positivism than that provided by the reflectivists. The aim has been to keep the concept of cause and, indeed, the idea of causal analysis as open as possible so that practising researchers and theorists can engage with their object of study armed with a more pluralistic ontological, epistemological methodological 'tool box'.

Nevertheless, the upshot of undoing the positivist premises of causal theorising is that the more reflectivist-influenced theorists, arguably, benefit the most. If the guidelines for 'social scientific causal theorising' advocated by mainstream IR are challenged on the basis suggested here, the 'marginalised' theorists in IR can be recognised as doing valuable and justifiable – and, indeed, causal – social scientific research. Paradoxically, the rethinking of the notion of cause can legitimise marginalised IR theories more effectively than their own frameworks can – because these frameworks are so fundamentally caught up in the divisive discourse themselves. As a result of the reconceptualisation of causation advanced here, the balance of argument can be seen to shift in IR and, indeed, the marginalisation of certain positions becomes more difficult to maintain. This, in turn, goes towards exposing the fact that IR is not a non-political, non-social, objective, discipline but a 'social structure' built around certain forms of thinking that have benefited some and marginalised others.

Besides posing a challenge to the empiricist/rationalist conception of science and causal theorising and, hence, provoking a re-evaluation of theoretical stances in the discipline, the reconceptualisation of causation here also poses far-reaching questions for the disciplinary 'self-image' of IR. This challenge comes on two levels: first, with regard to the internal disciplinary divisions in IR and, second, with regard to the external relations of IR with other social scientific disciplines.

The internal self-image of IR is challenged deeply by the refusal to accept the philosophical justification for the causal–constitutive theory division. As we have seen, we should avoid reifying the causal–constitutive theory division in IR by conceptualising the concept of cause in a wider way than is usual. On the basis of the meta-theoretical argument advanced here, the distinctions between causal and constitutive theorising are not as clear as most IR theorists think. It is crucial to note that, in the light of the approach here, causal concerns are always intimately tied to the 'constitutive' nature of objects. Indeed, what seem like causal questions, such as why-questions, are, on the basis of this approach, *fundamentally* interlinked with how- and what-questions; accounting for what caused something is to make claims about the nature of the objects involved. Making constitutive claims also entails making causal claims: this is because the way in which identities, practices, meanings and relations are 'constituted' is seen to have effects (causal powers) on concrete (non-conceptual) processes and actions.

The fact that causal and constitutive theorising 'collapse' into one another, or the realisation that they were never legitimately separated,[21] has some serious consequences for the discipline of IR. The 'divisive' discourse initiated by Hollis and Smith and followed by most IR theorists can be challenged. It can be seen that it legitimates an unhelpfully dichotomous understanding of forms of social inquiry, which in turn confuses and misdirects substantive theorising and research in IR.

Terminological walls between theoretical camps have played a crucial role in maintaining the patterns of disciplinary politics in IR: these walls have been produced and reproduced by marginalised non-causal theorists as much as by the positivist mainstream. In the light of the argument advanced here, it must be recognised that IR theorists all face the same world where complex things happen in complex ways, which is what they are trying to explain and understand. Putting all the theorists within the same 'causal fold', and advancing alternative conceptual tools for social analysis, provides the conditions for theorists to start engaging with each other more openly. It becomes much more difficult for theorists to hide behind the assumption that they are looking at different worlds, or that they are working on completely incommensurable criteria for knowledge. The fact that these terminological walls can be brought down, at least in some respects, should help the evaluation of theoretical and empirical merits of theoretical accounts. The evaluation can be based on the coherence of analysis and the persuasiveness of evidence rather than mere whim, terminological preferences or rigid pre-set criteria for valid knowledge. In a discipline constructed on the basis of the meta-theoretical grounding advanced here, political and theoretical differences will remain but the reduction of analysis of events and processes becomes harder and harder to justify in terms of clear-cut insulated theoretical -isms.

[21] For a similar argument see Colin Wight's (2006: 12) argument about the unnecessary nature of bridging the *via media* between positivism and postpositivism in IR.

However, doing away with disciplinary divisions may not be as easy as one might think. It must be recognised that a great deal of prestige, pride and effort has been put into maintaining the disciplinary divisions in IR. Disciplinary politics revolving around the causal–constitutive theory division have played an important role in structuring the field for more than a decade, during which time the theoretical identities of theorists have become deeply structured by this division.[22] A sceptic might argue that it is naive to expect that theoretical infighting will simply wane because of the rethinking of the meta-theoretical framing of IR: it is the nature of academic discourse to divide in order to debate and engage.

It is not my expectation that all theoretical infighting will cease, and that some sort of grand theory of world politics will emerge as a result. On the contrary, it is recognised here that it is natural to have contending interpretations of how and why things happen in the world. Causal analysis in both academic and everyday life is messy, contested and, indeed, a politically and normatively loaded affair. Although debate on causes remains, it is the hope of this work that some of the misleading avenues, including the debate over the legitimacy of the notion of cause, will be transcended so that efforts in IR theorising can be focused on more constructive lines of debate. Also, by recognising explanatory accounts as political, rather than pretending that they are beyond political contestation, makes social science more open and the debates more interesting. It should be noted, however, against the post-structuralists, that accepting causal accounts as politically situated and consequential does not mean that all causal accounts are 'equal': it is not the case that *anything* can be plausibly asserted about world political processes. Although many different explanations can be shown to be explanatorily and evidentially plausible within different conceptual and evidential frameworks, not all accounts can be upheld ontologically, conceptually or evidentially.

The 'self-image' of IR is affected by the reconceptualisation of the concept of cause, not only internally, but also in the discipline's external relations with the wider field of social sciences. There has been some contact between IR and the disciplines of history, sociology and economics. However, not only have these contacts been rather limited, but also it has been assumed that, although some theorists have

[22] As also noted by Wæver (2007).

ventured 'outside' the normal confines of the discipline, IR as a discipline is separable and self-sufficient. This argument is often justified on the basis that IR deals with a particular environment (interstate interactions) and particular agents (states). This justification is misleading, as it arises from a particular conception of the 'international problematique' that is seen to define IR.[23]

As was argued in chapter 7, this work rejects the traditional ontology of IR. Because of the wide and complexity-sensitive social ontology accepted here, including deep intertwining of social, economic, cultural and political social relations, it emerges that IR should be conceived of as a discipline focused on the study of the 'international' or rather 'world political' in a much broader sense than traditional IR allows. IR as a discipline should not be tied to the inside/outside-focused 'levels of analysis' framework that has dominated much of IR theorising, nor should 'what matters' be confined to mere state interactions, wars or institutional operation. Insulating IR and its 'objects of study' runs the risk of entailing misleadingly narrow and, indeed, implausible causal analyses of the complex social relations and processes that make up world politics. In order for IR inquiry to engage more effectively with the complex social relations and social structuring of world politics, the discipline needs to be opened up deeply to other social scientific disciplines, notably sociology, economics and history.

The goal here is not to do away with the discipline of IR, or to argue that what it inquires into is unimportant, but rather to reintegrate it with other areas of social inquiry (as was incidentally natural in the early discipline). IR as a discipline can be justified in that it asks questions that are often not dealt with deeply enough within other disciplines. However, because of the wide-ranging nature of its object of study (the international, the global), it is a fundamentally inter-disciplinary discipline that should draw deeply on other areas of social science. IR is but a part of the wider social sciences studying the complex social relations in the social world, and for this reason needs broader conceptual horizons and tools for conducting more holistic analysis of the international or the global.

The reintegration of IR with other disciplines is, however, not a simple matter. This is because other disciplines, too, have meta-theoretical shortcomings. It is important to note that because of the wide-ranging

[23] As also pointed out by Patomäki (2002: 82–5).

and deeply influential role of Humeanism in the modern philosophy of science and social science, the meta-theoretical confusions in IR are not unique. While reintegration with other disciplines is highly desirable, we must be wary of the terms within which this reintegration is conducted. What, for example, is the consequence of 'reintegrating' with economics if orthodox economics, with its closed system logic and atomistic social ontology, has to be accepted as a matter of course? Also, if integration with sociology and politics is looked for, we must seek to do away with the self-evidence of Humean and empiricist meta-theoretical assumptions, and the theoretical dynamics they give rise to, within these disciplines. It follows that Humean leanings in meta-theoretical bases should be identified, not just in IR, but also in other social science disciplines. Critical realists, and a few others, have sought to take on the task of challenging some of the seemingly self-evident but in certain respects problematic empiricist meta-theoretical assumptions that underlie many social science disciplines.[24] To the extent that this work seeks to advance a social theoretical framing on the lines of critical realism, and, indeed, aims to develop critical realism, it can offer potentially useful insights beyond the discipline of IR, thus aiding the difficult task of achieving the constructive reintegration of social science disciplines.

Possible objections and future directions

Wide-ranging claims have been made above about the impact that this retheorisation of causation has for IR theory and causal research. However, given that the issue of causation is a controversial one, and that many ontological, conceptual and even potentially political issues are at stake in how we study causes, it is likely that a number of objections will be levelled at the argument presented here. Let me take this opportunity to anticipate what some of these possible objections might be and how they might be responded to. I also want to make a note of the future research areas that this conception of cause opens up.

One objection that might arise is that the argument here amounts to nothing more than a purely semantic rephrasing of the idea of cause. Some 'strong' positivists might advocate this argument because for

[24] For efforts to reframe other social science disciplines see Lawson (1997); A. Sayer (1992, 2000); Hay (2002). See also Lloyd (1993) on history.

them the use of the term cause is itself vague and unnecessary in scientific practice: science strictly speaking does not require causal analysis but rather analysis of observable trends that we can use for predictive purposes. This is an interesting objection but one that is relatively easily rejected with reference to empirical evidence from the practice of science. Despite its controversial and contested meaning, the concept of cause has continued to play a central role in philosophy of science and in philosophy of social science and, despite numerous attempts by radically empiricist philosophers, for example, has not been eliminated. Indeed, nowadays most positivists and empiricists in IR, and in philosophy of science and social science more widely, recognise it is not possible to do away with the idea.[25] Despite its changing and multiple meanings, the concept lingers on in our everyday and in our scientific terminology. One conceptualisation of causation has been suggested here: while it would be presumptuous in the extreme to assume that this provides a final solution to the problem of causation, simply assuming away the concept, and all the language of consequences, production and forces that goes with it, would also be a very difficult move to maintain.

But what is the significance of rephrasing the meaning of the concept of cause? It is in some ways a semantic challenge: what is being challenged here is, indeed, the meaning of the concept of cause and the contexts within which it is used. However, it should also be noted that the ways in which we use the concept are not irrelevant: semantic uses exist in discursive contexts and discursive contexts have consequences for how we describe the world and how we debate our understandings of the world with others. When the idea of cause is thought of in different ways, new avenues, questions, ways of dealing with evidence and lines of debates between scholars arise, as we have seen in chapters 6 and 7. Also, as we have seen, other important issues, such as the normative consequences of the ways in which we talk about causation, are opened up. Conceptual reframing, then, is not a *mere* semantic exercise: I hope to have shown that, while reframing causation does not determine our causal theories or a specific understanding of world politics – discourses are not causally determining in a 'when A, then B' sense – it can enable different avenues for dealing with theories, evidence and methods.

[25] Nicholson (1983: 26–7); King, Keohane and Verba (1994: 75–6).

Another version of this objection focused on the significance of reinterpreting the meaning of causation, is one that is likely to be posed by poststructuralists: this is the argument that reframing causation, even just semantically, has a negative or dangerous influence in the discipline, in that it reifies a scientific discourse that fixes objects and realities in the social world. Some poststructuralists might argue that calling something a cause is both an unnecessary theoretical move and simultaneously a political act that justifies certain interpretations of the world over others.[26] I would accept that increased awareness and self-reflection on the political consequences of engaging in causal analysis is welcome: our social inquiries are, indeed, not void of political consequences. However, I would also re-emphasise that the conception of causation advocated here is a complexity-sensitive and dynamic one, and does not assume the fixity of causal forces: just because we point to a discursive determination of, say, a state identity in causal terms does not make this causal connection a law, a universal feature of social reality. Moreover, and more importantly, it has been argued here that even if one wants to avoid talking about causation, as the poststructuralists do, we all, including the poststructuralists, do still inevitably make causal claims (as was seen in chapter 4). Critical theories, as other theories, seem in fact to *require* that the conceptual determinations, discursive logics or forces of production that they study are in some senses causal on our practices and thought for their own theoretical and political claims to make sense. If discourses or reasons were not causal, what would be the point in analysing or criticising them? Importantly, recognising the causality of discourse or reasons does not lessen the 'meaningfulness' or 'contingency' and complexity of the social contexts we live in; it merely highlights their role and re-emphasises the importance of recognising that nothing, even our reasons for actions, arises from nowhere.

Another objection might be that arguing for depth and breadth in defining causation entails an increase in vagueness and imprecision. In reply, a key thing to note is that depth and breadth do not necessarily entail vagueness: indeed, the aim here has been to show that we can *specify* more effectively the kinds of causes we try to capture in our studies through the more expansive categories advocated here. Rather than collapsing different kinds of causes into a single monolithic

[26] This critique has been discussed in Kurki (2007).

description of causation, the categories advocated here specify different ways of causing. This approach allows the constitutive theorists, for example, to specify more adequately how the kinds of causes they study differ from mechanistic causes and processes studied by others.

Nevertheless, it is true that 'vagueness' in certain senses, specifically in reference to positivist criteria, is increased when causal complexity and unobservable causes are added to the picture. The rationalists certainly would object to talk of unobservable causes that cannot be tied to regular patterns of observations. It should be noted, however, that the very idea of science that informs the empiricist scepticism of unobservables is rejected here. Science, when understood through a philosophically realist lens, specifically requires dealing with unobservable objects: this is conceived to be unavoidable in the natural as well as in the social sciences. Philosophical realists see observational patterns as one aspect of scientific practice, but recognise that conceptualisation of unobservable realities constitutes the core practice of science. It is recognised, moreover, that, because of the dynamic and malleable nature of social objects, some level of imprecision will always be involved in the study of the social sciences.[27] It should be noted then that this critique only stands if one adopts the positivist understanding of science: an understanding that is far from self-evident as an accurate description or theory of the practice of science.

Of course rationalists might object further by arguing that the form of causation advocated here does not prove the falsity of their framework: it merely provides an alternative, and an alternative that in their eyes is inferior. This is a valid criticism in the sense that, although the weaknesses of the Humean framework have been pointed to, this work cannot in and of itself prove a philosophy of causation wrong, merely point to its shortcomings in regard to the ways in which it studies social reality. As has been noted throughout, the question of causation is not a problem that can be solved: it is merely a problem that can be solved in various different ways. Humeanism presents one answer, and the deeper and broader conception of cause advanced here presents another. The point here has been to argue that Humeanism has been accepted without reflection on the alternatives; that Humeanism has certain strengths but also certain weaknesses as a framework; and that an alternative discourse of causation can help us in clarifying the

[27] Sayer (1992).

nature of causation in IR and, hence, provides ways out of some of the discursive traps brought on by Humeanism. While this approach too can be seen to have its weaknesses when considered from alternative philosophical perspectives, it has been my aim to show that there are *good reasons* to consider the contributions of this approach to causation in IR. If nothing else, it is my hope that more open and self-reflexive debate on the kinds of assumptions that are associated with causation is engendered in IR by a philosophical discussion of this core concept.

Openings for further research

The meta-theoretical grounding and the conceptual system advanced here answer a number of important concerns that IR theorists have not managed previously to overcome (or dismiss). However, they also raise many more questions for further exploration.

First, *new empirical questions* are opened up for investigation, especially with regard to the complex nature and concrete role of various social relations in world politics. Such research is difficult and challenging but also vital. Constructing detailed empirical investigations, on the lines indicated in chapter 7, is important to demonstrate the practical and explanatory potential of this alternative approach to causal analysis. Also, in so doing, we should continue the search for more nuanced conceptualisations of the central concepts in IR (international system, state, capitalism, patriarchy, etc.) as well as in social theorising more generally (ideas, social structures, etc.). Important steps have been taken in IR towards multi-causal analysis by authors such as Heikki Patomäki, but much more remains to be done.[28] Furthermore, the consequences of this rethought conceptualisation of causation for the *theoretical frameworks in IR* need further clarification. We need to think further about how to shift theoretical assumptions in IR in more adequate directions. We need to ask, for example, how the political realist or the constructivist theoretical frameworks might be reframed towards more multi-causal explanatory terminology.

In the light of the analysis here, moreover, clarifying what the methodological implications of this approach are is central. Given the fact that the approach here is in deep disagreement with the dominant accounts of causal analysis, such as that of King, Keohane and

[28] Patomäki (2002).

Verba, it would be highly desirable to elaborate on *alternative research guidelines* that arise from this approach. Developing alternative prescriptions (even if open and flexible ones) for causal analysis in IR, and in the social sciences more widely, will allow future social and political theorists to develop more open, reflective and constructive research designs.

Another crucially important aspect of causal analysis that is in need of further investigation relates to the *normative and political consequences of causal analysis*. Although this issue has been left out of the discussion here, it should not be forgotten that in the history of philosophy of causation, the issue of causation has always been closely tied to the idea of moral responsibility. This is because, quite simply, how we explain the causes of something has an effect on how we allocate moral responsibilities to actors or structures. The normative implications of causal analysis have been, if you like, 'hidden' by the Humean discourse of causation because of the fact–value distinction that underlies it. However, when the non-normative Humean framing of the conception of cause is lifted we can see that political and normative debates become closely tied to the idea of cause and our conceptions of causal analysis. The moral and political consequences of engaging in causal analysis in particular kinds of ways has been by and large ignored in IR and in much of social science and should be subjected to further examination. It can be seen then that the issue of causality is not just an issue of meta-theory, methods or ontology but a question of normativity and ethics.

Much, then, remains to be done: the argument of this book presents but an opening towards new ways of dealing with causation and causal analysis in world politics.

Conclusion

The concept of cause has been under-philosophised in IR for too long. While dealing with philosophical issues is considered unnecessary and superfluous to their scholarship by some International Relations scholars, it has been argued here that it is important that IR scholars engage with some of the key debates in philosophy of science and philosophy of causation and, thereby, equip themselves to grapple with the central concepts they use in their analyses, such as the notion of cause, in more reflective and informed ways. This is crucial, not just for theoretical purposes, but because theoretical systems 'constrain and enable' the way in which we analyse the world. It follows that if causation is used in poorly conceptualised and unreflective ways, we run the risk not only of misunderstanding each other's explanations but also of misidentifying important causal forces or relations in world politics. Arguably, in current IR theorising certain trends towards (regularity-)determinist and reductionist causal analyses have been present. This work has sought to clear some of the theoretical and meta-theoretical ground surrounding the concept of cause in IR by providing an alternative to the Humean regularity conception of cause that has underpinned the disciplinary engagements with world political causes. On the basis of such a reconceptualisation of the concept of cause, it is hoped, we can open up paths towards more holistic and more constructive debates on complex forms of causation in world politics.

References

Achinstein, P., and S. F. Barker. (1969). eds. *The Legacy of Logical Positivism*. Baltimore: The Johns Hopkins University Press

Anscombe, G. E. M. (1957). *Intention*. Oxford: Blackwell

Anscombe, G. E. M., and R. Teichmann. (2000). *Logic, Cause & Action: Essays in Honour of Elizabeth Anscombe*. Cambridge: Cambridge University Press

Apel, Karl-Otto. (1984). *Understanding and Explanation: a Transcendental-Pragmatic Perspective*. Translated by Georgia Warnke. Cambridge: MIT Press

Aquinas. (1905). *Summa Contra Gentiles*. Translated by J. Rickaby. London: Burns & Oats

(2006). *Summa Theologiae, Questions on God*. Edited by Brian Davies and Brian Leftow. Cambridge: Cambridge University Press

Archer, Margaret. (1995). *Realist Social Theory: the Morphogenetic Approach*. Cambridge: Cambridge University Press

Archer, Margaret, Roy Bhaskar, Andrew Collier, Tony Lawson and Alan Norrie. (1998). eds. *Critical Realism: Essential Readings*. London: Routledge

Aristotle. (1970a). *Aristotle's Physics, Books 1 and 2*. Translated by W. Charlton. Oxford: Clarendon Press

(1970b). *Metaphysics*. Translated by J. Warrington. London: Everyman's Library

(1994). *Posterior Analytics*. Translated by Jonathan Barnes. Oxford: Clarendon Press

(1998). *Metaphysics*. Translated by Hugh Lawson-Tangred. London: Penguin

Armstrong, D. M., and N. Malcolm. (1984). *Consciousness and Causality: a Debate on the Nature of Mind*, Great Debates in Philosophy. Oxford: Blackwell

Ashley, Richard K. (1985). The Poverty of Neorealism. *International Organization* 38 (2): 225–86

(1989). Living on Border Lines: Man, Poststructuralism and War. In *International/Intertextual Relations: Postmodern Readings of World*

Politics, edited by James Der Derian and Michael J. Shapiro. Lexington: Lexington Books, pp. 259–321

(1996). Achievements of Poststructuralism. In *International Theory: Positivism and Beyond*, edited by S. Smith, K. Booth and M. Zalewski. Cambridge: Cambridge University Press, pp. 240–53

Aveling, Frank. (2001). Cause. *Catholic Encyclopedia* [cited 01.06.2007]. http://www.newadvent.org/cathen/ 03459a.htm

Axelrod, R., and R. O. Keohane. (1985). Achieving Co-operation under Anarchy: Strategies and Institutions. *World Politics* 38 (3): 226–54

Ayer, A. J. (1959). *Logical Positivism*. Glencoe, IL: The Free Press

(1968). *The Origins of Pragmatism: Studies in the Philosophy of Charles Saunders Peirce and William James*. London: Macmillan

(1974). *Language, Truth and Logic*. Harmondsworth: Penguin Books

Bain, William. (2000). Deconfusing Morgenthau: Moral Inquiry and Classical Realism Reconsidered. *Review of International Studies* 26 (3): 445–64

Baldwin, David A. (1993a). Neorealism, Neoliberalism and World Politics. In *Neorealism and Neoliberalism: The Contemporary Debate*, edited by D.A. Baldwin. New York: Columbia University Press, pp. 3–28

(1993b). ed. *Neorealism and Neoliberalism: the Contemporary Debate*. New York: Columbia University Press

Barkawi, Tarak, and Mark Laffey. (2001a). Introduction: the International Relations of Democracy, Liberalism and War. In *Democracy, Liberalism and War: Rethinking the Democratic Peace Debate*, edited by Tarak Barkawi and Mark Laffey. London: Lynne Rienner, pp. 1–24

(2001b). eds. *Democracy, Liberalism and War: Rethinking the Democratic Peace Debate*. London: Lynne Rienner, 2001

(2002). Retrieving the Imperial: Empire and International Relations. *Millennium: Journal of International Studies* 31 (1): 109–28

Bates, Robert H., Avner Greif, Margaret Levi, Jean Laurent Rosenthal and Barry R. Weingast. (1998). eds. *Analytical Narratives*. Princeton: Princeton University Press

Baumann, Zygmunt. (1978). *Hermeneutics and Social Science: Approaches to Understanding*. London: Hutchinson

Beauchamp, Tom. (1974a). Introduction: Manipulability Theories of Causation. In *Philosophical Problems of Causation*, edited by Tom L. Beauchamp. Encino: Dickenson, pp. 115–17

(1974b). Introduction: Modern Regularity Theory. In *Philosophical Problems of Causation*, edited by Tom L. Beauchamp. Encino: Dickenson, pp. 74–6

(1974c). ed. *Philosophical Problems of Causation*. Encino: Dickenson

Beauchamp, Tom, and Alexander Rosenberg. (1981). *Hume and the Problem of Causation*. New York: Oxford University Press

Beck, Nathaniel, Gary King and Langche Zeng. (2004). Theory and Evidence in International Conflict: a Response to de Marchi, Gelpi and Grynaviski. *American Political Science Review* 98 (2): 379–89

Beebee, Helen. (2006). *Hume on Causation*. London: Routledge

Bell, John S. (1987). *Speakable and Unspeakable in Quantum Mechanics*. Cambridge: Cambridge University Press

Benton, Ted. (1998). Realism and Social Science: Some Comments on Roy Bhaskar's Possibility of Naturalism. In *Critical Realism: Essential Readings*, edited by Margaret Archer et al. London: Routledge, pp. 297–312

Bhaskar, Roy. (1978). *A Realist Theory of Science*. 2nd edn. Brighton: Harvester

(1979). *The Possibility of Naturalism: a Philosophical Critique of the Contemporary Human Sciences*. Brighton: Harvester

(1989). *Reclaiming Reality: a Critical Introduction to Contemporary Philosophy*. London: Verso

(1991). *Philosophy and the Idea of Freedom*. Oxford: Basil Blackwell

(1993). *Dialectic: the Pulse of Freedom*. London: Verso

(1994). *Plato Etc.: the Problems of Philosophy and their Resolution*. London: Verso

(1998). *The Possibility of Naturalism: a Philosophical Critique of the Contemporary Human Sciences*. 3rd edn. London: Routledge

(2000). *From East to West: the Odyssey of a Soul*. London: Routledge

(2002). *Reflections on Meta-Reality: Transcendence, Emancipation and Everyday Life*. London: Sage

Bhaskar, Roy, and Rom Harré. (2001). How to Change Reality: Story V. Structure - Debate between Rom Harré and Roy Bhaskar. In *After Postmodernism: an Introduction to Critical Realism*, edited by J. Lòpez and G. Potter. London: Athlone, pp. 22–39

Biersteker, Thomas J., and Cynthia Weber. (1996). eds. *State Sovereignty as Social Construct*. Cambridge: Cambridge University Press

Bohm, David. (1984). *Causality and Chance in Modern Physics*. London: Routledge & Kegan Paul

Bohm, D., and B. J. Hiley. (1993). *Undivided Universe: an Ontological Interpretation of Quantum Theory*. London: Routledge

Bohman, James. (1991). *New Philosophy of Social Science: Problems of Indeterminacy*. Cambridge: Polity

Booth, Ken, and Steve Smith. (1995). eds. *International Relations Theory Today*. Cambridge: Polity

Born, Max. (1949). *Natural Philosophy of Cause and Chance*. Oxford: Oxford University Press

Brooks, Stephen G., and William C. Wohlforth. (2000). Power, Globalization, and the End of Cold War: Reevaluating a Landmark Case for Ideas. *International Security* 25 (3): 5–53

Brown, Chris. (2007). Situating Critical Realism. *Millennium Journal of International Studies* 35 (2): 409–16

Brown, M. E., S. M. Lynn-Jones and S. E. Miller. (1999). eds. *Debating Democratic Peace*. Cambridge: MIT Press

Bueno de Mesquita, Bruce. (1989). The Contribution of Expected Utility Theory to the Study of International Conflict. In *Origins and Prevention of Major Wars*, edited by R. I. Rotberg and T. K. Rabb. Cambridge: Cambridge University Press, pp. 53–76

(2002). Domestic Politics and International Relations. *International Studies Quarterly* 46: 1–10

Bull, Hedley. (1969). International Theory: Case for Classical Approach. In *Contending Approaches to International Politics*, edited by Klaus Knorr and James N. Rosenau. Princeton: Princeton University Press, pp. 20–38

(1977). *The Anarchical Society*. London: Macmillan

Bull, Hedley, and Adam Watson. (1984). *The Expansion of International Society*. Oxford: Clarendon Press

Bunge, Mario Augusto. (1959). *Causality: the Place of the Causal Principle in Modern Science*. Cambridge: Harvard University Press

(1979). *Causality and Modern Science*. 3rd edn. New York: Dover Publications

(1996). *Finding Philosophy in Social Science*. New Haven: Yale University Press

Burchill, Scott. (2001a). Introduction. In *Theories of International Relations*, edited by Burchill et al. 2nd edn. Basingstoke: Palgrave, pp. 1–28

(2001b). Realism and Neo-realism. In *Theories of International Relations*, edited by Burchill et al. 2nd edn. Basingstoke: Palgrave, pp. 70–102

Burchill, Scott, Richard Devetak, Andrew Linklater, Matthew Peterson, Christian Reus-Smith and Jacqui True. (2001). eds. *Theories of International Relations*. 2nd edn. Basingstoke: Palgrave

Butterfield, Herbert, and Martin Wight. (1966). eds. *Diplomatic Investigations: Essays on International Political Theory.* London: George, Allen & Unwin

Campbell, David. (1998a). *National Deconstruction: Violence, Identity and Justice in Bosnia*. London: University of Minnesota Press

(1998b). *Writing Security: United States Foreign Policy and Politics of Identity*. 2nd edn. Manchester: Manchester University Press

(1998c). MetaBosnia: Narratives of the Bosnian War. *Review of International Studies* 24 (2): 261–82

(1999). Contra Wight: the Errors of Premature Writing. *Review of International Studies* 25 (1): 317–22

(2007). Poststructuralism. In *International Relations Theories: Discipline and Diversity*, edited by Tim Dunne, Milja Kurki and Steve Smith. Oxford: Oxford University Press, pp. 203–28

Carlsnaes, Walter, Thomas Risse and Beth A. Simmons. (2002). eds. *Handbook of International Relations*. London: Sage

Carnap, Rudolf. (1950). *Logical Foundations of Probability*. London: Routledge & Kegan Paul

(1966). *Philosophical Foundations of Physics: an Introduction to the Philosophy of Science*. London: Basic Books

Carr, E. H. (2001 [1939]). *The Twenty Years' Crisis 1919–1939: an Introduction to the Study of International Relations*. With an introduction by Michael Cox. Basingstoke: Palgrave

(1986) *What History?* 2nd edn. London: Penguin

Cartwright, Nancy. (1983). *How the Laws of Physics Lie*. Oxford: Clarendon Press

(1989). *Nature's Capacities and their Measurement*. Oxford: Clarendon Press

(1999). *The Dappled World: Essays on the Perimeter of Science*. New York: Cambridge University Press

(2004). Causation: One word, Many Things. *Philosophy of Science* 71 (5): 805–19

(2007). *Hunting Causes and Using Them: Approaches in Philosophy and Economics*. Cambridge: Cambridge University Press

Carver, Terrell. (1991). ed. *The Cambridge Companion to Marx*. Cambridge: Cambridge University Press

Chalmers, Alan F. (1996). *What Is This Thing Called Science?* Buckingham: Open University Press

Chan, Steve. (1997). In Search of Democratic Peace: Problems and Promise. *Mershon International Studies Review* 41: 59–91

Chávez-Arvizo, Enrique. (1997). Introduction. In *Descartes' Key Philosophical Writings*, edited by Enrique Chávez-Arvizo. Ware: Wordsworth Classics of World Literature

Checkel, Jeffrey T. (1997). *Ideas and International Political Change: Soviet/Russian Behaviour and the End of the Cold War*. New Haven and London: Yale University Press

(2001). Why Comply? Social Learning and European Identity Change. *International Organization* 55 (3): 553–88

(2004). Social Constructivisms in Global and European Politics: a Review Essay. *Review of International Studies* 30 (2): 229–44

Chernoff, Fred. (2002). Scientific Realism as a Meta-Theory of International Politics. *International Studies Quarterly* 46 (2): 189–207

(2004). The Study of Democratic Peace and Progress in International Relations. *International Studies Review* 6: 49–77

(2007). Scientific Realism, Critical Realism, and International Relations Theory. *Millennium: Journal of International Studies* 35 (2): 399–407

Clark, Ian. (1999). *Globalization and International Relations Theory*. Oxford: Oxford University Press

Clatterbaugh, Kenneth C. (1999). *The Causation Debate in Modern Philosophy, 1637–1739*. London: Routledge

Cohen, R. (1994). Pacific Unions: a Reappraisal of the Theory that Democracies Do Not Go to War with One Another. *Review of International Studies* 20 (3): 207–29

Colaresi, Michael. (2007). The Benefit of the Doubt: Testing an Informational Theory of the Rally Effect. *International Organization* 61 (1): 99–143

Collier, Andrew (1989). *Scientific Realism and Socialist Thought*. Harvester: Lynne Rienner

(1994). *Critical Realism: an Introduction to Roy Bhaskar's Philosophy*. London: Verso

Collin, Finn. (1997). *Social Reality*. London: Routledge

Collingwood, R.G. (1940). *An Essay on Metaphysics*. Oxford: Clarendon Press

(1948). *Idea of History*. London: Oxford University Press

Collins, J. (2000). Preemptive Prevention. *Journal of Philosophy* 97: 223–34

Collins, John, Ned Hall and L. A. Paul. (2002). eds. *Causation and Counterfactuals*. New York: MIT Press

Cox, Michael, G. John Ikenberry and Takashi Inoguchi. (2000). eds. *American Democracy Promotion: Impulses, Strategies, and Impacts*. Oxford: Oxford University Press

Cox, Robert W. (1981). Social Forces, States and World Orders: Beyond International Relations Theory. *Millennium: Journal of International Studies* 10 (2): 126–55

(1987). *Production, Power and World Order: Social Forces in the Making of History*. New York: Columbia University Press

(1992). Multilateralism and World Order. *Review of International Studies* 18: 161–80

(1996). Realism, Positivism and Historicism. In *Approaches to World Order*, edited by Robert Cox and Timothy Sinclair. New York: Cambridge University Press

Cox, Robert W., and Timothy J. Sinclair. (1996). eds. *Approaches to World Order*. New York: Cambridge University Press

Crenshaw, Martha. (1995). ed. *Terrorism in Context*. Pennsylvania: Pennsylvania University Press

Crotty, Michael. (1998). *Foundations of Social Research: Meaning and Perspective in the Research Process*. London: Sage

Culler, John. (1982). *On Deconstruction: Theory and Criticism after Structuralism*. London: Routledge

Cushing, James T., and Ernan McMullin. (1989). *Philosophical Consequences of Quantum Theory: Reflections on Bell's Theorem*. Notre Dame, IN: Notre Dame University Press

Cushing, J. T., A. I. Fine and S. Goldstein. (1996). *Bohmian Mechanics and Quantum Theory: an Appraisal*. London: Kluwer

Danermark, B. (2002). *Explaining Society: Critical Realism in the Social Sciences*. London: Routledge

Dantzig, Tobias. (1954). *Henri Poincaré - Critic of Crisis: Reflections on his Universe of Discourse*. London: Charles Scribner's Sons

Davidson, Donald. (1980). *Essays on Actions and Events*. Oxford: Clarendon Press

Davis, James W., and William C. Wohlforth. (2004). German Unification. In *Ending the Cold War: Interpretations, Causation and the Study of International Relations*, edited by R. Hermann and R. N. Lebow. Basingstoke: Palgrave Macmillan, pp. 131–60

Delanty, Gerard. (1997). *Social Science: Beyond Constructivism and Realism*. Buckingham: Open University Press

de Marchi, Scott, Christopher F. Gelpi and Jeffrey Grynaviski. (2004). Untangling Neural Nets. *American Political Science Review* 98 (2): 371–8

Der Derian, James. (1995). ed. *International Theory: Critical Investigations*. Basingstoke: Macmillan

Der Derian, James, and Michael J. Shapiro. (1989). eds. *International/Intertextual Relations: Postmodern Readings of World Politics*. Lexington: Lexington Books

Derrida, Jacques. (1978). *Writing and Difference*. Translated by Alan Bass. London: Routledge

(1988). *Limited Inc*. Evanston, IL: Northwestern University Press

Des Chene, Dennis. (1996). *Physiologia: Natural Philosophy in Aristotelian and Cartesian Thought*. London: Cornell University Press

Descartes, René. (1997). *Key Philosophical Writings*. Translated by E. Haldane and G. R. T. Ross, edited by Tom Griffith. Ware: Wordsworth Classics of World Literature

Dessler, David. (1989). What's at Stake in the Agency and Structure Debate? *International Organization* 43 (3): 441–74

(1991). Beyond Correlations: Towards a Causal Theory of War. *International Studies Quarterly* 35 (3): 337–55

(1999). Constructivism within a Positivist Social Science. *Review of International Studies* 25 (1): 123–37

Deutsch, David. (1998). *The Fabric of Reality*. London: Penguin

De Vree, Johan K. (1999). On Some Common Misunderstandings about Democracy. In *Democratic Peace for Europe: Myth or Reality?*, edited by Gustaaf Geeraerts and Patrick Stouthuysen. Brussels: VUB University Press, pp. 41–60

Dews, Peter. (1987). *Logics of Disintegration: Post-Structuralist Thought and the Claims of Critical Theory*. London: Verso

Dickinson, G. L. (1917). *The Choice before Us*. New York: Dodd, Mead & Company

Dolhenty, Jonathan. (2007 [cited]). *Being and Existence: a Brief Introduction into the Nature of Reality*. Center for Applied Philosophy: The Radical Academy [cited 30.5.2007]. http://radicalacademy.com/ontologyg.htm

Dowe, Phil. (1992). Causality and Conserved Quantities: a Reply to Salmon. *Philosophy of Science* 62: 321–33

Doyle, Michael W. (2000). International Peace Building: a Theoretical and Quantitative Analysis. *American Political Science Review* 94 (4): 779–801

Dray, W. H. (1964). *Philosophy of History*. Englewood Cliffs: Prentice Hall

(1975). *Laws and Explanations in History*. Oxford: Oxford University Press

(1995). *History as Re-Enactment; R. G. Collingwood's Philosophy of History*. Oxford: Clarendon Press

Dunne, Tim. (1995). Social Construction of International Society. *European Journal of International Relations* 1 (3): 367–89

Durkheim, Emile. (1982). *The Rules of the Sociological Method and Selected Texts on Sociology and its Method, with an Introduction by Steven Lukes*. Translated by W. D. Halls. London: Macmillan

Easthorpe, Gary. (1974). *History of Social Research Methods*. London: Longman

Edel, Abraham. (1982). *Aristotle and his Philosophy*. London: Croom Helm

Edkins, Jenny. (1999). *Poststructuralism and International Relations: Bringing the Political Back In*. London: Lynne Rienner

Eells, Ellery. (1982). *Rational Decision and Causality*. Cambridge Studies in Philosophy. Cambridge: Cambridge University Press

(1991). *Probabilistic Causality*. Cambridge Studies in Probability, Induction, and Decision Theory. Cambridge: Cambridge University Press

Ekström, Mats. (1992). Causal Explanation of Social Action: the Contribution of Max Weber and of Critical Realism to a Generative View of Causal Explanation in Social Science. *Acta Sociologica* 35: 107–22

Ellis, Brian. (2001). *Scientific Essentialism*. Cambridge: Cambridge University Press

Elster, John. (1989). *Nuts and Bolts for the Social Sciences*. Cambridge: Cambridge University Press

(2000). Rational Choice History: a Case of Excessive Ambition. *American Political Science Review* 94 (3): 685–95

Emmet, Dorothy M. (1984). *The Effectiveness of Causes*. London: Macmillan

English, Robert D. (2000). *Russia and the Idea of the West: Gorbachev, Intellectuals and the End of Cold War*. New York: Cambridge University Press

(2002). Power, Ideas, and the New Evidence on the Cold War's End. *International Security* 26 (4): 70–92

Enloe, Cynthia. (1990). *Bananas, Beaches and Bases: Making Feminist Sense of International Politics*. Berkeley: University of California Press

(1993). *The Morning After: Sexual Politics at the End of the Cold War*. Berkeley: University of California Press

Evans, Peter B., Dietrich Rueschemeyer and Theda Skopcol. (1985). eds. *Bringing the State Back In*. Cambridge: Cambridge University Press

Ewing, A. C. (1924). *Kant's Treatment of Causality*. London: Kegan Paul, Trench, Trubner

(1987). *A Short Commentary on Kant's Critique of Pure Reason*. Chicago: University of Chicago Press

Farber, Henry, and Joanne Gowa. (1995). Polities and Peace. *International Security* 20 (2): 123–46

Farr, James. (1991). Science, Realism, Criticism, History. In *The Cambridge Companion to Marx*. Edited by Terrell Carver. Cambridge: Cambridge University Press, pp. 106–23

Faye, Jan. (1989). *The Reality of the Future: an Essay on Time, Causation and Backward Causation*. Odense: Odense University Press

Festinger, Leon, and Daniel Katz. (1965). eds. *Research Methods in the Behavioural Sciences*. New York: Holt, Rinehart & Winston

Feyerabend, Paul. (1981). *Realism, Rationalism and Scientific Method, Vol. I*. Cambridge: Cambridge University Press

(1989). Realism and the Historicity of Knowledge. *Journal of Philosophy* 86: 393–406

(1993). *Against Method*. 3rd edn. London: Verso

Fierke, K. M. (2005). *Diplomatic Interventions: Conflict and Change in a Globalizing World*. London: Palgrave Macmillan

Fine, Arthur. (1986). *The Shaky Game: Einstein, Realism and the Quantum Theory*. Chicago and London: University of Chicago Press

Finnemore, Martha. (1996). *National Interests in International Society*. New York: Cornell University Press

Finnemore, Martha, and Kathryn Sikkink. (1999). International Norm Dynamics and Political Change. In *Exploration and Contestation in the Study of World Politics*, edited by P. J. Katzenstein, R. O. Keohane and S. D. Krasner. London: MIT Press, pp. 247–77

Foucault, Michel. (1970). *The Order of Things: An Archeology of the Human Sciences*. London: Tavistock

(1972). *Archeology of Knowledge*. London: Tavistock/Routledge

(1991). *Discipline and Punish: the Birth of the Prison*. Translated by A. Sheridan. Harmondsworth: Penguin

Frankfurt-Nachmias, C., and D. Nachmias. (1994). *Research Methods in the Social Sciences*. London: Edward Arnold

Frei, Christopher. (2001). *Hans J. Morgenthau: an Intellectual Biography*. Baton Rouge: Louisiana State University Press

Gadamer, Hans-Georg. (1975). *Truth and Method*. Translated by G. Barden. 2nd edn. London: Sheed & Ward

Gaddis, John Lewis. (1992). International Relations Theory and the End of the Cold War. *International Security* 17 (3): 5–58

(2000). On Starting All Over Again: a Naïve Approach to the Study of Cold War. In *Reviewing the Cold War: Approaches, Interpretation, Theory*, edited by O. A. Westad. London: Frank Cass, pp. 27–43

Gasking, Douglas. (1974). Causation and Recipes. In *Philosophical Problems of Causation*, edited by Tom L. Beauchamp. Encino: Dickenson, pp. 126–32

Geeraerts, Gustaaf, and Patrick Stouthuysen. (1999). eds. *Democratic Peace for Europe: Myth or Reality?* Brussels: VUB University Press

Gellman, Peter. (1988). Morgenthau and the Legacy of Political Realism. *Review of International Studies* 14: 247–66

George, Jim. (1994). *Discourses of Global Politics*. Boulder: Lynne Rienner

Gerth, H. H., and C. Wright Mills. (1991). eds. *From Max Weber: Essays in Sociology, with a New Preface by Bryan S. Turner*. London: Routledge

Giddens, Anthony. (1974). ed. *Positivism and Sociology*. London: Heinemann

(1984). *Constitution of Society: Outline of the Theory of Structuration*. Cambridge: Polity

(1985). *A Contemporary Critique of Historical Materialism, Vol II: the Nation-State and Violence*. Oxford: Polity

(1993). *New Rules of Sociological Method*. 2nd edn. Stanford: Stanford University Press

Gilpin, Robert. (1981). *War and Change in World Politics*. Cambridge: Cambridge University Press

(1986). The Richness of the Tradition of Political Realism. In *Neorealism and its Critics*, edited by Robert O. Keohane. New York: Columbia University Press, pp. 301–21

(1989). The Theory of Hegemonic War. In *The Origin and Prevention of Major Wars*, edited by R. I. Rotberg and T. K. Rabb. Cambridge: Cambridge University Press

Gilson, E. (1984). *From Aristotle to Darwin and Back Again: a Journey in Final Causality, Species and Evolution*. Translated by J. Lyon. Notre Dame, IN: Notre Dame University Press

Gleditsch, Nils Petter. (1992). Focus on: Democracy and Peace. *Journal of Peace Research* 29 (4): 369–76

Goldsmith, A. A. (2001). Foreign Aid and Statehood in Africa. *International Organization* 55 (1): 123–48

Goldstein, Judith, and Robert O. Keohane. (1993a). Ideas and Foreign Policy: an Analytical Framework. In *Ideas and Foreign Policy: Beliefs, Institutions and Political Change*, edited by Judith Goldstein and Robert O. Keohane. Ithaca: Cornell University Press, pp. 3–33

(1993b). eds. *Ideas and Foreign Policy: Beliefs, Institutions and Political Change*. Ithaca: Cornell University Press

Goldstein, Judith L., Douglas Rivers and Michael Tomz. (2007). Institutions in International Relations: Understanding the Effects of the GATT and the WTO on World Trade. *International Organization* 61 (1): 37–67

Goodman, Russell B. (1995). ed. *Pragmatism: a Contemporary Reader*. London: Routledge

Gordon, Scott. (1991). *The History and Philosophy of Social Science*. London: Routledge

Gould, Harry D. (1998). What IS at stake in the Agency-Structure Debate? In *International Relations in a Constructed World*, edited by Vendulka Kubalkowa, Nicholas Onuf and and Paul Kowert. London: M. E. Sharpe, pp. 79–100

Gray, Mark M., Miki Caul Kittilson and Wayne Sandholtz. (2006). Women and Globalization: a Study of 180 Countries, 1975–2000. *International Organization* 60 (2): 293–333

Gribbin, John. (1991). *In Search of Schrödinger's Cat: Quantum Physics and Reality*. London: Black Swan

Grieco, Joseph. (1988). Anarchy and the Limits of Co-operation: a Realist Critique of the Newest Liberal Internationalism. *International Organization* 42 (3): 485–507

Grieco, Joseph, and J. Snyder. (1993). Controversy: the Relative Gains Problem for International Co-operation. *American Political Science Review* 87 (3): 729–43

Groff, Ruth. (2004). *Critical Realism, Postpositivism and the Possibility of Knowledge*. London: Routledge

Grovogui, Siba N. (1996). *Sovereigns, Quasi-Sovereigns, and Africans: Race and Self-Determination in International Law*. Minneapolis: University of Minnesota Press

Haas, Mark L. (2007). The United States and the End of the Cold War: Reactions to Shifts in Soviet Power, Policies, or Domestic Politics? *International Organization* 61: 145–79

Habermas, Jürgen. (1972). *Knowledge and Human Interests*. London: Heinemann

(1988). *On the Logic of the Social Sciences*. Translated by S. W. Nicholsen and J. A. Stark. Cambridge: Polity

Hacking, Ian. (1995). Three Parables. In *Pragmatism: a Contemporary Reader*, edited by R. B. Goodman. London: Routledge, pp. 237–47

Hall, S., and G. J. Ikenberry. (1989). eds. *The State*. Milton Keynes: Open University Press

Halliday, Fred. (1987). State and Society in International Relations: a Second Agenda. *Millennium: Journal of International Studies* 16 (2): 215–29

Hanfling, Oswald. (1981). *Logical Positivism*. Oxford: Basil Blackwell

Hankinson, R. J. (1998). *Cause and Explanation in Ancient Greek Thought*. Oxford: Clarendon Press

Harding, Sandra. (1986). *The Science Question in Feminism*. Ithaca: Cornell Unversity Press

Harré, Rom, and Roy Bhaskar. (1990). *Harré and his Critics: Essays in Honour of Rom Harré with his Commentary on Them*. Oxford: Basil Blackwell

Harré, Rom, and Edward H. Madden. (1975). *Causal Powers: a Theory of Natural Necessity*. Oxford: Blackwell

Harré, R., and P. F. Secord. (1972). *Explanation of Social Behaviour*. Oxford: Blackwell

Harré, Rom, and Charles R. Varela. (1996). Conflicting Varieties of Realism: Causal Powers and the Problem of Social Structure. *Journal for the Theory of Social Behaviour* 26 (3): 313–25.

Hausman, Daniel. (1996). Causation and Counterfactual Dependence Reconsidered. *Noûs* 30 (1): 55–74.

(1998). *Causal Asymmetries*. Cambridge Studies in Probability, Induction, and Decision Theory. Cambridge: Cambridge University Press

(1999). The Mathematical Theory of Causation. *British Journal of Philosophy of Science* 50: 151–62

Hay, Colin. (1995). Structure and Agency. In *Theory and Methods in Political Science*, edited by D. Marsh and G. Stoker. London: Bloomsbury

(2002). *Political Analysis: a Critical Introduction*. Basingstoke: Palgrave

Hay, Colin, and David Marsh. (2000). eds. *Demystifying Globalization*. London: Macmillan

Hedström, Peter, and Richard Swedberg. (1998). eds. *Social Mechanisms: an Analytical Approach to Social Theory*. Cambridge: Cambridge University Press

Heidegger, Martin. (1967). *Being and Time*. Oxford: Blackwell

Heisenberg, Werner. (1930). *The Physical Principles of Quantum Theory*. Translated by C. Eckart and F. C. Hoyt. Chicago: Dover

Hempel, Carl G. (1965). ed. *Aspects of Scientific Explanation and Other Essays in the Philosophy of Science*. London: Macmillan/Free Press

(1966). *Philosophy of Natural Science*. Englewood Cliffs, NJ: Prentice Hall

(1969). Logical Positivism and the Social Sciences. In *The Legacy of Logical Positivism*, edited by P. Achinstein and S. F. Barker. Baltimore: The Johns Hopkins University Press, pp. 163–94

(2001). *The Philosophy of Carl G. Hempel: Studies in Science, Explanation and Rationality*, edited by James H. Fetzer. Oxford: Oxford University Press

Henderson, Errol. (2002). *Democracy and War: the End of an Illusion?* Boulder: Lynne Rienner

Herrmann, Richard K. (2004). Learning from the End of the Cold War. In *Ending the Cold War: Interpretations, Causation and the Study of International Relations*, edited by Richard K. Herrmann and Richard Ned Lebow. Basingstoke: Palgrave Macmillan, pp. 219–38

Herrmann, Richard K., and Richard Ned Lebow. (2004a). What was the Cold War? When Did it End? In *Ending the Cold War: Interpretations, Causation and the Study of International Relations*, edited by Richard K. Herrmann and Richard Ned Lebow. Basingstoke: Palgrave Macmillan, pp. 1–27

(2004b). eds. *Ending the Cold War: Interpretations, Causation and the Study of International Relations*. Basingstoke: Palgrave Macmillan

Hitchcock, Christopher. (1993). A Generalised Probabilistic Theory of Causal Relevance. *Synthese* 97 (3): 335–64

(2002). Probabilistic Causation. *Stanford Encyclopedia of Philosophy*. Stanford University [cited 30.05.2007]. Available from www.plato.stanford.edu/entries/causation-probabilistic/

Hobbes, Thomas. (1905). *The Metaphysical System of Hobbes as Contained in Twelve Chapters from His 'Elements of Philosophy Concerning Body' and in Briefer Extracts from 'Human Nature' and 'Leviathan', Selected by Mary Whiton Calkins*. London: Kegan Paul, Trench, Tubner

Hobson, John M. (2000). *The State and International Relations*. Cambridge: Cambridge University Press

Hollis, Martin. (1994). *The Philosophy of Social Science: an Introduction*. Cambridge: Cambridge University Press

Hollis, Martin, and Steve Smith. (1990). *Explaining and Understanding International Relations*. Oxford: Clarendon Press

Holsti, Kalevi J. (1985). *The Dividing Discipline*. London: Unwin Hyman

Hopf, Ted. (1998). The Promise of Constructivism in International Relations Theory. *International Security* 23 (1): 171–200

Horsten, Leon, and Erik Weber. (2005). INUS-conditions. In *Encyclopedia of Statistics in Behavioural Science, Vol. II*, edited by Brian S. Everitt and David C. Howell. Chichester: John Wiley, pp. 955–8

Hume, David. (1955). *An Inquiry Concerning Human Understanding*, edited by Charles Hendel. London: Liberal Arts Press/H. Jonas

(1978). *A Treatise of Human Nature*. 2nd edn with an analytical index by L. A. Selby-Bigge. Oxford: Clarendon Press

Huth, Paul K., and Todd L. Allee. (2002a). *Democratic Peace and Territorial Conflict in the 20th Century*. Cambridge: Cambridge University Press

(2002b). Questions of Research Design in the Testing of Democratic Peace. *International Interactions* 28 (1): 31–58

Inwood, M. J. (1983). *Hegel*. London: Routledge & Kegan Paul

James, William. (1995). What Pragmatism Means. In *Pragmatism: a Contemporary Reader*, edited by Russell B. Goodman. London: Routledge, pp. 53–64

Jaki, S.L. (1984). *Uneasy Genius: the Life and Work of Pierre Dühem*. Hague: Martinus Nijhof

Jessop, Bob. (1990). *State Theory: Putting the Capitalist State in its Place*. Cambridge: Polity

(2002). *Future of the Capitalist State*. Cambridge: Polity

Joseph, Jonathan. (2003). *Social Theory: Conflict, Cohesion and Consent*. Edinburgh: Edinburgh University Press

Kant, Immanuel. (1964). *Immanuel Kant's Critique of Pure Reason*. Translated by Norman Kemp Smith. London and New York: Macmillan and St Martin's Press

(1993). *The Critique of Pure Reason: a Revised and Expanded Translation Based on Meiklejohn*, edited by Vasilis Politis. London: Everyman Library

Katzenstein, Peter J. (1996). *Cultural Norms and National Security: Police and Military in Postwar Japan*. Ithaca: Cornell University Press

Katzenstein, Peter J., Robert O. Keohane and Stephen D. Krasner. (1999a). *International Organization* and the Study of World Politics. In *Exploration and Contestation in the Study of World Politics*, edited by Peter J. Katzenstein, Robert O. Keohane and Stephen D. Krasner. Cambridge, MA: MIT Press, pp. 5–45

(1999b). eds. *Exploration and Contestation in the Study of World Politics.* Cambridge, MA: MIT Press

Keat, Russell, and John Urry. (1975). *Social Theory as Science*. London: Routledge & Kegan Paul

Keohane, Robert O. (1984). *After Hegemony: Co-operation and Discord in World Political Economy*. Princeton: Princeton University Press

(1988). International Institutions: Two Approaches. *International Studies Quarterly* 32: 379–96

Keohane, Robert O. (1986). ed. *Neorealism and its Critics*. New York: Columbia University Press

(1989). *International Institutions and State Power: Essays in International Relations Theory*. London: Westview Press

Keohane, Robert O., and Lisa Martin. (1995). The Promise of Institutionalist Theory. *International Security* 20: 39–51

Keohane, Robert O., and Helen V. Milner. (1996). eds. *Internationalization and Domestic Politics*. Cambridge: Cambridge University Press

Keohane, Robert O., and Joseph S. Nye. (1977). *Power and Interdependence: World Politics in Transition*. Boston: Little, Brown

King, Anthony. (1999). The Impossibility of Naturalism: the Antinomies of Bhaskar's Realism. *Journal for the Theory of Social Behaviour* 29 (3): 267–88

King, Gary, Robert O. Keohane and Sidney Verba. (1994). *Designing Social Inquiry: Scientific Inference in Qualitative Research*. Princeton: Princeton University Press

Klotz, Audie. (1995). *Norms in International Relations: the Struggle against Apartheid*. Ithaca and London: Cornell University Press

Knorr, Klaus, and James N. Rosenau. (1969). eds. *Contending Approaches to International Politics*. Princeton: Princeton University Press

Koslowski, Rey, and Friedrich Kratochwil. (1995). Understanding Change in International Politics. In *International Relations Theory and the End of the Cold War*, edited by Richard Ned Lebow and Thomas Risse-Kappen. New York: Columbia University Press, pp. 127–66

Krasner, Stephen D. (1991). Global Communications and National Power: Life on the Pareto Frontier. *World Politics* 43: 336–56

Kratochwil, Friedrich. (1989). *Rules, Norms and Decisions: On the Conditions of Practical and Legal Reasoning in International Relations and Domestic Affairs*. Cambridge: Cambridge University Press

(2000). Constructing a New Orthodoxy? Wendt's Social Theory of International Politics and the Constructivist Challenge. *Millennium: Journal of International Studies* 29 (1): 73–101

Krips, Henry. (1987). *The Metaphysics of Quantum Theory*. Oxford: Clarendon Press

Kubalkova, Vendulka. (1998). Twenty Years' Catharsis: E. H. Carr and International Relations. In *International Relations in a Constructed World*, edited by Vendulka Kubalkova, Nicholas Onuf and Paul Kowert. London: M. E. Sharpe

Kubalkowa, Vendulka, Nicholas Onuf and Paul Kowert. (1998). eds. *International Relations in a Constructed World*. London: M. E. Sharpe

Kuhn, Thomas. (1962). *The Structure of Scientific Revolutions*. Chicago: University of Chicago Press

(1977). *The Essential Tension: Selected Studies in Scientific Tradition and Change*. Chicago: University of Chigaco Press

Kurki, Milja. (2006). Causes of a Divided Discipline: Rethinking the Concept of Cause in International Relations Theory. *Review of International Studies* 32 (2): 189–216

(2007). Critical Realism and Causal Analysis in International Relations. *Millennium: Journal of International Studies* 35 (2): 361–78

Kurki, Milja, and Colin Wight. (2007). International Relations and Social Science. In *International Relations Theories: Discipline and Diversity*, edited by Tim Dunne, Milja Kurki and Steve Smith. Oxford: Oxford University Press, pp. 13–33

Laffey, Mark. (2003). Discerning the Patterns of World Order: Noam Chomsky and International Theory after the Cold War. *Review of International Studies* 29 (4): 587–604

Laffey, Mark, and Jutta Weldes. (1997). Beyond Belief: Ideas and Symbolic Technologies in the Study of International Relations. *European Journal of International Relations* 3 (2): 193–237

Lakatos, Imre, and Alan Musgrave. (1970). eds. *Criticism and the Growth of Knowledge*. London: Cambridge University Press

Lapid, Yosef, and Friedrich Kratochwil. (1996). eds. *The Return of Culture and Identity in IR Theory*. London: Lynne Rienner

Laudan, Larry. (1978). *Progress and its Problems*. Berkeley: University of California Press

Lawson, Tony. (1997). *Economics and Reality*. London: Routledge

Layder, Derek. (1990). *Realist Image of Social Science*. Basingstoke: Macmillan

Layne, Christopher. (1994). Kant or Cant: the Myth of Democratic Peace. *International Security* 19 (2): 5–50

Lear, Jonathan. (1988). *Aristotle: the Desire to Understand*. Cambridge: Cambridge University Press

Lebow, Richard Ned, and Thomas Risse-Kappen. (1995a). Introduction: International Relations Theory and the End of Cold War. In *International Relations Theory and the End of Cold War*, edited by Richard

Ned Lebow and Thomas Risse-Kappen. New York: Columbia University Press, pp. 1–21

Lebow, Richard Ned, and Thomas Risse-Kappen. (1995b). eds. *International Relations Theory and the End of Cold War*. New York: Columbia University Press

Lebow, Richard Ned, and Janice Gross Stein. (2004). Understanding the End of the Cold War as a Non-linear Confluence. In *Ending the Cold War: Interpretations, Causation and the Study of International Relations*, edited by Richard K. Herrmann and Richard Ned Lebow. Basingstoke: Palgrave Macmillan, pp. 189–217

Lemert, C. C., and G. Gillan. (1982). *Michel Foucault: Social Theory and Transgression*. New York: Columbia University Press

Lewis, David K. (1973). *Counterfactuals*. Cambridge, MA: Harvard University Press

(1999). *Papers in Metaphysics and Epistemology*. Cambridge: Cambridge University Press

(2002). Void and Object. In *Causation and Counterfactuals*, edited by J. Collins and L. Paul. New York: MIT Press, pp. 277–90.

Lewis, Frank A. (2001). Aristotle on the Relation between a Thing and its Matter. In *Unity, Identity and Explanation in Aristotle's Metaphysics*, edited by T. Scaltsas, D. Charles and M. L. Gill. Oxford: Clarendon Press

Lewis, Paul. (2000). Realism, Causality and the Problem of Social Structure. *Journal for the Theory of Social Behaviour* 30 (3): 249–68

(2002). Agency, Structure and Causality in Political Science: a Comment on Sibeon. *Politics* 22 (1): 17–23

Linklater, Andrew. (1990). *Beyond Realism and Marxism: Critical Theory and International Relations*. London: Macmillan

(1998). *Transformation of Political Community: Ethical Foundations of the Post-Westphalian Era*. Oxford: Polity

Linklater, Andrew. (2000). ed. *International Relations: Critical Concepts*. London: Routledge

Lloyd, Christopher. (1993). *The Structures of History*. Oxford: Blackwell

Locke, John. (1970). *An Essay Concerning Human Understanding*. Menston: Scolar Press

Loeb, Louis. (1981). *From Descartes to Hume: Continental Metaphysics and the Development of Modern Philosophy*. London and Ithaca: Cornell University Press

Lòpez, José, and Garry Potter. (2001a). After Postmodernism: the New Millennium. In *After Postmodernism: an Introduction to Critical Realism*, edited by J. Lòpez and G. Potter. London: Athlone, pp. 3–21

(2001b). eds. *After Postmodernism: an Introduction to Critical Realism*. London: Athlone

Lukes, Steven. (1982). Introduction. In Emile Durkheim, *The Rules of the Sociological Method and Selected Texts on Sociology and its Method, with an Introduction by Steven Lukes*. Translated by W. D. Halls. London: Macmillan, pp. 1–27

Lyotard, Jean-François. (1984). *Postmodern Condition: a Report on Knowledge*. Manchester: Manchester University Press

Mach, Ernst. (1959). *The Analysis of Sensations; and the Relation of the Physical to the Physical*. Translated by C. M. Williams. New York: Dover

MacKenzie, B. D. (1977). *Behaviourism and the Limits of Scientific Method*. London: Routledge & Kegan Paul

Mackie, J. L. (1974). *The Cement of the Universe: a Study of Causation*. Oxford: Clarendon Press

McKim, Vaughn R., and Stephen P. Turner. (1997). eds. *Causality in Crisis? Statistical Methods and Search for Causal Knowledge*. Notre Dame: Notre Dame University Press

MacKinnon, Catherine A. (1989). *Toward a Feminist Theory of the State*. London: Harvard University Press

McNeil, Russell. (1996) *Thucydides as Science*. Malapia University [cited 30.05.2007]. www.mala.bc.ca/~mcneil/lec18b.htm

Mahoney, James. (2001). Beyond Correlational Analysis: Recent Innovations in Theory and Method. *Sociological Forum* 16 (3): 575–93

Mann, Michael. (1988). *States, War and Capitalism*. Oxford: Blackwell

(1993). *Sources of Social Power: the Rise of Classes and Nation-States 1760–1914*. Cambridge: Cambridge University Press

Mansfield, E. E., and J. Snyder. (1995). Democratization and War. *International Security* 20 (1): 196–207

Maoz, Zeev. (1997). The Controversy over the Democratic Peace: Rearguard Action or Cracks in the Wall? *International Security* 22 (1): 162–98

Maoz, Zeev, and Bruce Russett. (1993). Normative and Structural Causes of Democratic Peace 1946–1986. *American Political Science Review* 87 (3): 624–38

Marchand, Marianne H., and Anne Sisson Runyan. (2000). eds. *Gender and Global Restructuring: Sightings, Sights and Resistances*. London: Routledge

Margolis, John. (1986). *Pragmatism without Foundations: Reconciling Realism and Relativism*. Oxford: Basil Blackwell

Marshall, I., and D. Zoher. (1997). *Who's Afraid of Schrodinger's Cat? The New Science Revealed: Quantum Theory, Relativity, Chaos Theory and the New Cosmology*. London: Bloomsbury

Marx, Karl. (1975). *The Eighteenth Brumaire of Louis Bonaparte*, New York: International Publisher

Matthen, Mohan. (1987). Introduction: the Structure of Aristotelian Science. In *Aristotle Today: Essays on Aristotle's Ideal of Science*, edited by Mohan Matthen. Edmonton: Academic Printing and Publishing

May, Tim. (1996). *Situating Social Theory*. Buckingham: Open University Press

Mearsheimer, John J. (1990). Back to the Future: Instability in Europe after the Cold War. *International Security* 14 (4): 5–56

(1995). The False Promise of International Institutions. *Intenational Security* 19 (3): 3–49

Meikle, Scott. (1985). *Essentialism in the Thought of Karl Marx*. London: Duckworth

(1991). History of Philosophy: the Metaphysics of Substance in Marx. In *The Cambridge Companion to Marx*, edited by T. Carver. Cambridge: Cambridge University Press, pp. 296–319

Menzies, Peter. (1999). Extrinsic versus Intrinsic Conceptions of Causation. In *Causation and Laws of Nature*, edited by H. Sankey. Dordrecht: Kluwer, pp. 313–29

(2001). Counterfactual Causation. In *Stanford Encyclopedia of Philosophy*. Stanford University [cited 30.5.2002]. Available from www.plato.stanford.edu/entries/causation-counterfactual

Meyer, Susan. (1993). *Aristotle on Moral Responsibility: Character and Cause*. Oxford: Blackwell

Mill, John Stuart. (1970). *A System of Logic: Ratiocinative and Inductive*. London: Longman

Milner, Helen V. (1997). *Interests, Institutions and Information: Domestic Politics and International Relations*. Princeton: Princeton University Press

Mohanty, J. N. (1995). The Development of Husserl's Thought. In *The Cambridge Companion to Husserl*, edited by B. Smith and D. W. Smith. Cambridge: Cambridge University Press, pp. 45–77

Morgan, Jamie. (2002). Philosophical Realism in International Relations Theory: Kratochwil's Constructivist Challenge to Wendt. *Journal of Critical Realism* 1 (1): 95–118

Morgenthau, Hans. (1947). *Scientific Man and Power Politics*. London: Latimer Press

(1948). *Politics among Nations*. New York: Alfred Knopf

Most, Benjamin A., and Harvey Starr. (1989). *Inquiry, Logiç and International Politics*. Columbia: University of Southern Carolina Press

Mousseau, Michael. (2003). The Nexus of Market Society, Liberal Preferences, and the Democratic Peace: Interdisciplinary Theory and Evidence. *International Studies Quarterly* 47: 483–510

Mueller, J. E. (1969). ed. *Approaches to Measurement in International Relations: a Non-Evangelical Survey*. New York: Meredith

Nadler, Steven M. (1993). *Causation in Early Modern Philosophy: Cartesianism, Occasionalism, and Pre-Established Harmony*. University Park: Pennsylvania State University Press

Nair, Sheila, and Geeta Chowdhry. (2002). eds. *Power, Postcolonialism and International Relations: Reading Race, Gender and Class*. London: Routledge

Navon, Emmanuel. (2001). The 'Third Debate' Revisited. *Review of International Studies* 27: 611–25

Neufield, M. (1993). Interpretation and the 'Science' of International Relations. *Review of International Studies* 19: 39–62

Neumann, I. B. (2004). Beware of Organicism: the Narrative Self of the State. *Review of International Studies* 30 (2): 259–67

Neurath, Marie, and Robert S. Cohen. (1973). eds. *Otto Neurath: Empiricism and Sociology*. Dordrecht: D. Reidel

Nicholson, Michael. (1983). *The Scientific Analysis of Social Behaviour*. New York: St Martin's Press

(1996a). *Causes and Consequences in International Relations: a Conceptual Study*. London: Pinter

(1996b). The Continued Significance of Positivism. In *International Theory: Positivism and Beyond*, edited by Steve Smith, Ken Booth and Marysia Zalewski. Cambridge: Cambridge University Press

Norris, Christopher. (1997). *New Idols of the Cave: on the Limits of Anti-Realism*. Manchester: Manchester University Press

(2000). *Quantum Theory and the Flight from Realism: Philosophical Responses to Quantum Mechanics*. London: Routledge

Norton, David Fate. (1993a). An Introduction to Hume's Thought. In *The Cambridge Companion to Hume*, edited by David Fate Norton. Cambridge: Cambridge University Press, pp. 1–32

(1993b). ed. *The Cambridge Companion to Hume*. Cambridge: Cambridge University Press

Onuf, Nicholas. (1989). *World of Our Making: Rules and Rule in Social Theory and International Relations*. Columbia: University of Southern California Press

(1998a). *Republican Legacy in International Thought*. Cambridge: Cambridge University Press

(1998b). Constructivism: User's Manual. In *International Relations in a Constructed World*, edited by Vendulka Kubalkowa, Nicholas Onuf and Paul Kowert. London: M. E. Sharpe, pp. 58–78

Oren, Ido. (1995). The Subjectivity of the 'Democratic' Peace: Changing US Perceptions of Imperial Germany. *International Security* 20 (2): 147–84

Osiander, Andreas. (1988). Rereading Early Twentieth Century IR Theory: Idealism Revisited. *International Studies Quarterly* 42 (3): 409–32

Outhwaite, William. (1987). *New Philosophies of Social Science: Realism, Hermeneutics and Critical Theory*. London: Macmillan

Owen, John. (1994). How Liberalism Produces Democratic Peace. *International Security* 19 (2): 87–125

Özkeçeci-Taner, Binnur. (2002). The Myth of Democratic Peace: Theoretical and Empirical Shortcomings of the Democratic Peace Theory. *Alternatives: Turkish Journal of International Relations* 1 (3): 40–8

Papineau, David. (1978). *For Science in the Social Sciences*. London: Macmillan

Patomäki, Heikki. (1991). Concepts of 'Action', 'Structure' and 'Power' in Critical Social Realism. *Journal for the Theory of Social Behaviour* 21 (2): 221–50

(1996). How to Tell Better Stories about World Politics. *European Journal of International Relations* 2 (1): 105–33

(2002). *After International Relations: Critical Realism and the (Re)Construction of World Politics*. London: Routledge

Patomäki, Heikki, and Colin Wight. (2000). After Post-Positivism? The Promises of Critical Realism. *International Studies Quarterly* 44 (2): 213–37

Peacock, M. S. (2000). Explaining Theory Choice: an Assessment of Critical Realist Contribution to Explanation in Science. *Journal for the Theory of Social Behaviour* 30 (3): 319–39

Pearl, J. (2000). *Causality: Models, Reasoning and Inference*. Cambridge: Cambridge University Press

Peterson, Spike. (1992). ed. *Gendered States: Feminist (Re)Visions of International Relations Theory*. Boulder: Lynne Rienner

Pettegrew, John. (2000). Introduction. In *A Pragmatist's Progress? Richard Rorty and American Intellectual History*, edited by John Pettegrew. Oxford: Rowman & Littlefield, pp. 1–18

Pike, Jonathan E. (1999) *From Aristotle to Marx: Aristotelianism in Marxist Social Ontology*. Aldershot: Ashgate

Plato. (1993). *Phaedo*. Translated by David Gallop. Oxford: Oxford University Press

Popper, Karl R. (1957).*The Poverty of Historicism*. London: Routledge & Kegan Paul

(1959). *The Logic of Scientific Discovery*. London: Hutchinson

(1974a). *The Open Society and its Enemies, Vol. I: the Spell of Plato*. 5th edn. London: Routledge

(1974b). *The Open Society and its Enemies, Vol. II: the Hightide of Prophecy: Hegel, Marx and the Aftermath*. 5th edn. London: Routledge

Porpora, D. V. (1983). On the Post-Wittgenstein Critique of the Concept of Action in Sociology. *Journal for the Theory of Social Behaviour* 13 (2): 129–46.

(1987). *The Concept of Social Structure*. Westport, CT: Greenwood

Powell, Robert. (1991). Absolute and Relative Gains in International Relations Theory. *American Political Science Review* 85: 1303–20

Psillos, Stasis. (1999). *Scientific Realism: How Science Tracks the Truth*. London: Routledge

Putnam, Hilary. (1975). *Philosophical Papers, Vol. I: Mathematics, Matter and Method*. Cambridge: Cambridge University Press

(1987). *The Many Faces of Realism*. La Salle: Open Court

(1990). *Realism with a Human Face*. Cambridge, MA: Harvard University Press

Quine, Willard van Orman. (1960). *Word and Object*. Cambridge, MA: MIT Press

(1969). *Ontological Relativity and Other Essays*. London, New York: Columbia University Press

Ray, James Lee. (1998). Does Democracy Cause Peace? *Annual Review of Political Science* 1: 27–46

Reich, Walter. (1998). ed. *Origins of Terrorism: Psychologies, Ideologies, Theologies, States of Mind*. Washington, D.C.: Woodrow Wilson Centre Press

Review of International Studies. (2001). An Interview with Cythia Enloe. *Review of International Studies* 27: 649–66

Risse, Thomas. (1997). Review: Cold War's End Game and German Unification. *International Security* 21 (4): 159–85

Risse-Kappen, Thomas. (1995a). Democratic Peace – Warlike Democracies? A Social Constructivist Interpretation of the Liberal Argument. *European Journal of International Relations* 1 (4): 491–517

(1995b). Ideas Do Not Float Freely: Transnational Coalitions, Domestic Structures and the End of Cold War. In *International Relations Theory and the End of Cold War*, edited by Richard Ned Lebow and Thomas Risse-Kappen. New York: Columbia University Press, pp. 187–222

Rorty, Richard. (1980). *Philosophy and the Mirror of Nature*. Oxford: Basil Blackwell

(1989). *Contingency, Irony and Solidarity*. Cambridge: Cambridge University Press

Rosato, Sebastian. (2003). The Flawed Logic of Democratic Peace Theory. *American Political Science Review* 97 (4): 585–602

Rosenau, James N. (1980). *The Scientific Study of Foreign Policy: Revised and Enlarged Edition*. London: Pinter; New York: Nichols

Rosenberg, Alexander. (1993). Hume and Philosophy of Science. In *The Cambridge Companion to Hume*, edited by David Fate Norton. Cambridge: Cambridge University Press, pp. 64–89

Rosenberg, Justin. (1994). *The Empire of Civil Society*. London: Verso

(2000) *The Follies of Globalisation Theory: Polemical Essays*. London: Verso

Ross, David. (1960). *Aristotle*. London: Methuen

Rotberg, R. I., and T. K. Rabb. (1989). eds. *The Origin and Prevention of Major Wars*. Cambridge: Cambridge University Press

Ruggie, John G. (1998). *Constructing the World Polity: Essays on International Organization*. London: Routledge

(1999). What Makes the World Hang Together? Neoutilitarianism and the Social Constructivist Challenge. In *Exploration and Contestation in the Study of World Politics*, edited by Peter J. Katzenstein, Robert O. Keohane and Stephen D. Krasner. Cambridge, MA: MIT Press, pp. 215–46

Rummel, R. J. (1995). Democracies are Less Warlike than Other Regimes. *European Journal of International Relations* 1 (4): 457–79

Rupert, Mark. (2001). 'Democracy, Peace. What's Not to Love? In *Democracy, Liberalism and War: Rethinking the Democratic Peace Debate*, edited by Tarak Barkawi and Mark Laffey. London: Lynne Rienner, pp. 153–72

Russell, Bertrand. (1962). *An Inquiry into Meaning and Truth: the William James Lectures for 1940*. London: Pelican

Russett, Bruce M. (1972). ed. *Peace, War and Numbers*. London: Sage

(1993). *Grasping the Democratic Peace: Principles of Post-Cold War World*. Princeton: Princeton University Press

Russett, Bruce, Christopher Layne, David E. Spiro and Michael W. Doyle. (1995). Correspondence: the Democratic Peace. *International Security* 19 (4): 164–84

Salmon, Wesley. (1984). *Scientific Explanation and the Causal Structure of the World*. Princeton: Princeton University Press

(1998). *Causality and Explanation*. Oxford: Oxford University Press

Sankey, Howard. (1994). *The Incommensurability Thesis*. Aldershot: Ashgate

Sayer, Andrew. (1992). *Method in Social Science: a Realist Approach*. 2nd edn. London: Routledge

(2000). *Realism and Social Science*. London: Sage

Sayer, Derek. (1979). *Marx's Method: Ideology, Science, and Critique in 'Capital'*. Atlantic Highlands, NJ: Humanities Press

Scaltsas, T. (2001). Substantial Holism. In *Unity, Identity and Explanation in Aristotle's Metaphysics*, edited by T. Scaltsas, D. Charles and M. L. Gill. Oxford: Clarendon Press, pp. 107–28

Scaltsas, T., D. Charles and M.L. Gill. (2001). eds. *Unity, Identity and Explanation in Aristotle's Metaphysics*. Oxford: Clarendon Press

Schlick, Moritz. (1959). Positivism and Realism. In *Logical Positivism*, edited by A. J. Ayer. Glencoe, IL: The Free Press

Schmidt, Brian C. (1998). *The Political Discourse of Anarchy*. New York: State University of New York Press

Schweller, Randall L. (1998). *Deadly Imbalances: Tripolarity and Hitler's Strategy of World Conquest*. New York: Columbia University Press

Scriven, Michael. (1969). Logical Positivism and the Behavioural Sciences. In *The Legacy of Logical Positivism*, edited by S. F. Barker. Baltimore: The Johns Hopkins University Press, pp. 195–210

(1975). Causation and Explanation. *Noûs* 9 (3): 3–16

(1991). *Evaluation Thesaurus*. 4th edn. Newbury Park: Sage

Searle, John. (1995). *The Construction of Social Reality*. London: Penguin

Shotter, J. (1983). Duality of 'Structure' and 'Intentionality' in an Ecological Psychology. *Journal for the Theory of Social Behaviour* 13 (1): 19–24

Singer, David J. (1965). ed. *Human Behaviour and International Politics: Contributions from the Social-Psychological Sciences*. Chicago: Rand McNally

(1990). *Models, Methods and Progress in World Politics: a Peace Research Odyssey*. Boulder: Westview

Skopcol, Theda. (1979). *States and Social Revolutions*. Cambridge: Cambridge University Press

Smith, Barry, and David Woodrow Smith. (1995). eds. *The Cambridge Companion to Husserl*. Cambridge: Cambridge University Press

Smith, David Woodrow. (1995). Mind and Body. In *The Cambridge Companion to Husserl*, edited by Barry Smith and David Woodrow Smith. Cambridge: Cambridge University Press, pp. 232–93

Smith, Mark J. (1998). *Social Science in Question*. London: Sage

Smith, Steve. (1987). Paradigm Dominance. *Millennium: Journal of International Studies* 16 (2): 189–206

(1995). Ten Self-Images of a Discipline: a Genealogy of International Relations Theory. In *International Relations Theory Today*, edited by Ken Booth and Steve Smith. Cambridge: Polity, pp. 1–37

(1996). Positivism and Beyond. In *International Theory: Positivism and Beyond*, edited by Steve Smith, Ken Booth and Marysia Zalewski. Cambridge: Cambridge University Press, pp. 11–45

(2000). Wendt's World. *Review of International Studies* 26: 151–63

Smith, Steve, Ken Booth and Marysia Zalewski. (1996). eds. *International Theory: Positivism and Beyond*. Cambridge: Cambridge University Press

Snidal, D. (1993). Relative Gains and the Pattern of International Cooperation. In *Neorealism and Neoliberalism: the Contemporary Debate*, edited by D. A Baldwin. New York: Columbia University Press, pp. 170–208

Sorabji, Richard. (1980). *Necessity, Cause, and Blame: Perspectives on Aristotle's Theory*. Ithaca: Cornell University Press

Sørensen, G. (2001). *Changes in Statehood: the Transformation of International Relations*. Basingstoke: Palgrave

Sosa, Ernest, and Michael Tooley. (1993). *Causation*. Oxford Readings in Philosophy. Oxford: Oxford University Press

Spiro, David E. (1994). Give Democratic Peace a Chance? The Insignificance of the Liberal Peace. *International Security* 19 (2): 50–86.

Spirtes, Peter, Clark Glymour and Richard Schienes. (1999). *Causation, Prediction and Search*. New York: Springer-Verlag

Steans, Jill. (1998). *Gender and International Relations: an Introduction*. Oxford: Polity

Steiner, George. (1982). *Heidegger*. Glasgow: Fortuna

Strawson, Galen. (1989). *The Secret Connexion: Causation, Realism, and David Hume*. Oxford: Clarendon Press

Suarez, Francisco. (1994). *On Efficient Causality: Metaphysical Disputations 17, 18, and 19. Edited by Alfred J. Freddoso*. Yale Library of Medieval Philosophy. New Haven: Yale University Press

Suganami, Hidemi. (1996). *On the Causes of War*. Oxford: Clarendon Press

(1999). Agents, Structures and Narratives. *European Journal of International Relations* 5 (3): 365–85

Suppes, Patrick. (1970). *A Probabilistic Theory of Causality*. Amsterdam: North-Holland

Sylvester, Christine. (1994). *Feminist Theory and International Relations in a Postmodern Era*. Cambridge: Cambridge University Press

Taube, Mortimer. (1936). *Causation, Freedom and Determinism: an Attempt to Solve the Causal Problem through a Study of its Origins in Seventeenth Century Philosophy*. London: George, Allen and Unwin

Taylor, Charles. (1985). *Philosophy and the Human Sciences: Philosophical Papers 2*. Cambridge: Cambridge University Press

Thayer, H. S. (1975). Introduction. In William James, *The Meaning of Truth*, edited by F. H. Burkhardt. London: Harvard University Press, pp. xi–xlvi

Thomas, P. (1991). Critical Reception: Marx Then and Now. In *The Cambridge Companion to Marx*, edited by T. Carver. Cambridge: Cambridge University Press

Thompson, Kenneth. (1976). *August Comte: the Foundation of Sociology*. London: Nelson

Tickner, Ann J. (1992). *Gender in International Relations: Feminist Perspectives on Achieving Global Security*. New York: Columbia University Press

Tilly, Charles. (1975). *The Formation of National States in Western Europe*. Princeton: Princeton University Press

(1990). *Coercion, Capital and European States, AD 990–1990*. Oxford: Blackwell

Tooley, Michael. (1987). *Causation: a Realist Approach*. Oxford: Clarendon Press

(1997). *Time, Tense, and Causation*. Oxford: Clarendon Press

(1999). *Laws of Nature, Causation, and Supervenience*. New York: Garland

True, Jacqui. (2001). Feminism. In *Theories of International Relations*, edited by Burchill et al. London: Palgrave, pp. 231–76

Van Bouwel, Jeroen, and Erik Weber. (2002). Remote Causes, Bad Explanations? *Journal for the Theory of Social Behaviour* 32 (4): 437–49

Van Fraassen, Bas. (1980). *Scientific Image*. Oxford: Clarendon Press

Vasquez, J. (1998). *The Power of Power Politics: From Classical Realism to Neotraditionalism*. Cambridge: Cambridge University Press

Vasquez, J., and M. T. Henehan. (1992). eds. *The Scientific Study of Peace and War: a Text Reader*. New York: Lexington

Viotti, P. R., and M. V. Kauppi. (1993). eds. *International Relations Theory: Realism, Pluralism, Globalism*. New York: Macmillan

Von Mises, Richard. (1956). *Positivism: a Study in Human Understanding*. New York: George Brazillier

Von Wright, Georg Henrik. (1971). *Explanation and Understanding*. London: Routledge & Kegan Paul

(1974). Causality and Causal Explanation. In *Philosophical Problems of Causation*, edited by Tom Beauchamp. Encino: Dickenson, pp. 133–7

Wæver, Ole. (1996). The Rise and Fall of the Interparadigm Debate. In *International Theory: Positivism and Beyond*, edited by Steve Smith, Ken Booth and Marysia Zalewski. Cambridge: Cambridge University Press, pp. 149–85

(2007). Still a Discipline After All These Debates? In *International Relations Theories: Discipline and Diversity*, edited by Tim Dunne, Milja Kurki, and Steve Smith. Oxford: Oxford University Press, pp. 288–308

Walker, R. J. B. (1993). *Inside/Outside: International Relations as Political Theory*. Cambridge: Cambridge University Press

Wallace, William. (1996). Truth and Power, Monks and Technocrats: Theory and Practice in International Relations. *Review of International Studies* 22 (3): 301–21

Wallace, William A. (1972a). *Causality and Scientific Explanation, Vol. I*. Ann Arbor: University of Michigan Press

(1972b). *Causality and Scientific Explanation, Vol. II*. Ann Arbor: University of Michigan Press

Wallerstein, Immanuel. (1984). *The Politics of World Economy*. Cambridge: Cambridge University Press

Waltz, Kenneth. (1959). *Man, the State and War: a Theoretical Analysis*. New York: Columbia University Press

(1979). *Theory of International Politics*. London: McGraw-Hill

(1986). In Response to my Critics. In *Neorealism and its Critics*, edited by R. O. Keohane. New York: Columbia University Press, pp. 322–46

(1993). The Emerging Structure of International Politics. *International Security* 18 (2): 44–79

Waterlow, Sarah. (1982). *Nature, Change and Agency in Aristotle's Physics*. Oxford: Clarendon Press

Weber, Cynthia. (1994). Good Girls, Little Girls and Bad Girls: Male Paranoia in Robert Keohane's Critique of Feminist International Relations. *Millennium: Journal of International Studies* 23 (2): 337–49

(1999). *Faking It: US Hegemony in the 'Post-Phallic Era'*. London: University of Minneapolis Press

Weber, Max. (1970). *The Interpretation of Social Reality*. Edited and with an introduction by J. E. T. Eldridge. London: William Joseph

Weinsheimer, S. C. (1985). *Gadamer's Hermeneutics: a Reading of Truth and Method*. London: Yale University Press

Weldes, Jutta, and Raymond Duvall. (2001). The International Relations of Democracy, Liberalism and War: Directions for Future Research. In *Democracy, Liberalism and War: Rethinking the Democratic Peace Debate*, edited by Tarak Barkawi and Mark Laffey. London: Lynne Rienner, pp. 195–208

Wendt, Alexander. (1987). Agent-Structure Problem in International Relations Theory. *International Organization* 41 (3): 335–70

(1991). Bridging the Theory/Metatheory Gap in International Relations. *Review of International Studies* 17 (4): 383–92

(1992). Anarchy is What States Make of it. *International Organization* 46 (2): 391–425

(1995). Constructing International Politics. *International Security* 20: 391–425

(1999a). *Social Theory of International Politics*. New York: Cambridge University Press

(1999b). On Causation and Constitution. In *Eighty Years' Crisis: International Relations 1919–1999*. Special edition of *Review of International Studies*, edited by Tim Dunne, Michael Cox and Ken Booth. Cambridge: Cambridge University Press, pp. 101–17

(2000). On the Via Media: Response to Critics. *Review of International Studies* 26: 165–80

(2003). Why the World State is Inevitable. *European Journal of International Relations* 9 (4): 491–542

Wendt, Alexander, and Daniel Friedheim. (1995). Hierarchy under Anarchy: Informal Empire and the East German State. *International Organization* 49 (4): 689–922

Westad, Odd Arne. (2000a). Introduction: Reviewing the Cold War. In *Reviewing the Cold War: Approaches, Interpretation, Theory*, edited by O. A. Westad. London: Frank Cass, pp. 1–26

Westad, Odd Arne. (2000b). ed. *Reviewing the Cold War: Approaches, Interpretation, Theory*. London: Frank Cass

White, Graham. (2005). *Medieval Theories of Causality*. Stanford Encyclopedia of Philosophy. Stanford University [cited 30.05.2007]. Available from http://plato.stanford.edu/entries/causation-medieval/

Wight, Colin (1996). Incommensurability and Cross Paradigm Communication in International Relations Theory: What's the Frequency Kenneth? *Millennium: Journal of International Studies* 25 (2): 291-320

(1999a). MetaCampbell: the Epistemological Problematics of Perspectivism. *Review of International Studies* 25 (1): 311–16

(1999b). They Shoot Dead Horses Don't They? Locating Agency in the Agent-Structure Problematique. *European Journal of International Relations* 5 (1): 109–43

(2004). State Agency: Social Action without Human Activity? *Review of International Studies* 30 (2): 269–80

(2006). *Agent, Structures and International Relations: Politics as Ontology*. Cambridge: Cambridge University Press

(2007). A Manifesto for Scientific Realism in IR: Assuming the Can-Opener Won't Work! *Millennium: Journal of International Studies* 35 (2): 379–98

Wight, Martin. (1966). Why is There no International Theory. In *Diplomatic Investigations: Essays in the Theory of International Politics*, edited by H. Butterfield and M. Wight. London: George, Allen and Unwin, pp. 17–34

Williams, Garnett P. (1997). *Chaos Theory Tamed*. London: Taylor & Francis

Wilson, Peter. (1999). The Myth of the first Great Debate. In *The Eighty Year's Crisis: International Relations, 1919–1999*. Special edition of *Review of International Studies*, edited by Tim Dunne, Michael Cox and Ken Booth. Cambridge: Cambridge University Press, pp. 1–16

Winch, Peter. (1990). *Idea of Social Science and its Relation to Philosophy*. 2nd edn. London: Routledge

Wittgenstein, Ludwig. (1961). *Tractacus Logico-Philosophicus*. Translated by D. F. Pears and B. F. McGuinness. London: Routledge

(1966). *Preliminary Studies for 'Philosophical Investigations', Generally Known as Blue and Brown Books*. 2nd edn. Oxford: Blackwell

(1967). *Philosophical Investigations*. Translated by G. E. M. Anscombe. 3rd edn. Oxford: Blackwell

Wohlforth, William C. (2000). A Certain Idea of Science: How International Relations Theory Avoids Reviewing the Cold War. In *Reviewing Cold War: Approaches, Interpretation, Theory*, edited by O. A. Westad. London: Frank Cass, pp. 127–45

Woolf, Leonard. (1916). *International Government*. London: Fabian Society, Allen & Unwin

(1917). *The Framework of a Lasting Peace*. London: Allen and Unwin

(1920). *Economic Imperialism*. London: Swarthmore

(1939). *Barbarians at the Gate*. London: Victor Gollancz

Wright, John P. (1983). *The Sceptical Realism of David Hume*. Manchester: University of Minnesota Press

Zalewski, Marysia, and Jane Parpart. (1998). eds. *The 'Man Question' in International Relations*. Boulder: Westview

Zehfuss, Maja. (2002). *Constructivism in International Relations: the Politics of Reality*. Cambridge: Cambridge University Press

Zimmern, Alfred. (1931). *The Study of International Relations: Inaugural Lecture*. Oxford: Clarendon Press

(1936). *League of Nations and the Rule of Law 1918–1935*. London: Macmillan

Index

Footnotes have been indexed only in those cases where substantial information on entries is provided in them and when specifically indicated (fn).

CAMBRIDGE STUDIES IN INTERNATIONAL RELATIONS

95 *Barry Buzan*
From international to world society?
English school theory and the social structure of globalisation

94 *K. J. Holsti*
Taming the sovereigns
Institutional change in international politics

93 *Bruce Cronin*
Institutions for the common good
International protection regimes in international security

92 *Paul Keal*
European conquest and the rights of indigenous peoples
The moral backwardness of international society

91 *Barry Buzan and Ole Wæver*
Regions and powers
The structure of international security

90 *A. Claire Cutler*
Private power and global authority
Transnational merchant law in the global political economy

89 *Patrick M. Morgan*
Deterrence now

88 *Susan Sell*
Private power, public law
The globalization of intellectual property rights

87 *Nina Tannenwald*
The nuclear taboo
The United States and the non-use of nuclear weapons since 1945

86 *Linda Weiss*
States in the global economy
Bringing domestic institutions back in

85 *Rodney Bruce Hall and Thomas J. Biersteker (eds.)*
The emergence of private authority in global governance

84 *Heather Rae*
State identities and the homogenisation of peoples

83 *Maja Zehfuss*
Constructivism in international relations
The politics of reality

82 *Paul K. Ruth and Todd Allee*
The democratic peace and territorial conflict in the twentieth century

81 *Neta C. Crawford*
Argument and change in world politics
Ethics, decolonization and humanitarian intervention

80 *Douglas Lemke*
Regions of war and peace

79 *Richard Shapcott*
Justice, community and dialogue in international relations

78 *Phil Steinberg*
The social construction of the ocean

77 *Christine Sylvester*
Feminist international relations
An unfinished journey

76 *Kenneth A. Schultz*
Democracy and coercive diplomacy

75 *David Houghton*
US foreign policy and the Iran hostage crisis

74 *Cecilia Albin*
Justice and fairness in international negotiation

73 *Martin Shaw*
Theory of the global state
Globality as an unfinished revolution

72 *Frank C. Zagare and D. Marc Kilgour*
Perfect deterrence

71 *Robert O'Brien, Anne Marie Goetz, Jan Aart Scholte and Marc Williams*
Contesting global governance
Multilateral economic institutions and global social movements

70 *Roland Bleiker*
Popular dissent, human agency and global politics

69 *Bill McSweeney*
Security, identity and interests
A sociology of international relations

68 *Molly Cochran*
Normative theory in international relations
A pragmatic approach

67 *Alexander Wendt*
Social theory of international politics

66 *Thomas Risse, Stephen C. Ropp and Kathryn Sikkink (eds.)*
The power of human rights
International norms and domestic change

65 *Daniel W. Drezner*
The sanctions paradox
Economic statecraft and international relations

64 *Viva Ona Bartkus*
The dynamic of secession

63 *John A. Vasquez*
The power of power politics
From classical realism to neotraditionalism

62 *Emanuel Adler and Michael Barnett (eds.)*
Security communities

61 *Charles Jones*
E. H. Carr and international relations
A duty to lie

60 *Jeffrey W. Knopf*
Domestic society and international cooperation
The impact of protest on US arms control policy

59 *Nicholas Greenwood Onuf*
The republican legacy in international thought

58 *Daniel S. Geller and J. David Singer*
Nations at war
A scientific study of international conflict

57 *Randall D. Germain*
The international organization of credit
States and global finance in the world economy

56 *N. Piers Ludlow*
Dealing with Britain
The Six and the first UK application to the EEC

55 *Andreas Hasenclever, Peter Mayer and Volker Rittberger*
Theories of international regimes

54 *Miranda A. Schreurs and Elizabeth C. Economy (eds.)*
The internationalization of environmental protection

53 *James N. Rosenau*
Along the domestic–foreign frontier
Exploring governance in a turbulent world

52 *John M. Hobson*
The wealth of states
A comparative sociology of international economic and political change

51 *Kalevi J. Holsti*
The state, war, and the state of war

50 *Christopher Clapham*
Africa and the international system
The politics of state survival

49 *Susan Strange*
The retreat of the state
The diffusion of power in the world economy

48 *William I. Robinson*
Promoting polyarchy
Globalization, US intervention, and hegemony

47 *Roger Spegele*
Political realism in international theory

46 *Thomas J. Biersteker and Cynthia Weber (eds.)*
State sovereignty as social construct

45 *Mervyn Frost*
Ethics in international relations
A constitutive theory

44 *Mark W. Zacher with Brent A. Sutton*
Governing global networks
International regimes for transportation and communications

43 *Mark Neufeld*
The restructuring of international relations theory

42 *Thomas Risse-Kappen (ed.)*
Bringing transnational relations back in
Non-state actors, domestic structures and international institutions

41 *Hayward R. Alker*
Rediscoveries and reformulations
Humanistic methodologies for international studies

40 *Robert W. Cox with Timothy J. Sinclair*
Approaches to world order

39 *Jens Bartelson*
A genealogy of sovereignty

38 *Mark Rupert*
Producing hegemony
The politics of mass production and American global power

37 *Cynthia Weber*
Simulating sovereignty
Intervention, the state and symbolic exchange

36 *Gary Goertz*
Contexts of international politics

35 *James L. Richardson*
Crisis diplomacy
The Great Powers since the mid-nineteenth century

34 *Bradley S. Klein*
Strategic studies and world order
The global politics of deterrence

33 *T. V. Paul*
Asymmetric conflicts: war initiation by weaker powers

32 *Christine Sylvester*
Feminist theory and international relations in a postmodern era

31 *Peter J. Schraeder*
US foreign policy toward Africa
Incrementalism, crisis and change

30 *Graham Spinardi*
From Polaris to Trident: the development of US Fleet Ballistic Missile technology

29 *David A. Welch*
Justice and the genesis of war

28 *Russell J. Leng*
Interstate crisis behavior, 1816–1980: realism versus reciprocity

27 *John A. Vasquez*
The war puzzle

26 *Stephen Gill (ed.)*
Gramsci, historical materialism and international relations

25 *Mike Bowker and Robin Brown (eds.)*
From cold war to collapse: theory and world politics in the 1980s

24 *R. B. J. Walker*
Inside/outside: international relations as political theory

23 *Edward Reiss*
The strategic defense initiative

22 *Keith Krause*
Arms and the state: patterns of military production and trade

21 *Roger Buckley*
US–Japan alliance diplomacy 1945–1990

20 *James N. Rosenau and Ernst-Otto Czempiel (eds.)*
Governance without government: order and change in world politics

19 *Michael Nicholson*
Rationality and the analysis of international conflict

18 *John Stopford and Susan Strange*
Rival states, rival firms
Competition for world market shares

17 *Terry Nardin and David R. Mapel (eds.)*
Traditions of international ethics

16 *Charles F. Doran*
Systems in crisis
New imperatives of high politics at century's end

15 *Deon Geldenhuys*
Isolated states: a comparative analysis

14 *Kalevi J. Holsti*
Peace and war: armed conflicts and international order 1648–1989

13 *Saki Dockrill*
Britain's policy for West German rearmament 1950–1955

12 *Robert H. Jackson*
Quasi-states: sovereignty, international relations and the third world

11 *James Barber and John Barratt*
South Africa's foreign policy
The search for status and security 1945–1988

10 *James Mayall*
Nationalism and international society

9 *William Bloom*
Personal identity, national identity and international relations

8 *Zeev Maoz*
National choices and international processes

7 *Ian Clark*
The hierarchy of states
Reform and resistance in the international order

6 *Hidemi Suganami*
The domestic analogy and world order proposals

5 *Stephen Gill*
American hegemony and the Trilateral Commission

4 *Michael C. Pugh*
The ANZUS crisis, nuclear visiting and deterrence

3 *Michael Nicholson*
Formal theories in international relations

2 *Friedrich V. Kratochwil*
Rules, norms, and decisions
On the conditions of practical and legal reasoning in international relations and domestic affairs

1 *Myles L. C. Robertson*
Soviet policy towards Japan
An analysis of trends in the 1970s and 1980s